This is the first study of the Zionist movement in Germany, Britain, and the United States which recognizes "Western Zionism" as a distinctive force.

From the First World War until the rise of Hitler, the Zionist movement encouraged Jews to celebrate aspects of a reborn Jewish nationality and sovereignty in Palestine, while at the same time acknowledging that their members would mostly "stay put" and strive toward acculturation in their current homelands.

The growth of a Zionist consciousness among Western Jews is juxta-posed to the problematic nurturing of the movement's institutions, as Zionism was consumed increasingly by fundraising. In the 1930s Zionism evinced questionable administrative motives and talents, which unsettled even its stalwarts such as Louis Brandeis and Henrietta Szold. While Zionist images assumed a progressively greater share of secular Jewish identity, and Zionism became normalized in the social landscape of Western Jewry, the organization faltered in translating its popularity into a means of "saving the Jews" and "building up" the national home in Palestine. This was the period in which the Jewish masses were approaching their most serious and ultimately fatal challenge.

Western Jewry and the Zionist project, 1914–1933

Western Jewry and the Zionist project, 1914–1933

Michael Berkowitz

CAMBRIDGE
UNIVERSITY PRESS

PUBLISHED BY THE PRESS SYNDICATE OF THE UNIVERSITY OF CAMBRIDGE
The Pitt Building, Trumpington Street, Cambridge, United Kingdom

CAMBRIDGE UNIVERSITY PRESS
The Edinburgh Building, Cambridge CB2 2RU, UK
40 West 20th Street, New York NY 10011–4211, USA
477 Williamstown Road, Port Melbourne, VIC 3207, Australia
Ruiz de Alarcón 13, 28014 Madrid, Spain
Dock House, The Waterfront, Cape Town 8001, South Africa

http://www.cambridge.org

First published 1997
First paperback edition 2002

A catalogue record for this book is available from the British Library

Library of Congress Cataloguing in Publication data
Berkowitz, Michael.
Western Jewry and the Zionist project, 1914–1933 /
Michael Berkowitz.
          p.   cm.
Includes bibliographical references.
ISBN 0 521 47087 0 (hardcover)
1. Zionism – Europe, Western – History.   2. Zionism – United States –
History.   3. Jews – Charitable contributions.   4. Jews – Travel –
Palestine.   I. Title.
DS149.5.E85B47   1996
320.5′4′095694–dc20   96-13024   CIP

ISBN 0 521 47087 0 hardback
ISBN 0 521 89420 4 paperback

For my mother,
Gloria Berkowitz,
and the memory of my father,
William Berkowitz (1917–1995)

It may be claimed that a nation, like an individual, is valuable only insofar as it is able to give everyday experience the stamp of the eternal. Only by doing so can it express its profound, if unconscious, conviction of the relativity of time and the metaphysical meaning of life. The opposite happens when a nation begins to view itself historically and to demolish the mythical bulwarks that surround it.

Nietzsche, *The Birth of Tragedy*

There is no set of maxims more important for an historian than this: that the actual causes of a thing's origins and its eventual uses, the manner of its incorporation into a system of purposes, are worlds apart; that everything that exists, no matter what its origin, is periodically reinterpreted by those in power in terms of fresh intentions; that all processes in the organic world are processes of outstripping and over-coming, and that, in turn, all outstripping and overcoming means reinterpretation, rearrangement, in the course of which the earlier meaning and purpose are necessarily obscured or lost.

Nietzsche, *The Genealogy of Morals*

Contents

Illustrations

Preface and acknowledgments

In my dissertation and book on the attempted nationalization of Western Jewry (*Zionist Culture and West European Jewry Before the First World War* [Cambridge: Cambridge University Press, 1993]), one of the recurrent themes is that early Zionism functioned, to a great extent, as a self-consciously male movement. In the course of my research, however, I noticed some intriguing women activists and groups of women who received scant attention in the historiography. I decided that my initial post-dissertation project would focus on these women and their role in Zionist nationalization.

A faculty development grant from St. Lawrence University in Canton, New York, allowed me in the summer of 1989 to delve into the Zionist women project, primarily at the Central Zionist Archives in Jerusalem. In examining material pertaining to Zionist popular culture, I became aware that the pre-1914 processes of constructing a Jewish national consciousness were already undergoing a dramatic change during the Great War. The deeper I dug the more I saw that there was a story to tell about the reception of Zionism among Western Jews in the 1920s and early 1930s – which might be critical in understanding how the movement assumed the shape it did in the West, well before the declaration of the State of Israel. I was particularly struck by four observations: that the movements in Germany, Britain, and the United States were not as dissimilar as suggested by the secondary literature; that Zionists in these nations perceived each other as sharing vital interests, separate from other Zionist constituencies; and that after 1921 fundraising came to dominate the practice of Zionism in each of these countries. Western-acculturated Jews furthermore shared a common stock of symbols and images through which they identified with Zionism.

In 1989–90 I enjoyed a Monkarsh Postdoctoral Fellowship at the University of Judaism in Los Angeles (then the West Coast affiliate of the Jewish Theological Seminary of America). I continued work on Zionist women, which became the red thread in my study of the interwar movement. A grant from the Lucius Littauer Foundation (1990) allowed me to return to the archives in Israel and see the larger contours of

---

the present study. After settling in Ohio, a Rapoport Fellowship from the American Jewish Archives in Cincinnati facilitated my foray into the history of Zionism in the United States; I perceived that it is impossible to untangle the American and West European Zionist experience, despite a body of historiography which asserts that the national strands of the movement are utterly distinct. A DAAD-Leo Baeck Institute award for the study of German–Jewish history and culture allowed me to work at the Leo Baeck Institute on the Upper East Side of New York, and a grant from Indiana University's Center for the Study of Philanthropy supported my research at the Hadassah Archives in midtown Manhattan. The bulk of research was accomplished while I was a fellow of the Wiener Library, of Tel Aviv University's Institute for German History, from October 1991 to March 1992.

In the midst of reading and gathering material for this book I presented papers on aspects of the project at numerous conferences and seminars. I wish to thank everyone involved in those occasions. Two of the presentations resulted in chapters (in edited works) which correspond to themes treated here. I would like to acknowledge the respective editors and presses for permission to reprint sections of those chapters: "The Invention of a Secular Ritual: Western Jewry and Nationalized Tourism in Palestine, 1922–1933," in *The Seductiveness of Jewish Myth: Challenge or Response*, edited by Daniel Breslauer (Albany: State University of New York Press, 1997), pp. 69–91, and "Transcending 'Tsimmes and Sweetness': Recovering the History of Zionist Women in Central and Western Europe," in Maurie Sacks, ed., *Active Voices: Women in Jewish Culture* (Urbana: University of Illinois Press, 1995), pp. 41–62.

There are several institutions and individuals deserving special praise and thanks: Yoram Mayorek and his staff at the Central Zionist Archives in Jerusalem, particularly my dear friends Pinchas Selinger and Reuven Koffler; at the Wiener Library at Tel Aviv University, Ms. Gila Michalowski; Dr. Abraham Peck and his staff at the American Jewish Archives in Cincinnati; the DAAD and the Leo Baeck Institute; the Jewish Historical Society in Waltham, Massachusetts; Ms. Pamela Brumberg of the Littauer Foundation; Drs. David Lieber and Elliot Dorff of the University of Judaism; Ira Daly at the Hadassah Archives in New York; the Melton Center for Jewish Studies, the Department of History, the College of Humanities, and the Graduate School of the Ohio State University. The visual materials are reproduced courtesy of the Central Zionist Archives and the Wiener Library in Tel Aviv.

Along with the readers from Cambridge University Press, many colleagues read (or heard) parts of the manuscript and offered wise counsel. It is a better book due to the thoughtful efforts of David Sorkin,

Steven Zipperstein, Derek Penslar, Mitchell Hart, Kevin McAleer, Claudia Prestel, Ursula Baumann, Billie Melman, Shulamit Volkov, David Cesarani, Alon Confino, Mark Levene, Gary Schiff, Mark Grimsley, Susan Tananbaum, Leila Rupp, Ken Andrien, Irina Livezeanu, Eve Levin, Marilyn Waldman, Jonathan Sarna, Michael Brenner, John Efron, Jack Kugelmass, Miriam Dean-Otting, Richard Freund, Mitch Levine, Bernard Friedman, Glenn Sharfman, George Vascik, Shelly Baranowski, Leslie Adelson, John Hoberman, David Luft, Miryam Glazer, David Brenner, Mark Gelber, Allon Gal, Melvin Adelman, Margaret Newell, Laurence Silberstein, Sean Martin, Mary McCune, Larry Bell, Kelly McFall, Steve Williams, Joy Scime, Joseph Galron, and Karen Anderson Howes. I am grateful to Laurence Silberstein for sharing with me his manuscript in progress, and through his good auspices, for seeing an unpublished paper of Yaacov Shavit on archaeology in Israel. Amy Alrich helped with the preparation of the bibliography. In addition to the funding agencies, the generosity of friends and relatives made this work possible. Eli Shai made my many stays in Jerusalem intellectually exciting and a pleasure; Dr. Ernest Oliveri (West Side) and Michael Littenberg (East Side) were wonderful hosts during several trips to the Big Apple; and Michael McHale graciously accommodated me in Boston.

Although he has been only indirectly involved in this work, my Doktorvater George Mosse serves as a great inspiration, mentor, and friend. I am fortunate also to have an understanding and good-humored editor, William Davies of Cambridge University Press.

Members of my family, especially my sister, Edie Needleman, were always willing to lend a hand wherever and whenever needed. Some of the photographs used in this volume (only a fraction of which are in these pages) were taken by the staff photographer at the Central Zionist Archives; some were taken in Columbus by my brother-in-law, Dr. Lawrence Needleman. My wife, Deborah Rozansky, did most of the painstaking photographic work for this volume in Jerusalem and Tel Aviv. But there is no doubt that her most wonderful "development" during the writing and research for this book was the birth of our daughter, Rachel. She's the supreme joy of our lives.

In nearing the completion of this book, I was greatly saddened by the death of my father. My friends helped me through a most difficult time. It is to my mother, Gloria Berkowitz, and the memory of my father, William Berkowitz, that this work is dedicated. Their unconditional love and support encouraged me to seek my heart's content. These now closed chapters are for my dear parents; those that lie ahead will be for my daughter and wife.

Abbreviations

AJA	American Jewish Archives, Cincinnati, Ohio
BJC	Bund jüdischer Corporationen
BZK	Bund zionistischer Korporationen
CZA	Central Zionist Archives, Jerusalem
DJJG	Deutsch-jüdisch Jugend-Gemeinschaft
FWZ	Federation of Women Zionists (of Great Britain and Ireland)
HA	Hadassah Archives, New York
IUJFGBI	Inter-University Jewish Federation of Great Britain and Ireland
IZA	Intercollegiate Zionist Organization of America
JA	Jewish Agency
JDC	American Jewish Joint Distribution Committee
JFB	Jüdischer Frauenbund
JNF	Jewish National Fund
JPS	Jewish Publication Society of America
KC	Kartell-Convent der Verbindungen deutscher Studenten jüdischen Glaubens (Union of German Students of the Jewish Faith)
KH	Keren Hayesod (Palestine Foundation Fund)
KJV	Kartell jüdischer Verbindungen
KKL	Keren Kayemet L'Israel (Jewish National Fund)
KZV	Kartell zionistischer Verbindungen
LBI	Leo Baeck Institute, New York
PBK	*Palästina-Bilder-Korrespondenz*
PC, CZA	Photo collection, Central Zionist Archives, Jerusalem
UJA	United Jewish Appeal
UPA	United Palestine Appeal
UZF	University Zionist Federation
VJJVD	Verband der jüdischen Jugendvereine Deutschlands
VJSt	Verein jüdischer Studenten
WIZO	Women's International Zionist Organization
ZOA	Zionist Organization of America

Introduction

One may think what one will about Zionism, but it cannot be denied that it is generated by latent power and energy, and an awakened self-consciousness.
                                                            Samuel Weissenberg (1900)[1]

Today Jewry lives a bifurcated life. As a result of emancipation in the diaspora and national sovereignty in Israel Jews have fully reentered the mainstream of history, yet their perception of how they got there and where they are is most often more mythical than real.
                                                            Yosef Hayim Yerushalmi (1982)[2]

This is a study of the historical construction and reception of Zionism between the world wars in Western Europe and the United States.[3] It is the first discussion of the movement outside Eastern Europe and Palestine which views Zionism in the Western nations as a distinct entity, as parts of an interwoven whole.[4] In taking this perspective I wish to underscore the notion that Zionism became a greater part of secular Jewish consciousness and a ground for charity and philanthropy among Western Jewry, as the movement sought to connect Western-acculturated Jews to an emerging Jewish sovereignty. It is not my objective to write a comprehensive history of Zionism;[5] or explore the travails of the movement in the wider worlds of politics and diplomacy;[6] or reconsider Zionist ideology, per se;[7] or examine how Zionism worked itself out in Palestine.[8] In certain respects, this book responds to questions raised in my first book, *Zionist Culture and West European Jewry Before the First World War*,[9] namely: how did Zionist-nationalism function for those Jews not seen by the movement, or themselves, as the likely immigrants to Palestine, and how was knowledge about Zionism, directed toward Western Jews, produced by the movement?[10] This study begins, however, with the changes wrought by World War I; it incorporates developments in the United States, as its Jewish community became more crucial to Zionist efforts, and extends the analysis until the advent of Hitler. The first book recognized and analyzed the Zionists' creation

1

of a "supplemental nationality" for West European Jews. The current book builds on that assumption in looking at the period 1914–33; but the main argument is that as the nationalization of Western Jewry proceeded apace, the component parts of the movement took on a life of their own, and that the sustenance of the Zionist Organization – especially its fundraising mechanisms – came to dominate the practice of Zionism for Western-assimilated Jewry. Zionism as an institution, I maintain, was accepted as a supreme value in itself, rather than as a means to securing the aims of the movement.[11]

This book confronts a historically perplexing problem: what accounts for the cohesion of those European and American Jews who called themselves Zionists, despite their apparent insulation from the threat of anti-Semitism, and the weighty differences between national and class-based contingents? What attracted them to the movement? What was it about Zionism that interested them? What exhilarated them? What might have bored them, or left them uninterested in the movement? How might one explain the uniformity of Western Jewish perceptions of, and ways of identifying with, the Zionist project in Palestine? How and why did Western Zionism's development influence its reception from the First World War until the early 1930s, resulting in a lackluster period for the movement? Obviously, Zionists in different countries acted and reacted differently; but the relationships and commonalties have commanded little attention. This book – encompassing popular culture, political symbolism, historical memories, imagery, fundraising, relief efforts, gender roles, militarism, education, politics, and charity – deals with the question of why Jews in Central and Western Europe and the United States, who were relatively assimilated and comfortable, bothered to bother with Zionism, which offered them little apparent advantage. Although I have included the experiences of individual men and women from France, Belgium, the Netherlands, and Italy, I have considered mainly Zionists and Zionism in the United States, Britain, and Germany, because the latter were the communities which Zionists usually perceived as the most formidable areas of the movement's support, among Westernized Jews, before 1933. It was only in the mid-1930s, for example, that Zionism in France seemed worthy of mention for something other than its dearth of popularity.[12] In sum, the movement was molded to fit Western Jews' demands for an ever more "platonic" type of Zionism.[13] Following the lead of Michael Brenner, Paula Hyman, and others, I wish to call into question the exaggerated image of patently "apolitical" Western Jewries, enthralled by delusions of hyperassimilation, which does little justice to the (broadly defined) Jewish political experiences of "emancipated" Jews in Europe and the United States.[14]

With the striking exceptions of Claudia Prestel's work on Zionist women, which covers Europe and Palestine from 1897 to 1933,[15] Yigal Elam's wide-ranging history of the Jewish Agency for Palestine,[16] and Ezra Mendelsohn's *On Modern Jewish Politics*, which features a comparative analysis of American and Polish interwar Zionism, the prevailing interpretations of Zionism before the Second World War stress its discrete components, such as the diplomatic maneuvering resulting in the Balfour Declaration and the British Mandate for Palestine, state and institution building in Palestine, biography and collective biography, and the unique character of the movement in Russia, Poland, Germany, Britain, South Africa, Argentina, the United States, and elsewhere. Over the past two decades, to be sure, there has been progress toward a more critical and synthetic body of historiography; important studies have appeared in Hebrew, English, and German.[17] But these works for the most part constitute an inner-group dialogue that rarely speaks to the non-Zionist community. Scholars of Zionism, with a few notable exceptions, neglect a rigorous comparative approach and confine themselves to a Zionist discourse.[18] Often the focus is on why and how Zionists differed and disagreed. Such tendencies reflect the concerns of an "in" group, and ignore modes of historical analysis that have proved fruitful in other settings. In particular cultural history and the "new" history have not had a great impact on Jewish scholarship in general.[19] My inclination (to borrow a phrase from Hobsbawm) is to see Zionism as an "invented tradition" which is remarkable for its adaptation to the circumstances of assimilated Jewries, and for devising diverse constituency-building strategies.[20] Simultaneously, the Zionists blurred the boundaries between belonging to an incipient nation, a religious group, a national movement, a local organization, a national organization, a fraternal order, a voluntary association, and a community determined by history and birthright. It may prove helpful, then, to look at the history of the Zionist movement in relation to the development of symbols, institutions, organizations, publicity, and popular community building that have been neglected in favor of mainstream "high" politics.

To carry out this study I have read the contemporary periodical literature and examined archives in Israel and the United States. Although the recent scholarship on Zionism is typically well researched, surprisingly few historians of the movement have systematically read the Zionist organs from Germany, Britain, and the United States, let alone the respective "propaganda and agitation" materials in the archives. I suspect that the lack of familiarity with different national settings of Zionism has bolstered claims of the uniqueness of Zionism in these countries. I base my analysis on the popular culture and perceptions of the movement, which along with the press includes consideration of promotional materials, graphic arts, iconography, and photography. I am particularly attuned to visual images, the manipulation of symbols, and the interpenetration of myth and reality, resulting in the processes by which certain perceptions became the common stock of Zionism.

In addition to filling a void in Zionist historiography, I wish to delve, as well, into some newer areas of inquiry. The first chapter focuses on the attempted appropriation of the First World War by the Zionist movement, showing that the Zionists reaped limited capital from the diverse war experiences of its constituents – despite the obvious political success represented by the Balfour Declaration. Chapter 2 is an excursion through the pantheon of heroic Zionist leaders in the West. My emphasis is on how the portrayal of these figures tended to produce an impression of harmony and consensus in the contentious movement. Above all, the organization seized on the image of Albert Einstein to highlight Zionism's professed affinity with the greatest hopes of human civilization and progress. Chapter 3, rather than clearing a new avenue of inquiry, instead turns to one of the better-trod paths in the history of interwar Zionism, that is, the "feud" between Chaim Weizmann and Louis Brandeis in the early 1920s, the creation of the Keren Hayesod (the Palestine Foundation Fund), and the reemergence of the opposition to Weizmann in the late 1920s. Although it was not my original intention to revise the judgments of Ben Halpern, Evyatar Friesel, and Jehuda Reinharz concerning what Halpern has termed "the clash of heroes," I nevertheless offer a rereading of this controversial episode.[21] I am not as concerned with exposing the inner workings of Zionist administration as much as I desire to explain the impact of the movement's politics on popular sentiments. Part of Zionism's frustrations in the interwar period were closely tied to this story, the "negative consequences" of which ran deeper than the "disarray" recounted in the historiography.[22] I think that this controversy led to a widespread disaffection of Zionists, primarily among the women of Hadassah. Except for Ezra Mendelsohn's *Zionism in Poland*, there are few scholarly studies of pre-state Zionism that illuminate the culture of fundraising in the diaspora.[23] Most work in Zionist historiography concerning the role of money raised in the diaspora has dwelt on the "nationalization of capital" in the Yishuv,[24] and the general literature on philanthropy only mentions Jewish organizations in passing.[25] The formation and subsequent evolution of the Keren Hayesod, as the chief financial instrument and tool of Zionist nationalization, cannot be underestimated as a factor in the reception of Zionism in the West. Chapter 4 analyzes the drives to raise money for

Zionism which were connected to polemics about catastrophe; this discourse established patterns of Western Jewish perceptions of Zionism and the reception of Zionist appeals.

The fifth chapter examines the interwar representations of Jewish Palestine. Images of the Jews' newfound preeminence in agriculture was a major part of this effort, while the Zionists' success in creating a new urban style also was triumphantly expressed. Chapter 6 discusses the unfolding of one of the most enduring dimensions of the Western-oriented Zionist project – the appropriation of Jewish tourism to Palestine. Primarily through improvising changes to existing tours, the organization engendered a secularized pilgrimage ritual to the Holy Land; many of its essential elements would not be fundamentally altered for more than fifty years. Chapter 7 deals with one of the most significant segments of world Zionism, its youth divisions in the West. Although important differences did exist from one nation to another, I argue that many characteristics were shared, and that there was a certain symmetry in Zionist youth groups in relatively acculturated societies. Organized Zionist youth not only reflected the world of its Zionist elders, but found its own means to adapt Zionism to life outside Palestine. British Zionist youth, for instance, was apparently the first section of diaspora Zionists to accommodate large numbers of Jewish returnees from Palestine into Zionist ideology and practice. Chapter 8 explores organized women in Zionism, focusing on the place of the German Kulturverband, Women's International Zionist Organization (WIZO), and Hadassah in the context of the history of women in Zionism. Particularly with regard to Zionism in the United States, my aim is not simply to add an account of women's "contributions," but to show how the integration of women affects the entire movement's history, and to consider the impact of the resistance to organized women in diaspora Zionism.

My main hypothesis is that, between 1914 and 1933, Zionism came to be styled increasingly as a rescue mission and object of philanthropy, and that the Zionist Organization and its preeminent institutions – especially its fundraising instruments – were held up by the movement as sacrosanct bodies. Given the Zionist goals of unifying Jews in support of the national home in Palestine and radically changing the modern Jewish condition, I wish to call into question the degree to which this kind of institutional development was propitious. While Zionism was creative and successful at making its aims and view of the world a part of Western Jewish life, Jews also lost faith in the movement due to its apparent mismanagement and obsession with fundraising. Yet however much Zionism may have declined in this period, it nevertheless assumed much of its principal shape with regard to Western Jewish integration in the movement – that is, before the birth of the State of Israel. The main questions with which I am concerned are: how did Western Jews, especially in Germany, Britain, and the United States perceive the Zionist movement? How did this perception change during the First World War, and from the war years until the rise of Hitler? What was the role of philanthropy and charity in the movement? How was it possible, with the Yishuv (the Jewish settlement in Palestine) assuming more and more a life of its own, to be a Zionist outside Zion? How might one evaluate the values, ethics, intellectual standards, and behavior of the organization in relation to its professed mission? I wish to illuminate the background of what Alain Finkielkraut perceives as "the apparent inconsistency of Western Jews" in the post-1945 world: "they're all Zionists, but they all stay settled right where they are . . . They see no contradiction between life in the Diaspora and love for Israel."[26] My study has led me to explore how diaspora Zionism – which might have been more widely interpreted as a contradiction in terms – was rationalized in the middle-class Jewish mind, and the processes by which it was made concrete in the lives of Western Jews from 1914 to 1933.

While the movement obviously gained power in the diaspora and disseminated a bold language of revolutionary, Jewish national transformation, Zionism also can be seen as inheriting many of the tendencies of pre-Zionist Jewish communal organizations and charities, which it had pronounced as a blight on Jewish self-help, and pointedly vowed not to replicate.[27] Many of the successors of the interwar Zionists vehemently denied that Zionism was a charity, yet they continued to rely on the charitable instincts of the Western Jewish middle class to explicitly or implicitly support the movement. A question to be raised, then, is whether or not there might have been any other means to rally Western Jewry under the banner of Zionism, or perhaps whether there should have been an attempt to redirect the course of the movement, or reformulate the original aims of Zionism. This was, in fact, the period in which the Jewish masses were approaching their most serious and ultimately fatal challenge.

1 Manly men and the attempted appropriation of the war experience, 1914–1918

In the summer of 1914, Zionists in both the Central and Allied powers responded enthusiastically to their nations' call to arms. Along with declaring that there was no contradiction between loyalty to the European nations and to Zionism, they rationalized that their own country's victory would hasten the conversion of Zionist dreams into reality. German and Austrian Zionists particularly were thrilled to engage the enemy who had trampled on their nations' honor.[1] Because one of their chief adversaries was the Russian Empire – the great tormentor of the Jewish masses, "the poorest of the poor" – the ardor of Zionists in the German *Kulturbereich* was fortified. Subduing the anti-Semitic tsar was portrayed as a life-or-death struggle between the "cultured world" of Central Europe versus Asiatic "barbarism."[2] Heinrich Loewe, the German Zionist stalwart, wrote that it was "only from the German side that the Jews will find protection and freedom."[3] Jonathan Frankel suggests that such fervor was not unique to the Zionists during the First World War, as

the experience of the Jewish people mirrored – but also magnified – that of the belligerent societies in general. The gulf separating the tangible realities of the Jewish situation from the way in which that situation was perceived proved time and again to be immense. Never before in modern history (specifically, since the expulsion from Spain) had the inherent vulnerability and weakness of the Jews as a scattered minority been exposed with such insistent brutality and impunity. Yet at the very same time, many Jews – movements, groups, individuals – came to the conclusion that the moment of emancipation or autoemancipation (national liberation, however variously defined) had arrived. The Jewish people had it within their grasp to solve the Jewish question.[4]

Before the British entry into the war, Zionists in Britain anticipated the country's joining with trepidation due to the predicted suffering that would be inflicted on Eastern Jewry, and objections to assisting tsarist Russia. Neither side in the unfolding conflict seemed very attractive to British Jews and Zionists. "We have no interest in the upholding of

Austria and far less in the debasement of Germany," ran an editorial in the London *Jewish Chronicle*:

For England to fight alongside of Russia would be as wicked as for her to fight against Germany, with whom she has no quarrel whatsoever. The plunging of Britain headlong into a melee, the prime object of which would be the upholding of Cossack rule, with its negation of all that human progress stands for would be such a stupendous affront to humanity, as well as to British interests, that we are astonished and aghast at its bare suggestion.[5]

As is often the case in politics, a turnabout quickly ensued when it seemed inescapable that the British would be allied with Russia. "In the Land of the Tsar," it was asserted, "the [Russian] army can never be the same prejudice-ridden institution as before it found itself in comradeship of arms with the British and French nations."[6] Now the ancillary objective, along with subduing the official enemy, became the transformation of the tsarist regime. With the war raging, the Allies and especially the Jews among them were desperate to hold up evidence of the Russian change of heart, that is, until the Revolution of 1917. For instance, allegations that the Russian army had instigated pogroms in Vilnius as soon as war broke out were denounced as "absolutely false."[7] The British Zionists' faith in this pre-revolutionary reform of tsarism was said to be validated by the fervor with which the Russian Jews rushed to defend their country, despite their oppression.[8] The tsar himself was claimed to be deeply moved and appreciative of the "loyalty and ability" of Jewish soldiers.[9]

Immediately the Anglo-Jewish press proclaimed that the heroism of Russian Jewry was brilliantly illustrated on the field of battle.[10] Of course, the record of the British Jews themselves was instantaneously judged to be one of shining honor and willing self-sacrifice. "I have been told by men of my corps who have just returned from convoy," read a letter quoted in London's *Jewish Chronicle*, "that the men in the Middlesex Regiment really love our men for their bravery and good work. They say that it is a credit to work with the Jewish soldiers, as they really have their mind on what they are doing."[11] A British soldier assured a reporter that the fine British Jewish soldiers were not unique, saying that he "came across a number of Jews in the British, French, and Belgian forces, and the very sight of them made me feel proud of my Jewish birth. These were splendid fellows and, without exaggeration, fine fighters and game to the last."[12]

But the attempt to put the best face on the Jewish war effort for Britain was obscured by the intermittent controversies which erupted over the issues of "alien conscription," that is, the drafting of Jewish immigrants from Eastern Europe and Russia in the spring of 1916, the proposed raising of a "Jewish Regiment," and finally, the actual creation of a "Jewish Battalion."[13] More than the Germans or Americans, British Jewry felt pressed to demonstrate that "the foreign-born Jew" of Britain was capable of serving with honor,[14] as the Russian emigrants in their midst were eventually faced with the specter of "enlistment or deportation."[15] The most distinctive "Zionist" contributions to the British war effort, however, comprised the research of Chaim Weizmann,[16] which was publicly recognized after the war, and the creation of a Jewish Battalion, which always was clouded by the "deep misgivings" British Jews and Zionists worldwide held over treatment which smacked of "discrimination or exceptionalism."[17]

The organization of separate Jewish troops under the British flag, typically referred to as the "Jewish Legion," had two main incarnations: first as the Zion Mule Corps, which served in Gallipoli (April 1915) and was disbanded after the Dardanelles campaign, and second, as the Jewish Battalion, known as the "Judaeans," which was supposed to participate in the fight for Palestine. As opposed to very scanty coverage allotted the initial force while it was in action, the second unit, the Judaeans, was extensively and sympathetically dealt with in the British and American Zionist press. By May 1918, it was reported that over 1,200 Jews from the United States (who did not possess US citizenship and therefore were ineligible for the draft) had volunteered.[18] In the end the unit served a more symbolic rather than substantive function, and the very insignias which represented the regiment were hotly contested.[19] Although it would later occupy a place of prominence in the discourse of Revisionist Zionism, neither the Mule Corps nor the Judaeans became a shared, lasting component of Zionist identity in the West compared to other aspects of the Zionist project.

The uniformed Jew whose star shone the brightest during the First World War was General (later Sir) John Monash, commander of the ANZAC (Australian and New Zealand) forces on the western front in 1918.[20] Monash, however, did not become involved in Zionism in Australia until the late 1920s,[21] and his legend was not widespread. The leading military hero who appeared to be representing Jewish and Zionist interests was General Allenby, a non-Jew, whose success "was as swift as it was brilliant" in delivering "almost the whole of Palestine from Turkish domination."[22] From the first reports it did not seem that the Jewish fighters had had any influence in the conquest of Jerusalem. Allenby, though, perhaps sensitive to allegations of anti-Semitism,[23] "made it clear in the later dispatches that not only Australians and New Zealanders had participated in the fight, but that the Jewish troops had taken a conspicuous part in driving the Turks back into Amman."[24] The general perception, nevertheless, remained that the Jewish Legion had been incidental, rather than critical, in Allenby's heralded campaign. It was, in the generous appraisal of David Vital, "something of a disappointment."[25]

When it became clear that the United States' entrance into the war was imminent, American Zionists heartily seconded "the break with Germany" articulated by President Wilson. Zionists harbored no thoughts of Jewish separatism in the United States; in fact, the very opposite was the case:

The Jews of America share the interests of the American people, of whom they are an integral part. Our love and loyalty go out to America not only because it has been a haven of refuge for our oppressed people, but because we have derived inspiration and strength from the ideals and enthusiasms that are America's contribution to modern civilization. The democratic education we have received here has strengthened our own movement for self-emancipation, for we have felt that American ideas give their sanction to the efforts of any people to secure itself against the future by making such sacrifices to-day as would render that future worthy. The Zionist movement runs parallel with the idealism of this land and is in fact a natural growth and the normal consequence of thinking in terms of democratic American idealism. In this land we have the opportunity for the first time in our history to realize our national hopes, living in a friendly environment. It is a source of Jewish gratification to find ourselves in perfect accord with the ideas and interests of the American people. We shall be among the first to come forward prepared to make our personal sacrifices for American national interests should the efforts of the President to avert war be unsuccessful, just as we have done in the past moments of national crises.[26]

By September 1917, the Zionist press boasted that contrary to "the impression" that "the Jews – especially the Yiddish-speaking Jews – are the prime movers in the pacifist propaganda in this country and that our young men are avoiding the draft," the general Jewish and the Zionist response could not have been more different. Jews evinced "an unmistakable enthusiasm for the war," in which "the Zionists are unusually well represented."[27] Within a few months of mobilization there were reported to be some 50,000 Jews under arms for the United States.[28]

Zionists throughout Europe, and eventually, the United States, seized what they saw as an opportunity to prove themselves on three levels. Firstly, as individuals, their manliness could be tested and demonstrated beyond a shadow of a doubt. The war rekindled the early Zionists' call for the creation, in Max Nordau's words, of a *Muskeljudentum*, a "Jewry of muscle." And as members of an embryonic nation, as Zionists, they could show their worth as a fighting force, deserving of their own nation and Jewish national honor. Furthermore, they also were fighting as Jews belonging to a particular nation. Overall, they were not immune from the larger passion, in the United States and elsewhere, to embrace unequivocal forms of masculinity and thereby to reassure themselves that modernity had not eroded manliness.[29]

Indeed, the Zionists, like everyone else in 1914, had little idea of what was ultimately in store for them. But what Zionists got out of the war bore little relation to their naive formula of fighting for manly honor.[30] This notion was rooted in the process of Jewish emancipation, in which many Westernized Jews firmly and optimistically believed it possible to earn respect and acceptance through changing their own attitudes and behavior – or at least through changing the perceptions of their thought and actions.[31]

The Zionists' very reaction to the war, and their attempts to use it as a springboard to their goals, outside the realm of diplomacy, was complicated and ambiguous. At least part of the reason why the movement failed to grow appreciably in Germany and Austria, and Britain from 1918 to 1933, stems from the difficulty of integrating the war experience into Zionism. Due to the late entry of the United States into the Great War, and the relatively contingent nature of its engagement, it did not figure as prominently in American Zionist discourse as was the case in Europe. After the Armistice, the movement was largely unable to exploit the war in its interwar polemics and imagery. This may be contrasted to the effective deployment of World War I-era symbols by right-wing and revanchist groups in Germany and Italy, and the mythologies of World War II appropriated by postwar communist regimes. Although Zionists during the First World War tried to construct a vision of a new Jewish warrior,[32] such a figure did not enjoy widespread recognition until the fight for the formation of the State of Israel in 1947–48, or later, through the remarkable Israeli victory in the Six-Day War of 1967.[33]

The second question this chapter addresses is: what did the Great War mean for individual Zionists?[34] To be sure, it gave rise to the expectation or wishful thinking that heroism could be translated into acceptance and rewards, and that the stereotype of Jews as disloyal, uncourageous, and constitutionally unfit as soldiers would be convincingly overturned.[35] Once the fighting began, however, other effects became evident: the war helped turn some Jews, who were not Zionists before, into Zionists; for others already identifying with the movement, the war instilled an even greater degree of sympathy. But what was the process which, along with the horrors of trench warfare,[36] steered the Jews who previously seemed uninterested in Zionism toward the movement? In addition, how did committed Zionists make sense of the war experience, and fit it into their Zionist *Weltanschauung*?

At the very beginning of the war, Jewish conscripts – in harmony with most of their non-Jewish compatriots – believed that the exposure to life in the military was good for them as men, and moreover, as national-minded Jews. Jewish separatism was understandably subdued, as it seemed more crucial to stress the successful Jewish integration into their country's armed forces. In a private letter (as opposed to the numerous published soldiers' letters), Robert Weltsch wrote Martin Buber that after a week in the battlefield and about a month on Russian soil, his health was holding up quite well, possibly even "restored."[37] A British soldier reported from training camp that "it is a very lively and healthy life here. For instance, we have plenty of good food and hard training. It's absolutely jolly from morn till night. I am a Jew boy called Sam, and I might say that every soldier in the camp treats me as an old friend."[38] Another recruit concurred that "I have all the comforts necessary. The food is good and wholesome and [there is] plenty of it . . . I am having the time of my life, finding that I can easily make friends among total strangers. We are all on very good terms."[39] American soldiers, too, found camp life to be strangely amicable, in which even the aesthetics of the military precision were immediately internalized by Jewish conscripts. "There is not a man here," wrote Maurice Samuel from Camp Upton, Long Island, "who is not looking healthier than when he arrived, and this despite the difficulty many of our boys experienced in habituating themselves to goyish food."[40] German Zionists tended to see their initiation in the military as consistent and complementary to their experience in Zionist youth groups and fraternities.[41]

In the heady first few weeks of warfare, when it seemed, as anticipated, to be a conflict of decisive victories and defeats, Jews confessed to being "thrilled" in the heat of battle.[42] By the onset of winter and the literal entrenchment of armies after three months of fighting, however, the tone of soldiers' accounts had markedly changed. Writing on November 7, 1914, Quartermaster Sergeant Charles Thompson assured the readers of the *Jewish Chronicle* from Belgium that he was "not complaining" and "not in the least sorry I am on active service." But as opposed to the cleanliness, vigor, and healthfulness that characterized the training camp experience for many, now he had not "had my clothes off for ten days. It's been nothing but trenches and saddle." The war was losing its glamour: "Whilst riding towards Nieuport, the sights I saw made me feel sick. The dead (Belgians and Germans) were lying piled up five and six deep, and the stench was something awful, the trenches in many cases having been utilised as graves."[43] The horror of the trenches, as is well known, would only grow. After 1915, if a soldier referred to "my mansion below the earth,"[44] it was with the blackest irony. Noting the fourth anniversary of the beginning of the war, the *Jewish Chronicle* painted its most nihilistic picture:

Standing on the brink of the abyss of the unknown which opens up to Mankind the fifth year of the world contest, minds the least contemplative must be filled with thought and with anxiety as to the future. The great disaster which destiny cast upon the world, like a huge smothering cloud, four years ago, has not yet spent itself. The darkness of war, with all that war comprises, still rests upon Mankind and the wickedness of war apparently must proceed, because its alternative remains undiscovered by man.[45]

"People in England," wrote a soldier, "cannot realise how awful it is without seeing it. The men in trenches are more than heroes; they are wonders."[46] Overall, the grotesque horrors of the trenches were understated – possibly so as not to incite greater alarm at the home front and among those who had not yet joined. "I was in the trenches 168 hours all told," wrote another Jewish soldier, "and then I was rendered almost incapable having been frost-bitten. I was sent to the base and then drafted to Rouen. After staying there a week I was marked up for an English hospital. So here I am anxiously waiting to be cured."[47]

The fighting on the eastern front engulfed significant areas in the Pale of Settlement, home to the Jewish masses.[48] Millions of soldiers had unprecedented exposure to the *Shtetl*. Jews, Zionist and non-Zionist, were witness to a vibrant but impoverished and unraveling Jewish world. Perhaps their most lasting impression was of the Jews' "frightful poverty" and destitution.[49] Due to the range of circumstances, it is difficult to generalize about these experiences. But there is evidence to suggest that what German Jews, especially Zionists, saw as the materially and morally depraved condition of Eastern Jewry was a spur to their Zionism, or at least gave them an image of a world they hoped fundamentally to transform.

The German and Austrian conscripts' war experience was particularly influenced by contact with Jewish girls and women during their tour of duty. One of the most frightful and humiliating aspects of the Russian troops' onslaught on the Jews of the Pale was their treatment of women. The worst atrocities were apparently perpetrated in the spring and summer of 1915 when the Russian army faced military disaster and forced the evacuation of the Pale – deporting hundreds of thousands of Jews eastward. Untold numbers of Jewish girls and women were raped and reportedly mutilated.[50] Surely the apparent singling out of Jewish women for such abuse during this frightful episode weighed heavily on the soldiers.[51]

As much as dealing with women is a memorable part of any soldier's experience, one can say that because of the ties between the German Jews and Eastern Jews, the nature of this meeting was distinctive. On the one hand, German Jewish men seemed to have internalized the stereotype of Jewish women held by the majority culture; they found Jewish women of Eastern Europe to be unusually beautiful, sensual, and alluring. "I believe," recorded Sammy Gronnemann, "that nowhere in the world can one find feminine beauty as in Kovno and Vilna [Kaunas and Vilnius]," that is, cities where he had been in touch with the large Jewish populations.[52] Although such evaluations are bound to be subjective, similar sentiments were recorded by numerous soldiers. In addition to the predictable romantic liaisons, there seem to have been a number of friendships struck up between German Jewish soldiers and Eastern Jewish women. German Jewish soldiers gained prestige in the eyes of their comrades, notably the non-Jews, when they showed themselves to be popular with the native Jewish girls.[53] Several soldiers' memoirs imply that the attention they received, and the level of intellectual engagement with the Russian and Polish Jewish women was beyond that to which they were accustomed at home with the Jewish women in their cohort. The intelligence, and depth and breadth of education, of many of these women were striking.[54]

But there was a disturbing underside to their encounter with Jewish womanhood in the Pale. German and Austrian Jewish soldiers came into repeated contact with Jewish prostitutes and pimps.[55] In the Jewish streets and inns, they were told with a wink that "anything their 'hearts' desired" could be theirs.[56] Certainly, the middle-class sensibilities of many of the soldiers were offended, even if Jewish prostitutes were a known element of Central European urban life.[57] It seems that the sheer number of them and their visibility was alarming.

Perhaps the most detailed account of Jewish prostitution on the eastern front is provided in a long letter from Robert Weltsch, "Im Felde," to Martin Buber in May 1916. "The war," Weltsch writes, "has disintegrated the inner structure of the Jewish people." One of its most dreadful consequences, a "national disaster" for the Eastern Jews, is its toll on girls and women. The soldiers' sexual energies, especially the officers, seem fixed on "the beautiful Jewess"; this is a prominent motif in the military humor newspapers. It obviously pains Weltsch that he cannot just dismiss these women as naive, as tramps, or simply as girls out looking for a good time. Clearly, they are more sophisticated; they seem all too aware of the tragedy in which they play a part. One is left with the impression that widespread prostitution has not just sprung up during the war – it has been in place for some time. When coming across a group of ten- to fourteen-year-old Jewish boys, after their initial

questions, "do you need something?," or "can I sell you something?,"
without losing a beat they ask: "Maybe you want to meet a pretty girl?"
Even if the boys are in religious garb, it is no preventative. To Weltsch,
the prevalence of Jewish prostitution, tacitly condoned as a necessity
across a broad spectrum of the community, signaled the pitiable
degeneration of the Jews.[58]

Another unnerving element was that boys who seemed to be the girls'
brothers fervently sought clients among the Jews and non-Jews – but
particularly among the officers. All of this gave rise, as well, to a stream
of apologetics concerning Jewish prostitutes. Some popular stories
asserted that many Jewish girls were not, in fact whores – they had no
intention of giving their bodies for a fee. It was, in one feminized maven
story, a clever ploy to dupe non-Jewish officers out of tidy sums or free
meals.[59]

Yet women, perhaps more so than men, also exemplified the potential
of Zionism for Jewish national transformation. Zionist women the
German soldiers met were still beautiful and mysterious – but they were
perceived as morally upright, well behaved, and displaying a keen sense
of purpose. In "a small East Galician town that had been almost totally
destroyed," Weltsch writes Buber, he by chance meets several Zionist
women, who first of all dazzle him with their fluency in modern Hebrew.
To Weltsch, these women "understand that nationalism is not a series of
slogans, but rather a philosophy of life, a determination to heal life, to
care and work for the health and purity of the community . . . Above all,
they realize that nationalism implies grappling with the vulgarity and
dishonesty in one's own heart and within a people."[60] Certainly this was
the best hope of the nation. Women became central in Weltsch's own
scheme of regenerated Jewry; he refused to countenance the institution-
alized debasement of Jewish women. His aspirations were shared by
other leaders, such as Louis Brandeis, who insinuated that Zionism was
at least part of the cure for the widespread Jewish prostitution in New
York.[61] On the surface, both men were ashamed and appalled; it is fair
to assume, however, that their rumination over the plight of Jewish
prostitutes indicated their recognition of a larger problem: the nexus of
power, gender, and anti-Semitism, which in this instance hurled young
women into the abyss.

Jewish men closest to the Central European soldiers, in terms of age,
did not seem to make much of an impression – not in a positive sense, at
any rate. Zionists were more inclined to reflect on their experiences with
women or older Jews. It was the encounters with older Jews that also
contributed to a developing Jewish national consciousness for some
German Jews, and galvanized the Zionism of others.[62] It is usually

recalled that the most significant chasm between Jewish and non-Jewish German soldiers came in the wake of the infamous "Jew count" among the German forces toward the end of the war. This survey resulted from complaints that Jews were shirking service, and engaging in smuggling and other unsavory business that was undermining the German war effort. But the argument might be made that a serious break came earlier. It is important to remember the timing of the conflict. In August troops were mobilized, and Jewish high holidays began several weeks later. Even for soldiers who were quite detached from Jewish observance, their first Rosh Hoshana and Yom Kippur in the field proved to be very profound – for Jews in all armies.[63] Modris Eksteins has poignantly rendered the strange, temporary brotherhood that broke out during the first Christmas of the war;[64] there is very little written about the extent to which Jews felt a part of, or alienated from, that unique episode. Jewish soldiers, during their holiday time, probably would not have suggested such fraternization among their enemy co-religionists, so as not to give rise to charges of dual allegiance or conflicting loyalties based on their "Jewish nationality."

Britain's Jewish soldiers were reminded that their allies, the French, had read the Rosh Hoshana service "on the battle-fields of France," when the Prussians soundly defeated them in 1870.[65] This, however, did not seem to be overly inspirational. Despite reports of the pains some took to participate in Jewish holiday services,[66] British Jews in uniform gained a reputation for ignoring or even displaying contempt for Jewish religious observance, which was yet another cause for public outcries and controversies.[67] Yet for a number of individuals, sharing the holidays seemed to quicken friendships between Jewish soldiers, and encouraged the feeling that they were separate from their non-Jewish peers.[68] German Jewish soldiers experienced this especially in the East where they developed a particular bond with local Jews. Often the locals reminded them of their grandparents; frequently, the soldiers expressed amazement at their conspicuous "high culture." Zionism was not uncommon among those they respected as the cultural elite, that is, the *Ostjuden* who identified with the German cultural heritage.[69] It is natural that the German Jewish soldiers, while recognizing a kinship with so-called foreigners, simultaneously estranged themselves from their comrades.[70] If such experiences did not convince them to be Zionists, many were sensitized to notions of Jewish cultural nationhood, which might have made them more accepting of Zionism. It led some, to be sure, to question their own identity as more complex than they had earlier assumed.

For a small but critical number of German and Austrian Jewish soldiers, the war turned into an intensive training in Zionist ideology and Jewish culture. In large part, responsibility lies in the efforts of the young Hans Kohn, at prisoner-of-war camps in Krasnaya Ryechka, Novo-Nikolayevsk, and Krasnoyarsk in Siberia, which were home to hundreds of Jewish prisoners.[71] From the publications of prisoners, and recollections of Hugo Knoepfmacher and Kohn himself we have a remarkably vivid account of this episode. In these camps a veritable Zionist university came into being; the educational circle around Kohn at Krasnoyarsk had about 370 members. When it swelled to its greatest numbers, the camp (including Jews and non-Jews) boasted three separate theater companies, a 65- to 70-piece orchestra, and a library of over 10,000 volumes.[72] It is daunting to think of how much of that library came from the Kohn family packages to their son; he wrote home to Prague every day, and requested several books, often multi-volume sets, in every piece of correspondence. He is kind enough to note his receipt of the most recent shipment, as well.[73] The first seminar which Knoepfmacher sat in on in Krasnaya was on Jewish mysticism; among the other memorable lectures of Kohn was one in which he discussed Jewish nationalism using illustrations from Anatole France, Ibsen, and Richard Beer-Hoffman.[74] Although it was not a mass phenomenon, it seems to have been a uniquely transfiguring experience for those who took part as instructors and as students.[75]

Women Zionists, for whom the war was a spur to their Zionist inclinations, also managed to work for the "cause" in European prisoner-of-war camps. Gertrude Van Tijn wrote that she "stumbled into work for war-prisoners" which mainly consisted of distributing kosher food to soldiers; after a few months, this project became "a big organization." She was able to cultivate contacts with the Red Cross and the American Jewish Joint Distribution Committee (JDC, or "the Joint"), which helped to build informal bridges between Zionism and the general relief work. Earlier Van Tijn had held an "important post" in the Jewish National Fund while it was based in Holland.[76]

Nothing approaching the vast scale of Kohn's Zionist enterprise materialized in any other setting. The potential for Zionist work among soldiers, however, was surely acknowledged. One American Jewish soldier wrote that "the hardships of military life utterly preclude [my own] taking the initiative in Zionist work." He implored the national and local Zionist organizations to supply "loads of literature" for "the men in camps" who "are now reading books they would never have dreamed of reading before. How eagerly would they satisfy through books their newly aroused interest in Zionism!"[77] For the most part, this demand was taken up by Hadassah.[78] Writing in January 1918 from Texas,

Henrietta Szold reported that "I have seen soldiers upon soldiers – at Waco, at Ft. Worth, [and] here [in San Antonio]. The population here has been increased 105,000 through the cantonments. Among them are 4,000 Jewish boys. Here and elsewhere many of the Jewish men have attended the Zionist meetings."[79]

German Zionists immediately publicized the exceptional Zionist educational work in the POW camps; the Zionist organizations in all countries also were anxious to show the Jews on the home front evidence of Zionist activity among those on active service. For example, soldiers were reported to be enthusiastic in joining in organizational and even fundraising work,[80] and Zionists at home were informed that drawings of the well-known Zionist E. M. Lilien adorned Jewish soldiers' magazines.[81] Predictably, biographies of individual Zionists in action were prominent in wartime Zionist organs,[82] and the movement attempted to keep Zionist soldiers abreast of developments in Palestine.[83] By the war's end, the Kartell jüdischer Verbindungen (KJV), the German Zionist student fraternity, reported that around 10 percent of its membership had been killed in battle.[84] Fallen soldiers also were incorporated into Zionist institutions, as their families were requested to commemorate their deaths by inscribing them in the "Golden Book" of the Jewish National Fund (JNF), or by honoring them with a tree or trees in Palestine.[85] Among the Jewish bystanders who were devastated by the war, it was claimed that the most effective relief work was spearheaded by Zionist groups.[86]

The United States, with its late entry into the war, consciously assumed the role as the bankroller of the movement in Europe and of Zionist enterprises in Palestine. In August 1914 Jewry in the United States was not called to arms, but rather to participate in "constructive work" to uplift the Eastern Jews who were caught in harm's way.[87] But even before the outbreak of war in August 1914, it was reported in the American Zionist organ, the *Maccabaean*, that anti-Semitism was "rampant" in Germany and pervasive among officers in the Austrian army. Before the war was enjoined on the side of the Allies, the harsh invective was also directed at Russia, and to a lesser degree France, for indulging in anti-Semitic rhetoric and acts.[88] Even though the drama of the war was not as heightened in the United States as it was in Europe, it certainly fit into the explicit Zionist goal to "restore the Self-Respect and proud Manhood of our Youth."[89] American members could take pride in the ability of German Jewish soldiers to handle a machine gun.[90]

Only months before the start of World War I Zionists in the United States ruminated about the relationship between Jewish soldiering and anti-Semitism, as three US Jewish soldiers were among the seventeen killed in the "active intervention in the civil war" in Mexico. Those who were killed constituted a

> proportion in excess of the mathematical share of Jews of this country. But this is in keeping with American tradition. The Jews of this country have always offered their lives in excess of their numbers in defense of their adopted country. They have been valiant soldiers and sailors . . . Even in Russia [Jews] have fought nobly, and fighting for Russia, hoped to convince that country of the injustice of regarding such defenders as aliens. So too, in perfidious Roumania, in Bulgaria, in France, in England. But more especially so in the United States. Let us not scoff at the Jewish youth who enlists in a dare-devil moment. Whatever the immediate motive for his enlistment, there is in him, probably a sub-conscious feeling, the desire to uphold the Jewish name. He fights as an American soldier to show the world that Jews have the fighting spirit. May this fighting spirit animate all Jews in doing battle for their own country, as well as for their adopted countries.[91]

Prior to the United States' tilt in favor of the Allied powers, the Zionists of the United States denounced both evils of "Pan-Slavism and Teutonism." The tasks of American Zionists were at first left very vague, which seemed to imply mainly financial support.[92] Zionists, possibly more than American Jews at large, wished to overcome the "serious concern" that Jews might not prove loyal to the United States in wartime due to their socialist leanings.[93] American Zionists had great difficulty remaining neutral in the first months of war.[94] Their earlier outcry that Russia had largely reneged on "its promise" to emancipate the Jews had to be reformulated when it seemed that the United States (for a brief moment) was to became the tsar's ally.[95] However much "the crisis of European Jewry also invigorated Zionism," it is difficult to imagine that the specifically Zionist effort toward relief was greatly distinguished from the general Jewish endeavor to assist their brethren, especially due to the creation of the ostensibly non-partisan JDC and the American Jewish Relief Committee in the midst of the war.[96]

Similar to all of the peoples at war, Zionists, too, tried to mobilize images for their cause. In the United States this effort was the spur to one of the most heated controversies of the war years. In January 1916, a cartoon appeared on the front page of the *Maccabaean* which inflamed a number of Zionists: it shows an apparently upper-class Jew, resembling many anti-Semitic illustrations with a pince-nez and hooked nose, large stomach, and top hat. He is trying to prevent the forward march of a group of proud, upstanding, good-looking, and youthful Zionists, who carry signs reading "nationality," "democracy," and "Zion." He and his cohort are aghast at the sight (figure 1). The motive behind featuring that cartoon, in a magazine which did not usually present editorial opinions in such a manner, is not entirely clear. Perhaps the editors were exasperated at the failure of their organization to draw larger numbers of Jews, and frustrated in the face of the more successful recruitment drives of the organizations founded to alleviate the suffering of Jews in the East, such as that of the American Jewish Committee.[97] At any rate, the overlap between this striking image and anti-Semitic drawings was not lost on the readers of the *Maccabaean*, a number of whom voiced their indignation. It was inexcusable, a number of Zionists argued, for the journal to depict its opinion through such means.[98]

During the war a number of other images, largely photographic, were introduced into the Zionist visual discourse. One particular motif depicted Jews fleeing their homes in the wake of battle. Pictures carried captions such as "On the March" and "Dispossessed."[99] In addition cartoons were used to try to portray the European Jewish predicament in the war, most frequently in magazines for Zionist youth.[100] These images did not, however, become a lasting part of the body of Zionist representation that circulated during the interwar period. The most memorable, graphic scene from the plight of diaspora Jewry until 1938 was probably the picture of bodies lined up after the Kishinev pogrom of 1903.[101]

In sum, the war could only have influenced Zionism in a number of ways. Predictably, the ravages wrought by the war in Palestine and Eastern Europe became a focus of fundraising, which consumed more and more of the movement's resources and energy. For propaganda purposes, the war offered the unique opportunity to testify to the Jews' mettle as able-bodied fighting men, and as a stock worthy of equal rights; no amount of proof, however, could undo the stereotypes among non-Jews of ill-will, especially in the defeated nations, of Jews as cowards, cut-throats, spies, and black-marketeers.[102] Furthermore, to the Zionist faithful the war could not serve as an unmitigated unifying factor. The Zionists' attempted appropriation of the war was obviously hampered by the division of their membership among the combatants. The commitment of the Jews, even the Zionists, to their European states was correctly read as genuine and deep seated. In the war's first year some half-million Jews were under arms.[103] How could the Russian army be completely vilified by Germans and Austrians when the Zionists also admitted that its forces included heroic Jewish soldiers?[104] The report in the British Jewish press that "a member of the Rothschild family in Vienna has been acting as a staff officer with the Austrian invading army at Krasnik (Russia)" was not simply meant to convey a curiosity, but the fact that Jewish allegiance and service in Central powers, too, cut across class lines.[105] There was at least one vague attempt of American Zionists ideologically to distance themselves from German Zionists,[106] but this

1 "How unJewish!": cartoon, *The Maccabaean* (January 1916): cover.

was an exception. One of the few things that could be agreed upon by all in the West was that Jews were treated in a "barbarous" way by Poles.[107] The pitting of Jew against Jew was unavoidable, and clearly painful.[108] The enemy could not be evil incarnate, with Jews and Zionists to be found nearly everywhere.

Perhaps more significantly, drawing on the war experience was not very effective because there was so little in Jewish tradition, and the liberal ethic out of which Zionism grew, to make militarism an organic part of the movement in the diaspora.[109] By the time Martin Buber called for the teaching and promotion of a different type of Jewish heroism – a heroism of the spirit, above all – the dogged brutality of the war made such pronouncements seem escapist.[110]

Although it would be glorified by a segment of Zionists in retrospect,[111] the Jewish Legion, grudgingly tolerated by the British, was initially denounced by the Zionist leadership. Because of its subservience to Britain and its vital link to the right-wing Revisionists and its identification with Vladimir Jabotinsky, Central European and American Zionists could not easily appropriate it.[112] There was at least one shining moment for the Jewish Legion: its dignified and colorful march through London's East End early in 1918.[113] But this scene was counterbalanced by Jabotinsky's utter failure to rouse enthusiasm for his plan. What probably stood out more clearly was the spectacle of Jabotinsky being "pelted with vegetables and jostled" by throngs of Jewish men whom he claimed to champion.[114] In the United States, the first extensive treatment of the Jewish Legion in the Zionist press was a review of Col. J. H. Patterson's book, *With the Zionists in Gallipoli* in August 1916.[115] "My chief object in writing this book," Patterson stated, "is to interest the Hebrew nation in the fortunes of the Zionists and show them of what their Russian brothers are capable, even under the command of an alien in race and religion."[116] Patterson was a non-Jew who was convinced that Jabotinsky was the most able and far-sighted Zionist leader. He wrote about the second incarnation of the Jewish military force in a later volume intended more for non-Jewish British readers, *With the Judaeans in the Palestine Campaign*, that

I felt that the Adjutant-General confided a great trust to me when I was selected for the command of this Jewish unit. It was a complete change from the command of an Irish Battalion, but the Irishman and Jew have much in common – temperament, generosity, love of children, devotion to parents, readiness to help those down on their luck, and be it noted, great personal bravery. These qualities will probably not appear out of place to my readers so far as the Irishman is concerned, but I imagine many will be surprised when they hear that they also apply to the Jew. It is true, however, and so should be more widely known. The soul-stilling deeds on the battlefield of such heroes as Judas Maccabaeus, Bar Kochba, and many others can never be forgotten.[117]

A German edition of Jabotinsky's memoir of his wartime travails appeared in 1930, replete with portraits of Patterson, Captain Joseph Trumpeldor, and Jabotinsky "as a Lieutenant of the 'Royal Fusiliers.'"[118] Although there was an attempt to revive the myth of the Jew as "warrior" through the Jewish Legion,[119] it did not seem to have a great impact. At best the pictures would evoke retrospective curiosity and nostalgia. "The Zion Mule Corps" and its successor, the "Judaeans," representing "a very small fraction of the half million Jews who are shedding their blood for both sides in the great conflict,"[120] did not broadly inspire the Jewish and Zionist faithful. Certainly the reputation of the Jewish Legionnaires was not going to be enhanced or preserved for posterity by the kind of sentimental poetry that it inspired. The following, entitled "The Jewish Legion," was penned by an American volunteer:

'Twas said that the glory of Israel was dead,
The mighty have fallen, the Shechina has fled,
Behold now, the militant soul of the Jew
By oppression long fettered yet rising anew!

From the most distant Ghettoes by destiny flung,
They come! Our own heroes, the daring and young,
And writ is their aim on our banners unfurled:
"For Israel! For Zion! For a free, righteous world!"

By strong faith encouraged, by loyal hearts blest,
To Zion they come now, our bravest and best,
All joyously eager to enter the fray,
To hasten the coming of freedom's new day.

From Dan to Beer-Sheba, from Jordan to the Sea,
O'er snowy-peaked Hermon in loved Galilee,
The spirit of heroes of ages gone by
Shall guard our brave legion and never be nigh.

By hero-blood nurtured through struggle and toil,
The fair flower of freedom shall rise from our soil,
Its fragrance will sweep over mountain and deep
And our world shall awake from its ages long sleep!

Gibore Israel! May the blessing of God
Enshroud those who fall on our land's sacred sod,
And Israel, unshackled, will tenderly keep
Most holy each spot where our fallen brave sleep![121]

It was only over time that all Western Zionists could share in the jubilation over the Balfour Declaration, which became a great rallying point for the movement.[122] Earlier promises for Zionist breakthroughs fell flat; a year or so into the war it was rumored that Germany might press for peace with "the granting of Jewish rights everywhere" as one of the conditions – which was taken seriously at that time.[123] A similar proposal was made by the American Zionist Horace Kallen, who called for the granting of universal Jewish rights and "something he obscurely called 'nationalization' in Palestine." This was another Zionist wartime paradox, in that emancipation and "equal rights" were not supposed to be the chief aims of Zionism; it was most likely a means to gain leverage for the Zionist position.[124] The Russian Revolution also muddled the movement's aim to appropriate the war for its own purposes; the question was raised in many minds: is Zionism necessary if the Jews of Russia are free?[125] A widely circulated pamphlet argued, in a rather pilpulistic way, that the movement would be even more popular among the newly liberated Jews.[126] By the war's end, the appeal for creating nation-states based on ethnicity helped to propel the movement forward.[127] But the Versailles deliberations underscored the movement's reliance on the Great Powers and laid bare the fragmented, international character of the movement. Sadly, the allegations of German anti-Semitism were more indicative of enduring trends than anyone could have imagined.[128]

To be sure, Zionists attempted to use the war to fight the stereotype of Jews as unfit for the manly art of warfare and unworthy of nationhood. The Jews fought, fought well, and died for their respective countries.[129] Their efforts, however, convinced few beyond the Jews themselves. The dominant tendency was to maintain that the Jews' religious/national identity overwhelmed their claim of loyalty to the European fatherlands. On balance, the mass death in the trenches did more to destroy European Jewish civilization and the Zionist dream of Jewish regeneration than the plodding Zionist diplomatic march toward their goals. This was eerily foreshadowed in an American Zionist proclamation of August 1914:

One issue of the World-War is not in doubt – the loss to human progress. Whoever is victor, no indemnity will pay for the destruction of cities built up during the patient centuries and the devastation of the fields trodden down by great armies. The great, young army of the dead, the youth of all lands and boundless potentialities cannot be replaced. No victory or gains the war can bring will fill the gaps. One doubts altogether the gains of bloody warfare. It must remain for the calmer and wiser spirits of all countries to lessen the pride of the victors and the bitterness of the vanquished, that neither insolence nor rancor may sow the seeds of a new hatred that will make of peace only a breathing spell for a new war.[130]

Compared to most of their Zionist brethren, the Americans were haunted by the specter of nationalism in Europe:

The most striking lesson of the war is the demonstration of the strength of nationalist feeling, to us in America too strong and terrible a force to be handed over to a few men in power to rise. The millions of Socialists fighting under their national colors, as Babel and Jaurès prophesied they would, shows how much stronger than aught else is the spirit of Nationalism. We must be united to maintain it not as a weapon of destruction, but as the great creative power it has always been since the Dawn of history.[131]

This stands in stark contrast to the Zionists' best hope that virile Jewish fighting men would help carry the movement to a swift victory and earn Jewry the acceptance of their countrymen.[132] Instead, the movement was forced to reformulate the legacy of the Great War upon which they hoped to build. Among the means they articulated to salvage the collective misfortunes of the war was to hope that the courage shown by Jewish soldiers in battle might be applied to Palestine, where a transformation was imminent from heroism in war to heroism in pioneering the

Yishuv.[133] And in addition to personal bravery, Zionists also had demonstrated an organizational zeal and brilliance – particularly the work of the
US "Provisional Zionist Committee" and Hadassah's American Medical
Unit in Palestine – which seemed to point to a brighter future and
constructive mobilization. These bodies had helped rescue Palestine and
would sustain it until the ultimate Zionist goals were met.[134] Ironically,
Hadassah's victories were mainly engineered by womanly women,
as opposed to the manly men writ so large in Zionism and other
nationalisms. Unlike other nationalists, though, Zionists for the most
part did not dream of a new breed of men rising out of the trenches. The
Great War had in many ways beaten them down and frustrated their
efforts. Except for the essential and "sacred" Balfour Declaration, the
Zionists could draw little from the wellsprings of the war experience
toward fortifying and spreading their movement in the West.

2   A new pantheon: the portrayal of Zionist leaders in the West

> There is not a single great man in history of whom the popular fancy has not drawn a picture entirely different from the actual man; and it is this imaginary conception, created by the masses to suit their needs and their inclinations, that is the real great man, exerting an influence which abides in some cases for thousands of years – this, not the concrete original, who lived a short space in the actual world, and was never seen by the masses in his true likeness.   Ahad Ha-Am, "Moses" (1904)[1]

Every political and social movement, especially in its germinal phase, has its heroic leaders. Zionism is no exception. As the movement took form in the late nineteenth century, Theodor Herzl (1860–1904) assumed the mantle as champion of Zionism and personification of the Zionist ideal.[2] Even Herzl's most ardent critics, including Ahad Ha-Am (1856–1927), were obliged to admit that the movement's rise never could have been imagined without the myth and reality of Herzl.[3] In Zionism's earliest days heroic stature also was accorded cultural critic Max Nordau (1849–1923), who was more famous than Herzl among both the general and the Jewish public of the fin-de-siècle. In large part the iconography of prewar Zionism comprises portraits of Herzl and Nordau, separately and together, and the movement's polemics are heavy with paeans to the leaders. After the death of Herzl in 1904, and with Nordau's subsequent falling out with the movement's heads, opinion-shapers in Zionism began to cultivate the legends of those who would become the new heroes. Lord Balfour (1848–1930), Chaim Weizmann (1874–1952), Nahum Sokolow (1856–1936), Louis Brandeis (1856–1941), Henrietta Szold (1860–1945), and Albert Einstein (1879–1955) were especially venerated in Western Zionism from 1914 to 1933. With regard to political symbolism, their portrayal served not only to highlight their status and achievements; the movement also magnified and exploited these personalities to create an impression that a broad consensus existed about the correctness, and likelihood of success, of the Zionist project. Each figure represented traits with which the movement wished to identify, and their public endorsement gave Zionism luster. A common thread which unites the projection of these figures, and complemented other efforts to nationalize Western Jewry, was the claim that they exemplified Zionism's affinity to a secular, humanistic culture. They were cited as exemplary of the movement's inextricable connection with the greatest fruits of human civilization and hopes for the Jewish nation's development as a "light unto the nations."

The selection of Balfour, Weizmann, Sokolow, Brandeis, Szold, and Einstein is not meant to slight the heroic acts or leadership roles of others.[4] To be sure, several individuals were regarded as Zionist heroic leaders, but they appealed to more limited constituencies. For instance, Martin Buber (1878–1965) was idolized by Zionist youth in German-speaking lands and by an intellectual elite in the movement.[5] The publication of his journal *Der Jude* was seen as a signal event in the intellectual maturation of Zionism.[6] He was also recognized, among those who fervently sought an accommodation between the Zionist movement and Palestine's Arabs, as a forceful voice for dialogue and reconciliation.[7] Buber's style, however, did not necessarily play well to the Zionist rank and file, and he did not regularly engage in publicity tours in the interwar years. Vladimir Jabotinsky (1880–1940), who was a spectacular Zionist publicist, also fostered a crucial group of loyalists – but in his case it was of the right wing, the opposite end of the political spectrum from Buber. Jabotinsky's disciples would move to the center of power in the realized Jewish state a generation after their mentor's death. Yet as much as support for Jabotinsky verged on the fanatic, the contempt he inspired was also immense, and his star never rose as high in Central and Western Europe and the United States as it did in Poland and South Africa.[8] Another figure who seems a likely candidate for inclusion in a pantheon of Zionist interwar heroes is Joseph Trumpeldor, who was killed in a raid on his settlement, Tel Hai, in 1920. Despite apparently insurmountable obstacles, Trumpeldor became an officer in the Russian army and was recognized for his bravery in the Russo-Japanese War; his arm was severed in battle. Yael Zerubavel writes that as a martyr, and because of his complicated make-up, Trumpeldor's image was especially malleable; it was held up like a prism by both the far left and far right, each one able to refract its own colors.[9] He therefore filled heroic functions that were substantially different from the individuals considered here, and his reputation was etched most deeply in Palestine and his native Russia.[10] Despite the mythologies of Trumpeldor and the Jewish Legion, the depiction of Zionist heroes had little to do with the war ethos which left so strong an impression on other national movements after the First World War. On the contrary,

Zionism's idealization of its post-World War I heroes as embodying the height of culture, democratic values, and refined civility – rather than being identified with power and brute force – was quite contiguous with the homage paid its pre-1914 leaders.

The figures discussed here were a living presence in Western Europe and the United States for most of the interwar years; they were ceremonial fixtures of Western Zionism from 1914 to 1933. The following analysis is, then, not an exercise in biography, or collective biography, in a conventional sense. Nor is it an attempt to detail their individual Zionist politics. Here I will be most concerned with their reception and presentation within the Zionist movement's organs and publicity. Although in many respects each of these figures epitomized some form of dissonance with mainstream Zionism, they typically were rendered to support Zionism's claim to be a most noble human endeavor, and the inter-Zionist tensions that they themselves embodied were downplayed or obscured. For instance, despite the bitter quarrels and palpable antipathy between Chaim Weizmann and Louis Brandeis, who firmly disagreed over their visions of Zionism, the fact that they stood under the tent of the same movement was regarded – particularly in retrospect – as overwhelming the differences between them.

One of the greatest watersheds in the history of Zionism, by all accounts, was the Balfour Declaration. It is obvious that Lord Balfour is a critical figure of interwar Zionism, due primarily to the fact that he penned the document which became the veritable cornerstone of the Jewish national home.[11] The reception of the Balfour Declaration is virtually inseparable from the reception of Balfour the man; a photograph of the typed letter of November 1917 was often reproduced in the Zionist movement's organs.[12] To the Zionist faithful, the Declaration was no less than a modern-day miracle, however much it was the product of years of diplomatic wrangling and crude calculations (and miscalculations) on the part of the British Foreign Office.[13] Especially to the minority of traditionally observant Jews who were aligned with the movement, it seemed that the messianic era "promised to the Jewish people had begun" with the Declaration, as Mordechai Breuer writes in his history of German Jewish orthodoxy.[14] To be sure, there were exceptions to the widespread chorus of approval. From Jabotinsky and his loyalists there was criticism that the pronouncement did not go far enough in advancing the movement's goals. This group, however, always had a circumscribed appeal in Germany, Britain, and the United States. Max Nordau, too, voiced his disappointment over the nebulousness of the Declaration, but after the First World War he was far less of a force to be reckoned with.[15] Nevertheless, pointed remarks against the

Declaration were usually aimed at the Zionists who accepted and praised it, rather than at its messenger. Few Zionists would have questioned Herbert Samuel's evaluation that "in the history of the Jewish people the name Balfour will enjoy unchallenged immortality, evoking comparisons with that of Cyrus, for the issue of the Balfour Declaration marked the opening of a new epoch in the annals of Jewry which will be recognized as such even in the remotest centuries to come."[16]

One of Balfour's biographers, Max Egremont, concludes that "Balfour often seemed strangely ornamental."[17] No one prized him more as an ornament than the Zionists. The name and image of Lord Balfour was mainly employed as a reminder of Britain's promise to help bring to life the Jews' national home. This vision was consistent with Chaim Weizmann's contention that the Zionist movement should above all trust the good intentions of the British to fulfill their pledge. Simultaneously, the myth was perpetuated that the Zionists would be shepherded by a wise and powerful patron, Britain, which was singularly adept at orchestrating Near Eastern affairs. Balfour was the most optimistic personification of this notion. The idealized relationship between them, rather than signifying the subordination of the lesser power, stressed that a partnership had been forged between the Zionists and the British. After issuing the Declaration, Balfour himself elucidated this view. "We are embarked on a great adventure," he told an audience at London's Royal Albert Hall, "and I say 'we' advisedly. By 'we' I mean on the one side the Jewish People, and I mean on the other side, the Mandatory Power of Palestine. We are partners in this great enterprise. If we fail you, you cannot succeed. If you fail us you cannot succeed. But I feel assured that we shall not fail you and you will not fail us."[18]

Such perceptions did not apply only to British Jews and Zionists; the significance of Balfour was likewise celebrated in the United States and Germany.[19] The many "Balfour Days" commemorated both the document and the man. In the store of Zionist icons, his was probably the most recognized non-Jewish countenance in the interwar years; he had snow-white hair and a well-groomed mustache[20] (figure 2). His was a visage of a sympathetic, dignified minister. Balfour's niece, Blanche Dugdale, who also was his biographer, probably was mistaken to assume that the Jewish masses had never known her uncle's face.[21]

In one of the most symbolically weighty and universally cheered moments of the movement's history, Balfour was honored by an invitation to open the Hebrew University of Jerusalem officially, which he did before a crowd of some 10,000 onlookers.[22] Irma Lindheim wrote in a published memoir that "Lord Balfour looked beautiful in his university gown of red velvet and a tam-o'-shanter of black. He is really

2 Reproduction of a portrait of Arthur James Balfour by G. Fiddes Watt, Eton College (1920), photo collection, Central Zionist Archives, Jerusalem.

one of the handsomest men I have ever seen. He has a noble, beneficent face, with wisdom and goodness clearly written upon it."[23] One of the most famous paintings in Zionist history, by Leopold Pilichowski, is of the colorful scene on Mt. Scopus, the convocation of the Hebrew University, with the robed figure of Balfour in the center[24] (figure 3). It conveys Lindheim's impression that "The setting was perfect. A master designer had planned and executed a set of unsurpassed beauty. It was drama at its highest."[25] "When Balfour rose to speak," writes Dugdale,

it seemed as if the cheering of the multitude would never cease. He was very much moved. And indeed it has seldom fallen to the lot of any statesman to see within his own lifetime the fruits of a policy so rooted in faith in the qualities of an untried nation as Balfour's Zionism had been. The Hebrew University (barred

3 The opening of the Hebrew University of Jerusalem; painting by Leopold Pilichowski, photo collection, Central Zionist Archives, Jerusalem, no. 16912.

to no one, whatever his race or religion) seemed about to fulfil all his hopes for a revival and a concentration of Jewish culture.[26]

The tie between Balfour, universalism, tolerance, and secular culture was captured in the scene and its remembrance.

Not surprisingly, his presence in Palestine was regarded as a magnificent occasion. Culture seemed to be the leitmotif of his journey: "In Tel Aviv Balfour attended a gala performance of the third act of 'Samson and Delilah.' In Jerusalem Handel's 'Belshazzar' was sung for him in Hebrew."[27] Wherever he appeared his words of support for Zionist efforts were heartening.[28] During a tour of the Jewish settlement of Nahalal in the days after the convocation, Balfour commented:

Can you pay a higher compliment to any population, to any set of men, than to say that, having been brought up under entirely different conditions, they nevertheless show such power of adaptation, such energy in work, such grasp of the new conditions under which they have to labour, that within three years they could turn this pestiferous wilderness into the smiling agricultural district which we now see around us[?][29]

Certainly Arthur James Balfour's quiet warmth and humility contributed to his appropriation by the movement. Upon the presentation of a statue of himself as a gift of the American Zionist Organization, Balfour was visibly emotional, and "expressed his deep appreciation of the action of the American Zionists." It was reported that, "He felt that he had hardly done enough to deserve all that had been said of him; in fact, he had not done a tenth of what he considered the cause deserved." An unabashed philo-Semite and pro-Zionist, Balfour stated his "disappointment at the opposition which Jewish aspirations had encountered, especially concerning how much the Jewish race had given, and was still giving, to the world, and what it received in return."[30] As both the spirit and the substance of the Balfour Declaration was revised as Arab opposition to Zionism grew, the document and its author were consistently recalled as "a beacon of light and hope."[31]

Balfour's death, which followed shortly after the Arab riots of 1929–30 in Palestine, elicited a tremendous response from Zionists worldwide.[32] Dugdale writes that "millions of poor Jews in the ghettoes of Eastern Europe and the slums of New York were bewailing with deep personal grief the loss of a British statesman . . . All over the world the ceremonial candles were lit in the synagogues and the prayer of Remembrance, the Azkarah, was chanted. Never in living memory had this been done for any Gentile."[33] In Britain a special volume of the Jewish National Fund's Golden Book was created to memorialize Balfour. Potential donors of £20 or more were informed that a replica of the "Balfour Golden Book" would "be offered to the British Museum," and that "all participating in this Memorial will receive a specially engraved certificate, to be issued solely for this occasion."[34] The Balfour Forest in Palestine was the most heralded tree-planting project since the inauguration of the Herzl Forest twenty-five years earlier.

Balfour was not, however, portrayed as operating in a vacuum. The evolving mythology of the movement underscored that it was primarily through the efforts of Chaim Weizmann that Balfour's declaration saw the light of day. Zionist pamphlets boasted that "no statesman in the history of the world" had accomplished what Weizmann had "without a state, without an army, and without the requisite financial means."[35] The founding of the Hebrew University had prominently featured Chaim Weizmann heading the procession, shoulder to shoulder with Lord Balfour. Furthermore, it became known that Weizmann, prior to Balfour's death, was Balfour's final visitor "from outside the circle of his family." Balfour's niece revealed that "no one but me saw the brief and silent farewell between these two, so diverse from one another, whose mutual sympathy had been so powerful an instrument in the history of a nation."[36]

Weizmann was, to a plurality in Zionism, "the living symbol of the Jewish Palestine movement of our generation"; he was not only "a leader," but "the Leader"[37] (figure 4). Although there is no shortage

4 "The XVI Zionist Congress" (unattributed drawings) in *Palästina-Bilder-Korrespondenz* (July 1929): 12; Chaim Weizmann in center; clockwise from top left: David Wolffsohn, M. M. Ussischkin, A. Hantke, Col. F. H. Kisch, Louis Lipsky, Lieb Taffe [sic], Nahum Sokolow, Max Nordau.

of self-consciousness in Zionist image-making, no Zionist leader committed so much of the resources of the movement to the construction of
his own mythical edifice as did Weizmann. An irony that has been
recognized in many quarters is that Weizmann initially gained prominence as a young man in the Zionist movement by calling into question
Theodor Herzl's "political Zionism," that is, the founder's fixation on
securing the diplomatic arrangements pursuant to Jewish settlement in
Palestine – which was precisely the role he took on himself.[38] Weizmann
was the first Zionist politician after Herzl to be widely perceived as a
respectable agent for the movement in the corridors of power. It was
frequently said that one of the hallmarks of Weizmann's leadership was
that he understood the British better than anyone else, and that the
British, in turn, placed a special confidence in him – which was critical
to the Balfour Declaration.[39] Although his relationship with American
officials would assume greater significance during and after World
War II, Weizmann also was reputed to inspire great confidence in
Washington.[40] It has become an open question in later historiography
whether Weizmann's single-minded focus on Britain as the guarantor
of Zionist interests was ultimately more harmful or beneficial to
the movement. David Vital has convincingly argued that it was the
expediencies of wartime, and the British overestimation of Jewish
influence over President Woodrow Wilson in the United States that
figured very large in the drama that culminated in the Balfour
Declaration;[41] in a classic essay Mayir Vereté stresses the dominating factor of Britain's imperial agenda, as opposed to Zionist self-assertion:
Britain "was ready to be seduced by any Zionist of stature."[42] Mark
Levene has pointed out the central role also played by Lucien Wolf as
a non-Zionist advocate for Jewry, and Levene clearly shows that the
Balfour Declaration also was wrought of anti- and philo-Semitic mis-
perceptions of Jewish power.[43]

At any rate, along with the acclaim of his brilliant statecraft, Weizmann
was touted, quite rightly, as a first-rate scientist. His identity as a "great
chemist" was seen as interwoven with his role as "a great statesman."[44]
In the chatty column, "Man and Matters" of the British Zionist paper,
Monthly Pioneer, Weizmann's brain-power was a favorite topic:

A close friend of the Zionist leader was once asked what was the dominant force
in his character. "His remarkable powers of concentration," was the reply. It is
perfectly true. I have seen Dr. Weizmann in his chemical laboratory watching an
experiment for hours on end. There was not the slightest indication that he had
any interest in life apart from the flask he was engaged in watching. I have heard
him speak in dozens of Zionist platforms, and neither in word nor smile did he
betray his chemical training or influence. This faculty of 100 percent concen-

tration upon the task of the moment is characteristic of the leader of men and affairs. When to this is added oratory, tact, and insight, we have a combination which readily explains Dr. Weizmann's personal triumph in so many difficult situations.[45]

Weizmann, after training at the technological university at Charlotten-burg, pursued a career in research in Britain, eventually assuming a position (but not a professorship, as is often said) at the University of Manchester.[46] His work was of no small significance to the British war effort in the development of a better acetone for explosives. Jehuda Reinharz has richly illuminated the relationship between Weizmann's politics and his science. There was widespread appreciation for his service, and his legend amplified this dimension of his persona. Through the comments of those speaking about him, and also by sprinkling his own speeches and writings with references to science or chemistry in particular, Weizmann sought to demonstrate that the Jews' return to Palestine was consistent with a "scientific" worldview, not simply a messianic-romantic illusion. He extrapolated and translated his own understanding of scientific principles into the ability to lead the movement in a most propitious direction.[47]

Despite his prominence as a scientist, no other Zionist figure simul-taneously bridged the worlds of modern civilization and a romanticized view of "authentic" Eastern Jewry as did Weizmann.[48] As opposed to Balfour, who was exotic from a Zionist perspective, Weizmann's countenance was reassuring and familiar (figure 5). He made the most of his *Yiddishkeit* origins. He was a child of the ghetto who had struggled to make his way in the secular world, in academic and applied science and politics, and he seemed to have mastered all provinces. After his rise in Zionist ranks, there was little recognition that Weizmann had envisioned Zionism as a rejection and transcendence of the ghetto, as is clear from his personal correspondence.[49] Nevertheless, the view of Weizmann as an *Ostjude* par excellence was trotted out numerous times during Weizmann's feud with Louis Brandeis and the so-called "Brandeis group." Weizmann was extolled as the leader who was most in touch with the true "folk soul" of the Jewish people.[50]

In the wake of this conflict which Zionist organs outside the United States preferred to minimize as "a purely local dispute,"[51] allegations against Weizmann were turned on their heads by his loyalists. At issue was Weizmann's attempt, challenged by Brandeis, to concentrate the capitalization of the whole Zionist movement under the auspices of a new fundraising and administrative body, the Keren Hayesod (KH, or Palestine Foundation Fund) (see chapter 3). Those who dared to question Weizmann were said to be motivated by their own "inferiority complex," as pitiable as "the pigmy attacking the giant."[52] Railing against the charge that Weizmann was obsessed with fundraising, earning him the title "King of the Shnorrers," one defender wrote: "O, if only the entire people were a people of such Shnorrers!"[53] His expertise and brilliance at garnering money for the cause were more typically seen as a great boon to Zionism;[54] among Zionist leaders he was famous for using his charm to leave his audience with starry eyes and empty pockets.[55] Parrying the frequent characterization of Weizmann as a "dictator," Adolf Boehm, one of the leading Zionist publicists, wrote that Weizmann did "not possess a dictatorial nature." On the contrary, he was "the leading advocate for democracy in the movement." Those who see Weizmann as a dictator, Boehm wrote, had misjudged the "prophetic" side of his personality and his "visionary power."[56]

To Weizmann's opponents within Zionism, most of the negative allusions previously mentioned seemed to fit the leader. His detractors saw him not only as the "King of the Shnorrers," but a master of Machiavellian intrigue whose concept of self-rule was detrimental to the aims of the movement.[57] Explaining to Julian Mack why he wished to leave his official post in Zionism in 1920, Stephen S. Wise wrote that he had begun

to feel a profound distrust of Dr. Weizmann. I could not feel satisfied of the wisdom and moral rightness of his acts as a leader. I was and remain persuaded that such is Dr. Weizmann's character as a leader as to make him undeserving of the confidence, which a movement such as ours must be able to place in its leader. Justice Brandeis has twice within the year dealt at close range with Dr. Weizmann [and] in a letter to you and me written in mid-July, Mr. De Haas indicates quite clearly that Justice Brandeis has come to share my own view of Dr. Weizmann, – that is, my entire distrust of the man.[58]

Although it is often stated or implied that the main opponents of Weizmann were "the Americans," that is, people such as Brandeis, Julian Mack, Felix Frankfurter, and Stephen S. Wise, there also were Zionist leaders in Europe and the Yishuv who felt that Weizmann's leadership was wrong-headed. In Eli Shaltier's biography of Pinchas Rutenberg, who masterminded the rapid electrification of Palestine, Weizmann is portrayed as not simply a political rival, but as a fellow scientist who failed to understand the needs and implications of Rutenberg's monumental endeavor.[59] On October 3, 1930, Rutenberg told Henrietta Szold that "Dr. Weizmann must resign from the leadership – he deals neither honestly nor seriously." She declined, however, to pass on this evaluation.[60]

Irma Lindheim, a president of Hadassah, offers a keen insight into why the views of Weizmann held by persons such as Brandeis, Wise, and

5 Portrait of Chaim Weizmann, photo collection, Central Zionist Archives, Jerusalem.

Rutenberg were not more widespread. "I understand why the word 'seductive' is often used in describing him," Lindheim observed. "His words, his meanings, are sharp, penetrating, incisive, but he speaks in a voice so melodious and low, so pleasing to the senses, that instead of arousing resistance which his militant words would ordinarily evoke, his voice insinuates itself into the consciousness of the listener."[61] Thousands upon thousands of Jews heard him directly, as Weizmann was a tireless campaigner on the stump for Zionism; his itinerary was loaded with stops in small towns as well as metropolitan centers.

As controversial as Weizmann was, his elder in the movement, Nahum Sokolow, was one of the least partisan leaders in Zionism. Perhaps Sokolow's boundless conviviality helps explain the scarcity of scholarly treatments of his career. He was not a member of one camp or another; he was not primarily a spokesman for any specific strand of Zionism. Sokolow was seen as above the fray in which nearly every other familiar name was connected with a particular party or clique. Sokolow was the most logical choice to head Zionism, then, when Weizmann was removed from the presidency in 1930. To a lesser degree than Weizmann, Sokolow was regarded as a foremost Zionist emissary to the world at large; he was said to have

stood before the leading statesmen of the world on terms of equality . . . There are few chancelleries in Europe where he is not persona grata and fewer still where his name is not unknown [sic]. For years, his has been the task to win over leading public men for the cause and the fact that Zionism to-day enjoys widespread support in all countries, is largely due to his labours. In Downing Street or in Washington, at the Vatican or at the Quai d'Orsay, it is to Mr. Sokolow that Dr. Weizmann frequently entrusts the delicate negotiations . . . and the acknowledged success of Zionist diplomacy is a tribute to his personality as well as to his powers of persuasion.[62]

Sokolow was perceived as an eloquent, sincere, and appropriate spokesman for the Zionist and general Jewish cause in the negotiations following the First World War; this was manifested in the homage accorded him during his speaking and fundraising tours in Germany, Britain, and the United States.[63] Perhaps because he was much older, it was not common to hear Sokolow referred to as Weizmann's lieutenant. But he was clearly a crucial senior figure, and often portrayed as having a moderating influence on the helm of the organization[64] (figure 6).

Also similar to Weizmann, Sokolow embodied a connection to Jewish life and culture in Eastern Europe; his career was more embedded in the worlds of Hebrew and Yiddish culture than any other Zionist leader involved in policy and "agitation":[65]

His family comes from Cracow and prides itself especially on one ancestor, the great rabbinical authority, Nathan Shapiro, author of a work called "Megalleh Amukoth" (Revealer of the Profound) . . . When the young Sokolow was only 11 years old, he was already famed as an "eelui," a "Wunderkind," a child prodigy. His vast knowledge of the folios of the Talmud and later rabbinic writings was amazing . . . As a statesman and national hero he belongs to the category of the greatest who have combined statesmanship with letters like Wilson, Balfour, Clemenceau, Masaryk, and Vizelos in our own time.[66]

Before becoming active in Zionism, Sokolow had been a well-known publicist in the Yiddish, Hebrew, and Polish Jewish press; he was acclaimed as one of the "creators of modern Hebrew journalism."[67] His original stance regarding the movement, as was well known, was that of a skeptic. Attending the First Zionist Congress in Basel (1897) as a

6 Sokolow is pictured (twice) here in a montage including Chaim
Weizmann, the president of the United States (Warren Harding),
David Lloyd George, Arthur James Balfour, Sir Wyndham Deedes,
Berthold Fiewel, Lieb Jaffe, in *Palästina-Bilder-Korrespondenz* (May
1929): 3; see also figure 4, which shows Sokolow to the immediate left
of Weizmann, and where, at the top of the drawings, are the faces of
Max Nordau and David Wolffsohn, to represent a tie to the earlier
group of leaders.

journalist, not as a delegate, Sokolow was won over to the cause by Herzl's charisma. He thereafter became a foremost advocate for Zionism and assumed the role as the first "great historian" of the movement, as the author of a "monumental" work on the background and early years of Zionism which was first published in 1919.[68] Sokolow's embrace of Zionism was claimed as representative of the intellectual shift among his generation.[69] His seventieth birthday, in the spring of 1931, prompted one of the biggest promotional campaigns of the interwar years which was not directly inspired by a perceived crisis or a fundraising drive. "Sokolow Month," the Hebrew month of Nissan, March 15 to April 15, 1931, was used to increase the membership of the organization which had been flagging worldwide; it also was meant to be a time in which serious questions were raised in Zionist forums about the future of the movement, such as "do we need an ideological renewal?" and "should the work of the youth groups be centralized?"[70] Although the publicity boasted that Sokolow was one of the more important Zionist thinkers, those in the thick of the polemics tended to see him as more of a dilettante than a weighty intellectual. It is not surprising that, despite his towering stature during the movement's infancy, Sokolow does not merit inclusion in the histories of Arthur Hertzberg and Shlomo Avineri, contemporary activist-scholars who in some ways are his heirs as popular historians of Zionism.[71] In no small measure, Sokolow's attractiveness as a Zionist spokesman and symbol derived from the perception that he was always well-mannered and congenial;[72] as opposed to the rough-hewn image of Eastern Jewish writers and news-papermen,[73] he was wonderfully respectable (figure 7).

If Sokolow filled the role of the dyed-in-the-wool Eastern Jew, showing the compatibility of Zionism and buttoned-up *Yiddishkeit*, whose reputation could stand independent of his Zionist attachment, Brandeis accomplished this with regard to the United States; he personified the compatibility of Zionism and Americanism[74] (figure 8). He was a true-blue American, whose credentials as a leading light of United States' legal theory and progressive social thought were impeccable.[75] Brandeis (1856–1941) endowed the movement with a sparkling intellectual grandeur, and demonstrated that Zionism was in harmony with the best minds and interests of the United States. Woodrow Wilson, to a great extent, relied on the "preachings" of Louis Brandeis in formulating his notion of progressivism – in which the "competitive order" was essentially preserved, but protection was accorded to the individual, small businesses, and property holders in the face of "established interests."[76] In particular, Zionist youth was thrilled by his appearance on the scene:

7 Nahum Sokolow, photo collection, Central Zionist Archives, Jerusalem.

To the American college youth of 1910, in the flush of the pre-war rebellion against the post-Victorian social order of vested interests, Brandeis, the battling lawyer was like a knight errant fighting the evil brigands who infested the highways. He was characterized by a simplicity of conduct, a directness of speech, a sense of justice, and a moral quality which set him apart as the highest type of the Lincolnian liberal fighting for the rights of the common people. We young students – Jew and non-Jew alike – were full of hero-worship. And when word came that he, Brandeis, had agreed to head the Zionist Organization of America, we [the incipient Zionists among the college students] were electrified. That the man symbolizing the best in American life of the day was ready to throw in his lot with his people and fight their battles with the same grit and fire that he had shown in his fight for his American fellow-men, that was as if the wildest fancy had turned to reality![77]

The path which led Louis D. Brandeis to a passionate interest in Jewish affairs quickly became part of Jewish and Zionist lore. In many respects his journey from what was seen as an abject secularism to a

burning interest in the Jewish question was reminiscent of Theodor
Herzl's life story. The prevailing theme of thumbnail sketches was that
he, like Herzl, Nordau, and a few other key leaders – reaching back to the
Biblical Moses – had "found his way back" to Judaism and the Jews; his
life could easily be interpreted according to the Zionist theme of exile,
return, and redemption. "In a crisis," wrote Louis Lipsky, who would
later be a staunch opponent of Brandeis,

the racial or national consciousness is awakened, and there is no escape for
the true man. So it was with Theodor Herzl, who, as he sat and listened to the
testimony in the Dreyfus case, felt stirring within him a feeling of kinship with the
people that was on trial with the unfortunate French officer. So it was with other
men in the Zionist movement, scientists, writers, orators, politicians. Max
Nordau came back to his people. Israel Zangwill found a place in Jewish Life
through the Zionist movement.[78]

Perhaps it is no accident that one of the best-known publicists of
Theodor Herzl in the English-speaking world was Jacob de Haas, who
was instrumental in arousing Brandeis's passion for Zionism. It is likely
that de Haas, quite literally, was responsible for introducing Brandeis to
more Zionist audiences than any other figure. De Haas's two-volume
biography of Herzl, published in 1927, was "dedicated to Louis D.
Brandeis on his seventieth birthday as a tribute to his full comprehension
of the unselfish life and high purpose herein unfolded [in the life of
Herzl]."[79] The comparison of Herzl and Brandeis did not exist only in
the imagination of de Haas. After his address concerning the Arab riots
of 1930, the "Zionist page" of *Der Tog*, the New York Yiddish daily,
reported that

It was a speech and reminder by a great patriot and statesman. Justly it can be
said that the epoch of the bloody events in Palestine may be divided into two
periods: Before the speech by Brandeis and after the speech. At the moment
when the speech reached the Jews world over, a spiritual transfiguration took
place within us. We have heard once again the call of Herzl, and anew in our ears
resounded the voice of World Zionism.[80]

Brandeis's family had fled Bohemia in the failed Revolution of 1848,
and he grew up in Louisville, Kentucky; the deepest influences on his
youth and education, which were not native to the United States, were
markedly German. Only a short time after graduating from Harvard Law
School, Brandeis gained fame as one of the most skilled and socially
conscious attorneys in the country. His curiosity about the Jewish
condition was sparked when he served as an arbitrator in a case
involving a largely Jewish garment workers' union; a few years later he
met Jacob de Haas. Inside and outside Zionist circles, however, Brandeis

8 Portrait of Louis D. Brandeis on a mass-produced postcard in photo
collection, Central Zionist Archives, Jerusalem.

was frequently credited with having "a characteristically Hebrew spirit"[81]
or "an intensely Jewish soul"; his role as a maker and molder of law was
seen as endemic to Jewry, a mark of the Jewish propensity for legal study
engaging its sharpest minds. It was no coincidence that in an earlier time
of crisis, the people of Israel were led by "judges," and during the trauma
of the Great War, Louis Brandeis stepped forward to lead.[82] One writer's
description of Brandeis as combining the characteristics of Moses
with Abraham Lincoln was typical of the Jewish–American synthesis
which Brandeis seemed to represent.[83] Even though Brandeis's first
unequivocal statement of support for Zionism did not occur until 1913,
and he did not offer to participate until the war was raging in Europe, de
Haas insisted that Brandeis had been sympathetic to the movement as
early as 1898.[84]

Similar to Chaim Weizmann, Brandeis also was perceived as a moving
force behind the Balfour Declaration;[85] the Weizmann legend, however,

seems to have left only a bit part for Brandeis and his impact on President Wilson in the Zionist historiography explaining the Declaration.[86] Inasmuch as the reception of Weizmann was influenced by attempts to disprove the allegations or insinuations that surfaced during his feud with Louis Brandeis, at least part of Brandeis's reputation was forged as a reaction to the charges of Weizmann and his loyalists. No doubt owing to the accusations that the Brandeis group was opportunistic, elitist, and arrogant, laudations of Brandeis – especially after 1921 – were sure to include mention of his zeal for democracy. He never failed, it was said, to canvass a whole meeting room "for everyone's opinion and this marked the introduction of a new method of common council."[87] Although testimonials and appraisals of Brandeis's Zionist career tended to gloss over, minimize, or ignore Brandeis's conflict with Weizmann,[88] de Haas used this dimension of Brandeis' legacy to demonstrate his linkage with Herzl. Like the malicious attacks the founder faced within Zionist circles, Brandeis, too, was forced to suffer the insult that he did not share or understand "the Jewish soul." Instead, de Haas argued, Brandeis, like Leon Pinsker and Theodor Herzl, not only possessed a Jewish soul, but his comprehension of the contemporary scene was so penetrating that many in the movement found his leadership threatening.[89]

Perhaps more than any other cultural hero in interwar Zionism, praise for Brandeis was an inadvertent double-edged sword. If one admitted the significance and insight of Brandeis, one could only surmise that Weizmann's ascendance was problematic. One could not worship both of them wholeheartedly. Some Zionists voiced a concern that Brandeis was not as devoted as he should be to Zionism because most of his energy had to be directed toward his role on the Supreme Court;[90] what seems more notable, in retrospect, is that he maintained such a high level of involvement in so many phases of Zionist affairs.[91] But there was another troubling side of the glorification of Brandeis. The fundamental shift during World War I in the respect accorded American Zionism was obviously the product of changes during the war years and the catastrophe of Eastern Jewry. But the importance of Brandeis's support for the cause could not be overestimated. Henrietta Szold recalled that

In the America of 1914 there was Zionist leadership, but it was not, in the true sense of the word, leadership. The generation itself lamented the fact that it had not the power to produce a leader. While the lament made itself heard, the leader appeared. He emerged from the ranks of Jews far estranged from their brethren and their brethren's aspirations, and he himself, the leader, had also been very remote from Jewish interests and problems. Yet it may be said, nevertheless, that from birth, by study and his activities, he had unconsciously been preparing himself for the leadership he assumed when two-thirds of his life had elapsed. Once he took over the leadership, he penetrated to the very core of the Jewish need and dealt with it constructively . . . Thirty years ago Zionism in America was far from being cognizant of its powers, even of its capacity to secure means for the development of Palestine.[92]

It would therefore be an admission of tremendous vulnerability for the Zionist Organization to affirm that its fortunes had rested to such a large extent on the shoulders of one individual. Worse yet, from 1921 to 1931, he was clearly in conflict with Weizmann, the leader of the World Zionist Organization, and Louis Lipsky, the president of the American Zionist Federation. In the years that Brandeis was a member of the opposition, the popularity of Zionism in the United States suffered a precipitous decline.[93] The connection of this phenomenon with the disaffection of Brandeis has rarely been examined.

One segment of the movement, however, which expressed no inhibition about acknowledging the indispensability of Brandeis was the Hadassah organization. Among the upper echelon of Zionist leaders, his "respect for women" was a distinguishing characteristic. He was singularly exceptional in his support for the women's Zionist organization in the United States. "He spoke at early Hadassah meetings and he observed Hadassah very closely from its inception. He often referred to Hadassah's early days as the classroom period when Henrietta Szold served in the role of teacher of the Central Committee of Associates." Brandeis, to the women of Hadassah, had made possible their very institutional life through his efforts in assuring that the American Zionist Medical Unit, the initial Hadassah project, was given the same official status as the American Red Cross by the United States' government. Brandeis's contribution of $10,000 toward Hadassah's anti-malarial work actually launched the organization, and helped assure Hadassah's emergence as an autonomous body, as opposed to being completely subsumed by the male-dominated Zionist Organization.[94]

As much as Brandeis was the most important patron of the Hadassah organization, there is no equal to Henrietta Szold, in any aspect of Zionism, who so successfully established a part of the movement in his or her own image (figure 9). Born into a prominent rabbinical family in Baltimore, Henrietta Szold was a prodigious worker, in several capacities, for the nascent Jewish Publication Society of America.[95] The gratitude expressed by the JPS, it was noted in the Zionist press upon her departure, did not come close to matching what Szold deserved for her efforts.[96] Shortly before the First World War Zionism became her consuming passion, and during the war years she devoted tremendous energy to organizing the American Zionist Medical Unit, which was the seed of Hadassah. In less than a decade Hadassah was one of the most formidable parts of world Zionism, a feat which is even more striking if one considers the dearth of women's participation earlier in the movement's history. From any perspective, Szold's accomplishment was astounding.[97] But the accolades she received rarely did justice to the obstacles she was forced to overcome from within the Zionist establishment (chapter 4).

Szold's seventieth birthday, in 1930, provided the occasion for a public assessment of her character and career. Julian Mack's birthday greeting was typical:

Henrietta Szold is and for many years has been the outstanding woman in Jewry. Founder of Hadassah, her life for nearly two decades has been devoted to Palestine. Disregarding all considerations of personal convenience, she courageously accepted a place on the Palestine Zionist Executive at a time when this body, weighed down by heavy debts, was faced with almost insurmountable difficulties. This is but one of many outstanding examples of her unflinching acceptance of Zionist responsibility. Hers is a life that is truly motivated by the finest and best in Judaism: American Jewish womanhood will confidently continue to turn to her for inspiration and leadership.[98]

Harry Sachar's tribute was unusual in noting the resistance that Szold encountered in Palestine. "Miss Szold's services as a member of the Executive," he wrote, "found least understanding and appreciation in the United States. In Palestine she had more critics and opponents, but all had some estimation of her value. In the United States there seemed to me to be a chill isolation. Even in the early months, those who had urged her into office, forgot and fell away in the most difficult hours."[99] Although her clash with "central groups" was obliquely recalled by others, for the most part in Western Europe and the United States there could be no mistaking the esteem in which she was held, although she seemed not to perceive it. Her combination of profound secular and Jewish knowledge, combined with an amazing grasp of practical problems and willingness to follow through was matchless.[100]

Henrietta Szold also was utilized as a symbol of Zionism as one of the world's first political movements "to base its constitution [sic] upon the principle of absolute equality for all adherents irrespective of sex," in which any position could be held by a woman. The example of Miss Szold allegedly testified to the affirmation of this tenet.[101] Everywhere women seemed to be striving for equality; Szold showed that in Zionism it had been achieved. But the idolization of Henrietta Szold was not exclusive to any single Zionist contention or agenda; she was seen as a pioneering humanist more than as a feminist. For instance, under her hand, Hadassah became famous for not discriminating between Jews and

9 Drawing of Henrietta Szold by Erna Grossman [?] in *Palästina-Bilder-Korrespondenz* (February 1930): 6; most of the photos of Henrietta Szold are of very poor quality.

non-Jews, for fostering an atmosphere and rigorously enforcing a policy which made all the people of Palestine feel comfortable using its services. Henrietta Szold, too, like Martin Buber, gained a reputation for advocating open dialogue and an empathetic understanding of Palestine's Arabs.

Not surprisingly, there were explanations of Szold's successes that were blatantly anti-feminist; at least one commentator traced her effectiveness to "her keen insight into the average feminine psychology." Szold realized, according to this interpretation, that "the reason why women's Zionist societies were constantly springing up and [just] as constantly melting away without leaving a trace" was because women, like children, must be given some specific task requiring increasing attention and concrete effort. The subtext was that Szold knew that her Hadassah ladies were incapable of higher-level thought and action.[102] In words meant to be taken as praise, Louis Lipsky wrote in 1917 that

There is women's work to be done in Zionism, which the men cannot do. Hadassah has added color and quality to the Zionist movement. The rough, uneven work dealing with miscellaneous elements by various methods – the work that must be done on the Jewish street – of necessity had to be done by the men. Hadassah has acted more quietly, more systematically, with more attention to detail, preferring a slow growth rather than a mass progress.[103]

Such comments tell us much more about male Zionist thinking about Hadassah rather than offering any insight into its substantial role. In fact, Hadassah, under Szold, was the source of the most demanding educational programs in the United States, in contrast to the generally superficial educational efforts of the mainstream organization.[104] Before her full-time commitment to Hadassah, her influence was so pervasive in the Jewish Publication Society of America that Jonathan Sarna has dubbed her tenure there as "the Henrietta Szold era."[105] Nevertheless, in the Zionist realm the intellectual power of Henrietta Szold was rarely as celebrated as her organizational skills. Partly this was a result of Szold's view of herself; she did not imagine herself as an important thinker in the movement. It is little wonder that Szold is not to be found in the standard works of Hertzberg and Avineri. Although Zionist polemics regularly attested to her paramount significance as an actor in the Zionist arena, the movement's historians, with the exception of Aaron Berman and Allon Gal, have rarely treated either Szold or her institution as a critical force.[106]

Above all, the figure treasured as diaspora Zionism's greatest claim to fame in the interwar years was Albert Einstein[107] (figure 10). Zionists the world over heartily agreed that Einstein was the most spectacular attraction of the movement. Einstein's importance in boosting Jewish pride in and confidence in the general direction of the Zionist movement defies comparison. He was untouchable and his reputation was unimpeachable. Few Zionists would have disputed Nahum Goldmann's view that Einstein was

the personification of every great quality a man can have: goodness of heart, honesty, and boundless love for all living creatures. It would have been almost impossible to discover a character defect in him. But perhaps his most amazing quality was his absolute simplicity. He was what he was in a perfectly natural way, without any effort.[108]

Despite the fact that his theories were incomprehensible except to a very narrow elite, it was generally known that he "introduced a new scientific conception of space and time and of their relation to the physical world." It was likewise known, particularly among Jews, that "the foremost Jewish genius of our age is a modest, unassuming, kindly gentleman, almost childlike in his simplicity, with a keen sense of humor."[109]

10 Albert Einstein, photo collection, Central Zionist Archives, Jerusalem.

Einstein's portrait became a universal symbol of scientific genius with a human face, and Zionists were ecstatic to be able to appropriate him as one of their own.[110] "One of the supreme joys which has come to the Jewish people in this modern era," remarked a leader of the American university-student organization,

is that Albert Einstein, indubitably one of the greatest of its sons, has recognized in his people and sympathizing with its difficulties, has labored earnestly time and again on its behalf. He has gloried in its heritage and has shown special interest in those idealistically motivated men and women who had pilgrimed [sic] their way to Palestine and have lived in the historic land of their fathers.[111]

They showed his picture and talked about him on every possible occasion.[112] Everyone wanted to soak up his wisdom, meet him, shake his hand, and be photographed with him. His presence at public Zionist functions always resulted in huge crowds that could barely control their adulation.[113] At the inauguration of the Einstein Forest in Palestine, even though Einstein himself was not able to attend, the delegation had its picture taken with a framed photograph of their hero[114] (figure 11). Whatever he had to say was taken as a solemn pronouncement to be pondered, regardless of its novelty or lack thereof.[115] Zionists also liked to believe that when Einstein spoke, the rest of the world listened intently.[116] Whenever he took to the road, his movements were tracked by Zionist organs with the fervor of gossip sheets looking for any scrap of information about a Hollywood celebrity.[117] Of course, his pilgrimages to Palestine were regarded as sacred events.[118]

Although the reputations of other figures were enhanced by their skill at raising money for Zionism, Einstein seemed to be the most powerful magnet to big donors – without making much of an effort appealing for funds. While others, quite understandably, found it difficult to encourage sizable donations in the midst of the Depression, with Einstein on the dais, the results were always extraordinary. Weizmann made a decided effort to demonstrate that Einstein was behind his plan for the creation of the Keren Hayesod.[119] When Einstein was on the stump, it was not simply a matter of local news in the host community or Zionist federation. Like everything Einstein did, it was worthy of front-page headlines in Zionist newspapers throughout the world.[120]

Along with Balfour and Weizmann, the figure of Albert Einstein was linked with the Hebrew University in Jerusalem. A number of his appearances were meant to garner material and moral support for the university project.[121] He was a member of the Hebrew University's founding faculty, although he never regularly worked there; Einstein's endorsement, nevertheless, translated into instant credibility and, for many, greatness.[122] Its library was the home of the original manuscript of Einstein's "Theory of Relativity," which also was given a Zionist slant: "This monumental document has revealed to the world a new truth, and it may well be that from Zion shall go forth to all humanity new values resulting from the development of the new Jewish homeland in Palestine."[123] The translation of his theory into Hebrew was treated as a profound Zionist act; it was crucial that when pressed for his response, Einstein himself affirmed its significance.[124] After the Nazis came to

11 "Inaugurating the Einstein Forest," *Pioneer* (May 1930): 23; the picture contains Einstein's portrait (figure 10).

power, however, Einstein turned down repeated invitations to take a post in Jerusalem. He publicly expressed, "to Weizmann and in interviews with a number of newspapers . . . all sorts of reservations and arguments against the Hebrew University; he settled in Princeton."[125]

Stories about Einstein, some of them apocryphal, became part of Zionist lore. The best known (true) story is from the State of Israel: in 1952, upon the death of Chaim Weizmann, Einstein was offered the presidency of the State of Israel, albeit a largely ceremonial position – despite the fact that he did not live, and had never lived, in the country.[126] Many of the Einstein stories revolved around the stereotype of the "absent-minded professor," while others focused on his penchant for riding a bicycle, playing the violin, and smoking inexpensive cigars. In his autobiography, Zionist Nahum Goldmann is overjoyed in relating that Albert Einstein was his personal friend. Goldmann recalled an anecdote he had told countless times:

One Sunday, I was taking a walk with him in Berlin, and he asked me for a cigar. I had none. The shops were closed, but we managed to find a little tavern where they sold cheap cigars. We entered. The owner was standing behind the counter, and when Einstein asked for a cigar, he said: "What kind? A twenty-pfennig cigar?" "Do I look like someone who smokes such expensive cigars?"[127]

Although there was no mistaking Einstein's colossal reputation, he was seen as a man who had to struggle continually, and still was not completely secure even in the face of his immense achievements. Goldmann also relates that

During the German inflation, when he was very badly off financially because his salary was devalued in the first few days of every month, I found him one day absorbed in an American magazine. "Look how terrible this is." He pointed in astonishment to the magazine – it was the *Saturday Evening Post* – which was offering twenty five hundred dollars for a few pages explaining the theory of relativity in popular terms. "Just think," he mused, "what that amount of money would mean to me." Then he confessed that he had been sitting for days, trying to figure out how to explain it in a way that readers could understand.[128]

Although Einstein often managed to make himself the object of his humor, no one would have described him as a *shlemiel* – one who is easily fooled or taken advantage of. Several stories stressed his dignity, such as when a park in Berlin was supposed to be dedicated to him in 1929. The British Zionist press reported that

Professor Einstein has refused the plot of land which the Berlin municipality proposed to buy for him on the occasion of his fiftieth birthday. The anti-Semitic Nationalist Party on the municipality opposed the gift . . . because the honoured recipient was a Jew. Though that attitude was far from representing the general feeling of esteem in which the distinguished Jewish scientist is held by the German people, his action is one which will commend itself to all who have regard for Jewish honour and self-respect.

This was seen as not simply an assertion of Jewish pride, but also Zionist identity – because he made a point of accepting an "Einstein Forest" in his honor in Palestine at the same time. He was hailed for placing the Zionists and the Jews "in a new light before the eyes of the world."[129]

Similar to the perception of Brandeis, Einstein, too, was seen as having a rather weak connection to Jewish culture and politics before his turn to Zionism.[130] But Einstein was a different type of symbol, in that he had no competing national identification – he was the epitome of a cosmopolitan. Although German Jews claimed him as one of their own,[131] he did not assign any special significance to his tie to German culture as did other Zionist notables from Central Europe such as Kurt Blumenfeld and Robert Weltsch. In fact, he became a Swiss citizen in 1901. Despite his sincere intolerance for chauvinism, he was explicit about the necessity of a national movement for world Jewry, and Zionism in particular:

Before we can effectively combat anti-Semitism, we must first of all educate ourselves out of our slave-mentality which it betokens. We must have more dignity, more independence in our own ranks. Only when we have the courage to regard ourselves as a nation, when we respect ourselves, can we win the respect of others; or rather, the respect of others will then come of itself . . . When I come across the phrase "German Citizens of the Jewish Persuasion," I cannot avoid a melancholy smile. What does this high falutin' description really mean? What is this "Jewish Persuasion"? Is there, then, a kind of non-persuasion by virtue of which one ceases to be a Jew? There is not.

Einstein claimed that what the description really meant was that those who adopted it desired "to have nothing to do with my poor (East European) Jewish brethren";[132] and second, that each wished "to be regarded not as a son of my own people, but only as a member of a religious community." Nevertheless, it was rarely his purpose to take a stance which was critical of German Jewry in general. It was more typical for him to inquire why they had come to be what they were and to extend his empathy.[133] His autobiography of 1933 was notably

dedicated to an appreciation of the German Jews. It must be remembered that we are concerned here with a body of people amounting, in numbers, to no more than the population of a moderate-sized town, who have held their own against a hundred times as many Germans, in spite of handicaps and prejudices, through the superiority of their ancient cultural traditions. Whatever attitude people may take up toward this little people, nobody who retains a shred of sound judgment in these times of confusion can deny them respect . . . Today the Jews of Germany find their fairest consolation in the thought of all they have produced and achieved for humanity by their efforts . . . no oppression however brutal, no campaign of calumny however subtle will blind those who have eyes to see the intellectual and moral qualities inherent in this people.[134]

Einstein clearly articulated the notion that to be a Jew, and to be a Zionist, required an unconditional love for the entirety of the Jewish people. "Let us just leave anti-Semitism to the non-Jews," he wrote, "and keep our hearts warm for our kith and kin."[135] Not since Herzl's early addresses and writings had a Zionist leader's call for Jewish unity been received as a sign of integrity, generosity, and compassion, as opposed to a tactical ploy.

Also like Brandeis and Herzl, Einstein embodied the notion of returning to the fold. In 1921 he wrote that it was not until his move to Berlin two years earlier that any "Jewish sentiments" were aroused in him, principally due to anti-Semitism. His biographer, Abraham Pais, concurs that "evidently Einstein's life and moods were strongly affected by the strife and violence in Germany in the 1920s." No doubt his friendship with Kurt Blumenfeld, the German Zionist leader, helped him to see Zionism as at least a partial solution to the problem.[136] Einstein was particularly struck by the fact that "the road to a safe existence" proved so hazardous to "the Eastern-born Jews in Germany, who were continually exposed to provocation." He perceptively realized, before the rise of the Nazis, the extent to which the *Ostjuden* had become unwitting pawns:

made the scapegoat of all the ills of present-day German political life and all the after-effects of the war. Incitement against these unfortunate fugitives, who have only just saved themselves from the hell which Eastern Europe means for them today, has become an effective political weapon, employed with success by every demagogue.

As a result of this recognition, along with his positive contact with *Ostjuden*, Einstein revealed that "the Jewish national sentiment" was "awakened" in him. "I am a national Jew in the sense that I demand the preservation of the Jewish nationality as of every other. I look upon Jewish nationality as a fact, and I think that every Jew ought to come to definite conclusions on Jewish questions on the basis of this fact." Again echoing the thought of Herzl, Einstein stated that "I regard the growth of Jewish self-assertion as being in the interests of non-Jews as well as of Jews. That was the main motive of my joining the Zionist ranks."[137]

Yet Einstein went further than any other Zionist leader in defining and condoning the existence of Zionism in the diaspora, which made him uniquely suited for heroic stature in the Western Jewish communities. His was the most lucid argument articulated in support of the diaspora, without intoning the pious Zionist hope that all Jewry would eventually settle in Palestine. The latter was a posture which provided a rationale for the bureaucratic European *Kulturarbeit* which Weizmann sought to protect. "For me," Einstein wrote,

Zionism is not merely a question of colonisation. The Jewish nation is a living thing, and the sentiment of Jewish nationalism must be developed both in Palestine and everywhere else. To deny the Jews' nationality in the Diaspora is, indeed, deplorable. If one adopts the point of view confining Jewish ethnic nationalism to Palestine, then to all intents and purposes one denies the existence of a Jewish people. In that case we should have the courage to carry through assimilation as quickly and as completely as possible.[138]

Although he freely admits his disdain for "undignified assimilationist cravings and strivings," Einstein nevertheless repeats Herzl, and in his own time, Brandeis's claim, that Zionism and other nationalities need not be mutually exclusive. There is no reason why the Zionist "who remains true to his origin" should not "also remain loyal to the State of which he is a subject. He who is faithless to one will also be faithless to the other."[139]

Despite the unprecedented adulation accorded Einstein, his thoughts about the kind of Zionism he wished to prevail in Palestine did not seem to have much impact.[140] He maintained his belief, even after the riots of 1929, that "friendly personal relations" could be both the spark and cement of Jewish–Arab understanding. This was not just a naive dream, but an idea which he thought could be sincerely and systematically cultivated within the framework of Zionist politics and institutions.[141] In terms of his efforts for conciliation with Palestine's Arabs, Einstein was on the margins of Zionist politics. Rather than challenging him, however, potential opponents usually made no comment when he aired his views on the subject.[142] Although he expressed some rather strong opinions, he was viewed as above the Zionist political skirmishes. "Einstein believed it was self-evident," Goldmann wrote, "that politics must rest on moral principles. He hated war, aggressive nationalism, and reaction. It was his profound humane impulses that made him a conscious Jew and led him to help in the settlement of Palestine."[143] Leon Simon concurred that Einstein's concept of nationalism allowed "no room for any kind of aggressiveness or chauvinism. For him the domination of Jew over Arab in Palestine, or the perpetuation of hostilities between the two peoples, would mean the end of Zionism."[144]

But in the end, Einstein, like his colleagues Weizmann, Brandeis, Szold, and Sokolow, and like Lord Balfour, genuinely and fervently believed in the goodness and the greatness of the Zionist project. Whatever their differences and personal reservations, all of them were seized by the "magic" of the movement's achievements in Palestine, which represented a magnificent striving toward the "peaceful reconstruction" of a nation, and the hoped-for salvation of the Jewish masses.[145] Because this Zionist refrain was central to all of their overtures, the overall message commonly heard was one of harmony, not dissent and discord.

3   Dollars and the changing sense of Zionism

The work of the Keren Hayesod [Palestine Foundation Fund] is not a work which will take weeks, but decades. It is not a tactic of a Shnorrer, but a service to the life of the Jewish people.   Ernst Marcus, 1922[1]

Thousands of loyal and zealous Zionists throughout the country are discouraged, discontented, and demoralized by an organization which has degenerated a political cause and economic task into a charitable proposition, animated by a schnorrer psychology.
                                                                Irma Lindheim, 1928[2]

The scholars who have either focused on or seriously discussed the inter-war Zionist movement in the United States for the most part accept the notion that American Zionism proceeded toward its goal – the establishment of a state of the Jews in Palestine, and the consolidation of support of diaspora Jewry – in a hard-fought, but relatively admirable and democratic manner.[3] This consensus is reiterated in a recent multi-volume history of United States' Jewry.[4] The chief obstacles that the movement faced, this and other accounts imply, were impositions from outside the Zionist or general Jewish realms, or tensions endemic to Jewry, over which the leadership of the movement had little or no control. Rarely is it admitted that Zionism in the United States and worldwide might have fared poorly due to leadership decisions or organizational processes deliberately embodied by the movement.[5]

In raw numbers, American Zionist ranks declined from over 200,000 in 1918 to less than 65,000 in 1929. Furthermore, as mentioned previously, the largest organized portion of the membership by the late 1920s belonged to Hadassah (45,000 in 1928), which had an identity in some ways distinct and alienated from the male membership.[6] Aaron Berman writes that "American Zionism went into a period of steady decline" during the decade and a half after the First World War, "largely because Zionists lacked an issue with which to capture the attention and loyalty of American Jews."[7] Although historians will never know for certain how inevitable was the diminishing popularity of American Zionism in the 1920s, I believe that there are insights to be gleaned from this tumultuous period by reexamining how the Zionists sought to navigate their own destiny and the various implications of their decisions.

The picture of American Zionism in the interwar years as presented in the scholarly literature hardly varies from the version of events as seen by the victors in Zionism's internecine debates. The view that prevails is essentially that of Chaim Weizmann as set forth in his problematic memoir, *Trial and Error*.[8] Weizmann was the president of the World Zionist Organization from 1920 to 1931, and was reelected in 1935.[9] The following interpretation of interwar Zionism in the United States, rather than tracing the career of Weizmann, emphasizes the tensions involved in sustaining the World Zionist Organization and American Zionist Organization, but above all, the care and feeding of the movement's fundraising mechanisms – which came to dominate the experience of Zionism for United States' Jewry. As opposed to the existing historiography on Zionist politics and institutions, I am most concerned with exploring the impact of the movement's politics on the attitudes of Western Jews toward Zionism.

If Zionism desperately needed money in order to accomplish its aims, how can fundraising be regarded as problematic? The fact of the matter was that although Zionists did raise a lot of money, they did not raise enough to accomplish many of their goals, and other non-Zionist bodies fared better. Henry Feingold states that

Between 1921 and 1925 the Zionist organizations launched four "appeals" but raised only $6 million compared with the [non-Zionist] Joint Distribution Committee's $20.8 million . . . Only the simultaneous failure of the JDC-sponsored Crimean settlement project and the emergency created by the Arab riots of 1929 gave Zionists an opportunity to enlist non-Zionists with their superior fundraising capacity, by welcoming them into the Jewish Agency for Palestine and by consolidating all fund-raising under the banner of the United Jewish Appeal (UJA).[10] But such a consolidation would require the continuing pressure of the crisis faced by world Jewry after the advent of the National Socialist regime in Germany.[11]

Concerning the period 1920 to 1945, Feingold comments that "Scholars have pondered the remarkable fund-raising apparatus of American Jewry, noting the traditional 'habit of giving' that was part of Jewish law and culture."[12] This "habit," to which a tremendous amount of energy in Zionism was directed, deserves careful consideration, beyond expressions of esteem, gratitude, and awe. The Zionist movement in the United States, since 1914, can be fruitfully examined from the perspective of the creation and function of fundraising bodies, and the relationship of Zionism to charity and philanthropy. It may thereby be recognized that the growing importance of fundraising in Zionism was inextricably tied to devaluing the intellectual content and ethical standards of the movement, in favor of nurturing an obedient, unquestioning membership primarily asked to give money to the cause.

In 1928, Hadassah president Irma Lindheim charged that American Zionism and the World Zionist Organization had spawned a "self-perpetuating body," fostering an institutional framework that was actually detrimental to the greater aims of the movement and the general well-being of world Jewry. Lindheim and others who comprised the Zionist opposition from 1920 to 1931 were profoundly disturbed by "the manner in which the Zionist Organization of America [was] being run." They saw themselves as representing the 100,000 members who had left the organization since 1919, and "the thousands of loyal and zealous Zionists throughout the country [who] are discouraged, discontented, and demoralized by an organization which has degenerated a political cause and economic task into a charitable proposition, animated by a schnorrer psychology."[13] In presenting Zionism to its existing and potential constituents, the movement was becoming ever more "cheap and huckstering."[14]

In Lindheim's contemporary definition, a "self-perpetuating body" did not signify a group that was routinely and openly reelected, but rather a leadership consisting of "a hierarchy of paid officials who were responsible to themselves alone." The paid officials were ostensibly responsible to the rulings of the annual convention, which was in fact

under the control of these paid executives who controlled the convention through the chair, which was held by the president [of the Zionist Organization of America] . . . In this way the administration was perpetuating itself while keeping up the semblance of election by popular vote, because it had control of the machine which controlled the votes and at the Convention gave the floor only to those who were "trusted" Zionists.[15]

In August 1927 the National Board of Hadassah, which was anything but a hotbed of radicals and malcontents, came to the conclusion that "the integrity of the Zionist Organization, as well as that of Hadassah, was being seriously menaced by the growth of a money-raising instrument which was responsible only to itself."[16] This problem, centering on the Zionist fundraising machine, however, has not typically been seen in retrospect as a major divisive force.

For the period beginning with the Jewish mass migration to the United States in the 1880s until the Second World War, tensions in American Jewish organizational life are often seen as stemming from the split between East and West. Historians and sociologists are accustomed to expounding the dichotomy between the earlier generation of Jewish immigrants, known by the shorthand "German Jews," versus their numerically overwhelming poor brethren, the East European Jews. Within the context of Zionism, Ben Halpern's *A Clash of Heroes: Brandeis, Weizmann, and American Zionism* is the capstone of scholarship on this subject. Halpern ascribes the friction between Brandeis and Weizmann to an inevitable collision of "Americanism," imbibed in a Germanic way, versus "Eastern European Jewishness." Most accounts of "the Weizmann/Brandeis controversy," following Halpern, relate that at the end of the First World War, "one group," the Brandeis faction, wanted to turn the Zionist Organization into an institution "run on banking lines" to promote Zionist enterprises in Palestine, solely according to business principles. The other group, led by Weizmann, stressed the need to preserve the "pioneering character" of Zionism by mobilizing "national capital" through donations from the Jewish masses.[17] The implication is that Brandeis, the German Jew, wanted to run Zionism from the top down, while Weizmann, the Eastern Jew and true democrat, wanted it run from the bottom up. A typical corollary claim is that Brandeis epitomized "the spirit of American free enterprise," whereas Weizmann advocated the "collectivist programs" embraced by Eastern European Jews.[18] Although it is usually recognized that Brandeis advocated the separation rather than the commingling of investments and donations, this is most often expressed as some sort of mania for efficiency at the expense of Jewish solidarity. Yet the conflict between Brandeis and Weizmann was a more complex and crucial episode in Zionist and Jewish history than many commentators intimate. There is a host of issues that figure into the conflict, such as what was perceived in Europe as a lack of sympathy or understanding for so-called cultural work (*Kulturarbeit*) in Europe. The main argument of the Brandeis faction here was that they wanted the same standards of accountability applied to the Zionist organization in Europe; for instance, they did not want money that American Jews had thought they had given for Palestine to pay salaried officials or subvent Zionist publications in Europe.[19] Nevertheless, it is rarely mentioned that Weizmann and his followers employed harsh, repressive, and disingenuous methods in maintaining control of the movement and particularly in controlling Zionist fundraising. This, too, left a permanent imprint on the movement.

However much "German" versus Russian and Polish or "uptown" versus "downtown" are useful categories for analysis, in the case of American Zionism in the 1920s, there are other fruitful strategies for investigation. The East/West model itself incites empathy for the self-styled "authentic" view of Chaim Weizmann, who claimed to epitomize the Eastern Jewish spirit. As effective a leader as Weizmann was, he was, to put it mildly, a bad historian – especially when his own role in the movement is concerned. Under Weizmann, as leader of the World Zionist Organization, and Lipsky, president of the Zionist Organization of America, principled dissent from the party line was systematically eliminated, alternatives to official policy were neutralized, and those seen as dissenters from its ranks were removed from positions of power.[20] These acts are often rationalized as the distinctive style of Eastern versus German Jews.[21] To blithely condone this line, however, is demeaning to Eastern Jews; it suggests a sort of authoritarianism as a hereditary trait of Russian Jews. Certainly it is possible to label such phenomena as nothing more or less than robust politics, to which the Jews have never been accused of being immune. But Zionism was not typically a movement that practiced apologetics for autocracy or preached the benefits of firm party discipline. If it were, it would be easier to subsume these actions into politics-as-usual.

It is indeed remarkable, and a point of pride among admirers of the Zionist movement, that various ideologies and forms of participation evolved and were welcome in Zionism. Yet the movement was akin to other organizations and national groups in trying to control what it perceived as pernicious in-group activity. Although David Ben-Gurion envisioned the Jewish state's graduation to "normalcy" when the first Jewish policeman arrested the first Jewish criminal, in the years before statehood, the Zionist leadership had achieved normalcy – in exercising an instinct for preserving what it deemed its "vested interests."[22] As Zionism developed into an ever more normal political entity from 1897 onward, with a growing bureaucracy and well-regulated party system, the avant-garde and iconoclastic edge was predictably and drastically dulled.[23]

The initial significant rift in American Zionist ranks arose over the creation of the Keren Hayesod in 1920–21, and the most notable subsequent eruption surrounded the opposition's attempt to reorganize the Zionist Organization of America in 1928. For the background of the founding of the Keren Hayesod, we must return to the years of the First World War. The formerly Berlin-centered Zionist organization was nearly shattered due to the difficulty of coordinating Zionist activities between the belligerent European states. Therefore, the Jews of the United States assumed the lion's share of financial responsibility for maintaining Zionist enterprises in Palestine and keeping the organization afloat in Europe.[24] Brandeis became the head of the Zionist Provisional

Committee, bringing the movement greater respectability and visibility among American Jews and non-Jews than ever before. By the war's end, while there was residual jubilation over Britain issuing the Balfour Declaration (1917), and tremendous relief that the Zionist work in Palestine had been salvaged, there was also concern that the settlement activity had not, in fact, progressed very far. This was puzzling to many American Jews, in light of the millions of dollars that had been donated to the cause, and the desperate need to resettle thousands of European Jewish refugees, whose fate was still hanging in the balance. After the war Brandeis went to Palestine to see the Yishuv for himself. He was deeply impressed – but at the same time, he was perplexed by what appeared to him to be inexcusable waste and mismanagement. For instance, he knew that a great deal of money had been given to combat the spread of malaria; he himself had anonymously given $10,000 for the Malarial Unit in 1919.[25] Particularly in light of this inside knowledge, Brandeis was shocked to find such work proceeding painfully slowly, or not at all – with a budget which represented a fraction of the money he had given and raised himself.[26] Henrietta Szold reinforced Brandeis's observations with her critique of "how Zionist funds were being squandered."[27] Although scholars such as Yigal Elam, Nahum Gross, Hagit Lavsky, and Jacob Metser have tackled the problem of administration and finance in Palestine, there has yet to appear a full-scale scholarly reckoning of the financial workings of the Zionist Organization, from the inception of pledges and donations, to the dissemination of funds in Palestine, Europe, the United States, and worldwide.[28]

At the behest of Brandeis and his faction at the London Zionist conference of 1920, a group of three – dubbed the "Reorganization Commission" – was dispatched to Palestine to evaluate the movement's work, and particularly to make recommendations and enact changes regarding the policies of the Zionist Commission, which had been the movement's chief instrument in Palestine throughout the war.[29] The main question animating the Commission was: to what extent is the Zionist Organization furthering the permanent settlement of the Jews in Palestine, as an independent, self-reliant, agriculturally oriented nation?[30]

The Reorganization Commission consisted of three members: Robert Szold, Julius Simon, and Nehemia de Lieme. Derek Penslar has characterized the Zionist settlement philosophy of de Lieme and Simon as "cautious progressivism";[31] Robert Szold embodied a similar approach. These men performed their tasks with great energy and care; their notes, which have been preserved, testify to their scrupulousness. What they found and reported could literally not be believed by most Zionists. The institutions in Palestine revealed severe structural faults; the commission called for "a complete reorganization of the Zionist work in Palestine."[32] Among their specific targets were sacred idols of the movement. For example, they found that the aforestation practices of the Jewish National Fund, which were so central to Zionist imagery and liturgy, were not based on any comprehensive, long-range plan. Compared to the funds disbursed, the institution contributed little to permanent Jewish settlement.[33] With "deep regret" they were "obliged to conclude that the farms of the JNF of which all Zionists had been taught to speak with pride, were, from the standpoint of future national colonisation, of limited value":[34]

The fault in the past has been largely in the system by which fixing the character of the settlement too early and equipping the farms too completely deprived the workers of their independence and initiative and reduced them to day-labourers. This does not mean that in the first stages the groups have not done beautiful pioneer service. Many have sacrificed their health and their lives to this work. The tragedy is that those who have sown do not always reap.[35]

In contradiction to the professed egalitarian aims of the new Jewish society, the Reorganization Commission was

particularly struck by the fact that the Yemenites, who were called upon to help erect new buildings for settlers at Nachlat Yehuda costing £350 each, were themselves at the same time housed in hovels of the most abominable character near Rischon. And this was permitted when our total annual expenditure exceeded £300,000.[36]

To its dismay, the Reorganization Commission observed that some of the most impressive aspects of the Zionists' propaganda – such as the forests and the far-flung settlements – had in fact done little to enhance the prospects of mass Jewish settlement. In Palestine, the Zionists had "combined and confused propaganda and practical work, to the degradation of both."[37] What looked good, and was effective for fundraising purposes, did not always coincide with the best forms of settlement activity. And as opposed to the vaunted ideal of the Jewish return to the soil and manual labor, they found that a substantial share of the movement's funds were devoted to the upkeep of growing bureaucracies – where few got rich, but many were able to hang on while doing little that actually served the cause of settlement, and devoured funds which did not engender "productive work."[38] Overall, they discovered the accounting procedures to be either highly questionable, incomplete, or nonexistent. In place of fiscal responsibility, the commission discovered an attitude bordering on contempt for budgets and guidelines from the central office.[39] In essence, they ordered a complete reorganization of the Yishuv and found the Zionist Organization to be seriously deficient in light of its goals. In a confidential memo, they went so far as to say that "We do not believe that the pre-war work has created a nucleus for the future work which the present circumstances now require." Efforts had been "scattered," and no system had been "planned before work was undertaken. Continuity of effort according to a plan, and careful administration, would have required specialization and economy." In part, this situation had emerged because the leaders believed that

the imagination is stimulated more by developing a seemingly broad system than by a limitation of effort. When, however, again and again, new stimulation is wanted, the work tends to extend beyond the available means, and becomes weaker and weaker. The system of propaganda adopted prevented a turning aside from ill-considered enterprises.[40]

The Reorganization Commission was very perceptive in determining that the Zionist Organization had reached a crisis stage,[41] and that the movement's propaganda and requirements in Palestine were out of joint. Clearly, there were fundamental problems with the organization, the rectification of which would have to be accompanied by drastic changes in the movement's propaganda – in particular, that devoted to fund-raising. This was not something the organization's European leaders would consider even momentarily. Along with this call to rationally disengage the propaganda from practical work was a demand for greater fiscal responsibility and accountability – which the movement's leadership, especially Chaim Weizmann, Menahem Ussischkin (a leader of the Zionist Executive in Palestine), and their loyalists opposed with all their power.[42] They vehemently denied the carefully garnered facts, and forcibly prevented the implementation of most reforms. The main polemic directed against the report was that it undermined the consolidation of the Jews' "national capital" for its necessary, uninhibited use by the Zionist Organization in Palestine.[43] Despite the assertion of Robert Burt and others that "the victorious Weizmann faction soon adopted all of the accounting and administrative proposals espoused by Brandeis and his defeated supporters,"[44] there is no hard evidence to support such a claim. It was, above all, the events surrounding the reaction to the Reorganization Commission report which prompted Weizmann's handling of the Keren Hayesod, and the removal of Brandeis and Julian Mack from the leadership of Zionism in the United States in 1921.

Had the Brandeis faction prevailed, the report might be considered among the seminal documents of the movement's history. Yet because the Brandeis group was defeated, and due to the methods employed to discredit it, this study has barely been noticed.[45] For historians, however, it should be seen as a critical document; it sets the scene for the clash between Weizmann and Brandeis. Essentially, Brandeis, Mack, and their cohort refused to tell the Jews to put their money into the hands of "those whose administration we could not trust."[46] Although they would never say so publicly, they regarded Chaim Weizmann and Louis Lipsky as untrustworthy.[47] In the stormy days of the London Zionist conference of 1921, Brandeis reportedly told Weizmann: "I do not trust you. I am done with you. I shall work with you for the sake of the cause, but I understand you and can never trust you again."[48] Some years later Stephen S. Wise confided to his daughter that "No matter what I said of Weizmann," and we may assume none of it was complimentary, "LDB [Brandeis] laughingly assented, though his laugh was rather grim and ferocious, and once he said, 'Nothing you can say is adequate to describe this Machiavellian being.'"[49] "From almost every point of view," Stephen S. Wise wrote at the end of 1928, "I consider Weizmann's leadership a tragedy."[50]

Weizmann's offensive against the members who produced and supported the report alleged that their only objective had been to "destroy" the existing organization for their own sake.[51] In part due to the "moral problems" which had been uncovered, Brandeis sought to impose a greater degree of "honest finance"[52] within the movement's fundraising, by clearly differentiating between "investments" in specific Palestinian enterprises, and donations which could be used at the organization's discretion. The Keren Hayesod, then, was conceived by Weizmann not merely to draw non-Zionists into the movement's orbit and to solicit larger contributions than those typically gained by the Jewish National Fund. He sought to quash Brandeis's plan to initiate public accountability in the movement. In a prescient assessment of the motives behind the founding of the Keren Hayesod, a Zionist who was present at its inception, Samuel Rosensohn,[53] wrote that "[Shmarya] Levin, [Menahem] Ussischkin, and Weizmann have through the instrumentality of the Keren Hayesod evolved a great dream of empire. The power is autocratic without any responsibility." They are demanding personal "loyalty to the officers of the Keren Hayesod . . . and anyone daring to criticize them or question their power will be deemed disloyal to the cause . . . Through it all the real point of the Zionist cause has been overlooked."[54]

In New York on May 20, 1921, Weizmann laid down his main lines of attack against Brandeis and Mack, which the Zionist Organization, and especially the Zionist Organization of America under Lipsky, would maintain until the 1930s. Rarely, however, would Brandeis's name be mentioned, due to his mythical stature in the movement. It seems that Julian Mack was forced to bear the brunt of the criticism. Adopting language that was alien to the sober, rationalistic tone of the Brandeis faction, Weizmann characterized the struggle over fundraising as a "war." In so doing he demonized, rather than debated, his opponents. What had been largely a demand for reform and accountability Weizmann expressed in terms of a devious, naked power struggle. In fact, however, it was Weizmann who undermined the officially sanctioned work of the commission through lying and temporarily inviting members of the Revisionist movement into the Zionist Executive in order to drive out the reformers.[55]

One of the "methods of warfare" that Weizmann accused his opponents of exercising, which was more graphic than describing their acts as "slander-mongering,"[56] must in retrospect be seen as an unfortunate analogy. He compared the campaign of the Brandeis faction to the use of poisonous gas:

You cannot see it. You can only protect yourself by closing ears, nose, and mouth. I know something about it. Those poisonous gasses have now been spread all over the country. I have heard all kinds of rumors, that there is no financial control, there is no efficiency, etc. Again I say, let these gentlemen specify instances . . . When you pin them down, you will see the poisonous gas entirely disappear, and I am determined to see it disappear.[57]

Weizmann knew what the specific charges were. It would be absurd to imagine he believed they were unfounded; in simple terms, he was lying. What he did was equate any criticism of the new fundraising mechanism, the Keren Hayesod, with high treason against the Zionist movement and the well-being of the Jewish people. Weizmann wanted to be sure that he himself, as leader of the Zionist Organization, held *carte blanche* in the disposition of funds. If one did not comply with his view, the result – as he put it – could only be increased "suffering" by the already depleted *Halutsim* (pioneers) of Palestine, who would no doubt bear their burden stoically.[58] Weizmann claimed that "no Jew worthy of the name" could decline to contribute,[59] and that refusing support for the Keren Hayesod was tantamount to obstructing "the coming of the Day of Redemption." As a mother is unconditionally devoted to nurturing her child, so too, he said, should the American Zionists support the Zionist leadership and the Keren Hayesod without asking hard questions.[60]

One of the elements of the Zionist Organization which was perceived by the administration as a chief threat after the defeat of the Brandeis faction at the Cleveland convention was Hadassah. The Lipsky administration, charging that Hadassah had refused to submit properly to the

Keren Hayesod, made a concerted effort to alter fundamentally the composition of Hadassah in the wake of the challenge to his authority in 1920–21.[61] On July 12, 1921, the Central Committee of Hadassah was notified by the General Secretary of the Zionist Organization of America that it had been "dissolved and that a new Central Committee was in course of formation." The Hadassah leadership was clearly taken aback by such a bold move – especially because it was issued no explanation. The deposed women retorted:

We are loath to precipitate legal action. We feel that factional differences in the Zionist Organization can best be settled within the organization, provided settled principles of fair play and just dealing are applied to such a settlement. When, however, seven elected representatives of thousands of women loyal to the Zionist Organization, individually, and as members of the Central Committee of Hadassah are advised that they have been removed from office without authority, without notice, without charges, without a hearing and without any opportunity to state their own position, and when this removal purports to come not from their constituents but from an organization claiming superior power, it seems to us that the time has come when self-respect and decency and loyalty to our constituents demand that before surrendering the trust that they have confided to us and the offices which they have conferred upon us, we determine definitely the character of the action purporting to remove us and dissolve the Central Committee.[62]

Although there was never a direct response to Hadassah's query, the conflict was eventually defused because of the women's overwhelming desire to reconcile with the administration.[63] In a letter to Lipsky which was drafted but never sent, the Hadassah leaders declared that "our attitude is by no means uncompromising, except as honor and fidelity to trust forbid compromise with falsehood and untruth. Apparently your whole action was based on false statements and false reports and is characterized by the injustice and illegality which usually inhere in actions so commenced." In this case, negotiations successfully returned the ousted women, and these criticisms of Lipsky never saw the light of day.[64] This did not, however, keep the Lipsky and Weizmann administrations from repeatedly attempting to undermine Hadassah through the creation of a (variously named) women's committee for the Keren Hayesod.[65]

The fires of criticism were never totally smothered. Dissatisfaction with the movement again came to a head seven years later in an attempt to "reform" the Zionist Organization of America. But the men and women leading the charge in 1928 were not necessarily the dissidents of 1921. Although Brandeis and Mack retained honorary titles, they and others had occupied themselves with building up the Palestine

Development Council to stimulate industrial development in the Yishuv. This was not, however, publicized as a substitute or an "opposing organization" to the official Zionist bodies.[66] Some of the more outspoken opponents of Weizmann and Lipsky after 1927 were party members who had more recently become distressed by the state of the organization. The impetus to reorganize the ZOA in 1928 was evidence of "gross mismanagement" both in the United States and in Palestine. Unwise and even shady financial operations had emanated from the highest Zionist offices, which were fueled by "undemocratic machine politics." Such "misdeeds and negligence" were perceived as "endangering the fate of Zionism and demoralizing American support for the movement."[67] There seemed to be little possibility of reform in either Europe or Palestine.[68] "It seems to me clear," Brandeis wrote in 1927, "that our friends cannot wisely assume control for the future if it means shouldering the huge indebtedness of the several organizations and institutions . . . You will recall the passage [of] Herodotus about the Persians. They considered lying the greatest of sins. And the next greatest was running into debt. For debts men lie."[69] A conservative estimate of the ZOA debt in 1930 was $150,000.[70]

One of Brandeis's confidants, Samuel J. Rosensohn, provided an assessment of the Fifteenth World Zionist Congress in Basel, 1927, which for the most part substantiated the earlier misgivings of the opposition, while also conceding that the organization had not remained totally static. Rosensohn was pleased to report that the delegates in Basel

did not seek to cover up the shortcomings and defects of the Zionist Organization, nor was it their aim to spare anyone connected with the Zionist administration. They regarded the economic condition of the Jews in Palestine with the gravest concern, and sought to remedy those conditions, and to restore public confidence . . . As a result of this attitude, real constructive progress was made.

Such advances occurred, however, only because the leaders' backs were to the wall. "The critical attitude of delegates was only a result of the notorious failure of Zionist work in Palestine, and did not arise out of the realization of the breakdown of the moral forces which were the foundation of the Zionist movement. The Executive was not changed because it had acted wrongfully, but because it had been unsuccessful."

The "reformers" such as Rosensohn were moved primarily because they believed that the movement lacked leadership: "first, because there were not persons with moral fervor requisite for such leadership; and second, because there was no people united in the promotion of a common ideal crying for leadership. The Congress was representative of the Zionists at large. As such, it was a Congress without idealism – almost a Congress without hope." Rosensohn believed, nevertheless, that a momentous shift of opinion had occurred: "the fiction of Weizmann's indispensability which has acted as a sort of incubus on the movement, has been completely shattered." The remainder of his synopsis, however, was bleak, and in particular, reveals a most unflattering portrait of Weizmann's leadership.

Rosensohn depicted Weizmann's reelection at the Zionist Congress as an unenthusiastic act of resignation:

The delegates divided themselves in four classes. (a) Those for Weizmann because they thought a change of leadership would interfere with the creation of the [Jewish] Agency, and might affect the attitude of the British Government. (b) Those for Weizmann because there was no other available candidate, and they did not wish to relieve him of the responsibility for the present critical condition of the movement. (c) Those who were for him because of their interest in the funds, and they felt that he could secure more funds than anyone else; and (d) those who were against him because they wanted the position of leadership for themselves, or because they had been kept out of the organization. Hardly anyone considered Palestine of the Zionist movement.[71]

This was made possible as

the direct result of Weizmann's policy to destroy all possible rivals to his position at the head of the Organization, and thus make himself the only available candidate. In carrying out this policy, he has destroyed all the truly critical and spiritual forces in the movement, and has practically destroyed Zionism. He has no program except that he should continue as the head of the Organization.[72]

Using the same devices that had served him in the past, Weizmann "even sought to prevent any possible criticism of his management, either by calling it *Ḥilul ha-Shem* [defiling the name of God], or that if that was ineffective, by threatening to resign. [Stephen S.] Wise's leaving the Congress was a distinct protest against this attempt to stifle freedom of discussion, and destroy the right of Zionists freely to criticize the Executive and the administration."[73] Rosensohn's final suggestion was obviously taken as a grim pronouncement:

What the Zionist movement needs today is not merely a program or a group of men who will see to it that the proper financial and economic policies are carried out in Palestine (although that is highly desirable) but a leader who will re-awaken the moral forces which have been stifled and almost destroyed. A change in the Palestine Executive and the adoption of the proper financial and economic principles, will in a measure restore public confidence, but they cannot revive the moral forces of Zionism. The Zionist movement must be re-created.[74]

Rosensohn's views are corroborated in the extensive correspondence of Henrietta Szold, who wrote in 1925 that "Zionism has fallen on evil times. The money-collections have watered it, dragged it down into the mud, cheapened it."[75] Although Weizmann would later publicly confess that "we have abused America as a moneygiving machine,"[76] he exacerbated, rather than rectified the problem.

In the Pittsburgh Convention of July 1928, Lipsky retained the presidency of the ZOA despite overwhelming evidence of poor and dishonest leadership. "It should be noted, however," read one of the most penetrating private analyses of the event,

that a large number of the delegates [who voted for Lipsky] were those whom we attempted to show . . . to have been fraudulently elected. The credentials committee of the convention, which Lipsky had named long before the convention assembled, threw out all protests and contests without ado and seated everyone whom Lipsky wished to have seated. It is largely in that way that he asserted himself the majority by which he won.[77]

It was only through spreading the lie that the opposition was set to bring the charges against him to court, outside the Zionist Organization, that Lipsky was able to convince a panel of "judges" to soften their findings of his improprieties. Lipsky, before and after, lambasted his accusers in the Zionist press. He labeled the character of his opponents as "something Goyish and something outlandish in Zionist life," who had been waging "guerrilla warfare" against him.[78] The campaign to hold on to his presidency was deemed an effort "to purge the movement of evil."[79] The opposition, he charged, was vindictive, hateful, and guilty of spreading *Rekhilut* (malicious gossip).[80] Continuing the haunting rhetoric of Weizmann from 1921, an ardent Lipsky supporter wrote that the opposition had initiated "a war of extermination, using camouflage at every step."[81] Weizmann himself denounced the opposition as "fratricidal."[82] This is particularly ironic considering that the Zionist Organization, which was in dire financial straits, poured around $38,000 into waging a propaganda battle with the opposition.[83]

Indeed, such attitudes contributed to the contention that any possible conflict with the fundraising mechanisms was tantamount to treason.[84] The umbrella organization United Palestine Appeal was wielded by Zionist authorities as "a club to enforce silence." Fundraising drives were "continuous the year around," and were used as an "excuse for an eternal silence about existing conditions" of Zionist affairs both in the United States and in Palestine.[85] Even when there was no threat to the fundraising bodies, the ruling clique saw enemies.[86] This was the impetus for a series of political dirty tricks, directed at Hadassah, on behalf of the Lipsky and Weizmann administrations. Sounding a note of conspiracy, Lipsky sent a "confidential" telegram to hundreds of Zionists claiming that a "small group abetted by several Hadassah national officers led by Mrs. Lindheim aims through creation of lack of confidence, disturbance, dissension, [and] public discussion to undermine the United Palestine Campaign."[87] Before the American Zionist convention of 1928, Lipsky attempted to postpone the national meeting of Hadassah (which was supposed to convene prior to the convention) until after the American Zionist Organization met, and furthermore changed the voting rules in order to disenfranchise some 5,000 members of Hadassah.[88] This became part of an extremely bitter, protracted campaign causing the leaders of Hadassah tremendous distress.[89] Essentially, Lipsky sought to prevent a public Hadassah vote on a platform which asserted that the women's organization was

dissatisfied with the Administration of the Zionist Organization of America, believing that it has been an ineffective instrument for the creation of a strong Zionist Organization in America, due to the faulty and inefficient method pursued, and due even more fundamentally to the fact that there are inherent weaknesses in the present form of Organization; and [that] Hadassah . . . sees the close relationship as of cause and effect between American Zionist affairs and certain unsatisfactory conditions in Palestine.[90]

An internal memo succinctly stated the failings of the ZOA: "1. It has not increased the membership in the Zionist Organization. 2. It is not able to draw to itself sufficient forces to work for Palestine. 3. It is not representative of all classes of American Jewry. 4. It has lowered the tone of Zionism in America."[91] None of the histories of the movement do justice to this chapter, in which the actions of the administration were in fact "radical" and "unjust."[92] At the Hadassah convention of 1928 (concurrent with the Pittsburgh conference), President Irma Lindheim railed against what she saw as the rank hypocrisy and misogyny of Zionism's central leadership.[93]

To no small degree, the polemics of this conflict also reflected the social and intellectual standing of the challengers relative to the administration. But this, too, is misleading. Weizmann had learned to mimic the ways of well-born circles in Britain, and the East European Jewish Americans, certainly the ones courted by Weizmann, were no poor *shleppers*. Still, the social position of those in the Brandeis faction was used to discredit it.[94] The criticism of "lawyers and judges"[95] was likened to the niggling of rabbinical authorities. There is some consistency to this complaint and Zionism's original attempt at a sweeping reform of Jewish life through a grand national ideal. Had Herzl not proclaimed "if you will it, it is not a dream"?[96] The movement's leaders regularly displayed a certain obstinacy when dealing with what they saw as encumbering details. The dreaded "weapons" of the "rancorous" Brandeis group featured "parliamentary procedure" and "pharisaical appeals to higher standards of morality." This was said to be so "unfair" as to justify any response by their adversaries.[97] The "prosecution tactics" invoked by Brandeis and Mack were unpalatable to many,[98] and the opposition was supremely guilty of acting like lawyers. Worse, this was at times tinged with condescension toward the officials from Eastern Europe.[99] But the slighting of the administration as some kind of social inferiors was very uncommon.

At any rate, the administration's case was taken up with more than a reasonable degree of vengeance. Simply put, the administration and its opposition were not playing by the same rules; it was as if Lipsky and Weizmann showed up at a tennis match with pistols. Their sustained vitriolic rhetoric was unprecedented in the movement and permanently changed the discursive parameters of Zionism. Zionists who used "Arithmetic," "Accounting," and consideration of "Method," according to Lipsky loyalist Maurice Samuel, show symptoms of "pathological treachery." The main indication of this was that the opponents had "sabotaged the collecting of funds."[100] It was repeatedly charged that the dissidents were by nature self-hating Jews; anything they said was a problem with Zionism actually was rooted in their own tortured personalities.[101] Upon the arrival of Weizmann to the United States in 1928, Lipsky unleashed his harshest invective to denigrate his rivals. He claimed that the "assimilated" opposition had proved itself to be completely alien from the Jewish "race" for refusing to swim with the main current of the movement: "They refuse to become part of the race and associate themselves with our problems." Echoing themes that were well worn by anti-Semites, Lipsky charged his foes with spreading "depression and doubt." Adapting a Wagnerian critique, he asserted that he and his followers truly represented "the creative forces in American Jewish life,"[102] having an "intuitive" sense of Zionism.[103] In perhaps the most bizarre twist of racist rhetoric, the Lipsky administration argued that "the moral standards of Zionists are different from those of the Nordic opposition."[104]

The Zionist version of gutter journalism did not go unchallenged. The National Board of Hadassah protested that the official Zionist organs, *New Palestine* and *Dos Yiddishe Folk,* were first and foremost "publicity sheets for the high officers of the ZOA and their close adherents. Latterly, they have become, also, means of attack and misrepresentation of those who have ventured to criticize the present administration." It was in part due to the irresponsible policies of these journals that Zionists were not aware of the severity of economic crisis in Palestine, and its relationship to problems of Zionist administration in the diaspora:

The *New Palestine* at no time published a definite statement about the economic crisis. It minimized, and so far as possible concealed the facts about non-employment. Not until returning tourists had made the facts known in their various communities was there anything published in the *New Palestine* concerning the situation . . . A flagrant instance of concealment was the suppression of Miss [Henrietta] Szold's article on the economic situation in Tel Aviv, the house shortage which compelled hundreds to live in unsanitary huts. The refusal of the editor of the *New Palestine* was on the ground that it would disturb the rank and file. May I comment here that the *New Palestine* is published for and circulated almost exclusively among organized Zionists, who have the right to know the actual situations in connection with the ideal they seek to serve and which they are willing to serve as these situations demand . . . How much information has been given in the periodicals of the ZOA about the currents and cross-currents in the Zionist world? How much information have they given about the parties, the factions, the "oppositionists" abroad, in Europe, in Palestine? How much space has been given to informing the newcomers in Zionism as to the spiritual content of the movement? "Let us go out and meet them" was the title of an editorial in the *New Palestine* when it first appeared in its new form. To the newcomers in Zionism it must seem that the whole aim of Zionism is fund-raising, and that, therefore, it is only another form of philanthropy. To them it must appear Zionism and controversy are synonymous.[105]

After the conflict which began around 1920 was finally quieted due to the 1929 convulsions of the Arab riots in Palestine, the stock market crash, and reverberations from the earlier charges against the ZOA administration, the Brandeis faction was called back to the leadership in 1930.[106] From the perspective of Hadassah, "no event in American Zionism caused such widespread, sincere rejoicing, and hope for intensification of Zionist feeling in this country" as the changing of Lipsky's guard in the United States.[107] The organs of the Zionist Organization predictably implied that the nine-year rift in the movement had been a mere trifle. The facts and spirit of such accounts are pure fantasy.[108] But in order to preserve both the affection for Lipsky and the stature of Brandeis as a hero in the movement, an uncensored history of their battles, and the unsavory way they were conducted – at least on one side – has not permeated Zionist history. As opposed to democratizing the movement, Weizmann was in fact cultivating a wealthy elite that had little to do with "Eastern" versus "Western" values,[109] and a lot to do with how much a person was willing to give – and to play by his rules.[110] Although there is no doubt that he believed himself to be motivating people of good will, and no matter how much he was admired for his intellect and scientific achievements, in no sense was Weizmann fostering an intelligentsia – that is, "an intellectual order from the lower ranks" which "stressed 'critical thinking' and opposition to established power."[111] In the words of one critic, "a man's value to Zionism was to be measured only by the size of his financial contributions."[112] Furthermore, the notion that Brandeis was unsympathetic to socialism in Palestine could not have been the true bone of contention. In fact, Brandeis's model for disseminating Zionist ideology was the British Independent Socialist agitation; his admiration for a great deal of "socialist doctrine" and state socialism was indisputable.[113] He made no secret of his support for the Histadrut, the union of labor federations in the Yishuv, or of the collective sick-care fund, the Ḳupat Ḥolim; his greatest hope was that all Zionist services and enterprises would be controlled and maintained locally, largely on a cooperative basis.[114]

Perhaps a more important motive for this conflict is to be found in the deep resistance to change, which Stephen S. Wise saw as endemic in the Jewish organizational world. Despite its desire to be perceived as a government-in-exile, Wise thought that the Zionist view toward its leaders bore little resemblance to modern political attitudes. He wrote:

People deal with the proposal to change the leadership, to introduce a new regime into the Zionist movement as though it were treason, and there are two things that lie behind this attitude. On the one hand, [there is] the feeling that it is ingratitude to a man and disgraceful to him to [remove him from office]. It is [reasonable] to say that both Clemenceau and Lloyd George rendered great service to their countries during the War and after, and still both of them have been retired from leadership. Yet there is no talk of ingratitude or injustice to either of them. Such are the fortunes of political life. But there is another cause that underlies this attitude. There is a certain moral and spiritual inertia, a change means effort and effort is deprecated. It seems easier not to make a change. The value that may accrue from the change is not weighed, but the change is avoided as if it were something wrongful in itself, as if it erupted into the peace of Jewish life. The value of that "peace" is, however, woefully exaggerated.[115]

Rather than making changes in the substance of their programs or policies, the organization usually responded by adjusting its propaganda, in order to make it seem as if the trouble had been overcome, or in fact never existed.[116]

The larger issue of resistance to change, in relation to obedience to fundraising appeals, is of a dialectical nature. Some members recognized that American Zionism had assumed its shape because of its peculiar relationship to Palestine, which consisted mostly of hearing glowing testimonies and appeals for money. This was accompanied by an attitude in the Yishuv which prevailed since the second decade of the century, and is encapsulated in Robert Szold's confidential assessment of Menahem Ussischkin's management style: "Mr. Ussischkin, in my opinion, can never learn to manage properly. He lives in a world of dreams and unreality. He neglects the immediate work of construction in his contemplation of the millions he imagines will be furnished from the Jews of America if only those who understand their psychology approach them."[117]

What were manifested in the 1920s as Zionism's "ruthlessly undemocratic methods"[118] should not be stereotyped as an Eastern Jewish trait. Beyond the typical interpretive framework of class distinctions and Eastern versus Western proclivities, it is at least as important to factor in the significance of gender, with Hadassah taken seriously as a participant in the unfolding Zionist drama. The preeminent source of antagonism between Brandeis and Weizmann was not, at bottom, Weizmann's "Eastern European Jewishness" versus Brandeis's "Americanism." Spurred by Weizmann's desperate attempt to secure his position, it was a struggle about fundraising and the control of money, and the degree to which Zionism's leaders believed that they had the right to total discretion over the funds entrusted to them. Weizmann won, in large part, because he refused to discuss the issues in a rational manner; he declared his view to be sacred, and denounced his opponents as not just illegitimate but evil incarnate, and undermined the possibility of debate. Weizmann's calculated subversion of Brandeis, and the retrospective discussions of this episode, has helped to disguise or bury critical problems – some of which remain unresolved.

The accounts emanating from Louis Brandeis and his cohort may be seen as offering a more reasonable critique of the contemporary events than has typically been assumed. To be sure, Brandeis and his crowd were no angels, and they too harbored strong opinions, prejudices, and resentments. Yet they were consistently better at sizing up the political landscape, and carrying out their programmatic ideas in an open and straightforward manner. Comparatively speaking the Brandeis group was less guilty of "misrepresentation and lying" than was the Weizmann and Lipsky group.[119] The Brandeis men and women were not so skilled, however, at keeping power within Zionism and making sure that the historical record accurately reflected their struggle. It is ironic that the Brandeis faction is regularly derided for being detached and aloof from Zionism,[120] while its main quarrel with the leadership was that Zionism was increasingly consumed by a fundraising machine which existed primarily for its own sake, as opposed to serving the original ideals of the movement. The Zionist Organization of America, stated an unsigned Hadassah memorandum, "is a money raising organization only without any spiritual content."[121] The allegation that the Brandeis group was hopelessly elitist also is contradicted by a confidential survey conducted by Hadassah, which registered around a two-thirds majority of its members in strong support of the "opposition."[122] Feelings toward the Brandeis group, then, seemed to matter in the question of the Zionist identification and sympathies of American Jews.

Certainly the "abnormal ascendancy of the Keren Hayesod" did not necessarily help either to popularize or to democratize Zionism.[123] Contrary to its characterization as the cement which bound American Jews with Zionism, fundraising seemed to many to be "ugly work."[124] The Zionist appeals and fundraising instruments aimed at American Jewry did not simply constitute a means of nationalization; it did, however, problematize nationalism and charity in a novel way.

Although the Brandeis faction was the most consistent in scrutinizing the fundraising arms of the movement, the feeling that "the Movement is not developing along healthy lines" due to the concentration on raising money also was aired in Britain and Germany. In *Pioneer*, a British Zionist organ, M. L. Perlzweig claimed to be speaking for a significant minority when he reported that

The ordinary man, fearful lest his loyalty to the [Jewish National Fund and Keren Hayesod] be questioned, or because poverty denies him a place among their conspicuous supporters, remains silent, though he knows that a system which puts the Funds first and Zionism second is indefensible . . . Our energies are absorbed in practical work, which is the current euphemism for collecting money; only a handful are concerned about making Zionists, or have shown any interest in the supremely important task of drawing out of Zionism all its latent moral values for the spiritual nurture of the Jew of to-day; and the political work is done in fits and starts under the spur of pogroms and betrayal.[125]

"Organizing a card party" for the Keren Hayesod or JNF was regarded as "a *mitzvah* of the highest order," while the Tarbut organization in Britain, "the only body seriously engaged in the dissemination of Hebrew culture," was "bankrupt." Augmenting his view of the "new mentality" of Zionism, Perlzweig wrote that the idea had been broached to dissolve the English Zionist Federation, because "the two Funds did all that was necessary, and the Federation only cumbered the ground." The author also had heard the comment of a higher-up in British Zionism, with some tie to the academic establishment, that "a man's value to Zionism was to be measured only by the size of his financial contributions." Perlzweig colorfully described those running the fundraising bodies as "a professional priestcraft jealous of its rights," and specifically, "new sects – Keren Hayesod men and JNF men – have developed their own theologies and orthodoxies." Their energies were consumed, if not by

raising money, then by "heresy hunting."[126] In Germany, similar concerns were articulated by a few dissenting voices such as Hans Kohn,[127]
and occasionally, it seems, percolated to the top of their ranks – because
Weizmann was compelled to defend his position vigorously, vis-à-vis the
Brandeis faction, to Robert Weltsch.[128] For the most part, however,
the Germans remained staunchly loyal to the movement's fundraising
bodies.[129]

The specter of Hitler's anti-Semitism and its staggering enactment in
no small way determined how the story of Zionism in the 1920s and early
1930s would be told. For the purpose of solidarity, the central figures
of the opposition to Weizmann and Lipsky, such as Irma Lindheim,
Henrietta Szold, Stephen S. Wise, Julian Mack, and Louis Brandeis, saw
fit to keep quiet, or at least not accentuate their conflicts with the
Zionist administration. All of them shared "a strong distaste for
conventional self-discussion and revelation."[130] The case of Stephen S.
Wise is representative: he

deliberately refrained from stressing differences between [himself] and the World
Zionist leadership . . . He held that these differences were less important than the
overriding need for unity in behalf of a Jewish state, which might have been weak-
ened had he revived or underscored them. It may further be stated that [by 1948]
such differences had diminished, and that he worked closely with Dr. Weizmann
during and after World War II.[131]

What was said and written in private against Weizmann rarely made its
way into print. There was no "opposition" equivalent to the short-lived,
mean-spirited journal, *New Maccabaean*, which was mainly created to
undermine the reputations of those in the Brandeis faction. The
reticence of the Brandeis group in the shadow of Hitler, and the
untimeliness of the death of Louis Brandeis in 1940, however, implicitly
bolstered the side of those who felt no such reservations about
announcing their opinion of Zionism's quarrels, namely Chaim
Weizmann and Louis Lipsky.[132] In addition to simply adding to the
credibility of the official line, the silence, or lack of consideration of
opposition voices, helps facilitate the selection of interpretive lenses
which exaggerate the Weizmann/Lipsky perspective. The reigning
perspective affirms that there was no alternative to Zionism's transformation in the West into a vehicle for fundraising – which was
undeniably colossal in conception but not necessarily awesome in its
results.[133] Ironically, the Zionists' main fundraising instrument, which
was a human product and loaded with faults and foibles, was the movement's ultimate sacred cow. Questioning the holiness, fecundity, and
nurturing power of the beast was never to be tolerated.

4   Fundraising and catastrophe

> It is now or never! Either the Jewish State rises now out of the ruins of
> the war, or it will never rise. Either the Jewish people is redeemed today,
> or its exile is eternal."[1]

This chapter explores the relationship between the depiction of, or
forecasting of, a Jewish crisis of devastating magnitude, and Western
Zionist fundraising from 1914 to 1933. The polemics attesting to Jewish
catastrophe assumed an ever larger role in Zionism from the First World
War until the rise of Hitler, and was virtually routinized in the development of Zionist fundraising. From the perspective of the movement's
leadership this strategy did not simply serve their principal aim of filling
their coffers. Undoubtedly, bonds of solidarity between disparate Jewish
communities and individuals and the movement were created or
strengthened, and raising money provided a clear goal for organizational
development.[2] Many Zionists genuinely felt that fundraising was an overt
sign of "real apostolic work,"[3] which was carried out with great
"strength," "joy," "courage," and a depth of commitment.[4] It was this
undergirding, Chaim Weizmann claimed, which energized his incessant
travel in search of donations. Yet on the other hand, due to the
obfuscated (and even denied) motif of charity as a part of Western
Zionism,[5] tensions emerged and were aggravated from the different
expectations involved in "giving to charity" and "helping," versus
"building a nation." Significantly, all of these ideas were laden with
secular-messianic implications. In meetings, the press, and in private
correspondence some diaspora Zionists expressed discomfort over the
"concentrated interest in the gathering of funds."[6] In certain respects
the constructed affinity between crisis and fundraising was part of
Zionism's studied appropriation of sentimentality and emotionalism.
    In sum, a kind of rhythm developed between the presentation of
disaster, involving all or a large share of European Jewry, or all of Jewish
Palestine – followed by impassioned requests for money to ameliorate or
avert the course of events. Indeed, many of the interwar crises were of

magnanimous significance, or life-threatening to vast numbers of Jews. The movement adopted a hyperurgent tone in attempting to respond to the crises of Jewish Palestine and Eastern Jewry, in order to harness the calamities to Zionism's greater goals.[7] The notion that the Jewish problem might be solved without Zionism, according to one official publication, was simply false. Jewish survival was claimed to be utterly dependent on the creation and sustenance of Zionist work in Palestine.[8] "A consideration of the annals of Jewish exile," asserted a widely circulated Zionist publication, "leads us to the conclusion that the wanderings and distress of the Jewish people would come to an end only if the Jews could settle upon a particular territory and establish a self-contained economic life of their own upon the basis of a peasant class."[9] The Zionist Organization insisted that the only permanent "constructive relief"[10] and the most rational solution for European Jewish masses was to prepare the ground in Palestine for their resettlement; and they believed that by the end of the First World War, public opinion was moving in their direction.[11] How could a Wilsonian world order be imagined without a place for the Jews?

But the establishment of the British Mandate for Palestine, obviously, did not effect a simple cure for the *Judennot*. Around a decade after the convulsions of the Great War, and before the Nazi takeover of power in 1933, Zionists also faced a series of downturns, beginning in 1929 with the Arab riots in Palestine. Furthermore, there was a growing dissatisfaction, manifesting itself as contempt and hostility, toward the mandatory power.

A discourse of disaster, giving, and "Redemption" was nurtured.[12] It seems as if the movement became dependent on crises to sustain the party faithful in the West, who apparently remained outside the realm of immediately threatening anti-Semitism or attacks on Jewish Palestine. Yet while this appeal sounded like a plea for *Tsedakah* (charity), a constant refrain from the movement insisted that philanthropy and charity had no part in their plan,[13] and some Zionist publicists attempted to distance the movement from any association with messianism.[14] The point here, however, is that the threat or perceived onset of catastrophe became an integral part of the fundraising process. One scholar suggests that all messianic movements share a similar, fundamental economy, if one may use such a term: that it is necessary to make an "investment," to offer a personal, material sacrifice, in order to facilitate a messianic future.[15] In that spirit Hadassah resolved that

our answer to the Passfield White Paper [1930], breaking faith and abrogating England's pledges to us shall be no verbal protest, but shall take the form of raising funds and more funds for the continuation of our program and the achievement of our purposes, so that a home shall be created in Palestine for the physical and spiritual regeneration of the Jewish people . . . We resolve to assume the raising of money this year as a solemn and exalted obligation.[16]

This notion also was embodied in Weizmann's contention that the best means to fight the Passfield White Paper was by giving more money to the Zionist cause.[17] Sacred duty was combined with giving as "a practical protest" against the British and as a symbol to the Arabs and the world of Jewish solidarity and Zionist steadfastness.[18] Giving to the Keren Hayesod was portrayed as a means of delivering "salvation" to the people and land of Israel.[19] Continuing a motif which was inaugurated in 1901 with the establishment of Zionism's initial money-collection agency, the JNF, the fundraising instruments themselves were seen as having a spiritual essence. The Jewish National Fund, Adolf Boehm wrote, "is material only in form, but in its real nature it is the expression of the sentiment of solidarity of all the Jews in the world, and it bears within itself the key that will unlock the fetters of the Jewish people."[20] At the Thirteenth Zionist Congress, in Carlsbad, August 1923, Nahum Sokolow proclaimed that the words "Keren Hayesod" have attained nearly equivalent significance for the Jewish people as the words "Shema' Yisra'el."

Especially in the United States the tie between crisis and the ascendance of Zionism was palpable. Somewhat exaggerating the prominence of the movement in the United States, the *Maccabaean* reported that

A great deal of this interest in Zionism, the reciprocal influence which has made Zionism the foremost idea in Jewish life, may be attributed to the war. Facing a great catastrophe, seeing thousands of our brethren ruined, and witnessing the collapse of hundreds of Jewish communities, the Jews not directly affected were made to feel that in Zionism they had the one constructive program which gave hope, courage, and vision. Thousands of Jews, overwhelmed by the calamity, have remained indifferent to the situation, for they felt that all human effort was useless to influence the perpetrators of the offenses against Jewish life; they saw nothing that could be done by puny individuals to relieve a calamity which seemed to be the work of superior malevolent forces. In Zionism, however, many hitherto impervious to Zionist appeals have found an outlet, have found something to make them feel that at least when the war is over, salvation is possible.[21]

What was left unsaid in this article was the change of heart which might be traced to the leadership of Louis Brandeis, and the broader context of the formative "ethnic politics" in the United States which was especially propitious for Zionism.[22]

To be sure, fundraising proceeded in more regular and businesslike cycles, as well, which historian David Cesarani sees as more character-istic of the British Zionists – which largely matches their sober self-perception.[23] There was some recognition, though, that British Zionists too "had to face a constant shower of urgent appeals for funds to cover deficits, to meet recurrent crises, and to avoid imminent disaster. The whole atmosphere in which the Zionist moves and lives was, and still is, filled with demands for money, money, and more money."[24] Jewish holidays, planned "bazaars and exhibitions," and important anniver-saries, such as Herzl's Jahrzeit, "Balfour Day," and the founding dates of the Keren Kayemeth and the Keren Hayesod, provided the pretext for fundraising year in and year out, with greater publicity accorded tenth and twenty-fifth anniversaries.[25] But the crisis theme punctuated the war years and the interwar period and seemed to determine the perception of the movement more markedly than the annual fund drives.[26]

The "Emergency Fund for Palestine," which was crucial in helping the Yishuv overcome some its most severe setbacks, owed its very existence "to the calamity of August 1929," the Arab riots. The success of this drive was traced to its organizers' perception that "the ever-recurrent Jewish tragedy had repeated itself."[27] Stephen S. Wise found it "grotesque" that in one drive for emergency relief in 1929 American Jews gave half as much as the maximum amount ever given for "Palestine upbuilding." "In other words," Wise wrote, "Arab hurt to the Jew has dictated the policy to the largest number of American Jews."[28]

Not only was giving money in the face of crisis (and planned drives) exalted among one's own organization and nation, but the raising of funds was also extensively reported across national boundaries as one of the principal activities of the movement. Zionists did not just experience the life of the *Halutsim* in Palestine vicariously – they vicariously shared in the exhilaration of fundraising in other parts of the diaspora as well.[29] Although the Germans were no strangers to bombastic appeals and giving generously to Zionism,[30] by 1922 the *Jüdische Rundschau*, in reporting on Keren Hayesod, began to use the (untranslated) American expression "cash and pledges."[31] It became typical in the German and British Zionist press for American fundraising to be deemed worthy of front-page articles; thereby, at times they took on the role of spectators, cheerleaders, and score-keepers. At any rate, Zionists in Western Europe certainly were not detached or oblivious to the Zionist activity among their relatively well-off brethren.[32] The United States, along with Palestine, was the primary stage upon which the Zionists' attention was fixed,[33] an implicit recognition that American Zionism, and by extension, money, was the most vital force of the move-ment.[34] Possibly an overestimation of the relative power of American

Jewry within the United States' political process figured into Zionists' fixation.[35] Nevertheless, the vast sums requested by the organization and huge bequests amazed the Europeans.[36] The visits of Chaim Weizmann were celebrated as occasions for extraordinary spurts of generosity by American givers.[37]

There was at least one instance when the Europeans were deeply moved by the American response to Jewish crisis, due to something beyond philanthropy: in the summer of 1930 some 50,000 New York Jews took to the streets, in searing heat, to register their protest against the British administration's limitation on Jewish immigration to Palestine. The multitude, comprising Jewish war veterans, rabbis of all denominations with their congregations, Halutsim, union members, school children, and fraternal orders, seemed to represent the entirety of United States' Jewry. (It was not said if the Halutsim were preparing to go to Palestine or if they had left Palestine for the United States.) The crowd, which appeared solid in purpose, joined in a rapturous singing of the songs of Jewish Palestine.[38]

There was little or no thought given to how this scene contradicted many of the stereotyped notions of American Jewry. Beginning with the stock market crash followed by the Great Depression of 1929, the reporting of Zionist fundraising was greatly subdued.[39] It was not until over a year after Black Monday, however, that the Zionist press broached the issue of the impact of the Depression on American Jewish contributions to Palestine.[40]

A decade earlier, upon the issuing of the Balfour Declaration, there were demonstrations at both the London Opera House and Carnegie Hall in New York City which were widely reported.[41] Although the Germans were understandably underwhelmed by the British response to the various fundraising drives,[42] the Zionists in Britain predictably lauded their own efforts.[43] As a "reply" to the White Paper of 1930, "over £11,000 was raised for the KH, in the United Kingdom, in a fortnight."[44] Not surprisingly, France was hardly noticed for its minor contributions, despite a stepped-up effort to interest French Jewry in the Keren Hayesod.[45]

One of the reasons why the Germans spoke so often about fundraising in the United States is because their own economic situation had plummeted so precipitously after the war, and because they did not wish to bring attention to the money that was being raised for Zionism among Jews in Germany.[46] The effort to adjust the giving schemes to hyper-inflation of 1923 came relatively late.[47] As opposed to the previous era when a large section of the Jüdische Rundschau listed the donations to the movement, after the war its editors were reticent about publishing anything that might inadvertently feed the allegation that Jews were less hurt than non-Jews by the inflation, and were hoarding wealth.[48] In fact, the American Zionists were acknowledged not only for raising money for Palestine: during the German inflation of 1923 they specifically supplied funds to maintain the German Zionist organ, *Jüdische Rundschau*, when it was on the verge of collapse.[49]

The essential backdrop for the beginning of this phenomenon in the interwar years was the wretched state of Eastern Jewry, which was spiraling downward from 1914 on – despite the optimism, in some quarters, aroused by hopes that Russia's alliance with the Western democracies would soften her anti-Jewish stance,[50] or that the Russian Revolution would put the Jewish masses on an entirely new, secure footing. World War I nevertheless brought about a dramatic shift in the status of the Eastern Jews.[51] "Wretched as the position of the [Romanian and Galician] Jews already was before the outbreak of the War," read a pamphlet by premier Zionist publicist Adolf Boehm,

they have now been reduced by it to utter beggary. Hundreds of thousands of Jews have been compelled by the Russian invasion to flee from Galicia to western districts, where they receive from the Government the barest accommo- dation and sustenance. The Jews who remained behind were harassed and ill-treated by the Russian soldiery in a brutal manner, the like of which is unknown in the history of the War.[52]

Although Jewry had faced disaster since their emancipation in Europe over a century before August 1914, it seemed as if there might be an impending catastrophe on the level of the expulsion from Spain of 1492, or the Chmielnicki Massacres in Poland of 1648 – a threat qualitatively more severe than the wave of Russian pogroms begun in 1881.[53] And it is important to remember that in the East, the war did not end with the armistice of November 1918; the Jewish masses were caught in the thick of the fighting between the Poles, the Ukrainians, and the Red and White Armies.[54]

The Zionist reading of the situation was predicated on the notion that the United States and Britain could not possibly absorb the refugees. Although emigrating to the United States was clearly a better alternative than remaining in Eastern Europe, in the United States, too, "much poverty and distress" could be found. Jews were "condemned to work under the worst conditions" in the country while anti-Semitism was on the rise, as was indicated by the "Leo Frank affair." In principle, despite being allowed "absolute liberty" in Britain and the United States, Zionist polemics charged that "there is no future for them there." And at any rate, both countries were "restricting the possibilities of Jewish immigration more and more."[55] It is important to qualify, however, that these dire predictions did not necessitate the 'Aliyah (emigration to Palestine) of those Jews who in the preceding years had decided to make their homes in the United States and Britain.

Simultaneously, during World War I, the threat and actual devastation of the Yishuv was prominent in Zionist reportage and polemics, and tied to fundraising efforts.[56] In 1914 Louis Brandeis implored American Jewry to recognize "the achievements of a generation are imperiled. The young Jewish Renaissance in the Holy Land, the child of pain and sacrifice, faces death from starvation."[57] The concept of postwar "reconstruction" in Palestine was not similar to alleviating the four-year devastation of the Great War, because the harm to Palestine was more severe, due to the 400-year combination of neglect and exploitation by its Turkish rulers.[58] Perhaps the most serious challenge to the Yishuv was the evacuation of Jaffa by the Turkish government in 1917, causing widespread destitution and starvation.[59] The treatment of Zionists in the Yishuv at the hands of Turkish authorities was compared to that of the Armenians. The *Maccabaean* reported that "Djemal Pascha, Military Governor of Palestine," swore

that the joy of the Jews on the approach of the British forces would be short-lived, as he would make them share the same fate of the Armenian[s] . . . By way of moral example, two Jews were hanged at the entrance of Tel-Aviv in order to clearly indicate the fate in store for any Jews who might be so fool-hardy as to oppose the looters [who were ransacking their homes] under the paternal eye of the authority.[60]

The suffering of the notable Aronson family was likened to that inflicted on Jewry during the Crusades:

In Samaria the search for spies was placed under the charge of the Kimakam, who had also learnt his trade in Armenia. One day about midnight he attacked Zichron Jacob with a company of soldiers. The Aronson family was tortured in a medieval fashion. The daughter, Sara Aronson, was mercilessly beaten before the eyes of her aged father, and after three days of the most terrible agony, she found an opportunity of escaping her tormentors by committing suicide.

In Lower Galilee the military doctor, Hassan Bey, was put in charge of the search for firearms. He also conducted it to the accompaniment of cruel tortures of old men and women. Hundreds of young men were sent to Nazareth, and from there to Damascus for a continuance of their examination.

Only the liberation of Judea and the capture of Jerusalem put an end to these persecutions. But before it could take effect some hundreds of young people were sent to Damascus. They had to pass many days in closed railway carriages without food and water. The dead and those suffering from infectious diseases remained among the living and healthy. In Damascus a special cemetery, with sixty graves, bears witness to the effects of this expulsion.[61]

"Despite the chaotic conditions," Zionists were assured in the United States, "the Zionist Provisional Committee is in possession of the means for the sending of relief to Palestine. It is sending aid to the refugees."[62] Perhaps due to the destruction of European Jewry in the Second World War, in which systematic starvation and deprivation of sanitation,[63] as well as "arrests, insults, and tortures,"[64] were obviously more widespread and had a greater impact on Western Jewish consciousness, this aspect of the Zionist experience in Palestine has largely been forgotten. The memory of Jews shipped off in sealed train cars would be almost exclusively associated with the Nazis, although it was part of the reality and discourse of the 1920s.

Only later, however, was the extent of crucial assistance by foreign counsels fully acknowledged, and in retrospect, the Zionist Organization would be hailed as a "tower of strength" in wartime.[65] In a number of instances, political and economic crises were exacerbated by natural crises – such as the "plague of locusts" around the holiday of Purim in 1917,[66] which was in turn aggravated by the failure of Arabs and Jews to coordinate their efforts in controlling the infestation.[67] As compared to the fundraising efforts for Palestine before the war, these drives were not geared primarily to building up the Jewish settlement: the goal was to sustain what had already been achieved.[68] No matter how short the movement fell from its ultimate goal, there was a great deal to lose in Jewish Palestine by 1914, where the essential, pre-national infrastructure was in place.

The challenges to Jewish Palestine, however, nearly always proved less popular than European relief efforts in rallying Western Jews. Their public's first priority, according to the JNF committee in Britain, was the "relief of the Polish refugees." This was clearly regarded as more important than the "relief of the Palestinian [Jewish] refugees."[69] Such views were widely shared in the United States.[70] "The opinion," related one representative report, "even among Zionists, [is] that all activities should be concentrated . . . only on our relief work. Our argument that the National Fund does relief work now does not seem to be effective."[71] During the war the American Zionist Provisional Committee was chastised by the paper *Forverts!* for earmarking a quarter of the money it collected, ostensibly for general Jewish relief, for work in Palestine.[72] Partly due to this clash, the Zionists' "Flag-Day" collection met with resistance from the "People's Relief Committee" effort of Jewish socialists.[73] The next year the Head Office of the JNF suggested that perhaps the organization should not publicize how much money it had collected, and from whom, because donors did not necessarily wish to publicize their support for the Zionist program.[74]

In 1901, the JNF had been established to purchase land for Jewish settlement, agriculture, and institutions in Palestine. The Zionist Organization, therefore, tactically shifted its focus when it called on the German and American offices of the JNF at least to partially redirect its efforts to relief work on European soil during and after the war.[75] The assistance offered to Eastern Jewry was depicted as an essential "phase" in the "struggle of the Jewish nation for its recognition and placement on an equal footing among all peoples."[76] Among the most poignant Zionist demonstrations in the United States were those devoted to European Jewish war relief, sometimes in conjunction with non-Zionist groups.[77] This was not merely a wartime phenomenon; in 1929, the Zionists saw fit to demonstrate their goodwill toward all Jews, with a joint appeal for European Jewry and Palestine.[78] Although events that signaled advances, such as the creation of the Jewish Agency for Palestine, also triggered funding appeals,[79] the period was more marked by the tie between overwhelming crises and fundraising.

As discussed in chapter 3 (on the birth of the Keren Hayesod), it was generally considered impolitic to discuss any averse effects of Zionist fundraising. Henrietta Szold was one of very few Zionists to muse over the connection between fundraising among the Jewish public and one's political fortunes in the Zionist camp:

Mr. Lipsky writes moderately: in six weeks collected $250,000 in cash, $2,500,000 in good pledges. At the same time Mr. Ussischkin in Germany boasts $1,000,000 in cash, 6 and 1/2 000,000 in pledges! Weizmann faints dramatically at Prague. That "faint" or "feint" will bring the Keren ha-Yesod so and so many delegates' votes at the Congress, for he was not going to have it all his own way there . . . Ugh![80]

In a public forum, the Zionist national poet C. N. Bialik also warned against the mingling of melodrama and fundraising. He blamed the lifelessness of the movement in the early 1930s on the exaggerated style of Zionist propaganda, which became quite predictable, and therefore easily dismissed, even by the Zionist faithful.[81]

The spokespersons for the fundraising instruments were not completely oblivious to such sentiments. They recognized that the movement included skeptics who

do not believe that our propaganda for funds can be successfully based on the deep-seated national consciousness of the people, that a collecting agency may indeed be a principal pillar of nationalism, indispensable to the whole Zionist movement. They say that our enforced concentration upon the collection of money has gradually destroyed the spirit of Zionism and made of the Zionist Organization merely a financial instrument . . . We have not ignored this menace: propaganda concerned only with the collection of funds is dangerous and it is evident that such propaganda has been conducted. There are speakers who make it appear that gold and nothing else is their object, under whatever conditions it is given.

Not only did this cheapen the movement, but it was not necessarily a consistently "successful" strategy for raising money over the long run.[82] Embedded in this critique, published in an organ of the Jewish National Fund, was not so much a self-criticism, as much as it seemed to be a stab at the tactics of the dominant fundraising body, the Keren Hayesod – although this was never stated explicitly. The reality of the "rival claims" of "entangling funds" of the greater and lesser fundraising bodies was rarely a topic of open discussion. Sometimes, however, the fact that different segments of the movement cast their own appeals was treated with disdain. Sephardic Zionists, in particular, were seen as "threatening the unity of the Zionist Organization" through separate campaigns.[83] Even before the Keren Hayesod came into being, the JNF Committee in Britain alerted the headquarters in 1915 that "You must bear in mind that three urgent questions are before our people at the present time: 1. The relief of the Polish refugees; 2. The relief of the Palestinian refugees; 3. The relief of the Belgian refugees. With these serious problems before the Jewish public, you will see that to some extent the National Fund work must be affected."[84] As opposed to the Keren Hayesod, which was always seeking to accommodate the non-Zionist Jewish public, the JNF styled itself as the most "Zionist" of the financial instruments, and thereby tried to maintain its distinct institutional identity.[85] Some years before, as the income accruing to the JNF dropped with the outbreak of the war and the establishment of the 1914 "Zionist Emergency Fund," the organization took a defensive stance – but still desired to encourage "a large amount of money" to be raised, "and raised almost entirely in America."[86]

The JNF, the author of a 1925 missive insisted, never lost sight of the main object of "making nationalists," not simply getting donations:

What is more simple than to move an audience to tears. A vivid description of a pogrom, with its awful details, is bound to prove effective. Once a propagandist cabled us: "Wonderful triumph: people wept!" It was not long before it became apparent that he could evoke tears but nothing else and as weeping was useless to the NF the enthusiastic propagandist was recalled . . . Others play upon the feelings of their listeners by describing the hardships of "our Haluzim," their hunger and suffering.

However much the JNF wished to distance itself from the methods which had obviously come to dominate the movement, it could do little to obfuscate the perception that Zionist fundraising had grown to rely on sporadically issued "superficial sentiment and emotion."[87]

In this model of disaster, giving, and redemption a number of additional caveats became apparent: the note of inevitable disaster, especially in the Yishuv, was sounded so often that the messages for help were homogenized, at least to some Western ears. It was difficult to differentiate the severity of one crisis from the next. Furthermore, there was competition between funds for the Yishuv and relief efforts in Europe.[88] Zionists were perturbed by the rivalry between themselves and the non-Zionist fundraising establishment, always imagining themselves on the short end.[89] This met with scorn and dismay which was not always publicly expressed.[90] Furthermore, Zionists felt themselves to be "under attack" due to their support for Palestine enterprises, while Jews were suffering in Eastern Europe.[91] At that time, and in retrospect, they wished to make clear that they, too, were engaged in significant relief work on the Continent, and had actually been the most vigorous defenders of the Jews.[92] At best, this final assertion is questionable.[93] Still, in the wake of the war, the notion that Zionism had played a uniquely heroic role was promulgated. The Zionist Organization said that it had been "willing and able to come to the rescue," as it "alone was in a position" to consistently render such service. "In the hour of danger," Zionism had "become the mainstay of the nation," the movement proclaimed.[94]

During the war, the reliance on American Jews for money was introduced; a self-conscious effort was inaugurated primarily to call on American Jewry for fundraising, and to seek out American Jewish notables and millionaires to assume leadership in the movement, and prime the pump for worldwide donations.[95] The great savior depicted in the Zionist press and touted in the fundraising promotions was American Jewry.[96] Not simply American Zionists, but all of America's Jews would contribute to Zionist efforts, first for Eastern Europe, and then for Palestine.

In a 1922 hardbound publication of the Keren Hayesod, *The Greatest Romance in History*, which featured the story of a budding Zionist who went from Eastern Europe to Vienna and then Palestine, the concluding section was specifically addressed to the Jews of the United States. Upon the founding of the KH they were admonished

it is now or never! Either the Jewish State rises now out of the ruins of the war, or it will never rise. Either the Jewish people is redeemed today, or its exile is eternal.

Tens of thousands of young Jews are ready to offer their lives in an effort to end long tragedy of our people.

Will you offer the means?

Shall the greatest romance in history close in darkness and failure, or in glorious success?

It is for you to say. It is for you to write the last chapter with your own hands.

The Jewries of Europe will offer their lives.

You, Jews of America, must offer the gold.

Forty centuries of Jewish history close with this question: Will you, Jews of America, redeem the Holy Land?

The promise that was made four thousand years ago is to be fulfilled through you, or it is to remain unfulfilled.

You are the guardians of Jewish history today. With you Jewish history ends, or through you it begins a new chapter.

Forty centuries of Jewish history are watching you today. The far-off generations look to you out of the twilight of the past. The warriors and prophets and teachers of ancient Judaea are watching you. The martyrs of Spain and Poland and Russia, they who died that our people might live, are watching you. The young heroes who fell on a hundred fields in the great war are watching you. The victims of a hundred pogroms, men and women and children are watching you.

In the eyes of all of them there is a single question:

"Will the land of our Fathers be restored to our people or have we lived and died in vain?"[97]

This piece of propaganda is unmatched in spelling out the consequences of non-compliance. The failure to give means nothing less than the end of the Jewish people. It was also unequivocal on the question of 'Aliyah for American Jewry. In response to the hypothetical question, "don't the Zionists want all Jews to emigrate to Palestine?," the tale asserts that Zionism does not advocate the "return" of "the entire Jewish people," but "only those who are oppressed, and those who feel they cannot live a full life except in Palestine."[98] This makes it all the more logical that before the official embrace of non-Zionists, when the "enlarged Jewish Agency plan" went to the drawing board, Zionist opinion was making allowances for American non-Zionists to have a wider role in their affairs – as long as they supplied the funds.[99] The Germans were implored to give in only slightly less menacing tones.[100] Perhaps due to their reputation for stinginess and "indifference" in Zionist matters, the British were not appealed to so stridently.[101] In the midst of the war, much of the "public excitement" among British Jews, due to the movement's stance regarding alien conscription and other issues, had been focused "against the English Zionist Federation and everything that is connected to Zionism."[102] This helped to make American-style appeals seem even less appropriate, even though such attitudes softened in the 1920s.

Perhaps most significantly the connection between Zionist fundraising and depictions of catastrophe helped establish the myth that any obstacle in the way of fulfilling the movement's mission could be overcome by a massive infusion of capital from the diaspora, combined with self-help within the Yishuv.[103] Such a mindset cast aside the existence of intractable problems or contradictions. One could, especially from the agenda of the fundraisers, say that the fundraising/catastrophe nexus was a productive formula: but at the same time it built up false expectations.[104] The movement requested diaspora Jews to invest in a messianic economy, where they expected messianic returns:[105] a world without misery, and more unreal, without contradiction or paradox. Diaspora Zionists were sometimes told that there were no grounds for a national conflict to develop between Jews and Arabs,[106] and that there was no inherent contradiction between the prevalence of Labor Zionism in Palestine and the apparent Jewish propensity toward economic individualism.[107] And in Zionist polemics, most threats facing the Jews were usually described as pogroms;[108] in fact, however, the crises in Palestine and Europe were in many ways profoundly different in character from the earlier persecution of Russian Jews.[109]

Built into this process, as well, was a system of guilt and recriminations for non-payment of one's messianic dues.[110] At one point, a Zionist official took this so far as to charge that the Arab riots of 1929 would not have occurred if diaspora Jews had given enough money. "The real lesson of the Jaffa events," asserted a memorandum to Zionist leaders, "is a reproach to the Jewish people for their failure to produce up to now the necessary means for a systematic and well-ordered immigration." The Jews must give substantially more "in spite of the financial crisis, or all of our prospects will be frustrated not by the ill-will of our enemies, but by ourselves . . . The [Zionist] Executive expects this point of view to be brought home by you to the Jewish masses with the stern emphasis it deserves."[111] This prescription was of a completely different order than that suggested by Henrietta Szold in the wake of the riots. "The chief onus does not lie upon us," she wrote to a colleague. "But we cannot hold ourselves guiltless. Visit our schools and then say whether our teachers are educating our children toward the solution of our race problem . . . the roots of our problem lie down deep next to the springs of justice and wisdom."[112] To the Zionist public she toned down the factor of race in Jewish attitudes as they were developing in Palestine. But she was clear about the steps that should be taken in order to achieve a society which more closely resembled the movement's utopian hopes:

We must learn to know our Arab neighbors and we must give them the opportunity of learning to know us. In the education of our children in our schools

every trace of chauvinism must be removed. The Arab language must be taught
to them seriously, and a knowledge of Arab literature and history, Arab customs,
and the Moslem religion must be made part of the cultural equipment of our
intelligent classes. We must acquire the secret of our forebears, our predecessors,
those who were associated with Arab writers and scholars at several epochs in our
history in interpreting the East to the West.

I maintain that not even you, the Zionists of the Diaspora, are exempt from the
task of bringing about a rapprochement with the Arabs. The Arab relations
should be made part of every program of studies set up for our young people.
That is work, I admit, not for a day, not for a year. Its completion will be the
reward after generations of effort as our whole Zionist undertaking reaches out
into a distant future. They are both Messianic tasks, as all peace and conciliation
is.[113]

Despite the best efforts of even the most farsighted, realistic, and humanistic of Zionists, the world they would engender and inhabit in Palestine
could only be fraught with contradictions, and scarcely fulfill the promise
of complete, secularized messianic redemption.[114]

Not even the Great Depression would have much of an impact on this
pattern of picturing a crisis and appealing for funds.[115] In comparison to
the frequent and intense calamities that were seen as inflicted on the
Jews from outside, only rarely would there be a mention of anything
approaching a "crisis" that originated in the Zionist Organization.[116]
Apparently without thought to its various implications, the movement
also helped shape the perceptions of those very catastrophes, which
became central to its secular liturgy. For many the catastrophic warnings
of Zionism added to its appeal, or inspired their interest in the
movement. At the same moment, however, the disaster, giving and
redemption paradigm directed energy toward the rationalization of a
greater and greater fundraising apparatus as a value in itself.[117]

Many of these notions would be replayed and amplified in the
tempestuous interwar career of the Keren Hayesod. Even outside
the ostensible domain of the fundraising instruments, the components
and discourses of the movement which bound Western Jewry to Zionism
– such as the perceptions of Palestine, Zionist-sponsored tourism to the
country, and the youth movements in the diaspora – developed along
lines that followed from, or were compatible with fundraising. The
diaspora Zionist discourse which seemed most disruptive to the fundraising imperative was that embodied by Zionism's organized women,
particularly the Hadassah organization in the United States. It was from
the American women's camp that the culture of fundraising and its
excesses were most clearly discerned and protested, and this earned these
women the movement's most severe reprobation from the centers of
power.

5 "From swamp to settlement": rural and urban utopian visions of Palestine

Palestine – a country of extremes: the contact of old and new civilizations; frontier life and dress-suit life; people on camels, asses, on foot, and in roaring autos and airplanes. Veiled women, and low shoes and high heels. Difficult to get a bath, yet dress suit required. Some few have telephones and others have to hoof it to get things sent and done, yet the telephone tempo is the standard.   Judah L. Magnes (1923)[1]

Tel Aviv was bursting at the seams with activity; I thought it an ugly place from an architectural point of view; every Jew had built there the house of his dreams, and the resulting mish-mosh of styles was truly awful. But its vitality was infectious and the pride of its citizens in this 100% Jewish town was understandable. On the streets, in the open-air cafes, in the shops, everywhere the modern Hebrew dominated.
                                                 Gertrude Van Tijn[2]

For Western Jews in the years 1914–33, even those who saw themselves as firmly rooted in the countries of Central and Western Europe and the United States, the multilayered discourses of Zionism came to be more and more interwoven in their national consciousness. The process of Zionist nationalization was not just political, in terms of Jewry supporting "the establishment of a national home for the Jews in Palestine."[3] Nor was it simply a matter of "the conquest of the communities," as Theodor Herzl put it in 1897, of Zionists wresting control of Jewish organizations in order to enlist them in the cause. The effort to integrate Western Jewry into Zionism comprised an inundation with Zionist "agitation and propaganda" of the written and spoken kind, and also, to a great extent, visual imagery, which was largely assimilated into secular Jewish consciousness.

The popular images of Zionist work in Palestine were not, and never could have been, an accurate reflection of the totality of the Yishuv. However much the mythical constructions of Jewish Palestine were wedded to the facts,[4] they were not one and the same. Nor were the images a "mirage" concocted by the Zionist Organization and its constituent elements, an ephemeral dreamland of the movement's faithful.[5] The images, overall, comprised a refraction of the Zionist project in Palestine, and the way it was projected for view to Western Jews was no doubt distinct from its representation inside the Yishuv and elsewhere in the Jewish world.

Zionism was conceived and matured in an age when advances in graphic technology, along with the popular press and, later, film, made possible a widespread dissemination of common images.[6] This was substantially abetted by the fact that Zionist publications showed the same pictures over and over again. Therefore, it is important to examine not only what Jews read and heard about Zionism, but also what they saw and experienced as Zionism.[7] The images were popularized through the Zionist press, and in pictorial newspapers created expressly for the purpose of conveying "the new Jewish Palestine."[8] Each picture in Zionist periodicals such as *Palästina-Bilder-Korrespondenz* and the *Palestine Pictorial Service* was numbered to make it possible for local organizations and other publications to make use of the Zionist photographic archive – a resource which was well utilized.[9] Furthermore there was a proliferation of brochures, produced mainly under the auspices of Zionist fundraising instruments, which regularly supplied its audience with a mixture of older and updated pictures of Palestine.[10] The photos were reproduced in a succession of nearly interchangeable publications and organs of the Zionist press.[11] Along with photographs, charts and graphs were extensively used to exemplify and document the movement's claim that under the Zionists, Palestine had developed "from swamp to settlement."[12]

In this chapter I will discuss the role that images of Palestine played in the formation of a Zionist identity for Westernized Jews. My main concern is with the visions of rural and urban life in the presentations of the Jewish settlement in Palestine, to analyze how "the new face of Palestine," which was claimed to have come into being by 1932, might have impacted on the national consciousness of Western Jewry. The self-consciously constructed image of Zionist-Jewish Palestine,[13] centering on the countryside and major cities, apparently played a significant role in the development of West European and American Jewish consciousness, not just as a means of enticing or preparing Jews to enter Palestine, but as a factor in Jewish identity itself.

Although the following treatment is not chronological, I do not mean to discredit the development of the Yishuv over time during the interwar period. Certainly the Yishuv changed and grew in important ways, and its transformations have been the subject of several studies. Here, though, I am less concerned with "social facts" than I am with the processes whereby Palestine was encountered by Western Zionists and the symbolic significance of that encounter.[14] What I hope to capture here is the sense of process, the making and remaking of a Zionist entity, as opposed to a comprehensive or static view of Palestine's material and cultural development. An idea which found expression in innumerable guises, from the end of the First World War until the early 1930s, was that Palestine was a land in flux, in the process of becoming something else, something even greater. In the imagery and supporting polemics, it emerges as a country in which its agricultural, urban, and industrial sectors are unfolding. Furthermore, while it increasingly is settled by Jews, it evinces to an ever greater degree a new secular, national Jewish life. Palestine's potential, it was said repeatedly, was being reaped, while its untapped possibilities remained to be cultivated. Irma Lindheim epitomizes this sentiment in her memoir of 1928, *The Immortal Adventure*:

Here there is beauty that can be reclaimed and peopled. The creation is not completed. You long to translate the aesthetic values into life. You turn from a view that is as unique as it is inspiring, and you plan and think of ways to make the spot on which you stand a garden instead of a waste place, a home instead of a stony mound. That is the secret, the thrill of the scenery of Palestine. It evokes action, it makes of man a creator.[15]

Although a main current of Zionist polemics affirmed that Palestine was yet to be "won," it was clearly shown as "being won." "It is an absurdity," Lindheim correctly asserted, "to say that Palestine is ours."[16] The much more important contention, proven in words and pictures, was that it was becoming "ours," that is, the possession of the Jewish people. The overriding purpose of telling about, and showing pictures of, Jewish Palestine for Western Jews was "to get a glimmer of the deep significance of the development going on in Palestine."[17]

At the beginning of the movement, which may be dated from 1881 or 1897, Zionists demanded, facilitated, and celebrated the Jews' return to the soil under their auspices. This was striking because one of the central tenets of modern anti-Semitism is that Jews are not, and can never be, at one with nature. Volkish nationalists in Germany (and elsewhere) believed that the landscape reflects the soul of its people and a people reflects its landscape. Jews were said not to share in the German landscape of mountain, meadow, river, and forest, having been doomed to suffer the fate of a race from the arid, wretched Orient. Furthermore, the most authentic type of person and member of the nation was idealized as the peasant who still lived directly off the land, despite the threat of industrialization, modernity, and death. The most feared agent alleged to be orchestrating these changes was the Jew.[18] Jews might have tried more forcefully to disprove this absurd but nevertheless compelling matrix of prejudices by rushing to the countryside. For a number of reasons, though, from the late nineteenth century to the advent of the Nazi regime, farming was not an option for appreciable numbers of Jews.[19] But a vocal minority among Western Jewry did identify, however vicariously, with agriculture as a means of transformation through Zionism. They became engaged in, or at least fascinated by, the idea of the Jews recreating themselves in their ancestral homeland as an agricultural people. The allure of the countryside of Palestine was enhanced for some Jews by the socialistic and communistic collectives, the *Kevutsot* (work groups; also kvutzah) and *Kibutsim* (kibbutzes).

Yet the gaze of Zionism was not fixed solely on pastoral settings. To be sure, the youth wing of the movement, particularly the Blau-Weiss of Germany, vociferously renounced the "materialism" of "big city life" and its detrimental effect on Jewry (chapter 7).[20] But the visual Zionist discourse also featured new Jewish cities, in which the greatest benefits of urban life were heralded as being transplanted in Palestine, and that the purposeful erection of urban centers by their own hand could also have a fundamental, transformative effect on Jewry as a nation. This, too, stood in stark contrast to the anti-Semitic assertion that Jews were, by their essence, not only denizens of but corrupters of the city. Zionism by no means rejected the city as a Jewish space, but instead claimed that an entirely new style of urbanity was being forged in Palestine. Thereby the Zionist vision was much more than a reaction to anti-Semitism and an exercise in an anti-urban discourse. Zionists claimed to be reinventing the very idea of the city in Palestine as a gleaming complement to their agriculturally based communal life, and as a means of suggesting that they had no intention of forsaking the prized aspects of their modern, secular lives in the cities of Europe.

In this way, too, they were mirroring trends in German nation-building, in which the modernization of cities such as Berlin and Munich was seen as part and parcel of nationalism's bounty. Physical structures of glass, steel, and stone, like in Weimar Germany, could conceivably serve as an "educational force" in the Yishuv.[21] At any rate, the Zionists triumphantly insisted that they were improving on cityscapes and making them their own, elegantly fusing the Occident with the Orient in the western suburbs of Jerusalem, the all-Jewish, bustling city of Tel Aviv, and the nascent gem of the Zionist enterprise, the port city of Haifa rising above the Mediterranean.[22]

We will turn first, however, to agriculture and the countryside. Beginning in the movement's early stage, artistic images of agriculture

12 Postcard from the Fifth Zionist Congress (1901), by E. M. Lilien, printed material file for the Fifth Zionist Congress, Central Zionist Archives, Jerusalem. The Hebrew quotation reads: "Let our eyes witness Your loving return to Zion" from the Amidah prayer). Reproduced in a slightly altered form in *The Maccabaean* (December 1929): 102.

played a substantial role in establishing paradigms for the reception of the Zionist project.[23] These portended a future order where true emancipation would emanate from the Jews' labor on their own soil. Each faction of the movement shared the belief that the regeneration of the Jews could only be attained in a society where they participated in all varieties of work, but particularly agricultural labor.[24] Although one of my purposes here is to argue that Zionism was not an anti-modern movement, it must be said that Zionists frequently employed romantic images of Jews in peasant garb broadcasting seed, plowing fields, or harvesting crops, without benefit of machinery, against the backdrop of a radiant sun above Zion – such as in the tremendously popular scene of E. M. Lilien, designed originally for the Fifth Zionist Congress commemorative postcard (figure 12).[25] Yet this and other such designs represented more than a reactionary posture: it underscored Zionism's stress on the development of a normal, self-sufficient, agrarian-based society – which was promised to occur by the early 1940s.[26]

In addition to the archive of images based on drawings and etchings,

13 Certificate for a wartime donation to the Jewish National Fund: "Landspende des jüdischen Nationalfonds, Kriegslandespendes-Diplom," JNF materials collection, A/3/6/7/1, Central Zionist Archives, Jerusalem.

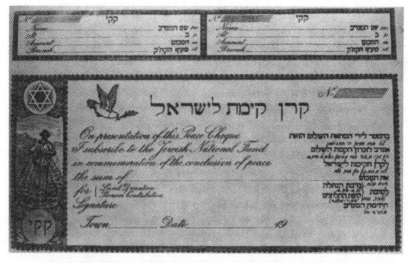

14 "Peace Cheque" from the Jewish National Fund, JNF materials collection, A/3/6/7/1, Central Zionist Archives, Jerusalem.

15 "View of the Emek Jezreel," in *Jewish Colonisation: Erez Israel 30 Years Keren Kayemet* (No place: Jewish National Fund, 1931).

which were often disseminated through postcards, or on certificates for donations to the tree fund and other specialized causes (figures 13 and 14), the Zionist movement was able to fix specific images of the landscape and the Jewish settlement of Palestine through the reproduction of photographs, and numerous slide-show and film presentations.[27] One of the principal aims of Zionist photography was to prove that a picturesque Jewish natural landscape did indeed exist which boasted beautifully tended fields (figure 15).[28]

But perhaps most important, similar to nationalist and "new life" movements of the late nineteenth and early twentieth centuries, Zionism purported to bring to life an entirely new man: a New Jew or a New Zionist.[29] Consistent with his depiction in Zionist art and polemics, in photographs and narratives as well, he was preferably seen as a bronzed farmer, in motion, working with hand implements in the field (figure 16).[30] Thereby Jews in their natural, national state could be seen as possessing a remarkable vital energy – again parrying an anti-Semitic stereotype. Jews on horseback or riding mules were favorite subjects, with those on horseback typically clad in keffiyehs and sometimes serving as armed guards of Jewish settlements (figure 17).[31] Jews were

16 Postcard: "Ein-Harod, the tobacco cultivation at the new colony founded by the JNF," 'En Ḥarod file, Central Zionist Archives, Jerusalem.

17 Postcard of "Nuris: Jewish Watchman," 'En Harod file, Central Zionist Archives, Jerusalem; the same image appeared as "On Guard: Jewish Watchman in the Galilean Hills," in *Palestine Pictorial Service* (May 1927): cover.

18 Postcard, "The Dagania Farm," Dagania file, Central Zionist Archives, Jerusalem; the same image was used in promotions for the Jewish National Fund before the First World War.

portrayed as adept at nourishing both crops and livestock (figure 18).[32] Photographs of Jews tending fields or baling hay were among the most prevalent, although in the 1920s they increasingly were shown atop tractors.[33] A substantial portion of photographs documented the idea that a younger generation of national Jews was growing up stronger and healthier in Palestine than they possibly could in Eastern Europe[34] (figure 19). The new Jewish youth sprouting in their ancestral land, healthy in body and spirit, was a dominant motif in the presentation of Palestine. It was said that a literal "metamorphosis" could be observed among the children in the colonies; they had progressed from being sickly in the East European *Galut* to being robust in their new homeland (figure 20).[35] It was also important that men and women were shown to be equally sharing the labor in this utopian vision, which was far from the case in reality (figure 21).[36]

In addition to redeeming the soil through physical labor, the life of the mind, at least in the projection of Zionism to Western Jews, was not diminished. One gets the impression, partly because of the numerous references to WIZO and Hadassah, that Palestine suffered no shortage of doctors, dentists, engineers, lawyers, and nurses.[37] But in addition to physicians and other academically trained professionals, who were to be found in the collective settlements, villages, towns, and cities, an

19 "The daughter of a Jewish colonist from Rechovoth in her father's orange grove," *Palästina-Bilder-Korrespondenz* (May 1931): cover.

extraordinary level of bookishness and secular learning was said to be pervasive among Palestine's Jews – even its manual laborers. One memoirist wrote that "The scholar-idealist finds the Palestine air peculiarly congenial; I met him in many interesting guises."[38] Another Zionist visitor recorded that she

paid a visit to the Gdud Avodah, the little colony of workingmen's huts which are clustered together in an isolation of uniqueness in the suburb of Rehavia. Dr. Kagan [a Hadassah physician] took me. She wanted me to meet one of the greatest of the pioneer women of Palestine, Rahel Yanaiet, the wife of Isaac ben Zvi. We walked in and around some of the huts of corrugated tin, passed workmen working on huge blocks of stone, women hammering and chiseling, making the stones ready for use, saw a house a little apart from the others, a house of tar paper and wooden strips, and we entered. We were in a library. Bookshelves reached from floor to ceiling. It was my first introduction to the home of a workingman in Palestine.[39]

Continuing a theme sounded before the First World War, secular educational institutions were prominently featured. Zionism had spawned a disproportionate number of "model" schools.[40] Yet it was

20 "A metamorphosis," *Palästina-Bilder-Korrespondenz* (June 1932): 67.

underscored that learning and self-cultivation occurred in the confines of homes and non-specifically "educational" institutions.[41] "I do not believe that there will be as many 'Babbitts' in Jerusalem as in New York," Lindheim wrote, supporting the notion of popular intellectualism – as opposed to anti-intellectualism – in the Yishuv. This dedication to the life of the mind was claimed to be harnessed to worldly matters, firmly wedded to the soil and social world of the *Halutsim*. Lindheim felt that most Jews in Palestine also were animated by a sense of communal purpose. The "saving grace" of the often rough-hewn people whom Lindheim encountered was their depth of character, aversion to crass self-interest, and adoption of a "spirit of service . . . such as I have never met with elsewhere."[42]

As much as politics was supremely important in the Yishuv and obviously penetrated most forms of intellectual and social life, in the way Zionism in Palestine was usually presented to the West, political divisions were not seen as all-important. Although it was assumed that some of the *Halutsim* were communists, it seemed more compelling that they all were "fearless, independent idealists who, often with bleeding hands and bleeding feet, sometimes even starving and freezing, [who had] set themselves joyfully to [road building] and similar tasks, in the glorious feeling that they were helping to upbuild the land of their fathers."[43] The tendency toward "cooperativism" was explained as having more of a vital tie to Judaism than to socialism or communism, as generic Zionism promised that "everyone may sit peacefully beneath his vine and beneath his fig tree," where "the ownership of the land belongs to the national community."[44] "Sharing" was an infinitely less threatening characterization of political culture in Palestine than was communism: "In a *Kvutzah* all labor is shared; it is an 'Institution of the Love of Comrades.'"[45] Lindheim continued:

The Kvutzah is creating a mold which is reshaping the instinct of possession. The young Jews who have come to Palestine from Eastern and Central Europe have been trained in the art of protest. Homeless spiritually, they have turned from one culture to another and have attempted to find satisfaction in the societies in which they have lived. They have evaluated many civilizations and have come to Palestine intent upon the building of a social order which will satisfy the needs they feel exist.[46]

Interestingly, one is hard pressed to find even the term "communism" in Western Zionist discourse, and before 1933 there are few if any vague allusions to the emerging order of the Soviet Union.

Even when the pictures were overwhelmingly of pre-modern agri-cultural work, as early as the first decade of the twentieth century the narratives accompanying the pictures offered a counterpoint to the peasant-type scenes. The texts asserted that the Jewish colonists were already showing great prowess and innovation in agriculture.[47] Although there were occasional successes, it is reasonable to assume that this was proclaimed far earlier than there could have been a basis for it – given the mixed results and climate of despair of many of the Zionist enterprises.[48] Zionist polemics repeatedly touted the hitherto untapped potential of the country; as late as 1929 one could read about "the possibilities of developing agriculture in Palestine," while it was argued simultaneously that agriculture already was in full flower. Jewish agriculture was metaphorically, then, continuously pregnant with revolutionary upturns.[49] The Jews' agricultural projects, specifically, were said to

21 "Harvesting grapes in Beth Alpha," in *Jewish Colonisation: Erez Israel 30 Years Keren Kayemet* (No place: Jewish National Fund, 1931).

exemplify the most modern scientific farming. For instance, in a number of pictures chemicals are being used to control pests or to fertilize crops.[50] This was one of the means by which the selected application of science was exalted in the presentation of the Yishuv.[51] In the 1920s, photographs of modern machinery and storage facilities would be increasingly interspersed with pictures of Jewish workers in the fields to bolster the image of the advanced stage of farming in Jewish Palestine.[52]

Despite the fact that much of Zionist historiography has dubbed the movement's relationship to the Arabs "the unseen question,"[53] Palestine's Arabs were not "unseen" in Zionist imagery of the country-side, as much as they were chronically underrepresented. Following the lines of most "Westernizing discourse,"[54] Arabs were, by and large, made to appear as less than vital elements of the Palestinian society.[55] This was achieved through photography and narratives that relegated them to marginality, as part of the romantic setting in a Jewish native landscape. It also was widely assumed that

the Arab is largely profiting from the capital and the enterprise which the Jew brings with him. He sells his land at a big profit; he has a better market for his crops; as workman he obtains a higher wage; his child has new advantages of schooling; the Jewish physician, the Jewish clinic, the Jewish district nurse, the Jewish milk station, serve him equally; he is admitted to the benefits of the Jewish library, he is learning from the Jewish workman how to organize.[56]

The pre-World War I Zionist view of Palestine depicted Jews as operating in a cultural void, that is, in a space where the indigenous population had not created a society with a unique character, or at least not discernible to European eyes – although Arab culture would be accorded greater respect and attention in Zionist media in the 1920s.[57] Repeatedly, Jewish farmers were claimed to be an especially important element of Zionism's so-called civilizing mission.[58]

As Arab opposition to Zionism became more pronounced after World War I, the "Arab problem" increasingly occupied Zionist thought and polemics.[59] From time to time Zionists were implored to take a broad view of the Palestine question and become acquainted with "the Islamic world."[60] The original Zionist slogan, "the land without a people for a people without a land" faded into oblivion as it was all too clear that there were, indeed, people on the land.[61] Some writers saw and recorded that "one is confronted," in Palestine, "with the problems of racial jealousy and labor competition . . . more or less in common with the rest of the world."[62] Irma Lindheim was taken aback to observe that the workers in the Jewish colony of Rosh Pina were "chiefly Arab women, who are paid, I hear, five piastres (25 cents) a day." Only occasionally, however, was the depth of the Arab struggle and organization against Zionism put into a less sanguine context, and it was rare to speak of an Arab "national movement." At one of the few times that nationalism among the Arabs was discussed in detail, it was happily proclaimed to be showing signs of accommodation with Zionism.[64]

Of course the attention to the "Arab problem" was most pronounced after the outbreaks of "riots" of 1929.[65] One of the means by which the horror of the riots was rationalized was through a strategy of evasion that probably was less the result of deliberate manipulation than it was the inadvertent consequence of wishful thinking. The violence of Arabs against Zionism was typically described as the work of "terror gangs" or hooligans who were not representative of the will of the Arab masses. It was reported that Arab village leaders wished to be dissociated from the violence.[66] After all, it was noted, to minimize the political dimension of the unrest, did not the Arabs even quarrel fatally among themselves?[67] Sometimes Arab violence was attributed not to deep-seated grievances against the Zionists, but to the failure of the British police to keep order, which in some ways was reminiscent of the pogroms in Eastern Europe.[68] There seemed to be an underlying mythology that Palestine consisted of both bad and good Arabs, and the Zionists tended to seize on those who they deemed "good" as normative. The myth thereby was perpetuated in the West that news of Arab opposition to Zionism tended to be exaggerated,[69] with most Arabs maintaining that "The Jews are our brothers and Palestine can never thrive without their financial and cultural help."[70] Indeed, an often reproduced scene in Zionist brochures showed Jews and Arabs working together on a construction project, although it was not always labeled as including both Jews and Arabs (figures 22a and b). Weizmann himself expressed confidence that "We have in times gone by co-operated with the Arabs in Spain, and we shall do so again in Palestine."[71] Conveniently, though, he did not recall that the Arabs had been in control. But even from the utterances of Zionists who were sincerely committed to dealing fairly with the Arabs, there was more than a hint of condescension in the manner in which Arabs are addressed. It was not unreasonable for Arabs to believe that they were being patronized as atomized individuals, rather than treated as a responsible people.[72] The unequivocal Zionist response, though, to the politically driven destruction of Jewish lives and property was not, according to the pogrom metaphor, to flee to a safe haven – but rather emphatically, to rebuild their lives in Palestine on an even firmer basis.[73]

For most Zionists the fact that the Arabs were willing to sell land to Jews and seemed to cooperate with them was taken as the sign that the Arabs' attachment to the soil was less profound than the Jews' eternal, cosmic connection.[74] In the 1920s and early 1930s, despite the obvious Arab resistance and rise of an anti-Zionist Arab national movement, Zionist representations of Palestine's Arabs for its Western audience tended to show the Arab population with more of a human, and less exotic face (figure 23).[75] Up until 1947 the movement in general tended to stress the evidence of Arab–Jewish cooperation, rather than using Arabs as an enemy to unify the fragmented movement[76] – the British came to serve that function more and more as the mandate wore on.[77] It was a point of pride for the movement that it continued to fortify the infrastructure of the national home despite the efforts of the British to thwart their attempts.[78]

Zionists stressed that they were reclaiming the land which had either been abused or lain dormant.[79] This reclamation, however, was only possible if the movement possessed the funds to purchase the land from its current owners. This was done mainly through the institutions which became entrenched in diaspora Zionist life, the Jewish National Fund (also known by the Hebrew Keren Kayemeth L'Israel or KKL, established in 1901) and the Keren Hayesod after 1921. A great part of Zionism's visual sensibility was therefore tied to the fundraising

Jews and Arabs working together on the Construction of Houses at Tel-Aviv.

22 (a) "Jews and Arabs working together on the construction of houses at Tel Aviv," in *Jewish Progress in Palestine: Four Years' Work of Keren Hayesod* (London: Palestine Foundation Fund, Keren Hayesod, 1925); it also appears with a caption identifying the workers as both Jews and Arabs in *Palästina-Bilder-Korrespondenz* (October 1928): 12; see also figure 27.

instruments.[80] Most of the films and slide shows were presented under the auspices of the Jewish National Fund (before World War I) and the Keren Hayesod (after the war).[81] Films were a prominent part of the numerous "Palestine Weeks" which also featured drama and poetry readings, lectures, concerts, art shows, plays, teas, sports festivals, and exhibitions of Zionist institutions.[82] Over 2,000 people attended the opening of the Berlin Palestine Week of 1919, which inaugurated a sixty-city European tour.[83] Therefore, it was relatively easy to participate in the agricultural regeneration of the Jews: one could see the work in action, and there were innumerable appeals to donate money. Even very small contributions were encouraged, and the movement claimed that this was enough to bind one to the land and people. Indeed, the donation of money, which was assumed to go primarily toward the purchase of land

HOUSEBUILDING.

(b) The same picture, this time labeled simply "Housebuilding," in *Jewish Colonisation: Erez Israel 30 Years Keren Kayemet* (No place: Jewish National Fund, 1931).

for agricultural settlement, was one of the most developed aspects of the Zionist project.[84]

However much the agricultural enterprise dominated Zionism's self-presentation to Western Jews, by the 1920s it was clear that the burgeoning cities of Palestine were also focal points of the Zionist initiative. Although in 1897 Herzl had conjured the image of toughened Jewish hands speeding a plow in Palestine, he also was careful to include a full-blown urban sensibility in his publicized dreams for the Jewish state. He assured his imagined constituency that Jews in the Old/New Land of Palestine would have the salt-pretzels and cafe society they enjoyed in Europe, professing that the Jews' cities would not be simple replicas of Europe: they truly would be cities of the future, bastions of high culture and sophisticated cooperativism. It was well known from his

23 "Arabs," *Palästina-Bilder-Korrespondenz* (October 1928): 19.

24 E. M. Epstein, "Dr. Herzl's Vision," and Harry Levin, "Prof. Abercrombie's Plans," *Pioneer* (July 1930): 12–13; the same image, with Theodor Herzl superimposed on a view of Haifa, appears in "Spezialnummer. Herzl und Haifa," *Palästina-Bilder-Korrespondenz* (May 1928) and again in *Pioneer* (July 1929): 12–13.

novel *Altneuland* that Herzl's own imagination seized on Haifa as the greatest embodiment of that dream, and indeed, in the 1920s, it seemed to be realizing that role (figure 24). Even before 1914, Haifa was home to the Yishuv's technical academy, which was famed for its fusion of moral and technical education, and Haifa also was the setting for some of its splendid building projects.[85] Indeed, for both Haifa and Tel Aviv, the sea-side was depicted as more than a potential economic resource, but as a site of regenerative power nearing that of "the soil" (figure 25).[86] Clearly, Haifa, Zion's city by the bay, was its greatest national, natural aesthetic treasure.[87] One Zionist from the West wrote that

For sheer beauty this Riviera of the Orient cannot be surpassed . . . A great convulsion of the earth must have given birth to the mount of Carmel. It rises steeply as a promontory out of the sea and extends seventeen miles back into Sharon and Samaria. It completes one end of the rhythmic curve which holds the bay of Haifa in its embrace. It welds into a horseshoe the length of silver shore which stretches from its sea-bathed point to Acre's pink and castellated walls. On its height are the Jews building their homes, at its base the old city lies drowsily watching itself grow . . . Haifa is ideally situated and has all the attributes of a

25 "Jewish sea-scouts near the bathing place, Tel Aviv," frontispiece in
Myriam Harry, *A Springtide in Palestine* (London: Ernest Benn, 1924);
in figure 23 the picture is labeled "Rudersport am Strand von Tel
Awiw," in *Palästina-Bilder-Korrespondenz* (October 1928): 19.

great seaport town. Its harbor can be dredged and made safe for the great ships
which carry their freight of passengers and goods to the near and far East and its
location allows for unlimited expansion and commercial development . . . Jewish
capital is building great modern factory buildings. Factories for the manufacture
of olive oil and soap and cement and building materials are already working full
blast. A beautiful flour mill of white stucco mills the wheat which is produced in
the Emek, and a building which is to house the next Rutenberg power plant is
near completion. Great travail is accompanying the birth of industry here because
of the lack of credit and capital, but there is a spirit of will and energy present that
presages a healthy development.[88]

References to Haifa's "drowsy" old city at the base of Mount Carmel was
shorthand for its Arab inhabitants.[89] In texts and captions there was no
mention of possible displacement or resettlement; they apparently were
untouched as the Jewish part of the city nearer the top of the mountain
grew beyond recognition. Although cities, including Haifa, would be
scenes of bitter conflicts and warfare between Zionists and Arabs, in the
Zionist popular literature there was little sense that the Jewish presence

26 "Interior of the 'Silicate' Sand-Brick Factory," in *Jewish Colonis-
ation of Erez Israel: After Ten Years Keren Hayesod* (Jerusalem: no
publisher [Keren Hayesod?], 1930); it is labeled "Chaluzim bei der
Arbeit in der Ziegelfabrik der Silikat-Gesellschaft" in *Keren Hayesod:
Tatsachen und Bilder aus dem neuen jüdischen Leben in Palästina*
(Jerusalem: no publisher [Keren Hayesod?], 1927).

in cities was contested as it was in the countryside. Certainly the
complicated reality was that the cities rose as a result of Jewish and Arab
labor, as well as by investments of the British mandatory power; but the
main impetus bore an unmistakable Zionist imprint. Ironically, the cities
were closer in spirit to the virgin space of which Zionists spoke than were
their prized agricultural settlements.

The burgeoning city of Haifa also seemed to epitomize the compatibility of the Zionist dream with industrialization.[90] A number of the
factories that were displayed in Zionist journals were those of Haifa
(figure 26). This too was meant to illustrate the manifestation of the
Jews' productivity and urge toward construction, in all its meanings, in
the Zionist sphere.[91] Factories were sometimes said to be prime sites
of Jewish–Arab cooperation, as was the case in a silk mill and leather
factory.[92] The various electrification projects of engineer Pinchas

Rutenberg were romanticized in the Zionist press, and typically described as the lifeblood of the Yishuv[93] (figure 27). Certainly Rutenberg's distinctive, visionary-futuristic political style contributed to the ready appropriation of his endeavors.[94] "I was happy to be in Haifa," Irma Lindheim wrote,

when the new Rutenberg power station was opened. It was a dramatic sight. Great, silent engines have been housed in a beautiful concrete building. In the half light of the early evening, they looked like monsters in repose. Two oil lamps shed a circle of light which intensified rather than lifted the shadows. As the dark settled down, people crowded into the engine room. Sir Herbert Samuel, Pinhas Rutenberg, and the builders were there, besides hundreds of others who had come to look on. Everything was in readiness. For one moment there was silence and darkness. A switch was turned and there was light. A new era had begun for Haifa. Electricity, power, industry. The Arabs fought against the installation of the power plant, but they too will soon rejoice in the day when this new force was put in their hands.[95]

As opposed to Haifa, which had a substantial Arab population, Zionists also prized the images of what was claimed to be the first "100% Jewish" city: Tel Aviv, which originated as a Jewish quarter of the Arab town of Jaffa.[96] By 1927 there were some 40,000 Jewish inhabitants; although its residents were mostly secular Jews, the city had a palpably Jewish rhythm.[97] The first photographs of Tel Aviv, from around 1910, boasted clean, wide streets, lined with white-washed buildings, with no trace of commotion.[98] But as the city grew, became congested, and incorporated a veritable "mish-mosh" of styles[99] – with little apparent central planning – the pictures rarely captured such changes (figures 28 and 29).[100] Some Zionist reporters went so far as to say that "one feels it a desecration to come upon false fronts, gawky patterns, hulky boxes of buildings, ridiculous towerlets and similar atrocities perpetrated by half-taught builders and overworked contractors at the pleasure of crude, ignorant property owners."[101] Apparently the Zionist publicity machine could not contain the city's reputation for being an affront to any aesthetic sensibility. In 1923, Julian Mack was happy to tell his family that while Tel Aviv "made no impression of beauty" on him, "it did not strike me as quite as ugly as I had been led to believe."[102] Nevertheless the movement's polemics praised its dynamic and "breathless" character.[103] Rather than claiming that it was unlovely or disordered, the captions of pictures explained that this was yet another expression of the unbounded energy that Jews were expending on their new home.[104] Tel Aviv, like Haifa, was praised for its success at industrialization:

It has the best electric light and power station in Palestine, a station which supplies power to some thirty factories, producing such diverse articles as silk,

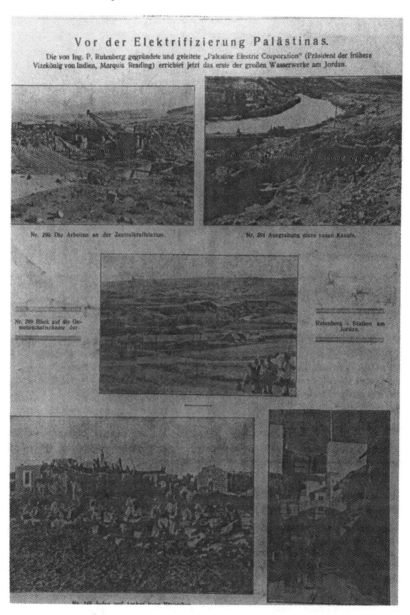

27 "Toward the electrification of Palestine," *Palästina-Bilder-Korrespondenz* (October 1928): 12.

28 "Tel-Aviv. General View," *Erez Israel* (London: Head Office of the
Keren Hayesod, no date).

chocolate, silicate brick, textile goods, finished leather; there is even, I understand, a workshop where small industries are provided with power. And all this
has been charmed, as if by magic, upon a soil that was deeply buried by yellow
sands, and soil which smiles with palms and orange trees and all the brilliant tints
of a rich flora as soon as the sand pall from neglectful ages is cleared away so that
the earth can bask again in that benignant sunshine.[105]

Zionist promotions frequently employed a succession of pictures of Tel
Aviv – of scenes of 1909, 1912, and 1922, for instance – to illustrate
vividly how quickly and successfully it had matured "from sand dune to
city" (figure 30).

Before the First World War Tel Aviv was often contrasted to Jewish
Jerusalem, which, ironically, seemed to exemplify the worst of the *Galut*.
A Zionist traveler in 1927 prefaced his comments about the city by
saying that

Jerusalem is a mere town of some seventy or eighty thousand inhabitants, a town
whose days of glory and of a modest measure of dominion belong to a distant
past, a town poor in wealth, reft of all power, rich in little beyond memories and
associations, but rich, above every other place in the world, in shrines of sanctity
which command reverence, respectively, of the three faiths that divide between
them the believing hosts of modern civilization.[106]

Its Jewish population, which comprised Jerusalem's majority since the
middle of the nineteenth century, was mostly impoverished, intolerantly

29 "Tel-Aviv. Montefiore Street," in *Erez Israel* (London: Head Office of the Keren Hayesod, no date).

orthodox, bitterly divided, and vehemently anti-Zionist.[107] In Jerusalem it was possible to face "the very depths of destitution and starvation."[108] It was this people, not the Arabs, who the Zionists presented as the most burdensome obstacle to the flowering of their plan, and who they treated to their harshest invective. But by the 1920s the presentations of Jerusalem were focusing more on the new buildings and commercial activity of "West" Jerusalem, as opposed to the Old City. Although the historic places and pictures of traditional Jews would always be a part of Zionist imagery, the ostensibly "regenerated" Jerusalem took on a new and profound significance for the movement.

Zionist media evinced a thrill to convey that the cities, including Jerusalem, were becoming bourgeois and middle class, and that life was for the most part "normal." One traveler wrote that "Suddenly as if by the waving of a magic wand, Palestine has become a place for life, a land where you and I and people like us are living in ways comparable with those which characterize our lives here," in the United States and Europe.[109] This was reflected in numerous pictures and postcards, in which the prominence of stores and businesses assured the audience that a Westernized, consumer-oriented society had definitively been established in the Holy Land (figures 31 and 32). Another traveler

30 Progression of images of Tel Aviv in *Jewish Progress in Palestine: Four Years' Work of the Keren Hayesod* (Jerusalem: no publisher [Keren Hayesod?], 1930). The same images appeared in several publications including *Jüdische Leistungen in Palästina. Tatsachen und Zahlen*, 3rd edn. (Berlin: Keren Hayesod Central European Division, no date), opposite p. 8; and as "Das Werden einer Stadt (Tel Awiw)," in Adolf Boehm, *Der Palästina-Aufbaufonds (Keren Hajessod)* (London: Head Office of Keren Hayesod, 1925), p. 30.

31 Postcard, "Jerusalem. Jaffa Road" (in author's collection).

32 Postcard, "Tel Aviv, Achad Haam Street" (in author's collection).

wrote that

No one can accuse Jerusalem of not being up-to-date. This morning we visited a beauty parlor equipped for manicures, shampoos, and facial treatments. It is a strange medley one finds here, the very old and the very new ... A Jewish woman with American initiative started this unusual venture of establishing a beauty parlor in Jerusalem. She was a trained nurse. She left Pittsburgh for Palestine when the first Hadassah medical unit was sent across. She worked in the hospitals and then decided that she wanted to settle down and stay. And so she opened this beauty parlor to counteract the effect of the sun and white dust of Jerusalem on the sensitive complexions of the tourists. It is not a key industry, essential to the upbuilding of the land, and yet it is good to see the spirit that made it possible and the will that had the tenacity to make it succeed.[110]

In addition to services specifically geared for tourists who had come principally to visit the holy and historic sites in the Old City, Jerusalem was also becoming a center of non-tourist-centered and secularized Jewish life. The Hebrew University had its initial growth spurt after its colorful founding in 1925,[111] and the Hadassah Hospital and Jewish Agency building were seen as embodiments of the new public life of Jewry which was taking form in the ancient capital.[112] Modern, clean-lined, Bauhaus-style buildings could be found in Haifa, Tel Aviv, and Jerusalem.[113]

The three major cities, however, were much more than showcases for "normalcy," eclectic architecture, human enterprise, and economic vigor. Clearly these were Jewish cities. Their synagogues may not have dominated the skylines as did churches and mosques in Christian and Muslim nations, but their houses of worship were certainly present. And Jewish motifs were intermingled in buildings besides synagogues, which distinguished the material society rising in Palestine from anywhere in Europe.[114] But perhaps more than its expressly religious character, the urban centers prominently revealed a "social conscience." Image upon image displayed various public welfare services – such as facilities for new immigrants, soup kitchens, schools, infant welfare centers, and clinics (figures 33 and 34).[115] The tie to any specifically socialist political agenda was left vague. Overall, the message was that this was a society that deeply cared for, and effectively dealt with, its most helpless and under-privileged constituents, in large part through the assistance of diaspora Jewry – particularly the women of organizations such as WIZO and Hadassah, respectively, the British and American women's Zionist organizations.[116] It furthermore was noted that many of these services served the old Jewish community which had been so opposed to Zionism, and Palestine's Arabs, as well as Jews. It was convincingly illustrated that

33 "From the work of Hadassah," *Palästina-Bilder-Korrespondenz* (May 1930): 2.

new life and hope are being brought to the East in the standards Hadassah is setting. It is amazing to see the most modern and hygienic methods of handling milk in practice here, in the midst of unspeakable ignorance and filth. The fairy wand of science is lighting up the dark corners of the earth, and the hand of woman is holding up the torch. Hadassah is certainly the Mother of Palestine

34 "From a WIZO children's home in Palestine,' in *Palästina-Bilder-Korrespondenz* "Spezialnummer WIZO" (January–February 1931): 1.

today. She is tending to her children and healing their ills. She has reduced the infant mortality and blindness from trachoma to a very considerable degree.[117]

These claims were bolstered by visual evidence of charts and graphs, sometimes quite ingeniously drawn, to give credence to these remarks (figure 35).

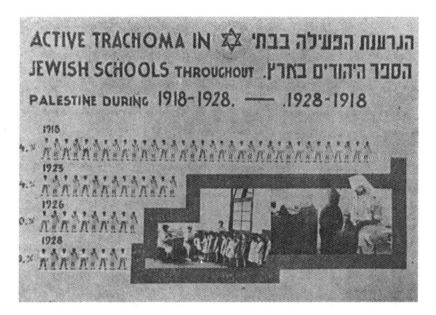

35 "Statistics of active trachoma in Jewish schools in Palestine, 1918–1928," in *Palästina Aufbaufonds* (Jerusalem: Keren Hayesod, 1928).

From the Balfour Declaration of 1917, to 1933, within the realm of Zionist projections of Palestine, the country was depicted as an increasingly realistic refuge for some millions of world Jewry in need of immediate evacuation and permanent resettlement – again, also portrayed by charts and graphs (figures 36 and 37). No longer were the Zionist enterprises in Palestine treated as mere philanthropic ventures or seedlings of a national Jewish life. On the contrary, Palestine was arguably the most logical area for mass Jewish settlement that had already attained the requisite institutions to nurture its growth. Where else did the Jews comprise such a large share of the population, and an important part of its agricultural class, at that?[118] Where else were they actually designing and constructing their own cities? This was cast in scientific and analytical terms, in addition to the language of Jewish messianism and appeals to the charitable instincts of Western Jews. To be sure there were obstacles: intransigent Jews of the Old Yishuv, the Arabs, and the British.[119] Even after the riots of 1929, the largest single impediment appeared not to be the country's Arabs, but the harsh physical environment of Palestine – which could only gradually be

36 "Jewish Palestine," inserted in *Jewish Pioneering in Palestine (What Our Haluzim are Doing)* (No place: Palestine Foundation Fund, 1922).

overcome:

Palestine is a poor country; men do not go there in order to "get rich quick." Its natural resources are conjectural. Oil may be hidden under the surface of the earth, there may be tremendous deposits of the Dead Sea, sufficient electric power may be developed for industry and irrigation, and the improved harbor facilities may make Palestine a gateway to the East. But Palestine as it stands is a land devastated of its wealth. Its forests have been cut down and its orchards and vineyards have been laid waste. It is not a land that men would seek out unless they wanted to pioneer in new fields.[120]

But the gallant pioneers were, so it was being documented, winning their "fight" for "progress and civilization" against their most implacable foe: the desert.[121] Ostensibly proving the normalcy of Jewish existence in Palestine, the Jews' turn to, and apparent success in agriculture, along with their concomitant achievements in devising and building "Jewish cities" allowed Jews in the West to affirm their place as a rooted, genuine people, engaged in healthy national pursuits, and propitiously wedded to modernity. To no small degree, this also represents an internalization of

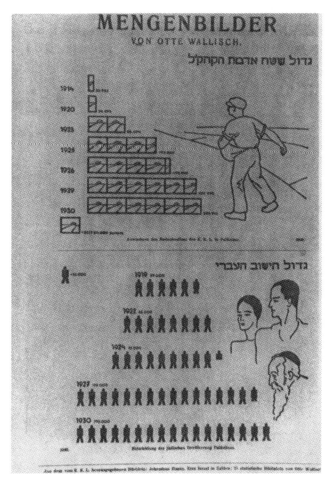

37 "Graphs" by Otte Wallisch, *Palästina-Bilder-Korrespondenz* (May 1931): 5.

the anti-Semitic stereotypes.[122] Yet it is difficult to draw a line, at times, between reaction to strictures imposed by the majority culture and the urge for national liberation and self- and communal expression. At any rate, the Zionist movement was able to effect a change in Jewish perceptions; some Jews began to see Palestine as a Jewish country, or an incipient Jewish sovereignty.[123] The perceptions of a Jewish "return" to agriculture, alongside the apparent Jewish proclivity for fostering humane and cosmopolitan urban environments, enabled a significant minority of Western Jews to envision a supplemental nationality and alternative national community for their East European brethren – but possibly also for themselves.

6   Nationalized tourism in Palestine

Before 1933, it was unusual for a Jew from Western Europe or the United States to consummate his or her participation in Zionism by settling in Palestine. The cases of those who attempted to do so, such as the Blau-Weiss youth from Germany, were truly exceptional, as indicated by the vociferous debate surrounding their decision.[1] In the interwar years, although Western Jews making 'Aliyah never constituted more than a trickle, the rush of German, British, and American Jewish tourists to Palestine became increasingly significant. Over 70,000 total visitors came to the country from the West during 1924, and in the spring of 1925, 1,200 were present on a single day.[2] Some 40,000, including an estimated 4,000 Jews, saw Palestine in 1930,[3] despite the ongoing Arab revolt and the deepening worldwide economic crisis.[4]

The steady increase of the tourist trade in Palestine, to a certain extent, resembles that of other Near Eastern and European locales in the interwar years. "The holiday-taking patterns of the privileged few,"[5] which took off on the Continent before the Great War, were adopted by a widening range of people, as "the vacation was ceasing to be the prerogative of the rich and well-off and was beginning to be considered the right of all."[6] There are aspects of the evolution of Palestine tourism, however, which make it distinctive; it does not neatly fit European models or those derived from "less-developed countries." Perhaps this helps explain why Jewish tourism to Palestine and the State of Israel is usually absent in the literature on travel.[7] "Tourism," Jonathan Culler argues, "is a practice of considerable cultural and economic importance . . . Yet despite the pervasiveness of tourism and its centrality to our conception of the contemporary world . . . tourism has been neglected by students of culture."[8] It is not surprising, then, that within Zionist historical scholarship, there is hardly any notice of the tourist trade,[9] despite the fact that it comprises a formidable share of the Jewish state's economy, it was and is a prominent means of Western Jewish integration in the movement, and it remains a vital part of Zionism's self-presentation and ceremonial forms.

A tradition of Jewish, Christian, and Islamic pilgrimage to their respective holy places in Palestine, especially Jerusalem, was well established by the 1880s when the Zionists arrived on the scene.[10] Travelers motivated by Islam, however, do not seem to have been within the ken of the movement's leaders. Especially after the British gained control over Palestine in the wake of World War I, Zionist officials articulated an awareness that the movement stood to gain in various ways through a Western-oriented tourist trade. What was the organization to make of the inadvertent observers of their fledgling nationalist project, and how might it deal with the country's obvious popularity as a tourist spot? Tourism was one of the few resources that could be immediately profitable. There existed the possibility that the Zionist Organization could convert non-Zionist Jewish travelers to Zionism,[11] and it was elated to show off the fruits of its efforts to non-Jews, including Christian pilgrims to the Holy Land.[12] Most of the movement's energy exerted on tourism, however, came to be channeled toward enticing Jews – who were already inclined to support the movement – to come to Palestine, and if they made the journey, to ensure that they carried away a favorable impression of the Zionist enterprise. "Tourism," a modern commentator writes, "is not just an aggregate of merely commercial activities; it is also an ideological framing of history, nature, and tradition; a framing that has the power to reshape culture and nature to its own needs."[13] What the Zionists attempted to do, and to a large extent accomplished by 1933, was establish a secular-Jewish pilgrimage ritual,[14] to endow the ancient historical sites with new national-Jewish meanings,[15] and furthermore to delineate a secularized "sacred geography" for Jews, which encompassed the entirety of Jewish life in the Yishuv.[16] The movement sought to assure that Jewish visitors were stimulated by "impressions of natural beauty and of human worth," and "the harmonious combination of Jewish and secular culture."[17] The collective traces of Israel's past, intermingled with signs of a regenerated Jewish nation, were to be "venerated as a fount of communal identity" for all Jews.[18]

To be sure, regardless of Zionism, Jewish travelers were inspired by the same core sentiments that had propelled Western Jewish tourists eastward since the early nineteenth century: to see Erets Israel, the birthplace of Judaism, the bedrock of antiquity, the veritable "cradle of civilization"[19] – in particular, to connect to their own primordial, religious tradition, and to take in sites of historical interest. The Zionist movement invigorated and then appropriated this phenomenon by actively encouraging Western Jews, even in places where Zionism was dormant, such as Switzerland and France, to see the movement's work in Palestine first-hand.[20] Despite intermittent pronouncements that tourist trips to Palestine were a prelude "to permanent settlement,"[21] any such pretension was subdued as tourism was integrated into the ideology and practice of diaspora Zionist nationalization. Further, a visit to the country was fashioned into the climactic ritual of the process of becoming a complete Zionist.[22] Indeed, this ceremonialized tour, which was both less and more than a pilgrimage, had been precipitated by the dissemination of Zionist artistic and photographic images in the West since Theodor Herzl wielded the techniques of mass politics in the upstart movement in 1897, helping to provide a richly textured view of Jewish life in Palestine.[23]

As opposed to a comprehensive treatment of the interwar tourist trade in Palestine, or an analysis of the "rediscovery" of the Holy Land,[24] what follows is a discussion of the attempted appropriation of tourism by the Zionist movement, and the evolution of its subsequent reception by Western Jews.[25] In particular, the focus is on institutional efforts to draw Western Jews, who had not been very involved in Zionism, into the movement's orbit, and to intensify the commitment of those already aligned with the movement by shaping their experience in Palestine. At first, the Zionist movement sought to add some exposure to the new Yishuv for those Jews who made their way to Palestine, mainly in the form of excursions to Jewish settlements. Such trips were made optional, or added to the preexisting schedule of visits to markets, historical venues, and holy places. Eventually Zionist officials made common cause with touring companies to include the sites of the Zionist project as regular stops on the Palestine, or Egypt–Palestine itinerary.

By the early 1930s, the movement so succeeded in fitting tourism into its general attempt to promote the movement among Jews that the earlier religious-historical impetus for seeing the country was subsumed into the greater scheme of showing off the Zionist efforts. Tourism was enshrined as a marvelous device of propaganda and fundraising. It furnished assimilated Jews with a way to connect with Jewish Palestine which made them feel as if they knew the inside story, and left some taste of the breadth of Jewish experience in the country. Zionist tourism fostered an ongoing information and propaganda network that for the most part worked to expand knowledge and sentimental attachment to the national project, and furthermore encoded paradigms for perceiving and grasping the Zionist movement which would prove to be remarkably resilient.

Obviously, Zionist interest in developing tourism in Palestine served multiple agendas, not the least of which was to develop the local Jewish economy. As elsewhere, the consequences of increasing tourism ranged from exploiting and disfiguring the indigenous peoples, environment, and cultures to creating pockets of prosperous elites or even communities where they had not before existed.[26] At any rate, tourism helped to transform all of Palestine, but before Zionism there had been a long tradition, primarily among the non-Jewish inhabitants of the country, of handling pilgrims and tourists. In fact, by 1872, "Egypt and Palestine had become so commercially important" to Thomas Cook Ltd. that Cook "could regard them as 'the two greatest features in our present programme.'"[27] Interestingly, the Zionist efforts to increase and consolidate tourism in Palestine possibly had a more disruptive effect on Jews than Arabs – for whom a tourist trade infrastructure was firmly entrenched.[28]

Nevertheless, on the ground in Palestine, control over tourism was one of the areas in which Jews competed with Arabs for money and the sympathies of outsiders; in addition, each wished to show their own specific vision of Palestine. The European-based touring companies usually observed the Arab boycotts of the Jewish sector, such as by excluding Tel Aviv from their itineraries. But on the other hand there also were numerous instances where Jewish–Arab tensions were said to be relieved due to cooperation in the tourist industry.[29] Undoubtedly, to the Zionists there were tremendous benefits to be reaped in making the Jews' ancestral home "one of the leading touring centres of the world." The development of public works, for one, had a reciprocal relationship with the growth of tourism.[30] In this way, the tourist industry in Palestine is comparable to that of innumerable other locales, such as Egypt and Greece. A unique feature, however, was that Zionist leaders hoped that a specific group among the visitors – Jewish tourists to Palestine – would disproportionately invest in existing businesses or initiate capitalist or cooperativist ventures, even if they did not plan to stay themselves.[31]

In addition to the easily understood economic motives, the use of tourism to bolster national pride and to demonstrate a nation's claims to legitimacy and greatness is not unique to Zionism. "National and communal efforts to recall and refashion a praiseworthy if not a glorious past," writes historian David Lowenthal, are "similar to the needs of individuals to construct a viable and believable life history. In reviewing alterations of the past, students of nationalism and psychoanalysis and literary criticism share an awareness that individuals, like states, must continually confront the competing pulls of dependence and autonomy, following and leading, tradition and creativity, infancy and maturity."[32] But along with these common traits is a distinctive Zionist variation on the familiar nationalist tune.

Regarding Western Jews who would come as visitors to Palestine, Zionist officials were not simply interested in their spending, perhaps investing, money and in their spirits being buoyed by the national achievements. The movement was committed to devising means to connect European and American Jews with the place, to create bonds that would lead to specific behaviors, including future visits and greater donations to the Zionist cause. Seeing Palestine was extolled as a more persuasive instrument for gaining adherents and promoting solidarity than any ideological argument. "Above all," it was proclaimed in the German Zionist organ *Jüdische Rundschau*, "it is important that every returning tourist from Palestine be an apostle for the idea of the building-up of Erets Israel," to establish "a personal connection of Diaspora Jewry with the new Jewry." Once home they should instinctively "arouse new Jewish life and a willingness to sacrifice for the purposeful construction of Palestine."[33]

To be sure, any pleasant visit to a foreign land might evoke curiosity, empathy, and sustained interest and good feelings toward the people and the place. The Zionists demanded no less, though, than for a Jew's visit to Palestine to become "the high point" of his or her life.[34] This included the imperative that Jewish visitors feel that they had visited the true home of the depths of their souls. Palestine was not to be another home away from home, or just a superb vacation spot – but the place Western Jews would recognize as their most authentic home.[35] Ideally, an inversion would occur, or at least the boundaries would be blurred in their mind's eye between concepts of "home" and "away," "we" and "they," "here" and "there."[36] Although after the establishment of the State of Israel, the concept "making '*Aliyah*" (literally, "ascending") would be understood as permanently settling in the country, earlier the notion was more vague; for instance, tourists, along with *Ḥalutsim*, were said to comprise the "'*Aliyah* from Germany" in 1923.[37] In effect, all one had to do was visit Palestine in order to undergo this spiritual transformation.

The attempt to institutionalize Zionist trips did not begin with a strategic or well-thought-out plan. The first attempts to modify Palestine tourism to fit the needs of the movement arose from complaints against the European-based tour industry in the early 1920s. Palestine was already a chief destination for travel,[38] according to a writer in the *Jüdische Rundschau*, but there was virtually no attention paid, within the existing structure of tourism, to any of the specific "Zionist addresses." The writer grumbled that "not a single Jewish colony or settlement is visited by the large tourist expeditions; they see nothing of the new Jewish life." This was attributed to the "anti-Semitic tendencies of the great international travel bureaus, especially [Thomas] Cook,"[39] which had been running tours to Egypt and Palestine since 1869.[40] A small measure that was taken to overcome this "evil" was the publication of Jewish travel guides by the Zionist Organization, so that tourists could see the Yishuv on their own. Tourism was said to have tremendous potential for business and propaganda value, which was at this point largely untapped.[41] It seems, however, that the touring companies began to sense that it was to their advantage to strike an agreement with the Zionist Organization.[42] This coincided with the fact that the base of clientele for tourism was expanding for Thomas Cook and other companies.[43] Up until the early 1920s, in explaining the touring firms' apparent antipathy to Zionism, it remains an open question whether they were animated more by anti-Semitism or a desire to cater to the desires of Christian pilgrims, or by simple indifference to the Zionist enterprise.

Bits of information about Palestine tourism could be found in nearly every Zionist journal by the mid-1920s, attesting to its popularity. Among the most publicized tours were those sponsored in conjunction with the biennial World Zionist Congresses held in Europe. One of the early programmatic statements concerning Zionism and the tourist trade appeared in the international Zionist journal *New Judaea*, published in London, in 1924. Interestingly, the announcement about tourism in Palestine was in the context of publicity for a film produced by the Keren Hayesod, called *The Land of Promise*. The medium of film, in the forms of still photography and cinema, and tourism, were seen as mutually supportive. They represented extraordinarily promising means of propaganda, and tours were devised with an eye to producing and reproducing certain images, which would have been long familiar to European and American Jews by the mid-1920s.[44] Readers were informed that

Arrangements are to be made to deal comprehensively with tourism from the Jewish point of view. It is sought to obtain the mutual co-operation of all bodies in Palestine which are affected, such as the Orphans Committee, Hadassah, the Building Loan and Savings Society, the JNF, as well as the Zionist Organisation and the Keren Hayesod. While the chief task here is to secure that the visitors have an opportunity of seeing Jewish Palestine, abroad there is much to do in getting the tourist to ask in advance for that opportunity. So many people travel according to programmes and itineraries prepared for them by agents or companies seldom unprejudiced against Jews or Zionism. In this respect Zionist offices in the various countries can help, for many a party misses seeing the Jewish colonies or towns through sheer ignorance. In Palestine those profiting from tourism are improving their methods, an instance of which is the union of hotel-keepers in Tel Aviv for the purpose of maintaining standards of comfort.[45]

The *Jüdische Rundschau* reported that Thomas Cook, in its promotional literature for Egypt and Palestine tours for 1924/25, gave special prominence to "the Jewish colonies in Palestine." "The tour leaders," the company stated, "have been instructed to give the travelers a picture of the development of the Jewish national home in Palestine, to show them the Jewish colonies." They will be exposed to "not only the old colonies, but those that had been erected by the Zionist Executive since the British administration in 1917 [sic], and upon request, Jewish tourists could have Jews as group leaders and interpreters." Apparently, the writer for the *Rundschau* editorialized, the company had taken to heart the dissatisfaction expressed by Jewish tourists and Zionist authorities, and assiduously tried to alter its standing in "Jewish circles." The writer, rather than simply applauding the shift, concluded that it remained to be seen if these modifications, in how the tour was described, were indeed realized.[46]

The Zionist Organization sought to attract greater numbers of Jews and Zionists to the country by lowering the cost of travel. The price up until the mid-1920s was apparently prohibitive for many middle-class and lower middle-class Jews.[47] This upper-class bias probably derived from Cook's tours to Egypt, which had originally been designed to be "grander and more luxurious" than their European tours, with a distinct "imperial" flavor.[48] Prices were lowered for many Jewish travelers by assembling larger and larger groups.[49] In 1927, the Fabreline cruise company advertised "surprisingly moderate rates" in American Zionist periodicals.[50] Some notices boasted "Cheap Mediterranean Cruises" to assure the non-wealthy that they were desired as clientele.[51] Besides working out a modus vivendi with Thomas Cook, which initially had been seen as hostile to Zionism, the movement also was able to work with the Cunard Line in offering excursions to Palestine beginning in 1921, a partnership which the Cunard firm hailed as a "phenominal [sic] success."[52] The joining of the "Palestine Express Company," touted as "the greatest Jewish tourist bureau" based in Palestine,[53] with the British "Palestine Lloyd Ltd." in 1925 was likewise regarded as a stunning victory for the movement. The Palestine Lloyd company, it was reported, was now "connected to Zionist financial institutions" through the efforts of the World Zionist Organization, and it was hoped that along with Jewish tourists, those with Near Eastern business interests would take advantage of the chance to see the Yishuv.[54]

Two years later, in 1927, a formal relationship was struck between "Palestine Lloyd" and the Palestine Office of the Zionist Organization, making it the official agent of the movement.[55] It seems that some tours were partially subsidized by the Zionist Organization to make them more accessible.[56] A main reason for the movement's elation over the partnership was that the non-specifically Jewish or Zionist tours were now to become "Zionistic." In the advertising, however, even in Zionist organs, mostly generic motifs, rather than Zionist symbols, were used. Stock images, like palm trees and keffiyeh-clad camel riders, adorned most advertisements.[57] The work of popular Zionist artists, such as E. M. Lilien and Hermann Struck, were rarely, if ever, applied to tourist promotions.

This is not to say, however, that Jewish symbols, and aspects of Jewish religious life and traditions were not utilized. The undergirding mythology, of course, was that visiting the Promised Land constituted a mitzvah for Jews. In conjunction with the Zionist Organization, Thomas Cook instituted a Palestine tour during the Passover holiday in 1929. A British Zionist journal promoting the tour wrote that

Pesach is a delightful season to pay a visit to the country. In the bright sunshine, with the land budding forth in luxuriant growth and the very atmosphere breathing the spirit of the Jewish Festival of Freedom, the Jew can see the New Palestine he has created under the most favorable climatic, economic, and psychological conditions. We are pleased to note that so universal a touring agency as Cooks should have found it advisable to arrange a special Jewish tour for this year.

So as not to single out Thomas Cook, it was reported that the Palestine Lloyd firm, as well, was dedicated to bringing "its quota of Jews to see the rejuvenated land of Israel." For those who for whatever reason could not make the trip, it was encouraged that they at least attend the Palestine Exhibition at the West London Bazaar.[58]

It is unclear what impact the statements and policies of Zionists had, compared with the efforts on the part of the companies to capitalize on the real or imagined windfall in the interwar Jewish tourist trade. Their interests were bound to merge. To be sure, though, a prevalent attitude among many in the movement's upper ranks was that tourism mattered; it was underdeveloped, and a concerted effort should be made to make it more useful in furthering the Zionist project. As a program in the celebration of "Sokolow Month,"[59] a long address about tourism was delivered in 1931 by Julius Berger. Given as a speech on the Zionist lecture circuit, and reaching others as a circular letter, this talk pointed out lines of possible expansion, but essentially summed up the endeavors already underway.[60] Overall, however, in the interwar years there is strikingly little evidence of long-range planning, concerning tourism, within the formative infrastructure of the Yishuv – despite the creation of a bureau with Fritz Loewenstein at its head in 1925. Rather, Zionist tourism emerged as a series of measures to improve on that which existed, and specifically, to respond to complaints of those whose visits to Palestine had been unpleasant or otherwise disconcerting. Tourist facilities that were not up to certain standards would undoubtedly detract from "the best propaganda for Palestine, a visit to the country,"[61] and Zionist officials in Europe, the United States, and Palestine were inspired to take action.

On a material level, the standard that many Zionists seemed to have in mind was Switzerland; they wanted facilities in Palestine to be as cheery and efficient as Alpine pensions, and thereby for Palestine to be considered a "Jewish Switzerland," or a "Swiss Corridor to Asia."[62] In 1925, Joseph Hirsch wrote in the *Jüdische Rundschau* that "on the basis of a four-week stay in Palestine," he believed that "the hotel industry in Palestine" was in need of "drastic reform and improvement." Hirsch asserted that he was not motivated by a desire to elevate the conditions in Palestine to those of other places merely for the comfort of European tourists, but that the impressions of tourists carried "great significance" in light of Zionism's attempt to win adherents and popular support. He noted a disposition among hotel proprietors that compounded the problem: they do not seem to care about the level of comfort or service, as long as they just provided clients with a room. Obviously, such an outlook would not go very far toward pleasing discriminating tourists, and worst of all, this behavior on the part of Jewish hotel-owners might discourage potential donors from giving more generously to the cause.[63]

Also writing on this theme, another correspondent for the *Rundschau* warned that Palestine was acquiring a reputation as an unpleasant destination. The guest-house and transportation problems made for numerous unsatisfactory experiences. There were still tour groups that would leave ignorant of the modernization taking place and of "the new type of Jewish man" preeminent in the Yishuv. This was not, as previously alleged, due primarily to the ill-will of the touring companies; the *Halutsim*, it seems, contributed to the shunning of the Zionist enterprise. Left to their own devices, members of the settlements were not very adept or patient at answering tourists' questions that, to them, were rather naive or repetitive. Although one should not expect the Yishuv's local leaders to regard enlightening tourists as their most crucial duty, the reporter continued that it was nevertheless unfortunate that visitors are rarely welcomed "with a joyful heart." It was desirable that Jewish tourists, in substantial numbers, should spend a few days in a collective settlement, to afford them more than a "fleeting glance" – so they could be won over to the system which counted numerous skeptics among middle-class Western Jews. While on the tour, visitors should meet the people who really know the country, and possibly see some kind of practical demonstration of the work of the *Halutsim*. Ironically, Christian visitors seemed to be treated more amicably than Jews, and there was occasional outright hostility toward non-Hebrew-speaking diaspora Jews. All of the organizational power of the movement, the writer concluded, must be focused on improving the reception of Jewish tourists in Palestine.[64]

There is little doubt that the brusque handling of eager tourists, and the repeated phenomenon of the inhabitants of Jewish settlements vanishing upon the arrival of their brethren from abroad,[65] helped to mold the programs intended to edify and cultivate the warm feelings of the next waves of Western Jewish visitors. In many of the settlements complaints were apparently acknowledged. As testimony to the rectification of such problems, Gertrude Van Tijn wrote about her experience at a Ḳibuts, where she delighted in getting to know the Ḥalutsim: "After dinner, spontaneously, somebody started to sing. Soon everybody joined in, and a few minutes later all were dancing the horrah, the Palestinian round-dance. It was an infectious, simple gaiety, coming naturally at the end of a hard day's work, without the help of alcohol or other stimulants."[66] This sort of experience, which might be characterized as "staged authenticity,"[67] became more and more typical; it represented a radical change from how Zionist tourists had been treated earlier, and the face of the Yishuv to which they were exposed. Van Tijn recalled: "I was really sorry to leave the colonies, although I felt that for the rest of my life I never wanted to look at another cow again. They are so proud of their livestock that every visitor has to spend a lot of time in the stables, just admiring cows."[68]

In the summer of 1927, Zionists in Europe and the United States learned that there was a steep rise in the number of rooms for tourists in Palestine.[69] By 1929, it was reported that there was no shortage of "simple, but perfectly middle-class hotels" available to groups.[70] The inadequacies of the Palestine hotel industry took a major step toward being overcome upon the completion of the King David Hotel in Jerusalem in December 1930. The funds for its construction were raised through the Palestine Economic Corporation, the independent development body of the Brandeis faction,[71] along with an Egyptian finance group. The 200-room hotel boasted a number of well-appointed conference rooms, salons, and space for business. It was thoroughly electrified and equipped with "the most modern kitchen" and storage space. The decor in both the public lounges and private rooms was an "oriental" style, and there were antiques from various periods and locales; the structure was modeled, nevertheless, on the most up-to-date European designs. The movement took pride that the greatest share of the £250,000 investment in the project had been raised in Palestine.[72] Although much of the movement's energy had gone toward attracting those who did not travel first-class, Jews (and Christians) who wished to be treated in grand style now had suitable lodging in Palestine.

Obviously the rooming situation was central to the Western Zionist tourists' experience. What else did the standardized visit entail, which included many characteristics that would persist for over fifty years? Upon arrival (or shortly thereafter) groups were met by a Zionist dignitary, often someone connected with a fundraising body.[73] On March 10, 1928, for instance, some 600 American tourists landed in Haifa, with 278 Jews among them. Henrietta Szold, who was then a member of the Zionist Palestine Executive, addressed the group at a banquet that evening; it is unclear if it included only the Jewish passengers, or the Christians, as well. She spoke about the extensive development of Palestine in the last decade. Szold stressed that their assistance in the Zionist effort did not constitute "an act of charity, but the fulfillment of their duty" as Jews.[74] The duty of welcoming and initiating the Jewish travelers seemed to fall upon Henrietta Szold, at least weekly, as early as 1922, and she tired of it.[75]

In addition to meeting an official with whom they might already have been familiar, at least by name, such as Henrietta Szold or Menahem Ussischkin, at several stops the tourists would be met by local officials or notables. If a known leader from abroad was with a group, this was likely to happen even in the early 1920s.[76] Indeed, a main impetus for Zionist engagement in tourism had been to show off the Jewish colonies and collective settlements that had formerly been off the beaten track. A number of such communities would be visited, with an emphasis on displaying the Jews' newfound prowess in agriculture and land reclamation. This part of the experience for many was remembered as a "romance" of the cows.[77]

Just as exemplary for displaying the human transformations wrought by the Zionist movement were its educational and cultural institutions. The Herzliya Gymnasium, Haifa Technikum, and Mikveh Israel agricultural school, and the Hebrew University, Bezalel Art Institute, and Hadassah hospital in Jerusalem (outside the walls of the Old City) were showcased as the most sparkling jewels of the new Yishuv.[78]

Sites of significance to Greco-Roman culture, Christianity, and Islam were included in Zionist-led tours. Although some recent critics have alleged that the goal of Zionism was to "possess" the treasures of other faiths,[79] the stress seemed to be on Jewry's suitability as a respectful caretaker, and a mediator between the major religions and their sects. On tours and in travel writing, it was wryly observed that Christians in particular were remiss in tending to their holy places, echoing Herman Melville's impression of the Holy Sepulcher as "A sickening cheat."[80]

Predictably, the emphasis in Zionist tours was on the evidence of Jewry's earlier incarnation as the biblical nation of Israel. Nowhere was this more striking than in the Old City of Jerusalem. The Wailing Wall, the remains of the western retaining wall around the Temple Mount in the Old City, carried the greatest symbolic significance. This was heightened after the riots of 1929, which had ostensibly broken out due to the denial of the Jews' right to pray at their holiest shrine.

Near the Wall Zionists were able to make use of British excavations which had begun in the middle of the nineteenth century. The inter-relationships of archaeology, the tourist trade, and brewing political formulas were formidable. Although Neil Silberman, Yaacov Shavit, Amos Elon, and others have reflected on the significance of archaeology in Israel (and elsewhere in the Middle East), there is hardly any discussion of archaeology's impact on Jewish consciousness outside the Yishuv or the State of Israel.[81] The claim that archaeology is inherently "neutral,"[82] from a cultural-historical perspective, is unconvincing. The European and American explorers and archaeologists had aimed to contribute to historical and religious knowledge about the Holy Land, and in so doing add to the glory of their own nations and themselves. Their labors, however, resulted in the equivalent of a goldmine for Zionist ideology, and the ongoing project of mediating the experience of travelers to Palestine. Overall, there can be little doubt that the intensification of archaeology – fomented by the advance of critical biblical studies and the termination of Ottoman restrictions and harass-ment – facilitated the rise of Zionist tourism.[83]

The British Palestine Exploration Fund had been founded in 1865; it vigorously "encouraged team efforts and sponsored a number of monumental surveys."[84] After the First World War, Britain reasserted its interest in Palestinian archaeology. Phillip King, the historian of the American Schools of Oriental Research, writes that "from the perspective of archaeology," the period between the wars was, and still is, considered "the 'golden age of Palestinian excavations.'"[85] In 1919 a Department of Antiquities was established by the mandate government, "and the British School of Archaeology in Jerusalem was the first successor of the old-established schools in Athens and Rome for the training of students and for research in countries overseas." More major excavations in Jerusalem were conducted during 1923–25.[86] The unflagging British mania for "Palestinology" was gleefully appropriated by the Zionists for touring purposes.

Predictably, in 1914 Zionists in Palestine established their own Exploration Society, which was tied to the nascent National Museum at the Bezalel Institute, under the direction of Nahum Slousch.[88] For the most part, however, the excavations initiated by the Zionist group were minuscule compared to those of the British, Germans, and Americans; they likely did not have the money for the undertaking. During this time, though, Jewish archaeologists who would later have a great impact on Zionism's backward glance, such as Nelson Glueck and Eliezer Sukenik, would receive their training.[89] They apparently learned not just the tools of the trade of archaeology in a technical sense, but its role in nation-building.[90] Noting the potential for intensified archaeology in her 1928 travel memoir, Irma Lindheim wrote that "A wealth of archaeological material lies waiting to be discovered in Palestine. I longed to dig beneath the surface to see the remnants of the civilizations buried away from our sight."[91] Later generations of Jewish tourists, particularly students, would include an archaeological dig among their "working" experiences in the State of Israel. Scratching the soil of an ancient site would carry at least the same level of Zionistic prestige as riding atop a tractor or picking fruit at an agricultural settlement.

Remnants of the enduring Jewish presence in Jerusalem, Zion itself, was the most irrepressible physical evidence propping up the movement's ideology. But Jerusalem, for all its inestimable value, was something of an enigma. The decrepit state of the Jewish Quarter, and its mostly religious inhabitants, was used to convey the message that the old Yishuv bore the ravages of years of neglect and deprivation; it was in drastic need of restoration and rejuvenation. The counter-image, to a certain extent, was represented by the new suburbs to the West of Jerusalem's Old City, accentuated by the erection of the Jewish Agency building.[92] The decay of Palestine also was counterbalanced by pointing out olive tree groves and forests planted by the Jewish National Fund.[93] Above all, however, the purest example of the new Jewish life breathed into the Yishuv was Tel Aviv.[94] The Tel Aviv/Jerusalem dichotomy would assume many forms in the history of Zionist discourse.

Important archaeological finds related to Jewish history certainly were not limited to Jerusalem, although the Old City ruins were the most spectacular. Sites that were sometimes considered by British archaeologists to be "minor excavations" were frequently "of great importance for the history of the Jewish people," and therefore prime Zionist tourist spots, such as "the ancient synagogues of Galilee" unearthed by the Deutsche Orient-Gesellschaft before the war.[95] The proximity of these ruins to the new settlements were essential in creating a composite of the new Jewish nation that stressed continuity from ancient to modern times, and assisted in endowing secular, domestic space with religious-national meanings.[96] One American visitor wrote, in a published memoir, that the beauty of Palestine was "as great (on its small scale) as Switzerland or

Colorado, as brilliant in places as Naples or Geneva, but a beauty, somehow, that is infinitely more appealing, especially in its setting of historic associations."[97] It was a great boon for a Jewish settlement to claim that it was located on or near a place where the Zionists' forebears had lived. Traipsing around on Zionist tours implied dizzying turns in time, but in a fairly circumscribed space.

In addition to the man-made features of the environment, tourists also enjoyed the natural wonders of the country, such as the Dead Sea, and the incredibly varied topography. Again, what made this notable was the existence of such a wide range of natural settings in a relatively small territory. Similar to the impact of British archaeology on Zionist tourism, the British development of Palestine's infrastructure during the mandate, such as refurbishing the port of Haifa and constructing breakwaters for the beaches of Tel Aviv, unintentionally served to make possible the ascendance of Zionist tourism.[98] Although Britain was surely looking out for its own interests, and there was substance to the claim that the mandatory power favored the Arabs over the Jews on economic questions, the fact remained that Zionists relied to no small degree on large-scale British enterprise, and that tourism in particular stood to benefit.

To be sure, those who toured Palestine under the auspices of the movement were strongly predisposed to see the country "Zionistically" due to the proliferation of images since the turn of the century. The flow of such pictures swelled during the interwar years, particularly through richly illustrated Zionist journals such as the *Pioneer* in Britain, *Young Judaean* in the United States, *Palästina-Bilder-Korrespondenz* in Central Europe, and the ubiquitous promotions of the Keren Hayesod. In Zionist periodicals and newspapers, more and more space was devoted to travel memoirs and notes from Palestine visitors. Travel to witness Zionism in action spawned a genre within Zionist literature of confessional, epistolary accounts of trips to Palestine, often in the form of juvenilia or quasi-scholarly reportage.[99]

Among the more popular Zionist books between the wars were travel memoirs by two women: *The Immortal Adventure* by Hadassah president Irma Lindheim and *A Springtide in Palestine* by Myriam Harry.[100] The advertisement for Lindheim's book stated that the author

has looked at Palestine in all its beauty and has gloried in the valiant struggle of her people for the rehabilitation of the soil of their forbears. Irma L. Lindheim has written "The Immortal Adventure" *so realistically that you will feel you are actually with her in the Holy Land.* Mrs. Lindheim takes us into every nook and corner which she herself has visited, and describes the valiant undertaking of the Zionist pioneers who are restoring the ancient tradition, culture, and life of Palestine with modern schools, hospitals, industry, and agriculture.[101]

In terms of descriptions of the place, Lindheim's *The Immortal Adventure* and Harry's *A Springtide in Palestine* are virtually interchangeable. Lindheim's book, possibly due to the general economic circumstances, only had one printing. Harry's memoir seems to have been a relative best-seller, and appeared in French and German as well as English. It recounts a young Englishwoman's trip to Palestine which results in her conversion to Judaism and enchantment with the Zionist movement. One would expect that the testimony of a convert – in this case a double conversion, to Judaism and Zionism – would be a lopsided paean to the new-found cause. Yet occasionally Harry seems to have removed her rose-colored lenses; her work is at times refreshingly nuanced. It actually raises questions about the core mythology of the movement she fervently embraces. For instance, she asks whether "Muslim fanaticism" could ever be reconciled with Zionism, and hints that the conflict was not simply over ownership of the land, but impinged on considerations of ethnicity and class.[102] Although it dispensed less saccharine than the fundraising promotions, the leadership of the Zionist movement proclaimed her novel as one of the most successful creative expressions of the interwar movement.[103] To a large extent both of these travelogues reinforced the impressions cultivated by the movement's policy-makers, except for striking an unusually empathetic tone toward Palestine's Arabs compared to the general run of Zionist travel literature.

However much there was a sincere effort on the part of some in the movement to impart an appreciation for the country and Jewish history and culture, for its own sake, Zionist authorities – with their eyes fixed on Western Jewry – continually returned to the implications for fundraising. "Improved tourism," it was widely understood, "means improved propaganda, and improved propaganda means improved fundraising."[104] "Propaganda work" which would strengthen the "financial instruments" of the movement was recognized, if not always explicitly mentioned, as one of the great benefits of tourism.[105] In a column, "American Tourists Visit Palestine" appearing in the *Hadassah News Letter*, it was reported that "several visitors were so impressed with the work of the [Hadassah] organization that they made contributions toward its support." The fifty-two individual contributors were listed with their amounts given, from $1 to $500.[106] Similar accounts appeared in numerous Zionist and general Jewish publications.

In fact, the "Zionist Information Bureau for Tourists," established in 1925, was founded under the auspices of not only the Jewish Agency, but also the Keren Hayesod and the Keren Kayemet L'Israel. This bureau issued a pamphlet, "Das jüdische Palästina," in hopes that it would replace or supplement the existing guides deemed oblivious to Zionism. It was billed as particularly shrewd in its restrained political tone and its "excellent understanding of the psychology of the tourist."[107] In 1931, though, a more extensive clearing-house type agency was suggested as a resource not only for tourists, but for those seeking information about investments, and to organize "fact-finding" missions for professionals such as teachers, engineers, doctors, archaeologists, journalists, and artists.[108]

In addition to using tourism to provide a greater incentive for people to give to the movement, fundraising was intertwined with tourism in other ways. It was quite common for tours to be conducted by officials of the Keren Kayemet or Keren Hayesod.[109] Contests were also established by which free trips to Palestine became the ultimate Zionist perquisite. Trips were usually won not by luck of the draw, but by collecting funds. In 1927, for example, twenty-five trips to Palestine were offered to Zionist youth who had been most dedicated to taking care of Jewish National Fund boxes.[110] *Propagandarbeit* and fundraising were always intimately interwoven.

Visits of notable personalities, both Jewish and non-Jewish, were frequently employed to publicize Palestine tourism. All of the various stops on journeys by Lord Balfour and Tomas Masaryk, leader of Czechoslovakia, were elaborately documented in the Zionist press.[111] The movement also considered it a minor victory when less well-known personalities, Jews and non-Jews, visited the country. There was no small pride in recognizing that seeing Palestine was worthy of people such as Dr. Emanuel Libmann, a heart specialist from New York, Sir John Russell, an agricultural chemist from Britain, Rabbi Max Heller of New Orleans, a "Zionist pioneer among the ranks of Reform Jewry," and businessman Samuel Lamport, who first came to Palestine to represent Brown University at the opening of the Hebrew University, and later returned to establish a loan society. There was no hint of irony in the reports of "visits" by famous Zionists, such as Max Brod, Martin Buber, and Albert Einstein.[112] In addition to judging the strength of the movement by the star quality of the visitors to Palestine, some in Zionism measured the well-being of diaspora Jewry by the number of tourists coming from their home nations. In other words, tourism to Palestine was perceived as a sign of Jewish vitality.[113]

Different segments of the movement, most often in political, professional, or age-based contingents, tailored tour packages to meet their specific needs.[114] As opposed to being seen as a kind of fragmentation, the movement's center generally condoned, and even applauded, such initiatives.[115] The Hadassah organization, for one, arranged tour packages for its members and their families "to see the comprehensive undertakings of Hadassah, its work in the schools, playgrounds, health centers, and hospitals."[116] Nima Alderblum wrote in the *Hadassah News Letter* that "Thomas Cook & Sons have made arrangements with me to give on board their Mediterranean Summer Cruise a course on the history of Palestine, its historic significance, and its present-day development. The itinerary in Palestine will be one that will acquaint the traveler with real Jewish life and will give him a full idea of the romance of the Zionist renaissance as well as of the historic background of the past." Consistent with Hadassah's endeavor to supply a serious educational component for young Zionists, Alderblum promised that the trip was "like sending the young folks to a Jewish university," and she backed up this claim by stating that attempts were being made for university students to obtain credits for the course. In fact, three levels would be offered, "one for adults, one for young folks, and one for children." Alderblum also informed her readers that "Hebrew-speaking clubs will be formed on board the ship so that tourists could become somewhat familiar with the language." And so that no one might think that one would have to rough it like a *Ḥaluts* for the whole trip, Alderblum noted that "Cook's cruises are well known for their comforts and luxuries." As opposed to treating Hadassah as marginal within the Zionist project, here "what Hadassah means to Palestine, to the making of Jewish history, and to the women in America" was at the very core of the trip's sensibility, as it was "permeated with the Hadassah spirit."[117] As a result of a similar trip in the winter of 1926, one woman was inspired "to remain in Palestine for six months, another for a year, and a third indefinitely." At least one woman visitor who had earlier not been particularly impressed by Hadassah decided to join upon seeing its work in Palestine.[118] Indeed, the Hadassah tours were remarkable not only in the history of Zionism and tourism, but in women's history. Although the experience of women travelers has gained the attention of historians, this episode stands apart from the journeys of individuals:[119] it is possibly one of the first international missions devised to highlight the contributions of women and a specific vision of womanhood and its potential. This may be seen in contrast to the general history of tourism and politicized travel in which anti-feminist stereotypes were more often than not propounded.[120]

Hadassah, like other factions of the movement, asserted that the "crown and climax" to its program of study was "a visit to Palestine." In 1932 it was able to report that "Travel to Palestine, today, can be accomplished with greater convenience and less expense than ever before. Nothing can so clarify one's outlook and stimulate one's interest as a vital and immediate contact with the *Yishub* [sic], no matter what the duration of one's stay." Along with highlighting its own institutions, two other features distinguish the Hadassah travel programs. Hadassah was adamant, and committed greater resources than any other touring group to their participants gaining some knowledge of Hebrew. Even more exceptional, however, was the importance it accorded to learning about the Arabs in Palestine. "While concentrating our thought upon the Jewish stake in Palestine," a Hadassah reporter urged, "we must not lose sight of the fact that in Palestine the preponderating element of the population is Arab and that surrounding Palestine, on all sides, is the great Arab world. It is imperative that we try to understand these neighbors. A course in Islamic culture and history ought to find a place in a complete and well-rounded scheme of Zionist study."[121] Although all Zionist trips included visits to the Dome of the Rock, Arab markets in Jaffa and Jerusalem, and occasionally, Arab villages, no other part of the movement devoted as much effort as did Hadassah to attempt to understand the Arab world as a viable and valuable civilization in its own right.

The left wing of the movement, Labor Zionism, also instituted its own tours, with an emphasis on participating, in some way, in the "labor" which was said to be invigorating the nation.[122] The brochure from this group proclaimed that "New forms of social existence have developed in Palestine in the course of its rebuilding," referring to the rise of *Kibutsim*, *Kevutsot*, *Moshavot* (collective farms), and various cooperatives. "The Seminar under the auspices of the League for Labor Palestine aims to acquaint its members with the new society based on self-labor. It will do more than merely 'tour' the country. The members of the Seminar will *live* the new social order as well as see it." Following the lead of the Thomas Cook Passover tour, the Labor League "Seminar" also took place over the holiday:

Almost as soon as we set foot on the soil of Palestine, we will celebrate the Passover Seder with the workers of Ain Harod. Then a week traveling through the Valley of Jezreel and through Galilee, living in workers' quarters, eating in community dining rooms, and sharing in all possible ways in the community life. The itinerary will include visits to [several] workers' settlements.

In addition to imbibing the institutions of Labor Zionism, most of the tour consisted of the typical itinerary: visits to "places rich in historic associations," such as "Safed, with its store of Hasidic traditions, the ancient synagogue at Kfar Nahum, Tiberias, the reconstructed synagogue at Beth Alpha, and other significant archaeological excavations." Other stops, among many, included the Jewish colonies Rehovoth, Rishon le Zion, and Ness Ziona; the agricultural school at Mikveh Israel; the famed Ruthenberg power station; Haifa, Old and New

Jerusalem, Jericho, and the Dead Sea; and Tel Aviv and its environs, particularly "the blossoming orange groves" and sparkling new suburbs of Herzliya, Ranana, and Kfar Saba. This trip boasted an exceptionally strong political-educational dimension, beginning on the cruise. Noted Labor Zionist leader Dr. Hayim Greenberg was to deliver several lectures on Zionism and "social movements" in Palestine, to be complemented by "lectures, informal talks, and discussions" once the members reached the country. These were arranged in conjunction with Histadrut, the union of Jewish labor federations in Palestine. "Our contacts," it was promised, "will not be those of sightseeing tourists; they will be warm, personal, human."[123] Indeed, the pledge to provide more of a human connection than the average foreign tour, combined with the opportunity to participate in the building of the society and sharing in the lives of its common people, became part of the stock in trade of Zionist touring to Palestine in general.

Along with the sponsorship of tours from the center of the Zionist Organization and by different factions, one of the consequences of the Zionists' efforts was the packaging of entire trips from "a Jewish point of view." These typically included a strong dose of Zionism. Often they were geared for teenagers or young adults, with the added attraction of making acquaintances with those from one's own social background.[124] Although the trend had been to make the journey more economically inclusive, here the incentive was exclusivity. Trips to Palestine could be part of the dating and mating conventions for Jewish young people which were less overt than other holiday trips, usually with one's parents, but essentially served the same function.[125] At any rate, a trip to Palestine became for many youth not only a Zionist, but a secular Jewish rite of passage.[126]

Prior to World War I, Zionism might or might not have made much of an impact on tourists to Palestine. Even those who were in search of a Zionist experience sometimes "would pass by the throbbing life of Palestine, unable to find its pulse."[127] In many respects comparable to the "conquest of the [diaspora] communities" achieved by the movement, Zionism also persevered in strongly influencing, if not over-whelming, the character of Jewish tourism to Palestine. The movement deemed it vital to its interest to combat the "threat of meaninglessness" and possibility of "disenchantment" for Jewish tourists making the journey.[128] The goal was for Jewish tourists to fall in love with the country, and to see Jewish sovereignty in Palestine as the preeminent means by which Jewry might obtain justice. "One cannot but love this land," an American rabbi wrote in 1927; "it has been martyred, as the age-old victim of war and barbarism; it will yet be maltreated, it is to be feared, for a long time; but the day must come when it will shine out, not only to the eye that loves beauty, to the soul that reveres holiness, but also to the heart which responds to the call of justice."[129] By the end of the 1920s, it would have been virtually unthinkable for a Jewish traveler to miss the "pulse" of Zionism in the country; indeed, the rhythm of the trip was likely to be dominated by Zionism – from inception to follow-up. Pictures of steam-ships bound for Palestine became a part of the archive of Zionist images (figure 38). In 1932, it was said that even the intense summer heat no longer dissuaded the surge of Zionist-inspired, Jewish tourists, and commentators were amazed by how many Americans made the journey.[130] However they might have *shvitzed*, their enthusiasm did not abate.[131]

Travel to Palestine became integral to inscribing "a moving, living picture" of Zionism in the mind of Western Jewry.[132] More of an effort, to be sure, might have been made to coordinate the films produced about the country with tour promotions, and certainly the institutions that existed could have been further coordinated and consolidated – to make Palestine "the focal point of all Zionist propaganda."[133] Nevertheless, tourism mushroomed, and after the early 1920s tourists were intention-ally intermingled with settlers as those who had "made *'Aliyah*," giving their act, as well, a cosmic significance.[134] No matter what the term, however, the movement would labor hard to assure that Jewish tourism to Palestine transcended the typical journey, to see that the mystique of Jewish national regeneration was indelibly imbued.[135] This sentiment permeates numerous promotions, which combine many layers of Jewish religious and national associations. For example, the following advertisement appeared in a British Zionist magazine:

> The Jewish New Year is coming!
> Make your resolution now.
> You must visit Palestine this year.
> The historical monuments are attractive.
> The religious places are fascinating.
> The sunny weather is very healthy.
> The Zionist achievements are wonderful.
> The modern improvements are amazing.
> The trading possibilities are increasing.
> The plantations and Industries are developing.
> Buildings and settlements are improving.
> The Glory of the Past and the Hope of the Future are calling you![136]

One of the most striking features of this terse advertisement is its imperative: "You must visit Palestine this year," which echoed the calls for all Jews to give money to the cause, along with the well-known

38 Postcard, "A steamship on the way to Palestine, commemorating the trip following the Fourteenth Zionist Congress (Vienna, 1925)," D.D.a, 2/1/1/14, Central Zionist Archives, Jerusalem.

injunction at the Passover seder "Next year in Jerusalem." As Zionists were told they must take part in the "conquest" of the soil of Palestine through facilitating the purchase of land and support of agricultural settlement, Zionists were not told that they should see that country, but that they must see it. As such it transcended any other "culturally induced need" related to vacationing.[137]

For years Zionist officials sought control over travel and tourism to Palestine, to make sure that visitors came in large numbers, had a comfortable stay, and saw things from a perspective that was favorable to the movement. Hence, the travelers would tell their friends and family about their wonderful experience and write a hefty check to the Zionist Organization.[138] In this time, the seeds were sown for one of the movement's great hopes and expectations – that the land, through the assistance of a well-developed, Zionist tourist industry, would become the center of world Jewish solidarity.[139] It was crucial that a Zionized view of Palestine embody "the fusion of past and present,"[140] integrated into Western Jewish consciousness as a place "not simply back there, in a separate and foreign country." It was to be assimilated into themselves, "and resurrected into an ever-changing present."[141]

Between the wars Zionism fabricated "touristic images" of Palestine which were "mobilized and modified in guided tours of the country." Thereby the "place" that tourists saw was not simply a real-life visage of their expectations, "or a real terrain, but the result of a dialogue between tourists and those persons and institutions which mediate between the tourist gaze and its object."[142] It is conceivable that one could view the Zionists' deliberate mediation of the Jewish experience in Palestine as manipulation, or worse, exploitation. But that would misrepresent their deep-seated quest for, and sincere belief in, the authenticity of their claims. This was, in the Zionist imagination, one of the chief means of national liberation for the Jews: they had to be able to see their potential as a people and a nation, quite literally, before their eyes – preferably in the best possible light, as a blossoming flower – in order to perceive themselves as fully human. It was not sufficient to view it from afar; they had to touch down on the ancestral soil of Palestine. The notion of migration, if only temporary, became a functional and symbolic motif of Western Zionism, which offered to many a kind of spiritual liberation and promise of ultimate fulfillment. It was, after all, a reformulation of a central myth of Judaism – exile, return, redemption – that so many non-Jewish peoples had internalized as their own heritage.[143] Zionists in the 1920s constructed an unprecedented, palpable Jewish public space in which Jews could experience their own people as an autonomous, thriving nation. This vision both mirrored and scraped against the reigning spirit of the age. The growing construct engendered by Zionist tourism nudged Palestine, as a modern Jewish home, toward the center of Western Jewish identity – while making it possible to remain a Zionist outside Zion for most of one's life.

7   Idealism, realism, and sociability in Western Zionist youth organizations

> At that time [around World War I] they used to say that, to marry off a daughter, let her join the Zionist organization.   Gertrude Van Tijn[1]

Almost by definition, youth implies vitality and optimism. Not surprisingly, nearly every organized cohort of Zionist youth in the West, from 1914 to 1933, issued remarkably similar, high-sounding pronouncements. They boasted of nurturing communities of youth in the throes of invigorating the Jewish nation, which would figuratively, if not literally, carry Israel on its shoulders toward a jubilant Zionist victory. This was heartily seconded in mainstream Zionist organs and meetings.[2] But the youth's oratory and programmatic statements, and the loquacious appraisals of its efforts, are sharply at odds with the stagnant character of the interwar Zionist movement outside Palestine and Eastern Europe.[3] If youth and student organizations were so vital, why were they not more effective in attracting a wider spectrum of Jewish youth? If Zionist youth organizations were, in fact, a wellspring of fresh thinking, why were they not more successful in infiltrating the mainstream bodies with their ideas and examples of their work? Why, with the possible exception of the German groups, were "the great issues of the time" so muted in the debates of Zionist students and youth?[4] What functions, then, did such organizations serve? What is the significance of the experience of their membership in the context of the formation of the Zionist project?

It is a long-held contention that for a modern nationalist or socialist movement to flourish, it must appeal to youth, and that a strong youth wing is necessary for sustaining an ostensibly mass-based political and social movement. Certainly the interwar European parties on the extreme left and right owed a great deal to ideologically motivated youth. Germany, above all, is recognized for the "youthfulness of the National Socialist movement and the widespread support it attracted before and after 1933 from young Germans."[5] To a lesser extent, youth and student organizations, particularly the Boy Scouts and Girl Guides, were important in Britain.[6] In the United States, organizations specifically geared for youth were not as significant as their European counterparts, no doubt owing to the diversity of the population and the relative non-politicization of its youth. Nevertheless, the YMCA and the Boy Scouts of America exerted a noteworthy influence on boys in the United States.[7] No matter what the country, however, Western Zionists maintained that it was crucial to mobilize youth in order to attain, or even strive toward, the aims of the movement.

In Zionist historiography and popular literature, the uniqueness of each nation's youth wing, corresponding to the self-proclaimed uniqueness of the national organizations, has been taken for granted. To be sure, the efforts to coordinate the Zionist youth movements worldwide were accompanied by colorful demonstrations but had little practical effect.[8] It is fruitful, however, to examine Zionist youth from Western Europe and the United States together, not merely for the purpose of contrast, but to illuminate aspects of commonalty and consensus. To their credit, Stephen Poppel, Moshe Zimmerman, and Hagit Lavsky have modified the earlier view of interwar German Zionism as single-minded preparation for *'Aliyah*.[9] Yet an even stronger case may be made concerning the extent to which Zionism in Germany and other Western countries was adjusted, in similar ways, for young people who would not make Palestine their actual home.[10] Therefore, while differences will be illuminated, I will concentrate here on the parallels between the German, American, and British youth movements that typically have not been acknowledged. Although the youth wings in each of these national settings professed the primacy of their Zionist nationalism, they were fundamentally wedded to their national contexts – a fact to which they were usually oblivious. The chief factors which unite them are that Zionism supplied a social center, a set of symbols and external trappings, and the opportunity for attaining Jewish cultural knowledge. Without question there existed a discourse of personal transformation for organized youth and students in Zionism. The movement endowed them with a strategy for building a subculture, and a means of alternative identity formation within the general societies of which they were a part. But for the most part the Zionist youth groups became a vehicle of further refining a pattern of assimilation which for all intents and purposes gave one a supplemental, but not a substitute, nationality. Until the cataclysmic events of 1933, the nationality that Western Zionists were born into was something akin to a gravitational force that pulled them back, or would not allow them to retreat from the spot on earth where they were born and raised.

It is difficult to determine precisely the organizational genealogy of

Zionist youth and student groups. Germany, as the youth movement nation par excellence, is a reasonable starting point, because the Zionist youth organizations there were comparatively autonomous, vocal, and noticed within Zionist affairs.[11] Several points of reference are pertinent in the German cultural context: the Burschenschaften (national-minded university student societies originating in the early nineteenth century), Wandervogel (free-spirited "youth among themselves," professing a rejection of politics and the bourgeois world of their parents), Bünde (the more self-consciously organized, politicized extension of the Wandervogel), Pfadfinder (scouts), Turnvereine (nationalist-oriented gymnastic and sport societies), Artamanen (agriculturally based youth settlements, for colonizing purposes), and the confessional youth groups. Further complicating the picture, Moshe Zimmerman and Marsha Rozenblit have shown that "the movements which paved the way to a national Jewish student movement" before the First World War "had their roots in Austria and not in Germany."[12] Outside the German cultural realm, in certain respects groups emphasizing character formation, as exemplified by the Boy Scouts and the YMCA, are also comparable to Zionist groups. Nevertheless, a strict, mutually exclusive description of each of these categories in the case of Jewish and other national and religious youth is problematic, because most of them aspired to a totality.[13] They shared the principal aim of influencing their members' complete way of life, so virtually nothing was untouched.

In the late nineteenth century, the initial stage of the history of the Jewish youth movements witnessed "the emergence of several groups independent of adult control and strongly impressed by the example of the Wandervogel." The largest organization in 1913 was the Verband der jüdischen Jugendvereine Deutschlands (VJJVD, Association of Jewish Youth Societies of Germany), which counted 14,500 members and at least 113 affiliated groups, operating under the auspices of B'nai B'rith. Although it had no formal political orientation, "the VJJVD possessed a powerful liberal and humanitarian flavour" and was non-Zionist before 1914.[14] Later, the VJJVD was surpassed in popularity by Kameraden, sponsored by the Centralverein deutscher Staatsbürger jüdischer Glaubens (Central Organization of German Citizens of the Jewish Confession);[15] the support of this group was part of a broader strategy employed by the Centralverein to thwart the efforts of their chief rivals, the Zionists.

The Blau-Weiss, Bund für jüdisches Jugendwandern (Blue-White, League for Jewish Youth Excursions) emerged as the dominant group in the Zionist camp by 1914, with a membership approaching 900. "Like the Wandervogel," the Blau-Weiss renounced "bourgeois society and its stiff conventions as well as urban civilisation and materialism. Other ideas and outer forms were also eagerly adopted from the independent German youth movement." The Blau-Weiss, however, had a dimension not shared by its German, and German-Jewish non-Zionist counterparts. It professed to reject the "assimilationist" stance of the older Jewish generation. As opposed to the world of their parents in which rationality and the rule of law were great beacons, the young people of Blau-Weiss "sought a new set of spiritual and cultural values" which were not traditionally religious, but a secularized and romanticized reformulation of *Judentum*. The philosopher Martin Buber was one of the ideological mentors of the movement.[16] Their parents' lives, according to the Blau-Weiss youth, comprised "another world."[17] Although Blau-Weiss claimed to have "found the answer to the problematical German–Jewish duality," replacing it with an affirmative Judaism,[18] this clear "answer" was not easily realized. It seems that Germanness (*Deutschtum*) could never be exorcised from Blau-Weiss, even when it was transplanted to the soil of Palestine.

The focus of Blau-Weiss activity was one-day-a-week or weekend excursions, by Jewish youth, into the German woods. Like the non-Jewish wandering youth, the Blau-Weiss emphasized singing as a means of expressing group solidarity, and collective and individual "spiritual renewal."[19] Although the members were encouraged to sing, even if just to pass the time as they hiked, they also were instructed that singing was not appropriate all the time, that not every song has the same cadence as a march, and that singing is not always enhanced by many voices. Singing had an aesthetic value which had to be learned as well as felt. "Loud singing," they were admonished, "is not always beautiful singing." In a romantic reaction against their perception that Judaism exalted the intellect above emotion, the Blau-Weiss songbook instructed its members that "feeling is everything. Only those who are sensitive to the essence of each song, the springtime rejoicing of hiking youth as well as the defiant song of our hopeful people, really knows how to sing."[20] The "defiant song" most likely is an allusion to the unofficial Zionist anthem, "Ha-Tikvah" ("The Hope"), which routinely closed Zionist gatherings.[21] Included in the Blau-Weiss *Liederbuch* were "songs of freedom," "Jewish folksongs," "general songs," and "restful songs." One student recalled that "the marching rhythms we sang on our hikes were interspersed . . . with sad and soulful Yiddish tunes and the early, exciting melodies of the Chaluzim."[22] Apparently there was not a firmly enforced boundary between *Yiddishkeit* and Zionism. Through learning the prescribed songs, and by imbibing the proper spirit, the Jewish "hiking youth" of the entire world were supposed to gain a consciousness of belonging to the rejuvenated Jewish nation.[23] The intensity of the songbook's nationalism is moderate; there are no direct references to weapons, enemies, or borders. Hebrew melodies are in the minority, mixed with a number of songs that were part of the repertoire of non-Jewish groups. The German versions of the Hebrew songs would be shared with Zionist youth in Britain, the United States, and other countries.[24] In some instances the "Jewish" songs were German national songs with Central European geography replaced with references to Palestine, or the "Jewish" songs were sung to familiar German tunes. Blau-Weiss leaders were also expected to possess the Wandervogel and Zupfgeigenhansl (guitar) songbooks. Beer-hall songs and modern operetta melodies were strictly forbidden.[25] Overall the cultural backdrop was unmistakably German.[26]

Along with the *Liederbuch*, a central text of Blau-Weiss was its guide-book for group leaders, the *Blau-Weiss Führer*. Not only is the German youth origin and atmosphere apparent in this guide; it is also clear that to no small extent, the Blau-Weiss internalized a segment of the anti-Semitic stereotypes concerning the degenerate state of Jewry. The opening manifesto reads:

> More urgently than German-Christian youth, our Jewish boys and girls need to obtain the physical and spiritual blessings of hiking in the open. Jewish youth on the whole is less physically fit and more nervous than other young people. A relatively greater number suffer from the pernicious influence of big-city life. Growing up in a milieu of materialism, among skeptical, ironic, and joyless people who are alienated from nature, in an atmosphere of the Jewish joke and Jewish ridicule, our boys and girls are a generation whose view of life has already been spoiled in their parents' home.

Although there is obviously a stronger sense of Jewishness in orthodox homes, "the orthodox parents have no understanding of the demands for bodily hygiene and a physical culture." Allegedly owing to the shameful Jewish past, but stemming more from anti-orthodox and *Ostjüdische* (Eastern Jewish) prejudices held by the more acculturated German Jews,[27] the orthodox were said not to honor the physicality the Blau-Weiss held so dear and lacked "an actual connection to nature."[28]

The notion of communing with nature is in large part a reiteration of the Wandervogel creed. The "natural" surroundings into which the youth is supposed to find peace and its "idealistic view of life" during its hikes and campouts is implicitly acknowledged as the German country-side. Although the ultimate goal, or the mythological aim, of the movement for all its adherents is settlement in Palestine, preparing for one's life in the ancestral and embryonic homeland does not preclude finding oneself in the German wood.[29] As compared to the "decadent" pursuits of assimilated Jews who were not part of their group, who observe the Ḥanukah holiday with "theater skits, raffles, dancing, and lame jokes," the Berlin Blau-Weiss is said to offer a striking contrast: they assemble on a hillside near Potsdam and make a bonfire, reviving the ancient Palestinian tradition of notifying distant communities of the onset of the New Moon. The central symbol, the menorah of this group, is nature.[30] One need not be in Palestine "to imbibe a new, happy, natural and honest view of life measured by what is beautiful and good, not by the standards of expediency and advantage," wrote one leader.[31] Included in the idea of achieving a "natural" state is abstention from smoking cigarettes and drinking alcohol.[32] After the influence of Blau-Weiss faded, a Jewish scout group would learn that one did not have to make a pilgrimage to Palestine in order to discover Jews in their "natural state"; with no small amount of nostalgia and romanticization, the Jüdischer Pfadfinder reported at length on their excursion to Kaunas (Lithuania). Similar to the feelings often aroused when Western Jews visited Palestine, the scouts from Königsberg (now Kaliningrad) were thrilled to see that Jews were engaged in all aspects of labor, and especially proud that a large portion of a courageous fire brigade was comprised of local Ha-Shomer ha-tsaʻir (Young Guards, a Zionist youth faction).[33] In extreme situations, it was not inconceivable that one could be involved in redemptive physical labor, and even a heroic Zionist outside the Holy Land.

The second major ingredient of Jewish youth's attempted revitalization in Blau-Weiss was shared in varying degrees with non-Zionist Jewish groups: it was imperative to cultivate joy and love though gaining a sense of one's Jewishness. Here the Zionists reflected the aims of the confessional organizations, especially groups such as the "Catholic Quickborn" and Protestant "Bibelkreise" (Bible Circle) that appropriated selected Wandervogel ideals.[34] The freedom the Blau-Weiss sought is described as a particularly Jewish freedom. For the young Jews' connectedness to nature to be enacted, a love of Jewry is essential. "A Jew without this love is hostile to nature, an uprooted creature." Each member "must be proud and happy when he thinks: I am a Jew"; he or she must "cultivate a consciousness of their Jewishness and answer the 'Heil' greeting of the Wandervogel with a 'Shalom.' It must be self-evident for him to demand that Jewish songs be sung, and to be on guard against anti-Semitism."[35] In addition to using the Hebrew greeting "Shalom" on the path and street, when one sits down to a meal, the German salutation "Mahlzeit" should be replaced with "Be-te'avon!"[36] Jewish self-consciousness and solidarity also was to be deepened through familiarity with Palestine, Jewish stories, literature, history, and the

Hebrew language. When playing games, one should attempt to infuse some "Jewish content." The singular route to a normal, Jewish national existence is through Zionism.[37] What was "Zionist" about their group's identity, however, was prone to characterization as a mere adornment, as articulated in Gershom Scholem's well-known critique of the movement.[38]

As opposed to other confessional groups, there was less debate in the Blau-Weiss about sex segregation. The Blau-Weiss leaders, at least in their official manual, were instructed that girls had a rightful place in the movement. This integration was to combat the supposed "unidealistic superficiality" to which so many Jewish girls were exposed, and allow them to live a more "harmonious" life.[39] There is no question, however, that the boys predominated. After the demise of Blau-Weiss, however, there was at least one attempt to create an organization exclusively for German Zionist girls.[40] On the more general question of organization, the independent model of the Wandervogel was praised, in comparison to that of the Pfadfinderbewegung (scout movement) or a more military-type leadership, although they later did adopt a militaristic tone, if not leadership style.[41] Like all such organizations, a uniform was required.[42] Even though the Blau-Weiss did not have the hard edge of militant nationalism found in many non-Jewish German groups, neither was it as self-consciously pacifistic as the Boy Scouts of America, who styled themselves as "peace scouts."[43]

The institutional mythology favored the notion that the Blau-Weiss was a body of "youth among itself," accepting neither orders nor directions from above. Although their ideology was prominently Zionist, the organization wished to avoid being treated as "an instrument" within a greater political scheme, and to have the youth seen as ends in themselves.[44] The desire for detachment from internecine Zionist politics is a characteristic which connects all of the youth bodies in the Western nations. Still, there was a tacit understanding that some elders would have to be engaged in the work of the group. "The most suitable are older Blau-Weisse, KJV-ers . . . and cultured (*gebildete*) business-men from the Herzl clubs or gymnastic societies (Turnvereine)." It was assumed that they would be "mature Zionists, with humane qualities, who take pleasure in hiking, with high educational qualifications. They must be well versed in and able to teach map-reading, camp-cooking, and other such skills." It was "extremely desirable" that the leaders have "musical ability."[45]

A substantial portion of the Blau-Weiss who were determined to become *Ḥalutsim* did indeed move their *Kommsitz* (campfire) to Palestine. In 1918, and more emphatically in 1922,[46] Blau-Weiss proclaimed that it would concentrate its efforts exclusively on establishing its own settlements in Palestine, which caused a few leaders to withdraw.[47] Vocational training centers were established to prepare members for careers in agriculture and crafts for their future lives in Palestine.[48] No doubt this scraped against the grain of the elite education in which most of them were engaged and was an upsetting departure from their lives in Germany. Certainly the former Blau-Weissers believed that the transition from will to reality would not exact such a high price, and that the community they elected to join would share their boundless idealism. Rather than an unconditional, warm welcome, many among the German youth felt a palpable alienation or rejection in the Yishuv.[49] Even on the organizational level, Blau-Weiss and Ha-Shomer ha-tsa'ir could not agree on a way of working together.[50] Most of the emigrants to Palestine returned after a year or two to Germany, due to the many-layered hardships of life in the Yishuv, such as the "terrible food and primitive conditions."[51] The focal point of Jewish settlement for German Jews, before their more substantial emigration beginning in 1934, was Givat Brenner, which numbered slightly over 200 members in January 1933.[52]

The problems in actually settling their members in Palestine did not lead the Blau-Weiss and others to give up on Zionism. Predictably, the unique contributions of the few German Jews to the Yishuv were stressed, as much as it was acknowledged that they were having difficulty assimilating.[53] In 1925 it was reported that Blau-Weiss was moribund, although there are references to it as a viable force until at least 1928. The group claimed to have evolved into Hamischmar ("The Watch"), which was a self-proclaimed "utopian" organization dedicated to building a "society of experts" to facilitate the dissemination of scouting-type techniques in Germany. It would also defend against anti-Semitism, and contribute toward long-range preparation for 'Aliyah. As opposed to the earlier clamor for settling Palestine, the importance of living in Erets Israel was left vague or subdued. For example, in the "geology" chapter of the Hamischmar handbook, the members were instructed to be conversant in general geological principles, and the specific features of Germany and France as well as Palestine.[54] Other groups, however, had appropriated much of the Blau-Weiss program, or at least the rhetoric of Palestino-centrism. Such groups included the Jung-jüdischer Wanderbund; Kadimah, Ring jüdischer Wanderbund Pfadfinderbünde (Kadimah, Jewish Hiking Groups' and Scouts Circle);[55] Zofim (Scouts); Berit ha-'olim (Covenant of the Olim, the immigrants to the Land of Israel);[56] and Ha-Po'el ha-tsa'ir (Young Workers). The last two groups attempted to merge radical political formulas with Zionism;[57] a substantial share of their recruits came from more recent East European Jewish immigrants to Germany, not the largely middle-class milieu of the Blau-Weiss.

Early in the interwar years the Zionist university students in Germany attempted to tap into the vitality of Blau-Weiss; many of them had helped in the founding of Blau-Weiss in the first place. The older students sought to formalize their relationship with the Zionist youth organizations, which was known in the student's jargon as "Fusion."[58] One reason why this proved fitful was because the Blau-Weiss perceived itself as the most committed to immigration to Palestine, while the others ostensibly espoused a diluted Zionism. Among the university men, there were occasionally charges that the Blau-Weiss leaders were "dogmatic" or immature,[59] and this was countered by Blau-Weiss accusations that the university men, even the Zionists, were captive to a ghetto mentality.[60] "Strictly speaking," a student wrote in 1925, the effort at Fusion was futile, because the union of Zionist university clubs did not constitute a Jugendbewegung (youth movement) in "the German spirit of the word" like the Blau-Weiss.[61]

The Zionist university students' groups grew out of the Kartell-Convent der Verbindungen deutscher Studenten jüdischen Glaubens, or KC (Union of German Students of the Jewish Faith), which was founded in Breslau in 1896. The KC had been established as a response to anti-Semitism in German student associations; Jehuda Reinharz writes that

its substantive Jewish identification was very vague. The KC's adherence to *Judentum* was more an adherence out of spite against the anti-Semites (*Trotz-judentum*) than out of a deep conviction of the value of the Jewish tradition. On the other hand, the KC's attitude toward *Deutschtum* was clearly defined; it stipulated that German Jews should seek complete acculturation into the German *volk* [sic]. It was simply adhering to the ideology professed by most German Jews.[62]

For the most part, the Jewish student associations were parallel institutions to the German groups from which they were excluded.[63] They imitated the non-Jewish student societies in holding "weekly drinking parties (*Kneipen*)"[64] and "in assertions of patriotism, in dress [and] manners." Furthermore, the Jews "attempted to establish their equality by outdrinking and outfighting" the non-Jews. The proof of *Satis-faktionsfähigkeit*, the evaluation of a Jew as a worthy opponent in a fencing duel (*Mensur*), was deemed a great achievement.[65] "The members were grouped hierarchically into *Fuxen* (freshman), *Bursche* (fully fledged members), and *Alte Herren* (old members who had left the university)."[66]

Mirroring developments in the Jewish organizational world at large, at the University of Berlin, a Zionist-dominated group, the Verein jüdischer Studenten (VJSt), was formed around 1895. It later merged with like-minded groups from Breslau, Munich, Freiburg, Marburg, Königsberg, and Strasbourg, forming the Bund jüdischer Corporationen (BJC) in 1900.[67] Other significant Zionist associations emerged as the Kartell zionistischer Verbindungen (KZV) (1906), and all of these were later amalgamated as the KJV in 1914, which claimed in its founding program to work toward "educating its members to strive for the national unity of the Jewish community and its renewal in Erets Israel."[68] Often the members of these groups intermingled, although their respective "alumni were organized in separate organizations."[69] In 1918 it was estimated that overall there were some 1,000 members of the Jewish nationalist student fraternities, and another 2,000 in Turnvereine (gymnastics clubs);[70] their numbers remained constant until 1933.

Although it is true that after the First World War the Zionist orientation "dominated" the KJV, it is misleading to generalize that "the remnants of the German students' habits were abolished and were replaced by Halutsiyut, whose aims were settling in Palestine and studying Hebrew."[71] One of the prominent aspects of the youth movement and previous organizations which remained ever present was the concern, if not mania, for physical development and sports.[72] Results of sporting events and notices of upcoming boxing tournaments, rowing races, and gymnastic exhibitions continued to fill the back pages of their journals in the interwar years, and reports of superior performances and club victories were counted among the "news" stories, as they were in non-Zionist groups.

From the outside, the BJC, KZV, and KJV seemed to be little more than imitations of the non-Jewish associations, or slight modifications of the KC model. But the members themselves attached great significance to the symbols they adopted, which they believed set them apart. Kurt Blumenfeld recalled a non-Jewish student's remark "that the real contribution of the Jews to German culture" in the realm of fraternity life "lay in their invention of the small glass of beer."[73] The Zionists' insignias and flags featured the colors blue and white – the official Zionist colors – as well as yellow, to symbolize an inversion of the medieval badge of shame into a mark of pride.[74] Yet the connection to Judaism and Zionism did penetrate, for most participants, more deeply than the colors one wore, or fighting for one's manly pride as a Zionist national Jew. The student groups were self-styled Erziehungsbünde (educational societies) as well as fraternal orders.[75] Despite a torrent of internal criticism of the instruction as either superficial or not well

enough coordinated,[76] they installed a curriculum with few equals in
the Western Zionist world. The students' reading list included, under the
heading of "literature on the question of nationalism," Jacob Burkhardt's
Kultur der Renaissance, Max Weber's *Politische Schriften*, and Friedrich
Meinecke's *Weltbürgertum und Nationalstaat*; on "the reason of state"
they were to discuss, among others, the works of Eduard Bernstein, Hans
Kohn, Tomas Masaryk, and Mahatma Gandhi.[77] It was noted that for
students whose regular course of study was in natural science, it was
particularly difficult to keep up with the regimen.[78] Probably the nearest
rival of the German students' curriculum, in terms of depth, was the
educational program developed by Hadassah.[79] Learning the Hebrew
language posed a particularly vexing problem, with the quality of
teaching and student commitment very uneven; one critic denounced the
state of Hebrew education in the KJV as in "complete anarchy."[80] Seen
as a whole, program designs were quite didactic and fitted to a Zionist
Weltanschauung; nevertheless, there were serious attempts to wrestle
with complicated issues, such as the diverse factors which account for the
textual tradition of the Middle Ages, and distinguished scholars often
taught courses. Furthermore, attention was paid to training students
according to the ideal of *Bildung*, of educating oneself as a part of an
ongoing process – not to provide simple answers.[81] In addition, there
were frequent, intelligent discussions of cultural-religious issues in
the pages of student journals, such as "Der Prophetismus als
Kulturgeschichtliches Problem" ("Prophetism as a Cultural-Historical
Problem"), submitted from the field during the First World War.[82]

One of the questions raised most often by the German university
student organizations was: to what extent should alumni of the
fraternities, the *Alte Herren*, be integrated, or even thought of, as a living
element of the Zionist youth contingent? One group of *Alte Herren* sought
to formalize their rejection of the Palestino-centrism of the KJV, and
renamed themselves the Bund zionistischer Korporationen in 1920;
there were affiliated groups in Berlin, Breslau, and Frankfurt. Although
the historiography of German Zionism tends to ignore them or see them
as somehow outside the fold,[83] it is important to remember that this
association perceived itself as Zionist, with a more authentic type of
Zionism than their brethren.[84] Eventually, the BZK would rejoin the KJV
in 1929, after a long period of general lack of enthusiasm for the Zionist
cause.[85]

A reason why the apparent aloofness of the *Alte Herren* might have
been so troubling to the students was that they were faced with a
discomforting vision: their predecessors in the fraternal ranks did not
turn out so differently from their parents.[86] There was also a convenient

myth circulating that if only the *Alte Herren* were more active, the whole
movement could be energized.[87] One student characterized this belief as
akin to the story of Sleeping Beauty (Dornröschenschlaf); but even if the
Old Boys were roused from slumber, they could not be the movement's
saviors. Predictably, there were some who denounced any official
affiliation of the alumni as a useless appendage, if not an embarrassment
to the rest of organized Zionist youth due to their "superficial interest"
in Zionism.[88] One commentator wrote that there had been great hopes
pinned on the university men in their student years; now that they had
reached maturity, what did they represent?:

Now this Jewish society exists; hundreds of *Alte Herren*, who for the most part
have married and established families, and raised them; now it is time for an
accounting of what it looks like. This society is no worse than any other Jewish
group in Berlin, in Frankfurt, Breslau, or elsewhere. They are certainly somewhat
better than some, and there are worthy men among them.

The question to be asked, which this writer answers in the affirmative, is:
do these men constitute a fundamental component for creating "a better
Jewish people," to insure that our totality "is not a facade, but a reliable
bridge to the Jewish future?" If one is to judge them, should one not
investigate their family lives, to see what kind of "humanistic and Jewish
values" they are cultivating in their children? Are their sons aware that
they are obliged to help in the building of the Jewish people in Erets
Israel? The conclusion is that if this is so, then there is no reason to
belittle the *Alte Herren*.[89] Indeed, there is almost a feeling of desperation
on the part of the students beseeching their older *Bundenbrüder* to
reaffirm their fealty to the group.[90]

The unstated implication is that the *Alte Herren* are living fruitful,
useful, Zionist lives in their German homes. Obviously they had been
inducted into a fraternal order, as opposed to an emigration-preparation
society, and many members would no doubt feel themselves responsible
and loyal well beyond their university years.[91] It was not, by any
stretch of the imagination, a complete way of life. Before 1933, the
disappointing failure of the Blau-Weiss settlements indicated to many of
the older students that impetuously uprooting oneself to stake a claim in
Palestine was inadvisable, and for the meantime, they should work to
resuscitate the Zionist youth movement in Germany.[92] "We must look
the facts square in the eye," wrote one KJV member in 1927, "and see
that the greatest portion of the current generation remains in the *Galut*,
and it is with this world that they are concerned. This is where they earn
a living and find their way, and thinking about Zionism, and Zionist
work" are secondary considerations.[93]

Although there is little doubt that the student societies in Germany had an identity distinct from the adults in the national federation, the extent to which the students' organizational life mirrored their elders should not be minimized. For instance, after the establishment of the Keren Hayesod in 1921, more and more student effort for the Zionist cause was devoted to fundraising, and there is no evidence of resistance to the idea that collecting money for the Keren Hayesod "must, among all KJVers, be the central task of their Zionist work."[94] In addition to involvement in fundraising, one of the preoccupations of university students as well as their elders was figuring out "how to achieve a synthesis between a profession and Zionism." One of the few concrete scenarios the students could envisage was that out of their ranks would arise a group of doctors, which would prove crucial in winning the respect and friendship of Palestine's Arabs at some point in the distant future.[95] This was consistent with the student organization's vaguely expressed sympathies for Jewish–Arab cooperation, even in the wake of the riots of 1929,[96] and indifference toward the Revisionist party despite the appeals of Richard Lichtheim.[97]

At the opposite end of the spectrum from the German university students, with regard to immersion in Zionist learning and affairs, were not, as one might think, the Americans, but the British.[98] Nevertheless, there are a number of common characteristics between Zionist youth in Germany and Britain. Like the German students, the British numbers were slight: in 1930, the University Zionist Federation of Great Britain recorded 384 dues-paying members.[99] In part their connection to the larger Zionist structures was maintained through contact with the fundraising instruments. A survey of the activities of British Zionist youth reveals that a great deal of their organizational zeal and energy was directed toward fundraising for the KKL and after 1921, the Keren Hayesod. The pressure to participate in the collection of funds was so intense that it actually elicited a backlash.[100] There was a tendency for student leaders to become "obsessed" with fundraising, and such "one-sidedness" was said to "detract from their own usefulness."[101] Numerous lectures and other events were held under the auspices of the KKL or KH, either for the express purpose of raising money, or for "education" about the work of the funds.[102]

Although the young British Zionists might not have approached the topic so scientifically, and as of 1932 had not produced a "badly needed" songbook of their own, the British youth also counted singing among their most important activities. The fact that the various youth groups were literally singing the same tunes, and that this held such a central place in their organizational life, should not be trivialized.[103] Organized sports, with the exception of the face-scarring *Mensur*, were also assumed to be integral to any program of *Tarbut*, or Hebrew culture.[104] Nature, too, was not forgotten. But as opposed to weekly outings, the "summer camp" or "summer school" experience was supposed to be a particularly intense period of one to two weeks when frolicking in nature was deliberately woven into one's social and educational program.[105]

Moreover, like the Germans, British youth made numerous speeches and published scores of articles about the importance of modern Hebrew. Although a few British students became dedicated Hebraists, such fervor was not widespread. In contrast to the anguish some German students expressed about their lack of progress in learning Hebrew, in 1932 the University Zionist Federation of Great Britain and Ireland boasted that "It has now become a definite part of the Federation policy to encourage Hebrew speaking."[106] In both locales, however, there was a tremendous gap between the polemics attesting to the importance of Hebrew and its actual progress as a spoken language.[107]

Other achievements were more honestly recognized. As in Germany, British Zionists boasted that many of its leaders arose in university circles. Stuart Cohen writes that, before the First World War,

Zionist societies had been established at the major universities, and although their membership was small, their very existence was considered to be one of the English Zionist Federation's most prestigious gains. Ultimately, these efforts bore more substantial fruit. For one thing, some of the second generation of native Zionist leaders first attained prominence at the university societies (Norman Bentwich at Oxford, Selig Brodetsky at Cambridge, and Leon Simon in London being the most obvious examples). For another, Zionism at the universities became altogether more respectable. At its third Annual Conference in 1920, the Inter-University Jewish Federation was persuaded to reverse its previous ruling against discussing politics. Instead, on Brodetsky's motion, it unanimously agreed to "welcome" the British mandate in Palestine and express "great gratification at the facilities now afforded for the reconstruction of Erez Israel."[108]

Cohen qualifies that "the extravagant self-congratulations" these advances elicited was "debatable."[109] The Zionist youth and student groups were at least as wedded to their British environments as were the Central European Zionist organizations to theirs. The British Zionist youth displayed characteristics of acculturation to diaspora existence that were or would later become emblematic of Zionist youth in general.

Clearly, the main means by which a connection to Palestine was fostered was not by participation in emigration societies, or through encouraging *'Aliyah* as the only authentic Zionism, but by devising programs in which it was possible to experience vicariously the life of settlers in Palestine, or to spend limited amounts of time in Erets Israel as either a tourist or visiting student.[110] As opposed to settling in the Yishuv, the goal was to "become acquainted" with Jewish Palestine.[111] German and American groups also initiated similar efforts to combine tourism and study, including a call to make a semester at the Hebrew University of Jerusalem compulsory for all Zionists.[112] Decades later a tongue-in-cheek Zionist publicity poster, featuring a pensive David Ben-Gurion, would read: "At least come here to study."

In Great Britain, as in Germany, there was an effort to coordinate the university groups with organizations of teenagers and children. The counterpart to the German endeavor at Fusion was labeled "The Habonim Scheme" in Britain.[113] "The founders of the scheme," it was reported in 1930,

have been impressed by the fundamental fact, that in order to make Zionists it is necessary to start moulding the available material early. At the same time, it is hopeless to instil into youngsters any intellectual ideal like Zionism unless it is combined with some interesting and amusing pabulum, in the form of games or sport. Hence the Habonim movement. It seeks to make youths of 11–15 interested in Zionism, and has gone to the scout movement for inspiration. The children are combined into troops and patrols, but everything they do is intimately connected with Jewish history and with Palestine . . . The movement, however, lacks leaders – young men of good Jewish knowledge who are prepared to sacrifice an evening a week for the sake of the Jewish nation. It seems to us that here is an opening which many members of the Federation might utilise with great benefit both to themselves and the Zionist movement.[114]

Despite the reservations about the compatibility of youth and intellectual challenges, in 1932 the British Zionist press asserted that "Habonim is a cultural movement" which "attempts to make Hebrew a living language to these young people and to instil in them a love for Jewish learning and culture." A framework for cooperation between the university students and teenagers was set, as the youngsters seemed "anxious to have the help of UZF members."[115] Rather than aspiring to influence the whole of students' lives, Habonim was conceded to be a "supplementary movement."[116] Not unlike other groups, Zionist activity was reserved for "an evening a week," special events, and one- to two-week conclaves in the summer.

Rebecca Sieff, a leading Zionist in Britain and moving force behind WIZO, the women's Zionist organization in Britain and worldwide, wrote an analysis of Zionist youth in Great Britain in 1924 which in many respects is representative of articles about youth groups in Western Zionist organs. Sieff begins her account of "the Youth Movement in England" with a grim picture of British Zionism in general, citing the "poverty of Zionism in this country in personnel, in spiritual forces, and in material results" which "has cast a depressing gloom in recent years over those who ostensibly lead the movement here." Attempting to discern the reasons for Zionism's stupor, she asserted that

It is evident that the poverty of intellectual life in Anglo-Jewry, together with the poverty of Jewish education, both qualitatively and quantitatively, have led to an indifference, to a lack of understanding of fundamental Jewish questions, which is deplorable. Until this state of affairs is remedied by one means or another the Zionist Movement can never be an effective force in Anglo-Jewry . . . Many of those who have anxiously watched the fluctuations of the Zionist movement in this country are convinced that until something akin to the Blau-Weiss arises, Zionism will never be a living force in Anglo-Jewry, though they are well aware that conditions here are somewhat different, and that difficulties of a special kind exist . . . In the first place, our student class has neither the tradition nor the cultural background of Jewish student life on the Continent. Its numbers have hitherto been comparatively small, and they have been for the most part occupied with their own private economic struggles outside their academic life. Consequently they have not exerted any moral or intellectual force on the community at large.[117]

Despite this bleak assessment, Sieff interjects: "But this is changing rapidly." Here she employs a polemical strategy that was prevalent in Zionism in general, and even more evident in discussions of Zionist youth. No matter how bad things seem, the organization is portrayed as being in a transition phase:

The students, whose numbers are growing, are feeling the necessity for self-expression, and that very young organisation, the "Inter-University Jewish Federation of Great Britain and Ireland" has made rapid progress during the last twelve months. Its recent Summer School showed quite conclusively that the aims of the Federation are Jewish and Nationalistic in the widest sense . . . Who can doubt that in the attempt to carry out [its] programme, and with the knowledge of what has been achieved elsewhere, the students will inevitably play an important role in the renascence of Jewish youth in England?

The main cause of this turnabout, however, was an influx of young people from Palestine. Without any hint that there might be a problematic aspect to this development, Sieff proudly announced that

there is considerable improvement in the methods and quality of Hebrew tuition and Jewish education in many Jewish centres. This is in large measure due to the presence of numbers of young Palestinians who have entered English universities, and who are in the meantime earning their livelihood by the teaching of Hebrew as a living language, and of Jewish history and literature.

"There can be no doubt," Sieff concluded, "that in a very short space of time there will be some hundreds of young people so imbued with

Jewish sentiment that they will provide an entirely new element in Anglo-Jewry."[118] Sieff does not speculate about what might have driven the "Palestinians" to Britain. The only consequence she envisions is the "vacuum" to be filled in the youth movement. By no means did she attempt to relate this boon to the British Zionists to any greater tendencies. Nevertheless it was possible to see such phenomenon from a very different perspective. In the summer of 1924, during his visit to the Jewish settlement Motzah in Palestine, American Zionist Julian Mack was shocked when the leader of the settlement broke down in tears before him. The elder settler exclaimed that the "greatest crime" being committed by Zionists, who he was certain had only the best of intentions, was "not doing everything possible to prevent the Haluzim from leaving the land." He was not speaking of settlers who fled the rural confines for Tel Aviv or Jerusalem, but had quit the country entirely and emigrated to the United States. The numbers, he pleaded, were already alarming.[119] Furthermore, British control over Palestine permitted at least several hundred Jews entry to Britain via Erets Israel, and many took full advantage.

A feature of university organizations in Britain, then, which would become a part of Zionist institutional life elsewhere in the diaspora, was the presence of numerous Jews who had recently come from Palestine. Prior to 1933 there is no indication of how many returned, or how many quit the country permanently by staying in Britain or making their way to the United States. When these students were mentioned, it was assumed that they were simply getting better prepared to resume their lives in Palestine. Little or no thought was given to the notion they had actually come to Britain to seek their fortunes outside the Yishuv. A myth developed that all Jews who left Palestine would some day return to the rebuilding of the homeland; they supposedly had gone abroad for very specific purposes, such as to receive a technical education. As early as 1920, though, there were reports that immigrants to Palestine were leaving in sizable numbers for the United States because their chances of "self-support" in the Yishuv "were very poor," and that the only reason they did not enter other countries, especially Britain, was because they were refused admission. "Zionists who have come" to Palestine, it was wryly noted in the non-Zionist journal, *American Hebrew*, "are looking for their first means of leaving."[120] One of the inadvertent effects of the British mandate was to open the way for hundreds of Jewish students from Palestine to enter Britain.

As Zionist organizations in the diaspora rationalized why these Jews had left Erets Israel, they likewise sought to integrate them, and the emigres therefore became part of the social landscape of the movement.

The formerly Palestinian Jews emerged as a formidable force in their own Zionist communities. At the University of Leeds, for instance,

the presence of nearly a hundred and fifty Palestinian students in our midst has often made the UZF members curious as to why so many Palestinians should study abroad. Information supplied by them shows they leave their beloved Erez Israel simply because the facilities for higher education are as yet very limited, particularly in subjects leading to a profession. The Jerusalem University is doing magnificent work, but, so far as scientific subjects are concerned, it is mainly a research institution.

Hundreds of other Jewish students from Palestine, the report continued, were studying in Italian, German, French, and Swiss universities; there was already a "small colony of them in California." There was no irony intended in relating that many of these students, "especially in Britain, are able to cover part of the cost of their education by teaching Hebrew,"[121] or that "the latest Hebrew songs" were taught by "an Edinburgh student hailing from Tel Aviv."[122] The *Halutsim*, then, were becoming the Hebrew teachers and songsters of the diaspora. They were said to be "doing invaluable work in spreading the Hebrew language and a love of Palestine among the Jewish youth of the world."[123] From other quarters, it was argued that the mythology and official organs of the movement did not allow for critical reports of the economic crisis in Palestine to be aired.[124] No doubt this contributed to the fiction that the hundreds of students were away for only a temporary period. In general, the two-way flow between Palestine and the diaspora has been chronically undervalued; rarely was it acknowledged that "not all" of the immigrants "became absorbed," and "many of them drifted away."[125] The American student Zionists, too, did not recognize that it might be paradoxical that some of their critical activists had come from Palestine.[126] Zionist youth movements in Europe, in fact, also "provided Eretz-Israel with Hebrew speakers and teachers," helping account for "the exponential growth of the Yishuv."[127] Clearly, the lines between the diaspora and Palestine were more fluid than static.

To what extent, though, did British students who did not come from Palestine even contemplate remaking their lives in Erets Israel? This issue was raised in a meeting in March 1930; it was decided that "some means of sending 'Halutzim' from England to Palestine ought to be found." In an uncharacteristic lack of pretension on the issue, it was reported that

While on all hands it is admitted that English Jews should be encouraged to go to Palestine and settle there, nevertheless members of the UZF may wonder whether it is wise at this juncture, to embark on any such project. There are many countries where the lot of the Jews is a far more unhappy one than here. Is it not better to use all available public funds for helping such Jews to emigrate to the Promised Land, than for attempting to send over English Jews, in whom the urge is, naturally, far less strong? This is a matter which requires some examination.[128]

Rarely was it stated so transparently that "to take a really active part in Zionist work"[129] did not necessitate going to Palestine oneself.

Although it would become commonplace in Zionism to hear that students in the United States were the least politically conscious, and tended to see Zionism as little more than an excuse for socializing, the social aspect of Zionism was not lost in Britain. At the highly touted Summer School of the British students, it was admitted that "the natural predominance of the social side of the School swamped much serious discussion of Jewish problems. A small group of keen Zionists tried to give the School something of a Zionist twist" by leading Hebrew song sessions, dancing the Horah, and improvising a "Hebraized popular jazz." Despite these efforts, as well as a "Hebrew study circle" and "JNF boxes" on the tables, it was determined that "Zionism was rather somnolent at the School."[130] Small wonder that the UZF, with dances among its frequent activities, was "a hive of romance!"[131] Whatever their intellectual posturing, the German Zionist students were likewise known for long lines at the "kissing booths" at their fetes – which were used to raise money for the Jewish National Fund[132] – and their enclaves were particularly noted as places for *höhere Töchter*, "girls from good families," to find husbands. "At that time," recalled a memoirist who moved from Berlin to the Hague, working as a translator for the JNF when it was headquartered in the Netherlands, "they used to say that to marry off a daughter, let her join the Zionist Organization."[133] Most likely this was not as prevalent an attitude in the groups with large numbers of relatively recent immigrants from Eastern Europe. Perhaps no Zionist youth contingent, however, was as consistently self-critical as those in the United States.[134]

Organized Zionist youth in the United States were apparently more troubled than their British counterparts by the notion that their group seemed more animated, at times, by socializing among themselves rather than political or intellectual concerns. No doubt this sensitivity was heightened due to repeated accusations that Zionism in the United States lacked intellectual depth. The stereotype, inside and outside Zionist circles, was that American Jewry, as an offshoot of the typical American mentality, was terminally shallow, crudely materialistic, and ruled by nouveau-riche proclivities. The "Summer School" approach, with its paean to beautiful natural settings, such as Lake George in the

Adirondack Mountains of upstate New York, was also a prominent aspect of American students' experiences.[135] Part of its appeal was its offer of excellent facilities for golf, tennis, swimming, canoeing, and riding.[136] Singing was integral to all of their activities, as in Germany and Britain.

Still, it is only with exaggeration that one could call the American Zionist student organizations that existed from 1914 to 1933 bastions of intellectualism, although some of the adult and student leaders were distinguished individuals. Like the British, the American Zionist youth were organized in the same way as other denominational or special interest clubs prevalent in American high schools and universities. By its very nature, any such club comprises only a small segment of the student's life. The first significant university-level union of Zionist groups of this period was the Intercollegiate Zionist Organization of America (IZA), which existed from 1917 to 1921.[137] Marie Syrkin, a main spokesperson for Labor Zionist and student contingents, characterized the IZA as "essentially a rallying point for sentimental affiliations. A Jewish student of a certain type went to the IZA meeting to sing the Hatikvah when he remembered Zion. To remember Zion in a vague, ineffable way, was the chief function of the Zionist student groups." It constituted, she wrote, little more than the embodiment of "sentimental affirmations."[138] The IZA had emerged during the height of nationalist passions in the First World War, and fizzled almost immediately upon the end of the United States' involvement in the conflict. A fear of being perceived as "un-American" undoubtedly played a role in the group's demise, when it became difficult to accentuate one's ethnic identity as the country was becoming increasingly isolationist and xenophobic.[139] But in retrospect, the work of IZA does not appear as meaningless as its successors would have it. Similar to the agricultural projects sponsored by the German groups, the IZA conducted at least one six-week "Summer Agricultural Course," which was comparable to the training centers in Central Europe. This was intended for future settlers of Palestine, but also designed "to give executives, educators, professional workers, and senior students an opportunity to do directed farming during their vacation." The accompanying educational program was fairly sophisticated, including attention to the varieties of soil in Palestine and the special problems of rural sociology.[140]

The organization which emerged in 1925 as a replacement for the IZA was Avukah. Avukah was publicized in Zionist organs as a substantial improvement over the lackadaisical IZA; Marie Syrkin wrote that it fortunately bore no resemblance to its predecessor.[141] But Syrkin's laudatory view of the group was not uncontested. From its inception, at least to some critical Zionist observers, Avukah also suffered from a superficial character. To succeed, wrote Morris Rivlin in the *New Palestine*,

the leaders must avoid the pitfalls of vagueness. Already, in its programme, there is so much vagueness that one can't help feeling for the ultimate success of the movement. Pledging the organization to help in the realization of the Basle Program, to help spread the Zionist doctrines among the Jewish youth of America, to help the Hebrew University, to promote the Jewish Youth Conference and so on down the line, is very nice and fine; but it is too broad in scope and too general to be called a definite and clear line of work.[142]

To be sure, a flawed founding program for Avukah was regarded as a grave matter. It was the only organization of its kind in the United States. A Jewish student society founded at Harvard University in 1906, Menorah, was the only other body which might compete for the students' loyalties; its activity, however, was concentrated in small study circles and its periodical, *Menorah Journal*.[143] The typical Zionist view was that Menorah was moribund and pretentious.[144] But seen from outside the Zionist fold, many Jews and non-Jews perceived Menorah as a Zionist group, and there were certainly students sympathetic to Zionism among Menorah members. One of American Zionism's intellectual luminaries, sociologist Horace Kallen, had been active in Menorah as an undergraduate.[145] The institution which would later emerge as the dominant Jewish force on the many campuses, B'nai B'rith's Hillel, was dismissed by hard-core Zionists as "churchy."[146]

Marie Syrkin's analysis of the failure of the IZA to nurture any intellectual substance was repeated in the later critiques of Avukah. Students who asked probing questions "were not considered an asset." The prevailing passion was toward conformity, "in trivial externals as well as essentials."[147] Within six years from its inception, Avukah saw itself at a crossroads, in many respects mirroring the dilemmas of the "adult" Zionist bodies: there were "basic differences of opinion" over "the nature of the organization" that best suited the movement's aims. The issue was said to be

summed up in the frequently used terms "selective" or "intellectual" versus "general" or "mass" membership. The "intellectuals" maintain that as a student organization Avukah must be concerned with the problem of future Zionist leadership, and that our task is the training of leaders through Jewish intellectual pursuits. Their opponents, however, argue that Zionism is a nationalist movement and therefore must not ignore the needs and demands of the average Jewish student. They contend, therefore, that the task of Avukah is to suit its program to the needs of the average student, regardless of his intellectual promise or capacity for leadership.[148]

To a lesser extent, a similar debate ensued in the largest Zionist youth organization, Young Judaea, over whether the organization should be more inclined toward "intensive" or "extensive" work.[149]

Included in the defense of the "mass" position was the pronouncement that "the American Jewish college man, like his fellow non-Jewish college man," is not a "student" in the European sense, and a decided contrast to his German counterpart. This evaluation, however, might have been based at least in part on a stereotype of German academic life as more arduous than that in American universities. Certainly the secondary school training of Central Europeans was more intense than even the relatively good, public secondary schooling of the Americans. But to judge the German collegiate experience as a cut above, intellectually, and much more demanding, is questionable at best.

American students, like the Germans and British, were particularly loathe to study Hebrew. By 1929 it could be publicly admitted in the United States that the resolutions in countless meetings exhorting their faithful to learn Hebrew could not be taken seriously.[150] In the American case, at least it was admitted that "college man, student, and intellectual" were far from synonymous concepts when it came to Zionist learning.[151]

In a stinging criticism of Avukah, Maurice Samuel, a leading Zionist propagandist, wrote that the "standard of intellectuality" in the movement was "extraordinarily low"; young intellectuals in the United States, from his perspective, had little reason to be interested in Zionism. This in part derived from what he saw as the paucity of intellectuals among American students. The Zionism espoused by Avukah, Samuel claimed, could only be "pseudo-intellectual," because it demanded a type of loyalty which did not allow for independent thought; instead, it championed a sort of organizational zeal which Samuel saw as anything but "spontaneous" and anathema to an intellectual frame of mind:

Get three American-Jewish students together and they elect a chairman, a secretary, and a treasurer; they issue a statement, they institute dues, they announce a nation-wide campaign, and they invite the local Rabbi and the chairman of the charities to address them.

Intellectuals scorn this type of action, not because "practicality and intellect" are somehow incompatible, but because it is unattractive to those in search of in-depth intellectual and political commitment. "At best," Samuel continued, "with its present constituency," Avukah can remain a rather superficial, loose educational body, "exerting a mild pressure on adults for funds." In his mind, "an intellectual student Zionist movement" had to be small and spontaneous, and not overly concerned with toeing the line of the official organizations and money-raising; its character should be informed, above all, "by intellectual curiosity combined with youthful vigor."[152] Ironically, although Samuel saw himself as a courageous intellectual, he was one of the main figures who helped fortify the mechanical, fundraising-centered cast of American Zionism under Louis Lipsky.

Another critic, S. L. Halkin, concurred that especially in light of the "great expectations" for intellectual renewal that were prompted by the founding of Avukah, its work was banal: "organizing campaigns, collecting funds, seeking greater and greater publicity: once again Zionism appears as an impersonal ideal, an ideal which does not nourish one's own soul, but is a means to be capitalized for the good of the much-suffering heroes, the *Chalutzim*." To Halkin, "a creatively joyous ideal" had been transformed into "unlovely social work."[153] Neither Samuel nor Halkin ever recognized that the failings of Avukah might be more directly tied to problems of the Zionist Organization of America. Aptly fitting the hackneyed American expression, in this case the apple did not fall far from the tree.

Most of Avukah's programming was designed to make students feel good about Zionism and its institutions. Concomitantly, among its membership, there was resistance to informed perspectives that conflicted with the central myths of the movement. The Ohio State University (OSU) Avukah chapter in March 1931 reported that

At yesterday's meeting, Dr. Herbert A. Miller spoke on "The Difficulties in Zionism." Dr. Miller, who is a professor of Sociology at OSU, is known as a national authority on race problems. He has made a number of trips to Palestine and has made a study of the Palestinian question and of Zionism . . . His talk aroused strong opposition, and one of the local rabbis, a native of Palestine, very tactfully and cleverly refuted many of the speaker's main points. He showed that Zionism was not an experiment but a people's long and cherished ideal that has been a vital force in its survival throughout many centuries.[154]

Eyewitness and expert testimonies that disrupted the official discourse of the movement were denigrated, if not shouted down, because of their ostensible lack of understanding of the movement or of the Jews. The students were, predictably, no more tolerant than the elders when it came to receiving views which did not conform to the party line.

There was a portion of American Zionist youth, however, which stood apart for its self-conscious anti-intellectualism. Along with wishing to detach themselves from any intellectual identification in order to gain the allegiance of the "average" student, there was, on the part of some in the movement, a vehement hostility toward intellectuals and the intellectual project – even from those within the Zionist camp. In

December 1931, an angry article in *Avukah Bulletin* declared that it was

high time that we free ourselves of the feeling of awe for the intellectual, regardless of his merit or contribution. Our task as Zionists is to inquire into the quality of the Jewish intellectual before we set him up to our youth as an ideal. The American Jewish intellectual, as we know him, emerges from the Zionist crucible a self-centered, powerless grumbler, who revels in the venom of his abuse against those who are under the yoke of Zionist responsibilities. Most of our intellectuals have fled the Zionist battlefield, but failed to build new "Jabnehs." What reason have we to glorify the Jewish intellectual? If anything, we should guard our youth against his disintegrating influence.[155]

One of the adult leaders of Avukah, Maurice Pekarsky of Chicago, succinctly characterized the organization's activities as "nothing more and nothing less than conventional American Zionist propaganda." It rarely strayed outside the boundaries of United Palestine Appeal (UPA) promotions,[156] and had likewise geared itself to "mass consumption." But for "the thinking minority of Jewish students who might be susceptible to Zionism," Pekarsky asserted, "this form of Zionist education – appealing slogans and sentimental blurbs about suffering Jews in Poland or the romance of cows in Palestine – is not acceptable."[157] In 1932 he wrote that

All about us there is discouragement and apathy. There is depression in the mind and heart of American Zionism. There is indifference and ignorance on the part of Jewish students. In the face of the numerous difficulties under which we labor Avukah calls for a pioneering minority, for intelligent and courageous leaders and members capable of self-forgetfulness in the service of Zionism.[158]

A critical student leader bemoaned the fact that Avukah members "do not think and create for Zionism."[159]

Even though Avukah was responsible for fostering what many would perceive as a minimal commitment to the movement, it too had its educational-cultural dimension. To some critics, even as late as 1932, it was hampered because most of the pertinent Zionist literature was in languages such as German and Hebrew, which were inaccessible to most students.[160] An underlying problem, though, seems to be that not all student leaders were even aware of the materials that were available. At any rate, its endeavors were focused on spreading the word about "Zionism and the Jewish National Home." Stephen S. Wise's son, James Waterman Wise, was active in this phase of the organization.[161] Avukah published a "Palestine Anthology and Zionist Text-book," as well as pamphlets, bulletins, and translations from the corpus of Zionist tracts. Like all parts of the movement, film was becoming more central in its

programs.[162] Avukah also sponsored "Palestinian nights," exhibitions
of Jewish art, concerts of Jewish music, and a national speakers'
bureau. The most novel aspect of its educational effort was to lobby for
the inclusion of Hebrew within the curriculum of high schools and
universities, which one commentator compared to the fight for
"minority rights" in Eastern Europe.[163] Although it is difficult to trace
the impact of this effort, because it likely coincided with similar moves
from other quarters, it seems that Avukah did find a way to integrate at
least some of its project into larger, permanent structures.

The most intensive educational program for American youth,
however, was conducted under the auspices of Hadassah. A Hadassah
"University Women's Group" became involved in

translating material in the Hadassah office from the Hebrew into English, and
from English into Yiddish, carrying on research in the field of public school
luncheons and infant welfare work in the United States, cooperating with the
cultural committee of Hadassah to formulate an educational syllabus for Junior
Hadassah groups, leading study circles in Junior Hadassah groups, furnishing
speakers and publicists . . . and raising funds to support the translation and
publication of text books for the Nurse's Training School in Jerusalem.

The Hadassah University women's first public educational program
featured its "Achad HaAm circle" presenting "a resume of its
discussions," followed by a forum "open to the group as a whole."[164] By
the end of 1925, the youngest Hadassah associates, Junior Hadassah, had
4,344 members in 140 chapters in 116 different cities.[165] Among the
Junior Hadassah was a select group known as the "Cultural Fellowship"
which was engaged in the most challenging educational regimen.[166]
Henrietta Szold, who privately admitted that the work of Young Judaea
was inconsequential,[167] believed that the Junior Hadassah was "growing
out of the status of a Youth organization."[168]

The young American Zionist women and men, like their German and
British relatives, had little patience for what they deemed politiciz-
ation.[169] Predictably, Avukah members were reluctant to take a stand
regarding the conflict between Labor Zionism and Revisionism; to do so
would have meant grappling with issues in a manner foreign to them.[170]
In what was described as an "important luncheon conference" in
1928, Avukah proudly reported that it had hosted "the first detailed
presentation of [Ittamar] Ben Avi's striking proposal that Fascism should
be adopted as a new plan for upbuilding Palestine."[171] Consideration of
the Zionists' friction with Palestine's Arab population, or the potential
confrontation with Arab nationalism, was rare.[172] The German student
organizations, in comparison, however much they underestimated Arab

nationalism and the threat of Revisionism to the liberal assumptions of Zionism, tackled these issues more frequently and with more gravity than their American counterparts.[173] This is possibly because some of their former members, such as Robert Weltsch, were sympathetic to the B'rith Shalom faction, which advocated a bi-national Jewish–Arab state in Palestine. Although Avukah's greatest claim to fame was that it had hosted the visit of Albert Einstein to the United States, the members did not seem to imbibe or even notice Einstein's compassion for Palestine's Arabs.[174] Not surprisingly, a student group meeting in Indianapolis was sympathetic to the contention of Goldie Meyerson (later Golda Meir) that although the Labor Zionists hoped "to create something finer and better" than that which currently existed, they could not "promise to the world to create or contribute something unique" in terms of relations with a hostile people, the Arabs. But at the same meeting, Manya Schochat apparently spoke more positively about the possibilities of "Arab–Jewish rapprochement," with a greater sensitivity to "the plight of the large masses of Arabs."[175] Moreover, the central syllabus of Avukah's curriculum, published after the Arab riots of 1929, stressed the evidence of reconciliation and friendship between Jews and Arabs, which they hoped would result in a "vision of a new Semitic society."[176] In this respect, the liberal-humanistic ethos of the organization was closer to that of their German brethren than has been recognized.

In addition to an urge to remain apolitical, despite the efforts of individual students to press the organization to side with a particular Zionist faction or to participate in the politics of class conflict,[177] the Zionist university students also resembled the Europeans in trying to enlist the forces of grade-school and high-school youth. The value of this formal bond, it seems, was always overestimated. From 1914 to 1933, the younger Zionist student groups did not generate much excitement in the United States. But this did not stop the claims, on the part of the movement's adult leaders, of their vast success.

The preeminent Zionist youth society in the United States was Young Judaea, which traced it origins to founding meetings in 1905 and 1909. The moving force behind the formation of the group was Judah Magnes, who would later emigrate to Palestine and serve as rector of the Hebrew University. In 1914 the Hadassah organization vowed to help the youth group and resolved that "a prime purpose" of their educational work was cooperation with Young Judaea.[178] In 1919 Young Judaea became a charge of the Education Department of the Zionist Organization of America, which was then headed by Henrietta Szold. This helps to explain the close connection between Szold's Hadassah organization and

Young Judaea, even though Hadassah had its own youth wing.[179] In 1924 Young Judaea formalized its ties with the mainstream Jewish scout movement in Palestine; a tangible consequence of this relationship was Young Judaea's publication of a Hebrew edition of the British Scout Manual.[180] Fundraising, not only for its own programs, scouting in Palestine, and special collections, but also for the Keren Hayesod remained a central function of Young Judaea[181] – even though "education" was claimed to be a higher priority than fundraising.[182] In a sign that Zionism was becoming more mainstream, and possibly that the politics of its youth wing were not very extreme, in 1926 the governing body of United States' Conservative Jewry, the United Synagogue, "encouraged" its members to support Young Judaea.[183]

At virtually the same moment when Rebecca Sieff proclaimed that the Zionist youth movement in Britain had been resuscitated, *New Palestine* announced in 1924 that

Among Zionist activities there is none which has caused more gratification – and astonishment – than the amazing revival of Young Judaea. Three years ago it was all but dead. Not only in numbers and finances did it seem to be approaching dissolution, but the spirit had gone out of it. There was no desire to carry on. Discouragement had done its worst. Within two years it has sprung again for a foremost place in Jewish youth activity. It has renewed its publication in an attractive and successful form. Its members have grown, and much more important, it has begun to radiate confidence and strength.

The most significant sign of the organization's vitality was that it was capable of raising $50,000 toward its annual budget.[184] As early as 1915, it was clear that fundraising, at that time for the Jewish National Fund, was a principal duty among the children of Young Judaea as it was for the European Zionist youth.[185] Also recalling the experience of its European counterparts, the children's branch was notable for disseminating various types of literature and paraphernalia including maps, pictures, plays, dialogues, books, pamphlets, pins, and buttons.[186] Artifacts of material culture should not be dismissed as ephemeral; symbols, flags, sashes, and badges were no small matter in developing a national consciousness for the rising generation.[187]

All of the American youth groups, but especially Avukah, regularly heaped praise upon themselves,[188] and apparently gauged their success by the extent to which they had generated "a lively interest and active participation in Jewish life on the part of many students who otherwise would not have found an avenue for such activity."[189] But if one traces the development of Avukah into the late 1930s, it is clear that the organization became more intellectually vital and less parochial without sacrificing its commitment to Zionism. Avukah's "Program for American

Jews" of 1938 displayed an impressive grasp of interconnected issues as well as a plan for action:

We must fight anti-Semitism by bringing out into the open the violation of the rights of the Jews as citizens, and the difficulties of their position. We must take part in the wider fight in defense of civil liberties, for many of the effects of anti-Semitism are infringements of these liberties and must be seen as such. Above all, Jews and Jewish groups must participate in anti-fascist action, and in the democratic and progressive movements which ward off fascism and which give promise of a fairer social order. Jewish organizations must be ready to do this, or new ones must be formed in their place.[190]

Nevertheless, even before the Nazi menace had materialized, the American student organizations displayed greater affinities to their continental counterparts than has usually been seen. Contrary to the stereotypes, many students in the United States, particularly women, did more in their Zionist conclaves than learn "the rhythmic intricacies of the Hora,"[191] and German students were not always engrossed in Zionist scholarship. All essentially conformed to their respective national models. All expressed an urge to overcome this conformity, which caused tensions. All struggled to include students' varying levels of commitment. Despite occasional modifications, all Zionist student groups were uneasy with the question: "Are you a contributor to the Cause if you do not intend to settle in Palestine?"[192] The movement, however, was adapted to the perceived permanence of the students' lives in the diaspora as it was for their elders.

8   Cold embrace: the reception of Hadassah and organized European women Zionists

The Women's Zionist Organization of America, commonly known as Hadassah, is recognized and respected as one of the most vital elements of world Zionism; it was instrumental in establishing and sustaining critical health, social welfare, and educational infrastructures for the pre-state Yishuv, and continues to serve this function in the State of Israel. The reception of Hadassah's founder, Henrietta Szold, was discussed in the earlier chapter on the symbolic significance of diaspora Zionist leaders.[1] To be sure, the notice paid to Hadassah before 1933 is not surprising, especially given the fact that overall, American Zionist ranks declined from over 200,000 in 1918 to fewer than 65,000 in 1929, while the membership of Hadassah rose dramatically in the same period. The latter figure includes some 45,000 "Hadassah ladies"; by a wide margin, therefore, they constituted the largest portion of Zionist membership in the United States between the wars.[2] In many respects the story of Hadassah interweaves the central themes of this study: it was a central and evolving symbol of the movement in the interwar years, which provided an increasingly important link between American Jewry and the Zionist project in Palestine. At the same time, the treatment of the organization in the wider scope of the movement illuminates how great was the gulf between Zionism's polemics, touting the movement's linear progress, and its more sporadic effectiveness. The early career of Hadassah shows how Zionism gained, and then squandered, much of its following in the United States. The problematic intersection between charity and Western Zionist nationalization is exposed most clearly in the conflicting Zionist perceptions of Hadassah.

Despite its impressive showing in Hadassah's first decades, the organization was far from unequivocally welcomed into the Zionist fold. Hadassah and Henrietta Szold frequently found their group under scrutiny, if not outright political and polemical attack as a deviant and even outlaw group by the administration of the Zionist Organization of America and the World Zionist Organization. On other occasions, however, various individuals and branches of the Zionist Organization would rush to praise Hadassah and its leader, often exaggerating their support for, and affinity with the American Zionist women. Since its inception in 1912, there was little fear that Hadassah would cease to exist; but its place within the interwar Zionist world was unsettled and fraught with tension. Despite the uneasiness with which the Zionist Organization received Hadassah, as well as the Zionist women's organizations from Europe, these groups had a decided influence on the development of the movement, and on the process of fabricating myths and symbols centered on women in Zionism. Organized women in Zionism did not simply "contribute" in their own way to the cause; their presence profoundly shook the male-centered movement, and their involvement led to the emergence of new secular Jewish mythologies. Women did not, however, make serious inroads toward power in Zionism during the interwar years.[3]

This chapter focuses on the perceptions of Hadassah and its European predecessors within the movement at large. I will deal, as well, with how Hadassah, WIZO, and the Central European women's groups promoted themselves, and in turn how they were used for propaganda and promotional purposes by the Zionist Organization. Earlier (chapter 3), I examined Hadassah's substantial role in the quarrels about fundraising in the organization.[4] Although it is acknowledged, even in the popular literature, that Henrietta Szold and her cohort faced an uphill battle, Zionist scholarship rarely considers Hadassah, and when the politics of Hadassah receives mention, the treatment is usually neither in depth nor judicious.[5] Most comment on Hadassah reflects the organization's reputation since the early 1930s, when it became widely known through its "Youth 'Aliyah" program, and thereby recognized as a leading humanitarian organization.[6] My inquiry here is directed toward how gender knowledge was produced within Zionism and how it might have influenced the overall development of the discourse of Zionism.[7]

It is helpful to begin an exploration of Hadassah in context, in both Jewish and Zionist frames of reference. Although its later claim to uniqueness would be well founded, Hadassah was not the most prominent Jewish or even Zionist women's organization in its early years. Worldwide, the most visible and effective leader of organized Jewish women was Bertha Pappenheim, the head of the Jüdischer Frauenbund, or Jewish Women's Organization in Germany. Although Pappenheim had little sympathy for Zionism, she advocated a kind of a national awakening and regeneration for the Jews within the nations of Europe. Specifically, she aimed to sever the networks which drew Jewish women into prostitution, to help Jewish women who were prostitutes to enter more respectable and less hazardous trades, to ameliorate the plight of

39 "Fieldworkers," in *Jewish Colonisation in Erez Israel: After Ten Years Keren Hayesod* (Jerusalem: no publisher [Keren Hayesod?], 1930).

impoverished Jewish women in Central and Eastern Europe, to challenge the status quo regarding *'Agunot* (abandoned wives unable to get a Jewish divorce), and dramatically expand the secular and religious knowledge, vocational opportunities, and general expectations of Jewish girls.[8] It was out of this atmosphere, of increased concern for feminist-inspired questions, and the transformation of social welfare service, largely through the efforts of Alice Salomon, that prompted the rise of Zionist women's organizations in the German-speaking world.

Indeed, the Zionist Movement in Europe since 1897 was a predominantly and self-consciously male affair.[9] Zionism was understandably beholden to the European order from which it was born, the endemic paternalism of Jewish life, and the governments its adherents wished to emulate. The women who took part in the movement were, therefore, a marginal element in a marginal force. Although Zionism proclaimed its openness toward women, Zionist women had difficulty making their voices heard once they were within the movement. This refutes part of the enduring legacy of women in Zionism: the image of a strong, assertive woman in the worldwide organization, in the social landscape of the incipient Jewish nation in Palestine, and later, in the State of Israel[10] (figure 39). Nevertheless, women's impact on the Zionist movement, while different from that of their male counterparts, was real and significant.

Organized Zionist women in Central and Western Europe and the United States had a distinctive influence on the course of Zionism and particularly on its reception among Western Jews. Especially because of their experience in social service, Central and West European Zionist women helped instill and disseminate the notion that modern social welfare was integral to the formative Jewish state and the movement's developing sense of nationalism. Hadassah, while reflecting these goals, furthermore stressed that different constituencies might, and had the right to, devise distinctive roles for themselves, such as their example of American women taking extraordinary responsibility for health care in Palestine.

Few scholars of Zionism, even those concerned with incorporating the history of women and strategies of the "new history," have integrated women into their analyses. In the histories of German and Austrian Zionism, with the notable exception of the works of Marsha Rozenblit and Harriet Freidenreich on Vienna, one is hard pressed to find a basic chronology of the establishment, main activities, and demise of Zionist women's organizations.[11] By comparison, the history of British Zionist women is more accessible, but largely from commemorative volumes produced expressly for the membership of the Women's International Zionist Organization.[12]

In the German-speaking world, as early as November 1898, the Wiener zionistische Frauenverein (Zionist Women's Organization of Vienna) was established, and its statutes were published in the Zionist organ *Die Welt*. Members of this organization were deeply impressed by Herzl's request for them to participate in an overtly "*political* venture."[13] Marsha Rozenblit informs us that in Vienna in 1896, a group of young women calling itself Miriam founded an organization to support Jewish colonization in Palestine, and another proto-Zionist group, Moria, directed itself to strengthening Jewish national consciousness by promoting "the study of Jewish history, literature, and the role of women in the Jewish past." In Berlin, the Jüdisch-nationale Frauenvereinigung also expressed interest in illuminating the role of women in Jewish history and literature.[14] Of greatest significance, though, was the Verband jüdischer Frauen für Kulturarbeit in Palästina (Jewish Women's Group for Cultural Work in Palestine) founded in 1907, which was also known as the Kulturverband für Frauenarbeit. To discern the origins of the latter group, we must look beyond the exclusively Zionist women's organizations to the role of Jewish women in social service in

Germany and Austria. It will be shown that there were similar influences on Zionist women's groups in Great Britain.[15]

As volunteers and professionals, Jewish women began to enter the field of social service in Jewish communities in the late nineteenth century, when social and economic changes and immigration from Eastern Europe prompted adjustments and growth in the social service structure. During this period the aim of social service was revised toward rooting out the causes of maladjustment and assisting needy individuals in regaining their economic footing. Susan Tananbaum shows that in Britain this was well under way by the 1880s.[16] In sum, "charity gave way to organized scientific philanthropy."[17]

Also beginning in the second half of the nineteenth century, the German feminist movement had a devoted following among Jewish women, many of whom became its leaders. In large part the movement was focused upon "social betterment through political activity," with the re-organization of the intellectual and technical training of girls and women as one of its basic demands. And whatever one might have felt about socialism, there is little doubt that increased social democratic agitation helped stimulate German Jewish women toward seeing Zionism as a possible forum for social and political action.[18]

The women who came together in auxiliaries of the newly established branch of the B'nai B'rith probably also had an impact on the formative Zionist women's organizations. B'nai B'rith women imitated newly devised non-Jewish programs in vocational and technical training, health care, nutrition, and education for specifically Jewish welfare activities. Their efforts also comprised an attempt to arouse "a Jewish mass-consciousness," and to make the notion of caring for one's co-religionists "socially fashionable." They accomplished this through combining fundraising functions, lectures on social welfare, and work projects with more purely social functions, such as banquets, teas, parties, and concerts. The allure of such activities was abetted by the bourgeois injunction that "a privileged woman has a moral duty to be benevolent." One might therefore see the B'nai B'rith as an institution which inspired and legitimated Jewish solidarity and sociability – for children, adolescents, men, and women – in a secular setting.[19]

As detailed by Marion Kaplan, the inauguration of the Jüdischer Frauenbund (JFB) (Jewish Women's Organization) in Germany in 1904, under its extraordinarily gifted and charismatic leader, Bertha Pappenheim, had a much weightier impact than the women of B'nai B'rith or any other group. Pappenheim was crucial in fusing and publicizing Jewish, feminist, and social welfare concerns, and in creating a nexus for mutual support. The JFB program of comprehensive social services and political agitation included "a wide-ranging journal, institutes and lectures on various aspects of Jewish culture," and most important, as a model for Zionists, "schools for farming and the household arts."[20]

The biographies of women Zionists demonstrate the extent to which their Zionist activities were fired in a Central European social welfare crucible. Gertrude Van Tijn, who rose to a relatively high position as a Zionist official, wrote that studying social work under Alice Salomon "had a lasting effect on me."[21] Siddy Wronsky and Anitta Müller-Cohen were leading figures among social workers and, later, Zionist women. Wronsky wrote extensively on social work in Germany and in other countries, and on the Jewish communal achievements in this field. She directed relief efforts for foreign Jews and helped establish the Bund zionistische Frauen ("Zionist Women's Organization") in the interwar years. Anitta Müller-Cohen founded a mutual aid society bearing her name. She ran kindergartens, soup and tea kitchens for thousands of local poor as well as Jewish war-refugees, and vocational schools where women refugees could learn trades; Müller-Cohen also marketed the wares produced by these women. For Rahel Straus in Munich, the path to Zionism was her work as a physician in public health.[22]

It was from this background that efforts to support the Jews of Palestine were initiated by the Kulturverband; they often ran a parallel course with relief efforts for refugees in Germany and Austria. With varying degrees of success, these programs were grafted onto the Yishuv, principally under the auspices of the Anglocentric WIZO, which subsumed the germinal Central European groups in 1919.[23]

Vowing to combat "the exploitation of women," the Kulturverband originally was concerned with the lace-making workshops that had been established by Sarah Thon in Jerusalem, Safed, and Jaffa. By 1913 there were some 400 women in the craft shops, most of whom were born in Palestine or had migrated from other parts of the Ottoman Empire. There is some indication that the German women had intended these workshops for girls from Eastern Europe, but their self-selected clientele turned out to be overwhelmingly Sephardic. The Kulturverband also sponsored women's agricultural training farms, a school for home economics, public kitchens, and health facilities for women and children; it partially financed and supervised kindergartens and Shaare Tzedik hospital in Haifa.[24] The Kulturverband was the first women's group to send a nurse to the Yishuv, which, along with its other work in the health field, partly inspired Hadassah's mission in Palestine.[25] Above all, though, it was the chief support for the institution that would become the most significant link between European Zionist women and their

Palestinian counterparts before and during the First World War: the
Girls' Training Farm in Kineret. It was especially from this institution,
which has been analyzed by Margalit Shilo, that the image and myth of
the working-woman pioneer was propagated.[26]

But the Central European women also sought to mitigate the
revolutionary and feminist fervor embraced by many of the women
immigrants in Palestine. The professed goal was to transform immigrant
women into productive workers and ideal mothers; they also wished to
replace "idleness" with productive work, promote literacy in Hebrew,
and to inculcate "a positive national identification" with Palestine. It was
important to the women of the middle class that the Halutsot (women
pioneers) learn "the value and delight of order, cleanliness, and good
taste." They feared the emergence, or even the appearance, of women in
the Jews' incipient nation as a shade too "red" for polite society. This
sentiment also revealed the ambivalence of many Zionist women, even
ardent activists, toward the idea of complete equality, and their fear of its
possible consequences.[27]

To a certain extent, the modifications of the Kulturverband
anticipated the shape the Zionist movement would assume in seeking to
enlist the sympathy of greater numbers of assimilated Jews in the 1920s
and 1930s. The promotions of the Kulturverband made a point, almost
from the outset, of trying to draw into their orbit all Jewish women of
Germany, whether Zionist or not. In this regard a leader of the Jüdisch-
nationale Frauenvereinigung, Edith Lachmann, suggested a need for
more "neutral" student and girls' organizations in order to provide a
common meeting ground for all Jewish youth. She also suggested that the
movement sponsor separate organizations for girls, to encourage their
independence because girls tended to be intimidated by boys in the usual
settings; to be on their own would enable them to speak and act for
themselves.[28] And after the Balfour Declaration (1917), it was from the
British women's camp that the strongest message was relayed that
the "building-up of the Jewish national home was a reality, whether one
had wished for it or not," and now every Jew was responsible for it
proceeding in the best and most constructive manner possible.[29]

Perhaps, though, a few German women as individuals – rather than the
organizations – gained greater notoriety in Zionism. Vienna's Anitta
Müller-Cohen was featured at a 1928 rally which drew an audience of
over 6,000, and she was a regular correspondent from a woman's
perspective in the Zionist press.[30] Müller-Cohen was the only woman of
this period whose oratory was captured on phonograph records used for
Zionist fundraising promotions. In many large European cities, events
billed as "women's evenings" could draw as many as 500 people.[31]

Helena Hanna Thon also emerged as a well-known analyst of Zionist politics, focusing on the situation of women in the Yishuv.[32] Predictably, there were a number of controversies aired by the German-speaking Zionist women's groups, but they tended to quarrel among themselves, rather than with the male leadership of the local and national organizations, or the central Zionist authorities. Although the women sometimes protested at being subordinate, the general sense from the men's perspective was that the women's groups for the most part accepted their secondary status.[33]

WIZO, a formidable British Zionist women's organization, also predated Hadassah; it dates its founding to 1920, 1917, 1909, or earlier.[34] Throughout the interwar period, WIZO was more prominent than Hadassah, in part because the center of European Zionist movement was Britain during Chaim Weizmann's stewardship, and it had visible connections to the embryonic women's movement in Palestine. Images and polemics exemplifying WIZO's welfare services for women and children made up a significant share of the movement's depiction of the "new Jewish life" in Palestine.[35] WIZO also gained attention as an actor in the struggle for women's suffrage in the Yishuv, another aspect of women's lives in Zionism which had some part in the wide-ranging political landscape of the movement.[36]

In Britain, the Federation of Women Zionists (FWZ) was established in 1918, but sporadic Jewish national societies, and committees dedicated to resettling Jews in Palestine, were inaugurated in the late 1880s. Among the earliest known groups was the "Western Women's Tent," which saw itself as adjunct to the efforts of the Hoveve (or Hibat) Tsiyon (Lovers of Zion). Scattered groups related to Hoveve Tsiyon emerged in the wake of the Russian pogroms of 1881; these societies were primarily interested in supporting the revival of Hebrew and colonization efforts to serve the incipient secular Jewish community in Palestine. In 1910, an organization emerged called the "Zionist Pioneer Women," which coalesced from the earlier bodies.[37] One of their members actually emigrated to Palestine after joining the group – with a ticket purchased from the club's treasury. This was a highly unusual course for a woman from such an organization in the prewar years. In the limited files of these groups, there are very few inquiries from prospective emigrants to Palestine, from their home nations of Britain, Germany, or Austria.[38]

A public "struggle for an equal and separate place" for women in the movement officially commenced in 1909, at the first Conference of Jewish Women's Organizations in Manchester, because, as one of their leaders admitted, "equal rights on paper did not necessarily bring them in reality."[39] Among the well-known women in the Manchester circle were Vera, the wife of Chaim Weizmann, and the Marks sisters (of Marks and Spencer fame), wives of Israel Sieff and Harry Sachar. Vera Weizmann had been involved in social welfare work as a physician; her communal activities provided valuable contacts for her husband's Zionist endeavors. She would later play a part in her husband's attempts to muzzle Hadassah and replace it with a "Keren Hayesod" women's auxiliary.[40] From a more expressly political perspective, Rebecca Sieff had been deeply influenced by the suffragette movement, an experience she also applied to Palestine. In 1917 these women, along with Henrietta Irwell, a child welfare worker, formed the core of the "Ladies' Committee" of the English Zionist Federation, which included a dozen women's groups.

Early in its organizational life, WIZO was embroiled in a conflict with the English Zionist Federation which would resemble the type of conflict that would shadow Hadassah: the mainstream Zionist organization and the principal fundraising bodies feared competition with the women's groups over the issue of where Jews and Zionists would donate their money. Although the men realized that women could be quite helpful in raising funds, a role euphemistically referred to as "recruitment," Zionist men were nevertheless anxious that money might be diverted by women from the "major funds" to the specific projects of the women.[41] The women resisted "recruitment" in favor of a more comprehensive role. "Recruitment" implied raising funds through membership subscriptions, which would go into the central body's coffers.[42] With surprising candor for this genre, one of the chroniclers of WIZO relates that

It took many years for the relationship between the English Zionist Federation and the Federation of Women Zionists to settle down: from its inception, with all the goodwill in the world, the situation was a slightly uneasy one. There are still many men, and indeed, some women too, who think the vast and complex task of the Zionist Movement calls for complete unity; that the splitting away of the feminine workers can only weaken the whole. Especially in fund-raising work there are those who still condemn any activity which they think might divert money from the major funds . . . The fruits of their co-operation have been far more numerous, as well as valuable and significant, than the many minor, often merely technical, points of difference.[43]

Shortly before World War I, there were several women's groups in Britain and elsewhere in Western Europe associated with the Kulturverband of the German Zionist women. After the war, "Mrs. Paul Goodman re-established connections with the Kulturverband branches in Germany, Poland, Holland, and Moscow as well as in Palestine, and succeeded in arousing their interest and sympathy in the plans for an

international body of Zionist women."[44] This sentiment materialized as
a conference in July 1920, calling WIZO into being, while the British
Federation of Women Zionists was maintained in a somewhat truncated
state. One WIZO account implies that in 1927, the ascension of
Mrs. Robert Solomon as "chairman" of the FWZ initiated an important
shift. Until this time, among women and men, the Zionist movement's
following had largely been from "newer immigrants from Europe," that
is, Jews of the lower classes – despite the middle-class outlook of many in
their ranks. The leadership, on the other hand, was mostly from the
assimilated bourgeoisie. With the Zionist conversion of Mrs. Solomon,
the movement was said to "broaden its base" considerably. It could now
draw in many more wealthy and highly assimilated Jews, who had earlier
scorned Zionism.[45]

As the Yishuv developed and demanded increasing financial support,
organized Zionist women became painstakingly concerned that the
audience of their promotions visualize the work that was being done
in Palestine – through photographs and narratives in slick flyers and
booklets, and through exhibitions, including scale models of their
facilities, examples from workrooms, and even a film entitled *Heldinnen
des Aufbaues* (Heroines of the Yishuv). They well understood the benefit
of presenting these images in both an aesthetically pleasing and realistic
manner, and for the most part they succeeded in fulfilling their
intentions. All of this helped make Jewish Palestine, and above all the
women's part in its re-creation, a "living reality" to the Zionist faithful
and the wider Jewish audience.[46]

The European women's organizations also showed Palestine as the
bastion of new cultural creativity for women, as a complement to their
newly found productive labor, and as rooted in their ancestral soil. This
was especially apparent in the British and German organs of WIZO,
which featured literature, poetry, drama, and art of the Yishuv women.[47]
These works contained an occasional radical reinterpretation of Judaism
and Jewish history from a feminist perspective. In a 1933 article, "Earth
– Mother of all Living," Ada Fishman wrote that "In days long since past,
indeed thousands of years ago, even before primitive man . . . woman was
the first to discover the secrets of the soil on which she lived and to turn
the richness and strength hidden in it to the use of mankind for his
bodily sustenance and strength." Zionist women were re-creating "that
bond of union between Woman and the soil which was first established
by [their] primitive ancestresses."[48] There is evidence, as well, that the
British and German organizations began to perceive the cultural fruits of
Zionist women living in Europe as having a distinctive value, ethic, and
voice.[49]

Although the Hebrew literature produced by men at this time included a tendency to be starkly critical and challenge many of the prevailing mythologies of the movement, the men at the helm of Zionism were not as ready as the women to spread such literature as part of official promotions. European women Zionists seemed more comfortable with exposing the movement's caveats and contradictions.[50] "In spite of the revolution in the life of the Jewish people," relates a WIZO booklet, "their conception of the woman [has] not fundamentally changed, even among the most progressive circles."[51] In one retrospective view, from a compilation of reports that appeared before 1934, the central myth of the emergence of the new woman is torn asunder: the texts proclaimed the Zionist woman "as a type does not yet exist." It was admitted that

the composition of Jewish womanhood in Palestine is a truly reflected image of the incongruity of the Yishuv. Differences of education, social standards, upbringing, and countries of origin present enormous difficulties in any attempt to unite women for a common aim and task. Even within the same social class, interests vary. An abyss seems to separate the Yemenite woman or the orthodox housewife from the woman worker of Russian origin or the professional woman from Eastern Europe.[52]

Yet even as they were more critical and attuned to realities of life in Palestine than the men, European Zionist women fostered a sort of unreflective detachment from the Zionist project. Along with Zionist men they too condoned the notion that a Jew in the diaspora could be fully integrated into the incipient Jewish nation simply by donating money to the cause – which helped lead to the patronizing style of "diaspora Zionists." European Zionist women championed the categorization of Zionists as "pioneers and helpers," praising Martin Buber for providing the theoretical underpinning for this idea. Women, then, also helped inaugurate a system which combined sentiments and elements of nationalism, charity, guilt, recriminations, and dependency, resulting in problems that have yet to be resolved.[53]

From the social service, charitable, and home economic underpinnings of most European women's Zionist work, it is understandable their brand of nationalism would be relatively inclusive, tending to appeal to a broader spectrum than the narrowly defined Zionist faithful. European women, followed by American women, were the first to press for the so-called de-politicization of Zionism, to make it more appealing to the greatest number of Jews.

As Hadassah was getting off the ground before the outbreak of World War I, European Zionist women had already succeeded in introducing a widely admirable model of a modern, independent Jewish woman, skilled in the sciences of home economics, hygiene, and education into the movement's discourse. Undergirding their efforts was a commitment to the specific needs and potentialities of women and children. To a great extent, however, they consciously or unconsciously accepted the male-centeredness of the movement. This is also true of the women who participated in the left wing of the movement, and women from the religious camp of Zionism, Mizrahi, who formed their own organization in 1925.[54] Although there was never any intention to subvert the male leadership of Zionism, Hadassah was certainly perceived as more threatening than the European women's groups of any political stripe.

Almost from its birth, Hadassah experienced friction with the central Zionist bodies. In 1914, Hadassah's request to use pictures from JNF promotions for publicizing their own events was turned down, on the grounds that it would lead to "confusion."[55] There was, however, never any reservation that the audience might be similarly confused when images of Hadassah were appropriated (from the 1920s onward) for general Zionist fundraising and promotional purposes.[56]

It seems that Hadassah first came to the attention of the worldwide movement with its contribution of medical help for Palestine during the First World War, when the Yishuv confronted what many saw as its darkest hour.[57] Its work, however, would soon fall under a harshly critical light when it became apparent that Hadassah was determined to steer a more independent course than had the earlier and existing diaspora women's organizations. After it was clear that the Yishuv had survived the specter of devastation, Hadassah ran afoul of the Zionist administration and Labor Zionist groups in Palestine. In 1919, owing to objections raised by Ha-Po'el ha-tsa'ir, the labor youth organization, a conflict broke out between the Hadassah's Medical Unit and Menahem Ussischkin, then director of the Palestine Zionist Executive. According to Ussischkin and the Palestine press, Hadassah had refused to subscribe to the "national discipline" required by the Zionist authorities, opting instead to take its orders "directly from the American organization." Similar complaints were regularly reported up to 1923, and became a point of contention in the Zionist press in the United States and Europe.[58] Around that time there were other grounds for singling out Hadassah for its apparent insubordination. As the Zionist movement became polarized around the figures of Chaim Weizmann, on the one side, and Louis Brandeis, on the other, Henrietta Szold and Hadassah were perceived as firmly in Brandeis's corner. Certainly Hadassah suffered a cool reception because of its persistent identification with the "loser," Brandeis.

The main motivation for Hadassah's sympathy for the Brandeis faction did not arise out of any particular fondness of Henrietta Szold for Brandeis himself, no matter how much she may have respected him and appreciated his efforts and unstinting support for her organization. Rather, it was her study of the conflict which incited Szold to question the arguments of the victors. Toward the beginning of the controversy over the Keren Hayesod in 1921, Szold wrote a colleague that "I hope that the American Zionist situation has cleared up by this time . . . I find myself unable to be an out-and-out partisan. I see right and wrong on both sides."[59] Slightly over a month later she would assert that "I have studied every document that came to me out of America, out of London, with the greatest care. If I had been in America my study of the documents would have compelled me to ally myself with Judge Mack and Mr. Brandeis . . . Not only the documents inclined me toward the 'American' attitude, but also my experience here [in Palestine]" influenced her stance critical of the administration.[60] She was unable, however, to translate her perspicacious view into policy.

By 1924 Hadassah was gaining prestige and influence within American Zionism, as the movement's dependency on American good-will and funds grew. The leader of World Zionist Organization, Chaim Weizmann, saw fit to praise Hadassah publicly for making possible the re-opening of the hospital in Tiberias, which was forced to close for over a year due to lack of funds. Weizmann also pointed out that Hadassah sought to serve the greater community, regardless of race or communal identification – in other words, it treated Arabs – and Hadassah had had a decided impact on the most impoverished Jews.[61] Hadassah was indeed demonstrating that its own power of the purse was formidable, and that it could make a serious difference in the life of the Yishuv. The organization would again attain notoriety in December 1925, when it provided relief for Syrian Druse following their flight from a religious conflict. Again, Zionist organs worldwide proclaimed with pride that Hadassah treated the victims without discriminating on the basis of confession.[62]

Predictably, though, the problem of Hadassah's relationship with the local administrative units in Palestine, the Va'ad ha-berit, and especially the main Labor Zionist sick-care fund, the Kupat Holim, would remain problematic.[63] Eventually Henrietta Szold was named as the culprit. She was charged with exacerbating the fragmentation of the Yishuv through her maintenance of Hadassah's autonomy, and accused of acting like the leader of a missionary society. This so-called "breach of discipline" was portrayed as especially ignoble because Hadassah and the Keren Hayesod had agreed to coordinate their fundraising since the Zionist convention in Philadelphia in 1925; the insinuation was that Hadassah was dishonestly siphoning money from the general fund. Szold's alleged insensitivity to the need for "self-sacrifice" was painted as a grave danger to the movement. Szold, her critics charged, "clever woman" that she was, could not distinguish between the "practical work" in Palestine, and the "Zionist work there," in the United States, of raising money.[64] This was sometimes attributed to Szold's "autocratic" character. Acting in such a manner may have been appropriate for fundraising among Jews in the United States, but it was not to be tolerated in dealing with Zionist authorities, especially in Palestine.[65]

To some degree, European women Zionists sought to stem the tide of criticism against Szold and Hadassah, defending the perceived independence of the American women Zionists.[66] They seemed in utter awe of Hadassah's budget, which reached one million dollars annually by 1928, and were impressed by the scope of its educational projects.[67]

The political loyalties of Zionist women, however, seemed to run deeper than any notion of sisterhood, at least as concerned support for Hadassah. The American Labor-oriented journal *Pioneer Woman* echoed the mainstream criticism of Hadassah's "defective organizational structure," arguing that it had become "a symbol of autocratic philanthropy":

Throughout all the years of its invaluable work the Hadassah has failed to make itself an organic part of Palestine and its Jewish community. It has remained an institution created from without and managed from above. It possesses no basis of public responsibility in the field of action. The spirit which pervades its activities is not that of modern public service, but of old-fashioned philanthropy.

The detractors of Hadassah refused to concede that the main motivation for Hadassah's refusal to relinquish control to the local authorities was due to its concern for efficiency, in order to make the most of its limited human and material resources.[68] Later, however, Henrietta Szold was hailed by the same faction as responsible for healing the rift between Hadassah and "organized labor" in Palestine,[69] and the mainstream leadership heaped praise on Szold when her ascension to the Zionist Executive was imminent.[70]

Hadassah would again be in a swirl of controversy in 1928 when it took the side of the so-called Brandeis group during that faction's attempt to "reorganize" the Zionist Organization of America (chapter 3). Suffice it to say that although the famous "split" between Brandeis and Chaim Weizmann over the founding of the Keren Hayesod had occurred seven years earlier, the conflict was never really resolved. In 1928 the rift came to dominate American Zionist politics because of specific charges of impropriety on the part of Louis Lipsky's Zionist administration, which was compounded by a fear that the organization had nearly been mismanaged out of existence, and there was a steep decline in popular support.[71]

Not only in the United States, but around the world, Hadassah was condemned as suffering from the manipulation of a "power-hungry" group of women, which had aligned its own "special interest" to that of the Brandeis group; Hadassah's position was also interpreted as a signal that Henrietta Szold had forsaken her promise to make her participation in the Palestine Zionist Executive her highest priority.[72] Again, Hadassah was painted as threatening the solidarity of the movement by seeking "domination," and was charged with being the main impetus of the opposition group.[73] By that time, however, any swipes at Szold could not be unmitigated; some of the same individuals who criticized her also recognized that Hadassah and its revered leader would necessarily play a crucial role in stemming the disintegration of the movement.[74]

It was in such a climate of opinion that any questioning of the fundraising mechanisms, especially the Keren Hayesod, was regarded by Zionism's central administration as an act of treason.[75] This was the ostensible reason for a series of political dirty tricks directed at Hadassah. Lipsky sent a "confidential" telegram to hundreds of Zionists claiming that Irma Lindheim and her Hadassah henchwomen were plotting "to undermine the United Palestine Campaign."[76] Before the 1928 convention, Lipsky attempted to postpone the national meeting of Hadassah (which was supposed to take place prior to the convention), and furthermore changed the voting rules in order to disenfranchise some 5,000 Hadassah members.[77] Essentially, Lipsky sought to suppress Hadassah's vote on a declaration that severely criticized his and Weizmann's rule, and asserted that the failures of American Zionism had resulted in the deterioration of conditions in Palestine.[78] At the Hadassah convention Irma Lindheim implored:

Ask yourself questions: *Why* was it treason for us to ask that the Zionist organization live up to the standards we impose upon ourselves? *Was* it wrong for us to reject a dual standard? . . . *Why* was it wrong for us to desire and work for a new leadership in the Zionist movement when we honestly believed that the present leadership was inadequate to meet the needs of Palestine? . . . *Why* should a Zionist public not protest against a political machine that crushes out the energies of those whose only desire is to work for Palestine?[79]

It became clear to Lindheim that in addition to a paranoid impulse to protect the fundraising instruments, the administration was driven by a fervent desire to exclude women from decision-making.[80] Early in its existence Hadassah women reflected on the condescension accorded their growing organization: "Even when [Hadassah's detractors] concede our claims to the Zionist heritage, they dub us lachrymose, whining sisters of a brotherhood that stands for staunch manhood and dignified self-assertion, and looks upon charity as a necessary evil at best."[81] Only on rare occasions, however, did Hadassah express the belief that the sexual division of labor in the movement was intended to subdue them. In 1928 they were compelled to lament that

The voices of the Zionist press, the Yiddish press, and the leaders of American Zionism are raised in clamor. "Hadassah is playing politics. Hadassah is sullying its skirts with dirty politics. Hadassah is interfering and causing trouble." This all sounds very much as though the gentlemen were in the habit of saying to their wives: "There, there dear, run along to your knitting and don't trouble your pretty head about these things. These things are men's work. You can't under-stand" . . . To them, we might reply . . . that we live in America in the twentieth century. Women do men's work in the community, efficiently and with full realization of their responsibility. To be womanly, in twentieth-century America, is to be comrade and partner. To be womanly in Zionism, means nothing less; to participate freely and completely in all that concerns the upbuilding of Palestine, to share the responsibility as well as the labor, to be fearless and resolute where the welfare of the Land of Israel is concerned.[82]

In addition to Hadassah's challenge to the Zionist Organization due to its relative independence and democratic character, combined with its incontestable results and brilliance of its leadership, Hadassah also exposed raw nerves in the intersecting nexus of philanthropy, social welfare work, and financial donations to the movement. Hadassah seemed to resolve the dichotomy between charity, on the one hand, which was seen as undesirable in the Zionist scheme, and institution- and state-building on the other, which was the primary object of the move-ment.[83] Their leader, Szold, was firmly entrenched in Palestine's day-to-day struggles, and its cadre of nurses and doctors were immediately uplifting the health and social welfare of Palestine. Yet there was no pretense that the organization in the United States was an insignificant backdrop for the work in Palestine. Hadassah proudly saw itself as an unabashedly American organization, most of whose members were committed to a Zionist life in the United States. Furthermore, Hadassah was threatening because its attitude regarding its members' donations was opposed to that of the leadership of the Zionist Organization and its main fundraising bodies. It was clear that the Hadassah women saw it as their right to take a far more active role in the dispensation of the funds they had given and collected. This was something the Zionist leadership refused to countenance; diaspora Jews, and especially Americans, were supposed to give money and keep quiet.

It seems that the perception of Hadassah's work as charity is essential for understanding its destabilizing role in the movement. Zionism categorically resisted defining the donations to its cause as philanthropy, although it certainly relied on the charitable instincts of the Jews, and sought to appropriate the tradition of *Tsedakah* for its own purposes.[84] One could not take national pride in being a recipient of philanthropy, but one might, however, not see it as charity if it were administered through local Zionist agencies in Palestine.[85] Nevertheless, with the American character of Hadassah so clearly evident, it was hard not to see it as a philanthropic venture. Some thoughtful critics, actually in line with the dominant ideas of Hadassah, intimated that the needs of women in Palestine could never be satisfied simply by raising money, but only by radically restructuring the social, political, and economic lives of men and women, allowing women "productive" roles outside the traditional realm.[86]

Most responses to the apparent proximity of Hadassah to charity work, however, were not very sophisticated. Hadassah's unavoidable "charitable" dimension typically induced a visceral, positive sentiment, or a negative reaction based on a view of the organization as irredeemably patronizing. Even the main voices denouncing Hadassah for autocracy and excessive intervention, the Palestine Executive and Kupat Holim, lambasted Hadassah for not setting up more clinics and offering more services.[87] To them, Hadassah was a magical cash cow that only needed to be milked for its endless riches; the success of the organization also incited unrealistic expectations.

Although Hadassah has principally been cited as living proof of how important women were and are in the Zionist movement, closer scrutiny of the organization's reception reveals the persistence of paternalistic attitudes. Hadassah, to a certain extent, destabilized the discourse of Zionism, but Zionist politics, overall, proved stubbornly intransigent. Much the same way as other forms of discrimination persist, despite the best efforts of marginalized groups to overturn a negative stereotype, Hadassah's successes were also used to legitimate women's subordinate status in the movement.[88] For much of her career, numerous Zionists wished that Henrietta Szold would either go away, or join the supposedly harmonious Zionist chorus, obsequious to the organization's leadership. Despite its tangible success in fostering a Zionist national consciousness among American women, and the group's unparalleled effect on the lives and health of people in Palestine, Hadassah in the interwar years could do very little to alter the prevailing male-centeredness of Zionism.

Henrietta Szold herself believed that the limitation of Hadassah's impact, compared to her best hopes for a comprehensive transformation of Palestine and diaspora Jewry, also stemmed from her own miscalculations and missteps of the well-meaning body. It was true, she confirmed, that Hadassah in many respects provided a useful model for other women's organizations. This was not, to Szold, a thorough vindication, as she wrote a colleague:

I was never satisfied with the way our attitude worked out in Palestine . . . the aloofness which we had assiduously cultivated . . . earned us all the reprobation and unfriendliness that have made our life here so bitter . . . here in Palestine an organic life is being developed. You and I may not like some of its manifestations. As a matter of fact I confess to you that some of its manifestations have aroused my indignation and destroyed my nerves. But for better or worse, that is the organic life that is being developed by Zionists here who are bone of the bone and flesh of the flesh of our ideal, the ideals we pursue in common with them. If we don't like some of the manifestations of their organized living, we can't withdraw to an island and gather up our skirts, and refuse to participate in their deliberations. We've got to get into their deliberations and influence their course and character. No "holier than thou" attitude produces positive results. And so it has been – the Hadassah Medical Organization as an administrative system has not taught the country good administration. As an administrative system it has locked its doors to everybody . . . Perhaps you can get me to admit that our drastic aloofness was justified ten years ago. It is not justified today, when the leaders of the community are wrestling gallantly if incompetently with the problems of the organization of Kenesset Israel, under the Communities Ordinance – that Kenesset Israel which is designed to take over from the Zionist Executive as soon as may be the responsibility for the health and education of the Jews in Palestine.[89]

In another burst of self-criticism, Szold wrote one of her successors, Mrs. Robert Szold, that

Hadassah, they say, has aroused criticism at the Congresses and in Palestine because it wants to control Palestine from a distance. The result has been that Hadassah has not contributed an iota to the education of the public in Palestine. One of the duties of Zionists in the Diaspora is to develop the Palestinian community to govern itself. We, Hadassah, by making the director of the medical work responsible to us in America, have given no opportunity to the people in Palestine to learn how to administer medical work. It will be a long time before Palestine can do without funds from the outside. But long before that time arrives, the community here should have learned how to use the funds put at its disposal.[90]

Although Henrietta Szold's self-evaluation is highly suggestive and perceptive, it also is unduly harsh. Szold and Hadassah, as well as the European women, were in an extremely difficult situation. It was as if they were always trying to put out fires while simultaneously training others in the skills of fire fighting. They could not relinquish the type of control they believed necessary, in order not to lose lives – but the price paid was not letting others truly help themselves. Although there was much to be gained, and much was achieved through their work, it was doubtful that they could have been both as effective and "educational" as Szold demanded they should be. She, too, could never overcome the fact that no matter how great the degree of solidarity between the Yishuv and the diaspora, they were dramatically different entities.

Despite declarations to the contrary, Zionist women in the United States and Europe were not simply just like men, nor were they merely better at men's tasks when they were given the chance.[91] Despite their self-consciously created myths extolling their unanimity with Zionist men, in important respects Hadassah and the organized Zionist women of Central and Western Europe came from a world different from their husbands and brothers. Even at that time, some women activists noted that a significant difference in "mentality" helped account for the varying Zionist outlooks and practices between women and men. They sought to transform the reality of the Yishuv, and its transmission to the Jews of Europe along the lines of their own middle-class virtues and values, according to a cultural framework with which they were familiar and believed to be most efficacious.[92] In their minds' eyes, and on the ground in Palestine, they engendered a different order from that of the men. They endowed Zionist nationalism with the image, idea, and praxis that public kitchens, infant welfare centers, and the physical, intellectual, and spiritual well-being of women are essential building blocks in the founding of a nation – which helped make it possible to assert that "Zionism is the social conscience in Jewry."[93] Hadassah raised this to an unprecedented level.

In sum, the Zionist movement represented a contest for power and knowledge in the wider world; within the movement, there also were such contests, not the least of which were organized in relation to gender.[94] The case of the reception of Hadassah and its European counterparts shows that a group can command knowledge, and prove its worthiness, but not necessarily be accorded power. Perhaps, however, that is more than one should expect. Hadassah's impact on selected individuals and on American women would be substantial, and would help fuel and occasionally disrupt the discourse about women in Zionism.

Conclusion

Zionism is not above all a political movement; it is primarily a moral movement. Its political power would be shaken if its moral content were to evaporate.   Robert Weltsch, 1922[1]

It cannot be emphasized too often or too strongly that what is needed for the advancement of the colonising of Palestine is money, money, money!   Adolf Boehm, around 1918[2]

I have attempted to illuminate a history of the institutionalization of a contradiction – of a permanent, self-re-creating diaspora Zionism, among a Jewish polity which was unlikely ever to set foot in Zion except as tourists. The forms of this lived contradiction developed within an organizational milieu which, akin to many political and social movements, studiously and vehemently sought to obliterate all traces of paradox and contradiction. Zionists understandably took great pride in, and were (and remain) defensive of, their movement's emergence as a political notion and in its achievements in Erets Israel. Its administration was vigilant in asserting that its course was the right one, and historians of Zionism have largely deemed that the leadership on the way to modern statehood was worthy, wise, and prudent. One recent commentator, although sympathetic to the Zionist movement, argues that

For the most part, scholarly studies of Zionism have tended to treat the Zionist definition of reality as an accurate depiction of historical processes, and the Zionist analysis of the Jewish problem as a valid description. Such attitudes, often written by confirmed Zionists, make no effort to critically examine Zionist discourse or question the categories through which it defines the Jewish condition. In general, the emergence of Zionism and its ascendancy to a hegemonic position is treated as a natural development in the history of the Jewish people.[3]

A result of this is that "Zionism has been highly effective in setting the discursive parameters for the ongoing struggle over Jewish identity not

194

only in Israel, but outside Israel as well."[4] This interpretation of interwar Zionism historically delineated these parameters of discourse, sociability, and political jockeying and its fallout in the West, to the extent that the years 1914 to 1933 constituted a formative period for the movement.

The self-estimation of Zionist work in Palestine, before the establishment of the State of Israel, is cogently expressed in Yosef Gorny's paraphrase of Martin Buber that the movement was "exemplary" in its "lack of failure."[5] Henrietta Szold, on the other hand, characterized the Zionist endeavors on the ground in Palestine in rather different terms: while its leaders were often "gallant," they proved "incompetent" in wrestling with numerous problems; she was unnerved by the amount of talent and resources routinely squandered.[6] Regarding Zionism in the Western diaspora, Chaim Weizmann thought that even among America's Jews, who were reputed to be aloof from the movement despite their significant financial contributions, there was evidence of selfless devotion and sincere commitment to the cause.[7] On the other hand, Irma Lindheim believed that by the late 1920s Zionism in the West had seriously compromised its self-proclaimed creed of democracy, public honesty, and responsibility toward Palestine and the welfare of the Jewish people; the confidence it had inspired during and after the First World War was severely eroded. The movement, she felt, had bowed to its entrenched bureaucracy and major fundraising instruments. The "ladies" of Hadassah, the mainstay of Zionism's all-important American constituency, were sapped of energy and treated with disdain. Ardently wishing to fulfill her Zionism, Lindheim took the extraordinary step of settling on a *Kibuts* in order to live the life of a pioneer, which brought her greater satisfaction.[8]

But can one neatly separate the Yishuv from the diaspora in speaking of pre-state Zionism, given the amorphous quality of the movement overall? Derek Penslar has convincingly argued that the designs and methods of Jewish settlement in Palestine, from 1870 until 1918, can best be understood in relation to the Central and Eastern European worlds from which the movement emanated.[9] Indeed, a truly comprehensive history of interwar Zionism, encompassing the diaspora and Palestine, remains to be written; until then grand judgments are at best tentative. At any rate, the emergence of a more thorough, judicious, and sophisticated historiography will not uncover anything like an essential truth of Zionism, but portends to yield a multiplicity of myths, counter-myths, realities, conflicts, and bases of consensus.

In interpreting a share of this history I have argued that it is plausible to look at the United States, Britain, and Germany as a loosely unified, but unselfconsciously cohesive force in the Zionist movement from the

First World War until 1933. (Hence later critics, such as Alain Finkielkraut, might unreflectively refer to "Western Zionism.")[10] Although most Zionists in these nations may have been oblivious to the extent that the movements in their countries were interconnected and alike, the practice of Zionism in the West comprised discernible processes of Jewish nationalization, replicated in other settings where Jews were largely acculturated. Western Zionists, for all their national distinctiveness, had common ways of seeing the Zionist project and developed similar strategies of ethnic mobilization, and perhaps more importantly, quasi-mobilization. Those who were not expected to emigrate to Palestine experienced common rites of initiation and participation in the movement. Their tangible connections to each other and to Palestine, outside the enterprise of collecting money that was headed to the same destination, were few. The elites mingled at Zionist Congresses in Carlsbad, Basel, or Zurich, and they were likely to meet as tourists to Palestine – maybe in the lobby of the King David Hotel or a *Kibuts* dining hall.

Most Western Zionists' experiences in the movement, however, were embedded in their national homes of Germany, Britain, and the United States. Zionism became a compartmentalized variant of Jewish ethnic identification, and a basis for local and international Jewish solidarity and sociability – and obviously, politics. It could be as vacuous for some as a means to improve one's chances for a date, to meet a suitable Jewish boy or girl in a Zionist youth or student group; it could, as well, lead to a cerebral engagement with a blossoming Hebrew renaissance, or Jewish philosophy, in a formal or informal study circle. Overall, as Zionism became further enmeshed in Jewish political and religious life in the West, it was presented as an umbrella for Jewish concerns well beyond the scope of the movement's initial goal of attaining a home for the Jews in Palestine. Partly due to the perception of Herzl as "fighting for the human rights" of the Jews along with attempting to secure Palestine as a Jewish national home,[11] Zionism came to be interwoven with Jewish anti-defamation.[12] There is ample evidence of clear, if not linear progress toward what Herzl called "the conquest of the communities" in the diaspora.[13] In part this may be traced to the ongoing development, since 1897, of an accessible, largely visual, symbolic language of the movement – conveyed mainly through photographic reproductions – which spoke to Western-acculturated Jewry in an unthreatening, even appealing, manner. Zionism did not simply occupy a space that had been taken by other loyalties; it did not replace Judaism. Zionism, instead, was a different entity – often intermingled with other secular and religious Judaisms – which Western Jews could easily condone to varying degrees, as men such as Lord Balfour, Louis Brandeis, and Albert Einstein were its champions, and as the Jewish settlement in Palestine was apparently attaining the character of an ever more normal, even grand, nation. It was easy to share in the honor of Jewish Palestine's unfolding success story.

But certain tensions, some of which were unique to Zionism and some of which were not, became apparent. Zionism was not immune to problems of other movements of political advocacy and ambitious social welfare and amelioration. It was pressed to deal with the dilemma of how to offer assistance without being patronizing; of how to present an image of strength, self-reliance, and honor, while at the same time arguing for rights and privileges of a people that had been historically victimized, and still mired in wretchedness.[14] In telling the Jews that they were simultaneously cursed and blessed by their distinctiveness as a nation, Zionists were compelled to restrain their self-assertion out of fear that they be judged by the non-Jewish world as chauvinistic and pushy. And having created a system in which the line was so clear between those Jews who were beseeched to give, and those to receive, how was it possible not to encourage arrogance, on one side, and resentment, on the other? *Shnorrers*, in the internal Zionist dialogue, was a designation reserved for the hangers-on of the "old Yishuv" and non-Zionist communal organizations – not themselves.[15] There is little doubt that many in the Zionist rank and file saw the movement as a kind of glorified *shnorring*. The Western Jews' sharing and basking in the achievements of Zionists in Palestine, and occasional visits to their poor relations in the burgeoning national home – even if the Westerners' solidarity was professed in a self-deprecating way – was not perceived outside the West as a Zionism on the same order as that embodied by the *Ḥalutsim*, the pioneers, hailing mostly from besieged Eastern Europe. And the sexual division of labor in the movement, between men and women, was no less stark than the rift between givers and takers in both Palestine and the diaspora.

All of this helped make a national movement which was in many ways distinctive in the West, in simultaneously assuming the roles of a voluntary association, a charitable society, a fraternal order for both men and women, a youth club, a proto-non-profit body, and a proto-special-interest lobby. Zionism was both supremely national and international. The convergence of Zionism and general Jewish interests also carried with it a diffusion of Zionist sentiments and energy. The fact that Zionism, despite the existence of a central address, was relatively undisciplined implied that it was more of a self-conscious hybrid than other political parties and nationalisms which had to refer to more single-minded systems of thought, loyalties, and concepts of fair play.

Weizmann's politics looked different from Boston and Washington than from London and Tel Aviv; Hadassah's efforts looked different from Jerusalem and Berlin than from New York or Baltimore. Zionism's scattered vantage points and contested sources of authority gave it the ability to generate a plethora of self-criticisms, only a fraction of which have been exploited in Zionist historiography. Although the movement's multivalent perspectives may not have always endowed it with greater flexibility, its protean nature made it easier for Jews throughout the world to find some connection with Zionism. It is not without reason that Ezra Mendelsohn has referred to interwar Zionism in Europe and the United States as "a kind of Aladdin's lamp."[16] After all, the community of Zionists did not represent a fixed group, but rather individuals and groups involved in, or at least exposed to a number of processes of nationalization which frequently required a minimal commitment of time and energy.

In dreaming up and manufacturing publicity the movement was tenacious and often brilliant, due to the real achievements on the ground in Palestine, and the residual theatrical impulses of Zionism's founders, Herzl and Nordau, which were no less dramatically swept up by Weizmann – despite his stated preference for the laboratory over the theater. But since the close of the First World War there was a growing consciousness of a gap between Zionist polemics and reality – and that something was amiss in the organization itself, particularly upon the rise of the mighty Keren Hayesod. By the early 1930s a note of sobriety and pessimism had even crept into the fundraising literature, which was usually ebullient. L. Jaffe wrote that if one has "close contact with the masses in every country" it is possible to see "the extent of the disaster that has befallen Jewry."[17] Zionism too was in decline. There was a need to reorganize its chief institutions, and the focus of the movement's propaganda efforts had to be rethought.[18] There was seemingly no choice but to cement further the explicit ties between Zionist and non-Zionist Western Jews,[19] despite the apparent radicalization and cries of separatism of the movement in Germany which had been brewing since before the First World War.[20] The movement showed its sanguine side by insisting that money collections necessarily symbolized unanimity with Zionism;[21] fundraising thereby was equated with nationalization:

the work so far done by the JNF, although it may not appear very extensive from the point of view of quantity, is of uncommon value as regards quality. It has not only wrought a complete change of mental attitude both in Palestine and among the Jews in the Diaspora, who after learning what has been achieved, have become more favourably disposed toward the colonisation; but it has also completely overcome the initial great difficulties that stood in the way of the further systematic colonising activity, which alone can constitute the aim of Zionism. The suitable institutions have been created for all undertakings and are directed in the proper spirit, so that all they need for the continuance and extension of their work is to be rightly developed and equipped with additional funds.[22]

Zionism was seen as an engine which could make itself go as long as it had the money.

It is ironic, but not surprising that Chaim Weizmann accused his foes in the movement of being "intellectually dishonest"[23] – whereas he himself seems to be one of the more creative sources of duplicity in interwar Zionism. His motives for throwing himself so forcefully into fundraising, and in bolstering the movement's fundraising instruments, were compelling to much of his constituency:

How can people possibly speak of forming a [Jewish] majority [in Palestine], and striving to obtain all that would follow from being a majority, if they don't throw in every ounce of energy which they possess, and every spark of idealism which still exists in them, in order to do the apostolic work of getting the necessary funds and forces together to give us a proper position in Palestine [?] This will remain always the central axis of my policy and everything else will be subordinated to this one view and to this one fact, which haunts me like a nightmare, and which makes me at the present time go through the ordeal of raising money in America and negotiating with non-Zionists for the Jewish Agency. I may say without boasting that I have not given up one iota of my idealist conception of the Movement as a Renaissance Movement of the Jewish people.[24]

Not everyone in the Zionist movement was willing to concede to Weizmann the notion that he could have both his obsession with fundraising and his cultural renaissance, existing only as complements to each other. Those who were resistant to his charms saw hucksterism, superficiality, and cheap sentimentality.

Still, the movement persisted in fostering the perception of its potential to bring ultimate healing to the Jewish people: "Its work is a work of peace and of true social progress. And hence it looks beyond the strife of parties within the Jewish people, and it will continue to form, in even a higher degree, a citadel of strength of despised and dismembered Jewry."[25] In the end, however, the results – however much they fell short of Zionist goals and potential – were real, and to a great many Jews and non-Jews, impressive. In 1930, Louis Brandeis wrote confidently that support among a majority of Western Jews "for the Jewish development of Palestine" was on its way to being "secure."[26] Where very little had existed before, outside remnants and memories for the Jews, there now was a palpable and pulsating national space, visible to all. The Zionist Organization and its many subgroups were accepted in the Jewish social landscape nearly everywhere in the West, and "non-partisan" Jewish organizations were appropriating more and more of the Zionist line. But what seems most clear from looking at Zionism in the United States, Germany, and Britain from 1914 to 1933 was that it adopted distinctive patterns to recruit, mobilize, and sustain its membership, and to reach out to the Jews at large. Although its successes and persistence were to be admired, its rigidity and authoritarian leadership styles, and obsession with fundraising, rarely have been scrutinized by scholars. Some would say that the utopian striving and all-inclusive vision of Zionism, as articulated by its founders, could only have foundered as the movement was forced to confront the real world. Historians of Zionism, however, might ruminate on the fact that even given the apparently overwhelming external forces, the movement, especially at a few key junctures, possessed a number of possibilities. Was the Keren Hayesod, essentially a top-down fundraising body, which was held to be sacred by its leaders and a Frankenstein monster by its detractors, the most appropriate flagship institution to connect the movement in the West with Palestine? Perhaps the best Zionist ideas and their progenitors, those with the greatest amount of foresight, those with the highest ethical standards, and even those who loved the Jewish people best, did not always triumph. Perhaps, despite its publicity to the contrary, the movement did not always adhere to the humanitarian impulses from which it had sprung, and this had some impact on its popularity among Western Jewries. After all, as Jonathan Frankel has written, "Zionist enterprises were heavily dependent for their survival and ultimate triumph on the West."[27] Zionism gave rise and prominence to a bourgeois fundraising device to enlist Western Jewry's support of an ostensibly radical socialist agenda. It is no wonder that there were such problems and frustrations in squaring the circle. The vague notion of "partnership," so favored by Zionist functionaries and even its historians, fails to do justice to a relationship which was carried over long distances and clouded by sloganeering and misleading euphemisms. Throughout much of the interwar years, Zionism, seen from the West, seemed to leave some of its best and brightest in the wings, or out in the cold. In retrospect it did build significant artifices of national consciousness, Jewish national culture, and material which bound Western Jews to their brethren in Eastern Europe and to the Zionist project in Palestine. Still, the movement was wont to waste precious moments.

Notes

INTRODUCTION

1 Samuel Weissenberg, quoted in John Efron, *Defenders of the Race: Jewish Doctors and Race Science in Fin-de-Siècle Europe* (London and New Haven: Yale University Press, 1994), p. 110.

2 Yosef Hayim Yerushalmi, *Zakhor: Jewish History and Jewish Memory* (New York: Schocken, 1989), pp. 99–100.

3 Although here I am most concerned with the integration of polemical and visual material in the construction of a national identity, investigations of "reception" in the literary-theoretical realm and the mediation of historical memory have informed my approach; see Gert Mattenklott, *Bilderdienst* (Munich: Rogner and Bernhard, 1976); Hans Robert Jauss, *Literatur als Provokation* (Frankfurt a.M.: Suhrkamp, 1970); Wolfgang Iser, "The Reading Process: A Phenomenological Approach," in *Critical Theory Since 1965*, edited by Hazard Adams and Leroy Searle (Tallahassee: University Presses of Florida, 1980), pp. 379–81; Russell Berman, *Modern Culture and Critical Theory: Art, Politics, and the Legacy of the Frankfurt School* (Madison: University of Wisconsin, 1990), p. 163; Berman, *Cultural Studies of Modern Germany: History, Representation, and Nationhood* (Madison: University of Wisconsin Press, 1993); Robert Holub, *Reception Theory: A Critical Introduction* (London and New York: Methuen, 1984); Ivan Gaskell, "History of Images," in *New Perspectives on Historical Writing*, edited by Peter Burke (University Park, Penn.: Penn State University Press, 1991), pp. 168–92; W. J. T. Mitchell, *Iconology: Image, Text, Ideology* (Chicago and London: University of Chicago Press, 1987); John Tagg, *The Burden of Representation: Essays on Photographies and Histories* (Amherst: University of Massachusetts Press, 1988); and Maurice Halbwachs, *On Collective Memory*, edited and translated by Lewis Coser (Chicago: University of Chicago Press, 1992).

4 There is a debate concerning the most fruitful means to compare Zionism in Europe versus the United States, but a stress on their similarities has been largely suggestive; see Allon Gal, "Independence and Universal Mission in Modern Jewish Nationalism: Comparative Analysis of European and American Zionism (1897–1948)," *Studies in Contemporary Jewry*, vol. 5 (1989): 242–74, which includes comments by Arnold Eisen, Arthur Goren, Yosef Gorny, and Ezra Mendelsohn and a "Rejoinder" by Allon Gal. Ezra Mendelsohn comes closest to the position I have assumed of including the

United States and Western Europe in asserting that "I do not believe in contrasting American Zionism with European Zionism. More meaningful is the dichotomy between East and West – with East meaning Eastern Europe, above all Poland–Russia–Romania and West meaning Central and Western Europe in addition to the new world," p. 267.

5 Walter Laqueur, *A History of Zionism* (New York: Holt, Rinehart, and Winston, 1972); Noah Lucas, *The Modern History of Israel* (London: Weidenfeld and Nicolson, 1974).

6 David Vital, *The Origins of Zionism* (Oxford: Clarendon Press, 1975); Vital, *Zionism: The Formative Years* (Oxford: Clarendon Press, 1982); Vital, *Zionism: The Crucial Phase* (Oxford: Clarendon Press, 1987); Jehuda Reinharz, *Chaim Weizmann: The Making of a Zionist Leader* (New York: Oxford University Press, 1985); Reinharz, *Chaim Weizmann: The Making of a Statesman* (New York: Oxford University Press, 1993).

7 Arthur Hertzberg, ed., *The Zionist Idea: A Historical Analysis and Reader* (New York: Athenaeum, 1977); Shlomo Avineri, *The Making of Modern Zionism: The Intellectual Origins of the Jewish State* (New York: Basic, 1981); Ben Halpern, *The Idea of the Jewish State*, 2nd revised edn. (Cambridge: Harvard University Press, 1969); Yaacov Shavit, *Jabotinsky and the Revisionist Movement, 1925–1948* (London: Frank Cass, 1988); Gideon Shimoni, *The Zionist Ideology* (Hanover, N. H.: Brandeis University Press of the University Press of New England, 1995); Laurence Silberstein, "Cultural Criticism, Ideology, and the Interpretation of Zionism: Toward a Post-Zionist Discourse," in Steven Kepnes, ed., *Postmodern Interpretations of Judaism: Deconstructive and Constructive Approaches* (New York: New York University Press, forthcoming).

8 Anita Shapira, *Ha-ma'avak ha-nikhzav: 'avodah 'Ivrit, 1929–1939* [The futile struggle: Hebrew labor, 1929–1939] (Tel Aviv: Tel Aviv University Press, 1977); Shapira, *Berl: The Biography of a Socialist Zionist*, translated by Haya Galai (New York: Cambridge University Press, 1984); Shapira, *Land and Power: The Zionist Resort to Force, 1881–1948*, translated by William Templer (New York: Oxford University Press, 1992); Israel Kolatt, *Ide'ologyah u-metsi'ut bi-tenuat ha-'avodah be-Erets Yisra'el, 1905–1919* [Ideology and reality in the labor movement in the land of Israel, 1905–1919], Ph.D. dissertation (Hebrew University, 1964); Yosef Gorny, *Aḥdut ha-'avodah, 1919–1930: ha-yesodot ha-ra'yoniyim ǫeha-shiṭah ha-medinit* [Aḥdut ha-'avodah, 1919–1930: its intellectual bases and its political system] (Tel Aviv: Tel Aviv University Press, 1973); Deborah Bernstein, *The Struggle for Equality: Urban Women Workers in Prestate Israeli Society* (New York: Praeger, 1987); Bernstein, ed., *Pioneers and Home-makers: Jewish Women in Pre-State Israel* (Albany: State University of New York Press, 1992); Mitchell Cohen, *Zion and State: Nation, Class, and the Shaping of Modern Israel* (Oxford: Basil Blackwell, 1987); Derek Penslar, *Zionism and Technocracy: The Engineering of Jewish Settlement in Palestine, 1870–1918* (Bloomington and Indianapolis: Indiana University Press, 1991).

9 Michael Berkowitz, *Zionist Culture and West European Jewry Before the First World War* (Cambridge: Cambridge University Press, 1993).

10 On the problematic distinction between Eastern and Western Jewries, see Jonathan Frankel, "Modern Jewish Politics East and West (1840–1939): Utopia, Myth, Reality," in Zvi Gitelman, ed., *The Quest for Utopia: Jewish Political Ideas and Institutions Through the Ages* (Armonk, N. Y.: M. E. Sharpe, 1992), pp. 81–103; Ezra Mendelsohn, *The Jews of East Central Europe Between the World Wars* (Bloomington: Indiana University Press, 1987), p. 7.

11 Mitchell Cohen, writing on the political developments in the Yishuv, asserts that "From being an essential means of liberation of the Jewish people," Labor Zionism "increasingly became a thing unto itself": *Zion and State*, pp. 3–4.

12 "Französisches Judentum und Zionismus," *Jüdische Rundschau* (hereafter cited as *JR*), October 1, 1935, p. 1; N. Hermann, "Notes from Paris," *New Judaea*, January 30, 1925, p. 158. A factor which was exclusive to France, which no doubt influenced the reception of Zionism, was the existence of the Alliance Israélite Universelle, which in many respects used a similar language of cultural regeneration and moral uplift as did the Zionists: see Aron Rodrigue, *Images of Sephardi and Eastern Jewries in Transition: The Teachers of the Alliance Israélite Universelle* (London and Seattle: University of Washington Press, 1993).

13 Ezra Mendelsohn, *On Modern Jewish Politics* (New York: Oxford University Press, 1993), p. 132.

14 Paula Hyman, "Was There a 'Jewish Politics' in Western and Central Europe?," in Gitelman, *Quest for Utopia*, p. 106; Michael Brenner, *The Renaissance of Jewish Culture in Weimar Germany* (New Haven: Yale University Press, 1995).

15 Claudia Prestel, "Frauen und die Zionistische Bewegung (1897–1933): Tradition oder Revolution?," *Historische Zeitschrift* 258 (1994): 29–71.

16 Yigal Elam, *Ha-Sokhnut ha-Yehudit: Shanim rishonot* [The Jewish Agency: the formative years] (Jerusalem: Ha-Sifriyah ha-Tsiyonit, 1990).

17 The following are among the significant works not mentioned elsewhere in this chapter: Steven Zipperstein, *Elusive Prophet: Ahad Ha-Am and the Origins of Zionism* (Berkeley and Los Angeles: University of California Press, 1993); Mark Levene, *War, Jews, and the New Europe: The Diplomacy of Lucien Wolf, 1914–1919* (Oxford: Littman, 1992); Naomi W. Cohen, *The Year After the Riots: American Responses to the Palestine Crisis of 1929–1930* (Detroit: Wayne State University Press, 1988); Stuart A. Cohen, *English Zionists and British Jews: The Communal Politics of Anglo-Jewry, 1895–1920* (Princeton: Princeton University Press, 1982); Jehuda Reinharz, *Fatherland or Promised Land: The Dilemma of the German Jew, 1893–1914* (Ann Arbor: University of Michigan Press, 1975), and Reinharz, ed., *Dokumente zur Geschichte des deutschen Zionismus, 1882–1933* (Tübingen: J. C. B. Mohr, 1981); Hagit Lavsky, *Be-terem pur'anut: darkam ve-yihudam shel Tsiyone Germanyah, 1918–1932* [Before catastrophe: the unique path of Zionism in Germany, 1918–1932] (Jerusalem: Magnes Press, Hebrew University, Ha-Sifriyah ha-Tsiyonit, 1990); Stephen A. Poppel, *Zionism in Germany, 1897–1933: The Shaping of a Jewish Identity* (Philadelphia: Jewish Publication Society of America, 1977); Norman Rose, *Chaim Weizmann: A*

Biography (New York: Viking-Penguin, 1986); Melvin Urofsky, *American Zionism from Herzl to the Holocaust* (Garden City, N. Y.: Anchor/Doubleday, 1975); Urofsky, ed. *Essays in American Zionism, 1917–1948* (New York: Herzl Press, 1978); Ruth Kozodoy, David Sidorsky, and Kalman Sultanik, eds., *Vision Confronts Reality: Historical Perspectives on the Contemporary Jewish Agenda* (New York: Herzl Press, 1989); Naomi W. Cohen, *American Jews and the Zionist Idea* (New York: KTAV, 1975); and Yonathan Shapiro, *Leadership of the American Zionist Organization, 1897–1930* (Urbana: University of Illinois Press, 1971); Haim Avni, *Argentina and the Jews: A History of Jewish Immigration,* translated by Gila Brand (Tuscaloosa: University of Alabama Press, 1991); Gideon Shimoni, *Jews and Zionism: The South African Experience, 1910–1967* (New York: Oxford University Press, 1980).

18 Among the most successful at grounding a discussion of Zionism in the European context are Derek Penslar in *Zionism and Technocracy,* Claudia Prestel in "Frauen und die Zionistische Bewegung," and Ezra Mendelsohn, in *On Modern Jewish Politics;* the latter richly illuminates both European and American Zionism with thoughtful comparisons to non-Jewish groups.

19 A great deal of the excitement that has been generated in scholarship on Zionism has involved recently released documents from the early years of the State of Israel; see Benny Morris, *1948 and After: Israel and the Palestinians* (Oxford: Clarendon Press, 1990); Avi Shlaim, *Collusion Across the Jordan* (Oxford: Oxford University Press, 1988); on the appropriateness of the term "revisionism" regarding this literature, see Morris, *1948 and After,* pp. 6–7.

20 Eric Hobsbawm and Terence Ranger, eds., *The Invention of Tradition* (New York and Cambridge: Cambridge University Press, 1983).

21 Ben Halpern, *A Clash of Heroes: Brandeis, Weizmann, and American Zionism* (New York: Oxford University Press, 1987); Evyatar Friesel, "Lel ha-mashber ben Weizmann le-ven Brandeis" [The crisis in leadership between Weizmann and Brandeis] in *Ha-Tsiyonut* 4 (1975): 146–64; Friesel, *Ha-Mediniyut ha-Tsiyonit le-aḥar hats'harat Balfour, 1917–1922* [Zionist policy after the Balfour Declaration, 1917–1922] (Tel Aviv: Tel Aviv University Press, 1977); Jehuda Reinharz, *Chaim Weizmann: The Making of a Statesman;* on the actual fragmentation of the "Brandeis group," see Naomi Cohen, *The Year After the Riots,* pp. 79–81. See also Deborah E. Lipstadt, "The Zionist Career of Louis Lipsky, 1900–1921," Ph.D. dissertation (Brandeis University, 1976); Samuel Halperin, *The Political World of American Zionism* (Detroit: Wayne State University Press, 1961); Robert A. Burt, *Two Jewish Justices: Outcasts in the Promised Land* (Berkeley and Los Angeles: University of California Press, 1988), pp. 14–18.

22 Evyatar Friesel, "Pinsk and Washington," *Studies in Contemporary Jewry,* 6 (1990): 328.

23 Ezra Mendelsohn, *Zionism in Poland: The Formative Years, 1915–1926* (New Haven: Yale University Press, 1981).

24 Hagit Lavsky, *Yesodot ha-taḳtsiv la-mif'al ha-Tsiyoni: Va'ad ha-tsirim, 1918–1921* [The budgetary bases of the Zionist enterprise, 1918–1921] (Jerusalem: Ben Zvi Institute, 1980); Jacob Metser, *Hon le'umi le-vayit*

le'eumi, 1919–1921 [National capital for a national home, 1919–1921] (Jerusalem: Hebrew University Press, 1979); Friesel, *Ha-Mediniyut ha-Tsiyonit*; "Simon–Friesel Correspondence," in Julius Simon, *Certain Days*, edited by Evyatar Friesel (Jerusalem: Israel Universities Press, 1971), pp. 327–72; Jacob Metser and Nahum Gross, "Public Finance in the Jewish Economy in Interwar Palestine," *Research in Economic History* 3 (1978): 87–159.

25 See Peter Dobkin Hall, *Inventing the Nonprofit Sector and Other Essays on Philanthropy, Voluntarism, and Nonprofit Organizations* (Baltimore: Johns Hopkins University Press, 1992); Teresa Odendahl, *Charity Begins at Home: Generosity and Self-Interest Among the Philanthropic Elite* (New York: Basic, 1990); Robert Bremner, *American Philanthropy* 2nd edn. (Chicago: University of Chicago Press, 1988); cf. Eliezer D. Jaffe, *Givers and Spenders: The Politics of Charity in Israel* (Jerusalem: Ariel, 1985).

26 Alain Finkielkraut, *The Imaginary Jew*, translated by Kevin O'Neil and David Suchoff (Lincoln: University of Nebraska Press, 1994).

27 David Myers, in writing on the Zionist attempt to fashion a new, Zionist history, has similarly concluded that despite adopting a posture of transformation, the historical work itself coming from the "Jerusalem school" was largely beholden to earlier views of history; see Myers, *Re-inventing the Jewish Past: European Jewish Intellectuals and the Zionist Return to History* (New York: Oxford University Press, 1995).

1 MANLY MEN AND THE ATTEMPTED APPROPRIATION OF THE WAR EXPERIENCE, 1914–1918

1 "Österreichische Zionisten im Felde," *JR*, October 16, 1914, p. 389; Heinrich Loewe, "Die Juden im Kriege," *JR*, September 5, 1914, pp. 357–58; Ludwig Strauss, "Reichstreu und Volkstreue," *JR*, October 16, 1914, p. 387; see George L. Mosse, *The Jews and the German War Experience, 1914–1918* (New York: Leo Baeck Institute, 1977).

2 "Aus aller Welt – Antisemitismus unter russischen Kriegsgefangen," *JR*, October 16, 1914, p. 391; Loewe, "Die Juden im Kriege," p. 357; and Loewe, no title, *JR*, August 7, 1914, p. 343.

3 Loewe, "Die Juden im Kriege," p. 357.

4 Jonathan Frankel, "The Paradoxical Politics of Marginality: Thoughts on the Jewish Situation During the Years 1914–1921," *Studies in Contemporary Jewry*, 4 (1988): 4.

5 *Jewish Chronicle*, July 31, 1914, p. 7.

6 *Jewish Chronicle*, September 4, 1914, p. 5; one of the more tepid responses was that of the Czechs: see Hans Kohn, *Living in a World Revolution* (New York: Trident, 1964), p. 86.

7 "The War. Alleged Pogroms in Russia. 'Absolutely False.' An Enemy's Concoction," *Jewish Chronicle*, September 4, 1914, p. 10.

8 "Russian Jews' Enthusiasm" and "The Russo-Jewish Hero Katz," *Jewish Chronicle*, September 18, 1914, p. 28; "The War. Russian Jews and the Conflict. Loyal Jewry Astonishes Russia. March of Jews to the Tsar's Palace," *Jewish Chronicle*, August 28, 1914, p. 10.

9 "The Tsar's Thanks to the Jews," *Jewish Chronicle*, October 9, 1914, p. 16.
10 "The War. News from All Quarters. More Russo-Jewish Heroism," *Jewish Chronicle*, October 16, 1914, p. 12; "Russo-Jewish Heroes," *Jewish Chronicle*, October 23, 1914, p. 23.
11 "Bravery of Jewish Soldiers," *Jewish Chronicle*, October 23, 1914, p. 23.
12 "Bravery of Jewish Soldiers," p. 23.
13 See Stuart Cohen, *English Zionists and British Jews*, pp. 218, 252–54; David Vital, *Zionism: The Crucial Phase*, pp. 133, 140–61, 228–33, 250, 259, 272, 344; Eugene C. Black, *The Social Politics of Anglo-Jewry, 1880–1920* (Oxford: Basil Blackwell, 1989), pp. 374–78; David Cesarani, *The Jewish Chronicle and Anglo-Jewry, 1841–1991* (Cambridge: Cambridge University Press, 1994), pp. 114–33; David Yisraeli, "The Struggle for Zionist Military Involvement in the First World War, 1914–1917," *Bar Ilan Studies in History*, ed. Pinhas Artzi (Ramat-Gan: Bar Ilan University Press, 1978), pp. 197–213; Sharman Kadish, *Bolsheviks and British Jews: The Anglo-Jewish Community, Britain, and the Russian Revolution* (London: Frank Cass, 1992); Levene, *War, Jews, and the New Europe*; Geoffrey Alderman, *Modern British Jewry* (Oxford: Oxford University Press, 1992); Bryan Cheyette, *Constructions of "The Jew" in English Literature and Society: Racial Representations, 1875–1945* (Cambridge: Cambridge University Press, 1993).
14 "How the Foreign-born Jew Fights," *Jewish Chronicle*, January 7, 1916, p. 11.
15 "Enlistment or Deportation," *Jewish Chronicle*, July 14, 1916, p. 18.
16 Reinharz, *Chaim Weizmann: The Making of a Statesman*, pp. 40–72; Reinharz, "Science in the Service of Politics: The Case of Chaim Weizmann During the First World War," *English Historical Review* (July 1985): 572–603.
17 Cesarani, *Jewish Chronicle and Anglo-Jewry*, pp. 119–21.
18 "The Jewish Battalion," *Maccabaean* (May 1918): 119.
19 "The 'Judean' Regiment," *Jewish Chronicle*, February 22, 1918, p. 5; David Cesarani, *Jewish Chronicle and Anglo-Jewry*, p. 120.
20 See Geoffrey Serle, *John Monash: A Biography* (Melbourne: Melbourne University Press, 1985). I wish to thank Leo Dougherty for this reference and his insight into Monash's significance in military history.
21 Entry for "Sir John Monash," in *Encyclopaedia Judaica* (Jerusalem: Encyclopedia Judaica, Keter, 1971), 16 vols.
22 N. Syrkin, "General Allenby's Sweeping Victory in Palestine," *Maccabaean* (October 1918): 292–93.
23 J. H. Patterson, *With the Judaeans in the Palestine Campaign* (London: Hutchinson, 1922), pp. 249–58.
24 "Palestine Liberated," *Maccabaean* (October 1918): 286.
25 Vital, *Zionism: The Crucial Phase*, p. 146.
26 "The Break With Germany," *Maccabaean* (March 1917): 169.
27 "Zionists and American Patriotism," *Maccabaean* (September 1917): 336–37.
28 "Welfare Work for Jewish Soldiers," *Maccabaean* (November 1917): 383.
29 See Michael C. C. Adams, *The Great Adventure: Male Desire and the Coming of World War I* (Bloomington: Indiana University Press, 1990); Margaret

Higonnet, Jane Jenson, Sonya Michel, and Margaret Collins Weitz, eds., *Behind the Lines: Gender and the Two World Wars* (New Haven: Yale University Press, 1987).

30 To a great extent, this was true for Jewish soldiers in general; see Ulrich Dunker, *Der Reichsbund jüdischer Frontsoldaten, 1919–1938: Geschichte eines jüdischen Abwehrvereins* (Dusseldorf: Droste Verlag, 1977), p. 154; Egmont Zechlin, *Die deutsche Politik und die Juden im Ersten Weltkrieg* (Göttingen: Vandenhöck and Ruprecht, 1969).

31 See Michael Meyer, *The Origins of the Modern Jew: Jewish Identity and European Culture in Germany, 1749–1824* (Detroit: Wayne State University Press, 1984); David Sorkin, *The Transformation of the German Jewry, 1780–1840* (New York: Oxford University Press, 1987).

32 Cover and cartoon: "The Old Sword in Jew Hands," *Young Judaea* (April 1918): 226.

33 See Paul Breines, *Tough Jews: Political Fantasies and the Moral Dilemma of American Jewry* (New York: Basic, 1990).

34 See "German-Speaking Jews and Zionism," *LBI News*, no. 53 (Winter 1987): 5–6.

35 On this subject, see the works of Sander Gilman, such as *The Jew's Body* (New York and London: Routledge, 1991), pp. 38–59; and George L. Mosse, *Nationalism and Sexuality: Respectability and Abnormal Sexuality in Modern Europe* (New York: Howard Fertig, 1985).

36 Paul Fussell, *The Great War and Modern Memory* (New York and London: Oxford University Press, 1975), pp. 36–74.

37 Robert Weltsch to Martin Buber, "Im Felde in Russisch Polen," July 18, 1915, AR 7/85, Folder 8, Box 2, Leo Baeck Institute, New York (hereafter cited as LBI).

38 "A Jew Boy in Kitchener's Army," *Jewish Chronicle*, October 23, 1914, p. 20.

39 "The Time of My Life," *Jewish Chronicle*, October 16, 1914, p. 16.

40 Maurice Samuel, "Soldiering at Yaphank: A Letter from a Zionist Soldier," *Maccabaean* (November 1917): 396.

41 *JR*, August 7, 1914, p. 343; Eugen Tannenbaum, ed., *Kriegsbriefe deutscher und österreichischer Juden* (Berlin: Neuer Verlag, 1915), p. 138.

42 "A Jewish Soldier's Thrilling Experiences," *Jewish Chronicle*, October 16, 1914, p. 16.

43 "Letters from Jewish Soldiers. From Quartermaster-Sergt. Thompson," *Jewish Chronicle*, November 20, 1914, p. 14.

44 "My Mansion Below the Earth," *Jewish Chronicle*, October 23, 1914, p. 23.

45 "In the Communal Armchair. The Fourth War-Anniversary," *Jewish Chronicle*, August 2, 1918, p. 7.

46 H. V. Levin, "Letters from the Front. Many Jews in the Trenches," *Jewish Chronicle*, March 5, 1915, p. 12.

47 Baron Nunes Martin, "Letters from the Front. Many Jews in the Trenches," *Jewish Chronicle*, March 5, 1915, p. 12.

48 The definitive treatments, with substantial bibliographies on the encounter of German Jewry and East European Jewry are Steven Aschheim, *Brothers and Strangers: The East European Jew in German and German-Jewish Consciousness 1800–1923* (Madison: University of Wisconsin Press, 1982),

pp. 80–99; and Jack Wertheimer, *Unwelcome Strangers: East European Jews in Imperial Germany* (New York: Oxford University Press, 1987).

49 Sammy Gronemann, "Erinnerungen," LBI; A. Williner, "Palästina memoir collection," p. 271, LBI; *Die Juden im Krieg: Denkschrift des jüdischen sozialistischen Arbeiterverbandes Poale-Zion an das Internationale Sozialistische Bureau* (The Hague: no publisher, 1917), pp. 3–4.

50 "The Jews in the War," *Maccabaean* (September 1915): 80.

51 James Fuchs, "Eight Months of Cossack Rule in Galicia," *Maccabaean* (September 1915): 92.

52 Gronemann, "Erinnerungen," p. 273.

53 Gronemann, "Erinnerungen," pp. 272ff.

54 Gronemann, "Erinnerungen," p. 273.

55 Gronemann, "Erinnerungen," pp. 273–74.

56 Gronemann, "Erinnerungen," p. 271.

57 See Edward J. Bristow, *Prostitution and Prejudice: The Jewish Fight Against White Slavery, 1880–1939* (New York: Schocken, 1983), and Marion Kaplan, *The Campaigns of the Jüdischer Frauenbund, 1904–1938* (Westport, Conn.: Greenwood, 1979).

58 Robert Weltsch to Martin Buber, May 1916, Folder 6, Box 2, LBI AR 7185, pp. 3–7.

59 Gronemann, "Erinnerungen," pp. 275–76.

60 "German-Speaking Jews and Zionism," *LBI News*, no. 53 (Winter 1987): 5–6; Weltsch to Buber, May 1916, pp. 9–10, LBI.

61 Louis Brandeis, "Zionism and Patriotism" (1915), p. 6, Box 6, Nearprint file, special topics, Zionism, American Jewish Archives, Cincinnati, Ohio [hereafter cited as AJA]; see Ruth Rosen, *The Lost Sisterhood: Prostitution in America* (Baltimore: Johns Hopkins University Press, 1982).

62 Tannenbaum, *Kriegsbriefe deutscher und österreicher Juden*, pp. 4–5.

63 Tannenbaum, *Kriegsbriefe deutscher und österreicher Juden*, pp. 35–37, 49, 66; "Feier des Jom-Kippur im Felde," *JR*, October 30, 1914, p. 407.

64 Modris Eksteins, *Rites of Spring: The Great War and the Birth of the Modern Age* (London: Black Swan, 1990), pp. 159–68.

65 "Rosh Hashana," *Jewish Chronicle*, September 18, 1914, p. 9.

66 "A War-Time Seder," *Jewish Chronicle*, April 10, 1918, p. 16.

67 "The Jew Soldier and Judaism," *Jewish Chronicle*, March 22, 1918, p. 8.

68 Tannenbaum, *Kriegsbriefe deutscher und österreicher Juden*, pp. 12–13, 21.

69 Tannenbaum, *Kriegsbriefe deutscher und österreicher Juden*, pp. 119–21.

70 To a lesser extent, this was also the case on the western front; see "Feldpostenbriefe Jomkippur in der französischen Kirche," *JR*, October 23, 1914, pp. 396–97.

71 Hugo Knoepfmacher, "Some Recollections of My Encounter with Hans Kohn in Siberia (1917–1919)," AR 7172, LBI; "Zionistische Propaganda in Kriegsgefangenen-Lagern," *JR*, August 31, 1917, p. 291; "Tätigkeitbericht I, II," 1919, Robert Weltsch archive, AR 7185, LBI; Georg Schutz, "Jüdische Erlebnisse in Sibirisches Kriegsgefangenschaft," *Jüdische Wille*, 12 (1919): 101; see Kohn, *Living in a World Revolution*, pp. 89ff.; Kohn attempted to escape from the camp at Samarkand; when he was recaptured he was sent to a more secure outpost.

72 "Bericht über die am 4. Mai im Cafe Gartenbau abgehaltene Versammlung der Vereinigung-Angehöriger Kriegsgefangenen Gruppe Krassnaja-Rjetschka-Chabarowsk," Hans Kohn archive, AR 259, 23/10, LBI.

73 Hans Kohn archive, AR 259, 23/3, 4, LBI.

74 Knoepfmacher, "Some Recollections," p. 3.

75 "Hans Kohn zu seinem 27 Geburtstage in tiefer Dankbarkeit der ZsidoSondolat Nowo-Nikolajewsk Westsiderien, 15 September 1918," Hans Kohn archive, AR 259, 23/5, LBI.

76 Gertrude V[an] Tijn, "Oh Life of Joy and Sorrow, Laughter and Tears," ME 643, typescript in LBI, pp. 29–30.

77 A. B. Makover, "From a Zionist in Khaki," Maccabaean (September 1918): 267.

78 "Books for Jewish Soldiers," Hadassah Bulletin (April 1918): 3.

79 Henrietta Szold to Jessie Sampter, January 14, 1918, Record Group 7, Folder 44, Box 5, HA.

80 George Wollstein, "KJVer Feldbriefe," Jüdische Wille, 1 (1918): 136–37.

81 "Eine jüdische Kriegschronik," JR, September 25, 1914, p. 374.

82 "Ein zionistischer Generalmajor in Österreich," JR, September 5, 1914, p. 358; "Das Testament eines gefallenen zionistischen Offiziers," JR, December 4, 1914, p. 445.

83 "An unsere Gesinnungsgenossen im Felde!" [leaflet], September 1915, KKL 1/85, Central Zionist Archives, Jerusalem (hereafter cited as CZA).

84 "Der I. Kartelltag des 'Kartells jüdischer Verbindungen,'" JR, March 4, 1919, p. 127.

85 Memo [from the Zionist Central Office in] the Hague to Jewish National Fund bureau, December 21, 1915, England, KKL 1/40, CZA; Erez Israel: Sondernummer: Die Kriegslandspende (Vienna: Jewish National Fund, 1916); Eli Rothschild, ed., Meilensteine: Vom Wege des Kartells jüdischer Verbindungen in der Zionistischen Bewegung (Tel Aviv: Präsidium, KJV, 1972), p. 73.

86 "Unsere Hilfsaktion," JR, September 11, 1914, p. 364; E. W. Tschlenow, Der Krieg, die Russische Revolution und der Zionismus (Copenhagen: Bureau of the Zionist Organization, 1917), p. 6; S. Bernstein, Zionism, Its Essential Aspects, and Its Organisation (Copenhagen: Office of the Zionist Organisation, 1919), p. 42.

87 Maccabaean (August 1914): cover.

88 Maccabaean (March 1914): 90.

89 Maccabaean (April 1914): cover.

90 Abraham Burstein, "The Prayer in the Trenches," Young Judaean (June 1915): 11.

91 Maccabaean (May 1914): 131.

92 Maccabaean (August 1914): 47.

93 Gerald Sorin, The Jewish People in America. A Time for Building: The Third Migration, 1880–1920 (Baltimore and London: Johns Hopkins University Press, 1992), p. 134.

94 "Our Own Neutrality," Maccabaean (November–December 1914): 155.

95 Cf. Maccabaean (October 1914): 121.

96 Sorin, Jewish People in America, pp. 200–01, 207.

97 Hyman Segal, "Interpretations of a Cartoon," *Maccabaean* (February 1916): 36.
98 "Reviews and Comments. The January Cartoon," *Maccabaean* (February 1916): 40; George J. Horowitz, "Letters to the Editors," *Maccabaean* (September 1916): 37.
99 "On the March," *Maccabaean* (January 1916): 6; "Dispossessed," *Maccabaean* (February 1916): cover; cartoon, "For Whom?" in *Maccabaean* (March 1916), cover.
100 "The Guardian of Israel," *Maccabaean* (April 1916): 91; "If You Will It It Is Not a Dream," *Young Judaean* (July 1918): 323; "With the Might of the Lion," *Young Judaean* (August 1918): 349; see also an untitled picture with the caption: "Although Poland itself is under the heel of the oppressor, it still finds time to carry on its mean, anti-Jewish policies," *Young Judaean* (February 1918): 159.
101 Robert Goldstein, "Advertising the Zionist Movement," "Letters to the Editor," *Maccabaean* (January 1917): 135.
102 Jacob Segall, *Die deutschen Juden als Soldaten im Kriege, 1914–1918: Eine statistische Studie* (Berlin: Philo-Verlag, 1922); *Jüdisches Archiv* (Vienna: R. Loewitt, 1915); "The War: Jewish Heroism: Tributes to Jewish Loyalty," in *Jewish Chronicle*, September 11, 1914, p. 10.
103 "Jews in the War," *Maccabaean* (August 1915): 59.
104 "Momentbilder aus Russland," *JR*, October 30, 1914, p. 404.
105 "A Rothschild in the Austrian Army," *Jewish Chronicle*, October 9, 1914, p. 16.
106 Eugene Kohn, "Jewish Nationalism and German Kultur Cult," *Maccabaean* (October 1917): 336–37.
107 "The Polish Atrocities," *Maccabaean* (January 1915): 9.
108 "Die Juden in englischen Heere," *JR*, December 11, 1914, p. 456.
109 Cf. "Die Juden im österreichischen Kriegsdienste," *JR*, August 21, 1914, p. 358. For how this issue played in the Yishuv, see Shapira, *Land and Power*.
110 Martin Buber, in *JR*, January 5, 1917, p. 5.
111 Elias Gilner, *War and Hope: A History of the Jewish Legion* (New York: Herzl Press, 1969).
112 "Das jüdische Regiment in England und der Zionismus," *JR*, October 26, 1917, p. 348; A. Wolliner, "Palästina und die jüdische Legion," *Volk und Land*, July 10, 1919, p. 877; "REPORT," December 23, 1915, p. 11, DD a 2/3/6, CZA.
113 "London's Welcome to the 'Judeans,'" and "The War. The 'Judeans.' March Through London. Enthusiastic Reception," *Jewish Chronicle*, February 8, 1918, pp. 5, 13; "London Cheer Jewish Battalion," *Maccabaean* (March 1918): 89.
114 Vital, *Zionism: The Crucial Phase*, p. 229.
115 "Book Reviews," *With the Zionists in Gallipoli* by J. H. Patterson (New York: George Doran and Co., 1916), in *Maccabaean* (August 1916): 17.
116 Patterson, *With the Zionists in Gallipoli*, pp. v–vi.
117 Patterson, *With the Judaeans in the Palestine Campaign*, pp. ix–x; other accounts include Redcliffe N. Salaman, *Palestine Reclaimed: Letters from a*

Jewish Officer in Palestine (London: George Routledge and Sons, and New York: E. P. Dutton, 1920).

118 Wladimir Jabotinsky, *Die jüdische Legion im Weltkrieg* (Berlin: Jüdischer Verlag, 1930); this edition was a translation from the Russian which was originally published in Paris; the American edition did not appear until 1945, as Vladimir Jabotinsky, *The Story of the Jewish Legion*, translated by Samuel Katz (New York: Bernard Ackerman, 1945). Joseph Galron supplied this reference. Jabotinsky's *Turkey and the War* (London: T. Fisher Unwin, 1917) was received warmly, but he was depicted as highly partisan; see "Books – Old and New," *Maccabaean* (October 1917): 375.

119 Shmarya Levin, "The Warrior," *Maccabaean* (December 1915): 140.

120 "Book Reviews," *Maccabaean* (August 1916): 17.

121 Morris Freilicoff, "The Jewish Legion," *Maccabaean* (November 1918): 322.

122 "Eine Erklärung der englischen Regierung für den Zionismus," *JR*, October 16, 1917, p. 369; cf. "Eine Erklärung der deutschen Regierung," *JR*, January 11, 1918, p. 1.

123 "Editorial: Germany and Jewish Interests," *Maccabaean* (September 1915): 65.

124 Levene, *War, Jews, and the New Europe*, pp. 87–88.

125 See Leo Motzkin, "The Russian Revolution and the National Question," *Maccabaean* (April 1917): 200–03; Motzkin, "Jewish Factions in Russia," *Maccabaean* (May 1917): 233–36, 244.

126 Tschlenow, *Der Krieg, die Russische Revolution und der Zionismus*, pp. 12–13.

127 Nahum Goldmann, *Die drei Forderungen des jüdischen Volkes* (Berlin: Jüdischer Verlag, 1919).

128 "German Atrocities Against Jews at Kalish," *Jewish Chronicle*, August 28, 1914, p. 11; "The Jews in the War," *Maccabaean* (December 1915): 155.

129 Franz Oppenheimer, "Alt und neue Makkabaeer," *JR*, August 28, 1914, p. 353.

130 *Maccabaean* (August 1914): 53.

131 *Maccabaean* (August 1914): 54.

132 *Die Juden im Kriege*, pp. 3–4.

133 Adolf Boehm, "Zionistische Arbeit in Palästina," *Erez Israel* (Vienna), p. 24; S. Bernstein, *Zionism*, p. 67; Kurt Blumenfeld, "Hochschule des Zionismus (Rede gehalten auf dem ersten Katelltag des KJV, 16 Februar 1919)," in Rothschild, *Meilensteine*, pp. 74–77.

134 Samuel Lewenberg, "Our Organization in War Time: The Story of the Provisional Zionist Committee," *Young Judaean* (February 1917): 163–66; Joseph Krimsky, *Pilgrimage and Service 1918–1919* (printed privately, no date); "The 'Hadassah' Unit," *Jewish Chronicle*, July 12, 1918, p. 6.

2 A NEW PANTHEON: THE PORTRAYAL OF ZIONIST LEADERS IN THE WEST

1 Ahad Ha-Am, "Moses," quoted in Daniel Jeremy Silver, *Images of Moses* (New York: Basic, 1982), pp. 289–90.

2 Berkowitz, *Zionist Culture*, pp. 99–103.

3 See Ahad Ha-Am, quoted in David Tartakover, ed., *Herzl in Profile: Herzl's Image in the Applied Arts* (Tel Aviv: Tel Aviv Museum, 1979), p. 51; Jacques Kornberg, ed., *At the Crossroads: Essays on Ahad Ha-Am* (Albany: State University of New York Press, 1983); Zipperstein, *Elusive Prophet*.

4 For an alternate selection of heroes see Benjamin Harshav, *Language in Time of Revolution* (Berkeley and Los Angeles: University of California Press, 1993), pp. 87–88.

5 Berthold Feiwel, "Zum ersten Heft des 'Juden,'" in *JR*, May 5, 1916, p. 143; Alons Paquet, "Martin Buber," *Die Tat* 5 (1921): 362–65; Maurice Friedman, *Martin Buber's Life and Work: The Middle Years, 1923–1945* (New York: Dutton, 1983); Friedman, *Encounter on a Narrow Ridge: A Life of Martin Buber* (New York: Paragon, 1991); Steven Kepnes, *The Text as Thou: Martin Buber's Dialogical Hermeneutics and Narrative Theology* (Bloomington: Indiana University Press, 1992); Laurence Silberstein, *Martin Buber's Social and Religious Thought: Alienation and the Quest for Meaning* (New York: New York University Press, 1989).

6 "Der Weg des 'Juden,'" in *JR*, May 19, 1916, p. 161.

7 Martin Buber, *A Land of Two Peoples: Martin Buber on Jews and Arabs*, edited by Paul Mendes-Flohr (New York: Oxford University Press, 1983).

8 See Shavit, *Jabotinsky and the Revisionist Movement*.

9 See Yael Zerubavel, "The Politics of Interpretation: Tel Hai in Israeli Collective Memory," *AJS Review* 16 (Spring–Fall 1991): 133–59.

10 Dina Clementine Mayer, "Trumpeldor," *JR*, April 13, 1920, p. 172; "Joseph Trumpeldor. Zu seinem 10. Todestag," *JR*, March 11, 1930, p. 133; Solomon Schiller, "Joseph Trumpeldor," *Pioneer* (March 1930): 10; see Mendelsohn, *On Modern Jewish Politics*, pp. 106–07.

11 For Balfour's Zionism in the context of his life and politics, see Ruddock Mackay, *Balfour: Intellectual Statesman* (Oxford: Oxford University Press, 1985); Sydney Zebel, *Balfour: A Political Biography* (Cambridge: Cambridge University Press, 1973); Max Egremont, *Balfour: A Life of Arthur James Balfour* (London: Collins, 1980).

12 "Balfour-Deklaration," *Palästina-Bilder-Korrespondenz* (hereafter cited as *PBK*) (March 1928): 6.

13 Cartoon, "Light Out of Darkness: Israel Hails England's Declaration in Regard to Palestine as a New Miracle," reprinted in *Young Judaean* (January 1918): 124.

14 Mordechai Breuer, *Modernity Within Tradition: The Social History of Orthodox Jewry in Imperial Germany*, translated by Elizabeth Petuchowski (New York: Columbia University Press, 1992), pp. 392–93.

15 See Nordau's interview with Herman Bernstein in Bernstein, ed., *Celebrities of Our Time* (London: Hutchinson, 1924), pp. 254ff.

16 Herbert Samuel, Foreword, in Balfour, *Speeches on Zionism*, edited by Israel Cohen (London: Arrowsmith, 1928), p. 6.

17 Egremont, *Balfour*, p. 340.

18 Quoted in *Pioneer* (June 1930): iii.

19 "Balfour-Feiern in der ganzen Welt," *JR*, November 8, 1927, p. 628; "Das Balfour-Dinner in London," *JR*, November 15, 1927, p. 642; "Zehn Jahre Balfour-Deklaration," *JR*, November 18, 1927, p. 648; "Presentation to

Lord Balfour," press release from Zionist Organization Central Office, November 21, 1923, London, DD 2/3/4/1/1, CZA.

20 "Lord Arthur James Balfour," *PBK* (April 1930): 1.

21 Blanche Dugdale, *Arthur James Balfour* (New York: G. P. Putnam's Sons, 1937), p. 303; "To Liberate the Smaller Nationalities," *Maccabaean* (May 1917): 232; "The Jewish Magna Charta," *Maccabaean* (December 1917): 47.

22 "Von Eröffnung der Universität," *JR*, March 24, 1925, p. 217; "Der Universität Jerusalem," *JR*, April 4, 1925, p. 243.

23 Irma Lindheim, *The Immortal Adventure* (New York: Macaulay, 1928), p. 34.

24 The painting, now in the foyer leading to the University Senate chamber of the Hebrew University of Jerusalem, is rarely reproduced in biographies of Balfour.

25 Lindheim, *Immortal Adventure*, p. 82.

26 Dugdale, *Arthur James Balfour*, p. 271. For Balfour's address, see "The Opening of the Hebrew University," in *Opinions and Argument from Speeches and Addresses of the Earl of Balfour, 1910–1927* (Garden City, N. Y.: Doubleday, Doran, and Co., 1928), pp. 229–38.

27 Egremont, *Balfour*, p. 331.

28 "Lord Balfours Empfang in Tel Awiw," *JR*, April 4, 1925, p. 249.

29 Quoted in *Pioneer* (June 1930): iii.

30 "Presentation to Lord Balfour," p. 2.

31 Chaim Weizmann, quoted in "Presentation to Lord Balfour," p. 1.

32 *JR*, March 2, 1930, p. 153ff.; "Lord Balfour," *New Judaea* (March–April 1930): 106; Mrs. Edgar Dugdale, "Lord Balfour as a Zionist," *Pioneer* (April 1930): 5.

33 Dugdale, *Arthur James Balfour*, p. 303.

34 *Pioneer* (June 1930): iii.

35 *Weizmann der Führer: Anlässlich seines Besuches in Brünn im Januar 1925* (Prague [?]: Keren Hayesod in Czechoslovakia, 1925), p. 8; Israel Cohen, "Weizmanns Aufstieg. Sein Verhältnis zu dem Staatsmännern Englands," in *Weizmann der Führer*, pp. 11–15.

36 Dugdale, *Arthur James Balfour*, p. 303.

37 *Weizmann der Führer*, pp. 5, 3.

38 S. M. Melamed, "Chaim Weizmann: Man and Zionist," *Maccabaean* (December 1917): 427.

39 "Editorial Comments. Dropping the Pilot," *Pioneer* (July 1931): 3.

40 "Weizmann in Washington," *JR*, January 28, 1927, p. 51.

41 Vital, *Zionism: The Crucial Phase.*

42 Mayir Vereté, "The Balfour Declaration and its Makers," in *From Palmerston to Balfour: Collected Essays of Mayir Vereté*, edited by Norman Rose (London: Frank Cass, 1992), pp. 1–38; the quote is from p. 26. In addition to arguing that Weizmann's role has been overstated, Vereté argues that Balfour has been assigned too prominent a role. Derek Penslar referred to this important work.

43 Levene, *War, Jews, and the New Europe.*

44 *Weizmann der Führer*, p. 6ff.

214   Notes to pages 35–38

45 A. D. Lineator, in *Monthly Pioneer* (August 1928): 8.

46 Melamed, "Chaim Weizmann."

47 Chaim Weizmann, "Lay Down Your Arms," *New Maccabaean*, May 20, 1921, p. 23–24.

48 "Chajim Weizmann: zum 50. Geburtstag (27. November 1923)," *JR*, November 27, 1923, p. 575.

49 See Chaim Weizmann to Theodor Herzl, May 6, 1903, in *The Letters and Papers of Chaim Weizmann, II*, edited by Meyer Weisgal (general ed.) (London: Oxford University Press, 1971), pp. 312–13.

50 "American Zionists Welcome Dr. Weizmann: Reception in New York City Marks First Public Appearance Since Arrival Here as President of the World Zionist Organization: Louis Lipsky Scores Zionist Detractors," *New Palestine*, April 6, 1928, p. 402.

51 "Editorial Comments. Zionist Leadership," *Monthly Pioneer* (June 1928): 5.

52 A. D. Lineator, "Men and Matters," *Pioneer* (February 1933): 4.

53 "Chajim Weizmann: zum 50. Geburtstag."

54 "Editorial Comments. Dr. Weizmann Returns," *Pioneer* (June 1932): 1; "Chajim Weizmann und der Keren Kajemeth," *JR*, January 14, 1927, p. 28; Viscountess Erleigh and Paul Goodman, "Dr. Chaim Weizmann: Appreciations," *Pioneer* (November 1931): 11, 14.

55 Stephen S. Wise to Julian Mack, April 7, 1924, MSS col. 19, 25/13, AJA.

56 Adolf Boehm, "Weizmanns Führerpersonlichkeit," *JR*, November 27, 1923, p. 576.

57 "Why an Opposition," *Zionist Free Press*, June 12, 1928, p. 3; Stephen S. Wise, letter to Justine and Lee [his children], April 10, 1928, A 243/20, CZA; Stephen S. Wise to Richard Gottheil, December 7, 1928, MSS col. 49 3/7, AJA; Samuel Rosensohn, letter to Felix Frankfurter, April 28, 1921, A 264/34, CZA.

58 Stephen S. Wise to Julian Mack, August 24, 1920, Stephen S. Wise Collection, Folder 3, Box 114, American Jewish Historical Society, Waltham, Massachusetts.

59 See Eli Shaltier, *Pinchas Rutenberg: Ḥayim u-zemanim, 1879–1942, vol. I* (Tel Aviv: Am Oved, 1990), pp. 275–94, 119–27; cf. Yosef Gorny, *Shutafut u-ma'avak: Chaim Weizmann u-tenu'at ha-'avodah ha-Yehudit be-Erets Yisra'el* [Partnership and conflict: Chaim Weizmann and the Jewish labor movement in Palestine] (Tel Aviv: Tel Aviv University Press, 1976).

60 Henrietta Szold, notes from "Conversation with Mr. Pinchas Ruthenberg [sic], Jerusalem, Friday, October 3," A 125/55, CZA.

61 Lindheim, *Immortal Adventure*, pp. 22–23.

62 A. D. Lineator, in *Monthly Pioneer* (April 1929): 6.

63 "Begrüssung für Sokolow: zionistische Massendemonstration in Berlin," *JR*, October 14, 1921, p. 595.

64 See also "Zeichnungen von Erna Grossman 'Kongress-Köpfe,'" *JR*, September 13, 1927, p. 325.

65 "Nahum Sokolow. Zu seinem 70. Geburtstag," *JR*, January 23, 1931, p. 31.

66 "Nahum Sokolow," *Boston Hebrew*, August 9, 1931, p. 1.

67 "Sokolow-Monat," January 20, 1931, DD a 2/3/4/1/4, CZA.

68 There are several versions of this work in different languages; the most recent edition is published in one volume: Nahum Sokolow, *History of Zionism, 1600–1918* (New York: KTAV, 1969).

69 "Nahum Sokolow. Zu seinem 70. Geburtstag," *JR*, January 23, 1931, p. 31; Heinrich Loewe, "Geschichte des Zionismus," *JR*, July 25, 1919, p. 404.

70 "Sokolow-Monat der zionistischen Organisation," February 5, 1931, from the Zionist Office, London, DD a 2/3/4/1/4, CZA.

71 Hertzberg, *Zionist Idea*; Avineri, *Making of Modern Zionism*.

72 A. D. Lineator, in *Monthly Pioneer* (April 1929): 6.

73 Leon Simon, *Ahad Ha-Am: Asher Ginzberg, A Biography* (Philadelphia: Jewish Publication Society of America, 1960), pp. 14, 70, 78, 107, 135–37.

74 Bernard Richards, "Louis Brandeis," *JR*, November 20, 1914, p. 437.

75 On Brandeis's early career see Allon Gal, *Brandeis of Boston* (Cambridge: Harvard University Press, 1980); Gal, "Brandeis, Judaism, and Zionism," in *Brandeis and America*, edited by Nelson L. Dawson (Lexington: University Press of Kentucky, 1989); Philippa Strum, *Brandeis: Beyond Progressivism* (Lawrence: University of Kansas Press, 1993); Strum, *Louis D. Brandeis: Justice of the People* (Cambridge: Harvard University Press, 1984).

76 Richard Hofstadter, *The American Political Tradition and the Men Who Made It* (New York: Vintage, 1960), pp. 225, 255, 258–9.

77 I. J. Klingler, "Louis D. Brandeis," *Yedioth Hadassah* (October–November 1941); translated excerpts in Brandeis file, Folder 1, Box 2, Hadassah Archives, New York (hereafter cited as HA).

78 L. L. [Louis Lipsky], "Mr. Justice Brandeis," *Maccabaean* (November 1916): 79.

79 Jacob de Haas, *Theodor Herzl: A Biographical Study*, 2 vols. (Chicago and New York: Leonard, 1927).

80 "Brandeis in Leadership," editorial in *Der Tog*, August 14, 1930; translated English typescript in A 406/94, CZA.

81 Jacob de Haas, "Louis Dembitz Brandeis – Zionist," *Jewish Tribune*, November 12, 1926, p. 5.

82 Jessie Sampter, "A New Leader," *Young Judaean* (December 1914): 4, 12.

83 Mrs. Sol Rosenbloom, in *Jewish Tribune*, November 12, 1926, p. 4.

84 de Haas, "Louis Dembitz Brandeis – Zionist."

85 "Brandeis im Zionismus," *JR*, March 23, 1928, p. 174.

86 Most scholarship reflects Weizmann's perspective; see Jehuda Reinharz, *Chaim Weizmann: The Making of a Statesman*, pp. 190–93.

87 Bernard Richards, "Louis D. Brandeis on His 70th Birthday," *Jewish Criterion*, November 12, 1926, pp. 7, 39. Earlier articles written by Richards about Brandeis were reprinted in the Zionist press; see *JR*, November 20, 1914, p. 437.

88 "Louis D. Brandeis: Zu einem 70. Geburtstag," *JR*, November 12, 1926, p. 638; *New Judaea* (July–August 1930): 206–07.

89 de Haas, *Theodor Herzl*, p. 202.

90 Communication from JNF of America to Zionist Organization, January 31, 1916, KKL 1/11, CZA.

91 Cf. Burt, *Two Jewish Justices*.

92 Address delivered by Henrietta Szold at the Brandeis Memorial Meeting, 'En Hashophet, October 16, 1941, Brandeis file, Folder 9, Box 1, HA.
93 Cf. Aaron Berman, *Nazism, the Jews, and American Zionism, 1933–1948* (Detroit: Wayne State University Press, 1990), p. 18.
94 All in Mrs. Edward Jacobs, in Brandeis Memorial Session, 27th Annual Convention of Hadassah, Hotel William Penn, Pittsburgh, November 2, 1941, pp. 4–11; Folder 9, Box 1, HA, New York.
95 Jonathan Sarna, *JPS: The Americanization of Jewish Culture, 1888–1988* (Philadelphia: Jewish Publication Society of America, 1989), pp. 47–94.
96 "Miss Szold's Retirement," *Maccabaean* (June 1916): 124.
97 There is a tremendous amount of work in progress on Hadassah. A number of scholars are exploring the life and career of Henrietta Szold, as well as that of Irma Lindheim, the next most important Hadassah figure after Szold; among the scholars with articles and work in progress on this issue are Claudia Prestel, Joyce Antler, Naomi Lichtenstein, Shulamit Reinharz, Yaffa Schlesinger, Mira Katzburg Yungman, and Miriyam Glazer. The unpublished scholarly works on Hadassah include Donald H. Miller, "A History of Hadassah, 1912–1935," Ph.D. dissertation (New York University, 1968), and Carol Bosworth Kutscher, "The Early Years of Hadassah, 1912–1921," Ph.D. dissertation (Brandeis University, 1976). Joan Dash's biography *Summoned to Jerusalem: The Life of Henrietta Szold* (New York: Harper and Row, 1979) is one of the more authoritative accounts; earlier biographies of Szold include Irving Fineman, *Woman of Valor* (New York: Simon and Schuster, 1961); Rose Zeitlin, *Henrietta Szold* (New York: Dial, 1952); Elma Levinger, *Fighting Angel* (New York: Behrman, 1946). What we have in the meantime are primarily Hadassah-generated products which are informative and often compelling, but lack detachment from the subject, and are of limited value and access to historians. Existing first-hand accounts include Marvin Lowenthal, ed., *Henrietta Szold: Life and Letters* (New York: Viking, 1942), and Irma Lindheim, *Parallel Quest: A Search of a Person and a People* (New York: Thomas Yoseloff, 1962). The larger theoretical frameworks for investigating the role of women in Zionism, particularly in reference to the pre-state Yishuv are best explicated in the works of historian Claudia Prestel and sociologist Deborah Bernstein; see Deborah Bernstein, *Struggle for Equality* and *Pioneers and Homemakers*; for broader conceptual considerations see Judith R. Baskin, ed., *Jewish Women in Historical Perspective* (Detroit: Wayne State University Press, 1991); Lynn Davidman and Shelly Tenenbaum, eds., *Feminist Perspectives on Jewish Studies* (New Haven and London: Yale University Press, 1994); Adrienne Baker, *The Jewish Woman in Contemporary Society: Transitions and Traditions* (New York: New York University Press, 1993); Maurie Sacks, ed. *Active Voices: Women in Jewish Culture* (Urbana: University of Illinois Press, 1995).
98 "Greetings. The National Board Greets Henrietta Szold with Love and Esteem," *Hadassah News Letter* (December 1930): 3.
99 Harry Sachar, "Henrietta Szold," *Hadassah News Letter* (December 1930): 13.
100 "Henrietta Szold 70 jahrig," *JR*, December 20, 1929, p. 667; "Miss Szolds 70. Geburtstag," January 6, 1931, p. 1.

101 "Men and Matters," *Monthly Pioneer*, March 1929, p. 9.

102 "Upbuilders of the Land. Henrietta Szold at Three Score and Ten," *Our Fund*, January 1931, p. 31.

103 Louis Lipsky, "Hadassah's Anniversary," *Maccabaean* (February 1917): 145.

104 Louis Brandeis to Robert Szold, August 19, 1930, A406/79, CZA.

105 Sarna, *JPS*, pp. 47–94.

106 See Aaron Berman, *Nazism, the Jews, and American Zionism*; Allon Gal, "Medinat Yisra'el ha-ide'alit be-ene Hadasah, 1945–1955" [The ideal State of Israel in the eyes of Hadassah, 1945–1955], *Yahadut Zémanenu* 4 (1987): 157–70. These works, however, deal with the period after 1933.

107 On the reception of Einstein, from a cultural perspective, see Alan J. Friedman and Carol C. Donley, *Einstein as Myth and Muse* (Cambridge: Cambridge University Press, 1989); Gerald Holton and Yehuda Elkana, eds., *Albert Einstein: Historical and Cultural Perspectives* (Princeton: Princeton University Press, 1982), pp. 281–343.

108 Nahum Goldmann, *Mein Leben als deutscher Jude* (Munich: Langen Müller, 1980), pp. 177–78.

109 Herman Bernstein, *Celebrities of Our Time*, p. 243.

110 Stephen S. Wise to Julian Mack, December 17, 1930, MSS col. 19, 25/15, AJA.

111 M. S. Fisher, quoted in "Professor Einstein Gives Avukah Students Views on Palestine in International Broadcast – Organization Selected for Exclusive Radio Address," *Avukah Bulletin* (December 1930): 1.

112 See, for example, the portrait of Einstein by Max Liebermann on cover of *Menorah* (a Paris Zionist organ), April 1, 1928.

113 *JR*, June 24, 1921, p. 359; "Der Aufbau Palästinas als Aufgabe der Judenheit: Eine jüdische Massenkundgebung in Berlin," *JR*, July 6, 1921, p. 371.

114 "Einstein Forest," *New Judaea*, February 28, 1929, p. 86; "Professor Albert Einstein: Forest to be Planted in His Name," *Monthly Pioneer* (March 1929): 4.

115 "Professor Einstein über sein Eindrücke in Palästina," *JR*, April 24, 1923, pp. 195–96; "Eine Botschaft Einsteins. Die Antwort auf das Weissbuch muss verdoppelte Arbeit sein," *JR*, December 5, 1930, p. 644.

116 See "Das Echo des Einstein-Briefes," *JR*, October 22, 1929, p. 555, on the impact of Einstein's letter to the *Manchester Guardian* of October 12, 1929.

117 "Prof. Einstein fährt nach Palästina," in *JR*, October 6, 1922, p. 521; "Einstein in Singapore," *JR*, January 5, 1923, p. 5; "Einstein in Wien," *JR*, September 26, 1924, p. 551; "Einstein in New York," *JR*, December 19, 1930, p. 672.

118 "Einstein in Palästina," *JR*, February 16, 1923, p. 75.

119 "Professor Einstein über die Universität Jerusalem: seine Stellung zu Palästina um zu Keren Hajessod," *JR*, March 30, 1921; "Einstein und Keren Hajessod: Einstein begleite Weizmann nach Amerika," *JR*, February 25, 1921, p. 107; Stephen S. Wise to Richard Gottheil, April 27, 1921, p. 3, MSS col. 49, 3/5, AJA.

120 "Eine Botschaft Einsteins," *JR*, January 29, 1929, p. 45; "Das Einstein-Bankett in Amerika. Übertragung durch 44 Sender 200000 Dollar gesammelt," *JR*, February 10, 1931, p. 121.
121 "Einsteins Amerikareise," *JR*, March 1, 1921, p. 115.
122 "Professor Einstein über die Universität Jerusalem"; "Einstein und Keren Hajessod"; "A Hebrew University in Jerusalem," *Jewish Progress in Palestine: Four Years' Work of Keren Hayesod* (London: Palestine Foundation Fund, Keren Hayesod, 1925), p. 10. This picture includes a sketch of a main building of the university by Patrick Geddes which was never built, and the caption incorrectly identifies the site as the Mount of Olives.
123 "Professor Einstein," *Avukah Bulletin* (December 1930): 1.
124 "Einstein hebräisch," *JR*, June 15, 1926, p. 340.
125 Tom Segev, *The Seventh Million: The Israelis and the Holocaust*, translated by Haim Watzman (New York: Hill and Wang, 1992), p. 36; Ronald W. Clark, *Einstein: The Life and Times* (New York: World, 1965), pp. 474ff.
126 Yitzhak Navon, "On Einstein and the Presidency of Israel," in *Albert Einstein, Historical and Cultural Perspectives: The Centennial Symposium in Jerusalem* (Princeton, N. J.: Princeton University Press, 1982), pp. 293–96.
127 Goldmann, *Mein Leben als deutscher Jude*, pp. 178–79.
128 Goldmann, *Mein Leben als deutscher Jude*, p. 174.
129 "Editorial Comments: Prof. Einstein's Refusal," *Monthly Pioneer* (June 1929): 3.
130 Goldmann, *Mein Leben als deutscher Jude*, p. 178.
131 "Professor Albert Einstein: Forest to be Planted in His Name," *Monthly Pioneer* (March 1929): 4.
132 See Aschheim, *Brothers and Strangers*, and Wertheimer, *Unwelcome Strangers*.
133 Albert Einstein, *The World As I See It* [originally published as *Mein Weltbild*], translated by Alan Harris (New York: Covici Friede, 1934), pp. 164–66.
134 Einstein, *The World As I See It*, pp. xv–xvi.
135 Albert Einstein, "Assimilation and Nationalism" (1) (1920), in *About Zionism*, edited and translated by Leon Simon (London: Soncino, 1930), pp. 23–24.
136 Abraham Pais, *Subtle is the Lord: The Science and Life of Albert Einstein* (New York: Oxford University Press, 1982), pp. 317, 315. See also Zev Rozenkranz, "Albert Einstein be-'ene Tsiyone Germanyah, 1919–1921" [Albert Einstein in the eyes of German Zionists, 1919–1921], in *Yehude Weimar: ḥevrah be-mashber ha-moderniyut, 1918–1933* [Weimar Jewry and the crisis of modernization, 1918–1933], edited by Oded Heilbronner (Jerusalem: Magnes Press, 1994), pp. 108–21.
137 All the above citations are from Einstein, "Assimilation and Nationalism" (2) (1920), in *About Zionism*, pp. 27–28.
138 Einstein, "Assimilation and Nationalism" (2), p. 28.
139 Einstein, "Assimilation and Nationalism" (2), p. 37.
140 "Professor Einstein," *Avukah Bulletin* (December 1930): 2.
141 Einstein, letter to the *Manchester Guardian*, October 12, 1929, in *About Zionism*, pp. 58–59.
142 "Einstein an die arabische Welt," *JR*, January 31, 1930, p. 57.

143 Goldmann, *Mein Leben als deutscher Jude*, p. 178.
144 Leon Simon, introduction to Einstein, *About Zionism*, p. 18.
145 Einstein, letter to the *Manchester Guardian*, October 12, 1929, in *About Zionism*, p. 55.

3 DOLLARS AND THE CHANGING SENSE OF ZIONISM

1 Ernst Marcus, "Der Keren Hajessod und die Zionisten," *JR*, October 10, 1922, p. 533.
2 Irma Lindheim, "Why an Opposition," *Zionist Free Press*, June 12, 1928, p. 3.
3 On American Zionism, see Ben Halpern, *A Clash of Heroes*; see also Melvin Urofsky, *American Zionism from Herzl to the Holocaust*; Urofsky, *Essays in American Zionism*; Gal, "Brandeis, Judaism, and Zionism"; Friesel, *Ha-Mediniyut ha-Tsiyonit*; Metser, *Hon le'umi le-vayit le'eumi*; Lipstadt, "Zionist Career of Louis Lipsky"; Halperin, *Political World of American Zionism*, p. 337; Naomi Cohen, *American Jews and the Zionist Idea*; Yonathan Shapiro, *Leadership of the American Zionist Organization*; and Burt, *Two Jewish Justices*, pp. 14–18. A general tendency of many of these works is to end with Lipsky's rise to power in 1921, rather than following his checkered career; see Friesel, "Pinsk and Washington."
4 Henry L. Feingold, *The Jewish People in America, Volume V. A Time for Searching: Entering the Mainstream, 1920–1945* (Baltimore: Johns Hopkins University Press, 1992), pp. 155–88.
5 Howard M. Sachar, *A History of the Jews in America* (New York: Knopf, 1992), p. 508.
6 See chapter 5 in this volume.
7 Aaron Berman, *Nazism, the Jews, and American Zionism*, p. 18.
8 *Trial and Error: The Autobiography of Chaim Weizmann* (New York: Schocken, 1966), pp. 248–78. A small volume is devoted to "correcting" the "errors" in *Trial and Error*; see Oscar K. Rabinowicz, *Fifty Years of Zionism: A Historical Analysis of Dr. Weizmann's "Trial and Error"* (London: Robert Anscombe, 1950).
9 Ironically, Weizmann himself would have to settle for the figurehead position of president devised by David Ben-Gurion, the dominant leader of the Jewish settlement in Palestine, the Yishuv, and the first prime minister of Israel. At the time, at least to insiders, Weizmann's "presidency" symbolized his powerlessness in relation to Ben-Gurion in his later years.
10 It may be argued the Crimean project did not "fail" until well into the 1930s, and not entirely until the Nazis invaded the Soviet Union. Derek Penslar pointed out this alternative view.
11 Feingold, *Jewish People in America, Volume V*, pp. 164–65.
12 Feingold, *Jewish People in America, Volume V*, p. 166.
13 "Why an Opposition," *Zionist Free Press*, June 12, 1928, p. 3. "Shnorrer" is a derogatory term meaning "beggar," but not necessarily someone who begs due to poverty. "Shnorring" can imply anyone who asks for money.
14 Stephen S. Wise to Alexander [Sachs?], August 22, 1920, A 404/168, CZA.

15 Irma Lindheim to Pearl Franklin, April 8, 1928, Record Group 4, Folder 7, Box 1, HA; Zip [Zipporah, alternately known as Mrs. Robert F.] Szold to the Presidents of the Hadassah Chapters, April 8, 1928, Record Group 4, Folder 3, Box 1, HA; "Head of Hadassah Joins Zionist Split," *New York Times*, March 31, 1928; extract from letter of Dr. Adolf Friedmann to Mr. De Haas, April 16, 1921, A 405/1, CZA.

16 "National Board Statement," *Hadassah News Letter*, August 1927, p. 3.

17 "Keren Hayesod," in *Encyclopaedia Judaica* (1971 edition), vol. X, pp. 914–15.

18 *The Autobiography of Nahum Goldmann: Sixty Years of Jewish Life*, translated by Helen Serba (New York: Holt, Rinehart, and Winston, 1969), p. 120.

19 See, e.g., Nahum Goldmann, "Der dreizehnte Zionistenkongress und die Zukunft des Zionismus," *Der Jude* (1924): 564; cf. Robert Szold, A 405/19, "Supporting Memorandum on the Politics of the Zionist Organization of America," August 1919, p. 4 (apparently page proofs of an article for the *New Palestine*).

20 "Statement by Dr. Stephen S. Wise, President of the American Jewish Committee, Rabbi of the Free Synagogue of the Reasons for His Resignation from the Administration and Executive Committees of the Zionist Organization of America," A 243/20, CZA; cf. *New Judaea*, November 18, 1927, p. 50: "Stephen Wise, whose services to Zionism are inestimable, has found it desirable to launch an attack on the Zionist Executive at the Conference of the United Palestine Appeal in Cleveland . . . the statement that any attempt was made to stifle freedom of discussion and to destroy the rights of Zionists to criticise the Executive and the Administration, will, we feel certain, be strongly resented."

21 Burt, *Two Jewish Justices*, pp. 14–18.

22 "Editorial Comments. The Zionist Enquiry," *Monthly Pioneer* (February 1929): 3.

23 Vital, *Zionism: The Formative Years*, pp. 3–4; this is especially apparent in Vital's *Zionism: The Crucial Phase*.

24 KKL 1/40, July 27, 1916, memo from the Hague to JNF Comm. for England, CZA; KKL 1/9, circular, November 1914, CZA; *The Greatest Romance in History* (New York: Keren Hayesod, 1922), pp. 86–89.

25 Rose G. Jacobs, "Our Tribute to Louis Dembitz Brandeis," *Hadassah News Letter*, November–December 1931, p. 2.

26 There were ongoing revelations of a similar character, such as reports that funds designated for the Hebrew University were never put to their intended use: Harry Levenson to Jacob de Haas, May 18, 1921, A 405/1, CZA.

27 Harry Barnard, *The Forging of an American Jew: The Life and Times of Judge Julian W. Mack* (New York: Herzl Press, 1974), p. 263.

28 The most judicious evaluation of claims and counterclaims of the differing parties would have to marshal a vast sweep of evidence. Scholarly treatments – as opposed to polemics – of "Zionist finances" have focused mainly on the administration of funds in Palestine, and like the material on Zionist politics, much of it does not extend into the 1920s and early 1930s. For the most part, Zionist institutions in the diaspora are treated separately from the

Zionist bodies on the ground in Palestine. See "Zionistische Finanzinsti-
tutionen" in *Zionistisches Handbuch*, edited by Gerhard Holdheim, for the
general contours of the main institutions in the early 1920s (Berlin: Bureau
of the Zionist Organization, 1923), pp. 93–138. On finance in Palestine see
Lavsky, *Yesodot ha-taḳtsiv la-mif al ha-Tsiyoni*; Metser, *Gibush ma'arekhet
ha-minum ha-tsiburi ha-Tsiyoni: 1919–1921* [Crystallization of the Zionist
public finance plan: 1919–1921] (Jerusalem: Hebrew University, 1976),
and Metser, *Hon le'umi le-vayit le'eumi*; Metser and Gross, "Public Finance
in the Jewish Economy in Interwar Palestine"; Yigal Elam's study extends
to the 1930s; see his *Ha-Sokhnut ha-Yehudit*.

29 The Zionist Commission was set up after the Balfour Declaration
(November 1917), before the formal establishment of the Mandate, and
was headed by Chaim Weizmann; see Vital, *Zionism: The Crucial Phase*,
pp. 310–20.

30 Nehemia de Lieme, Julius Simon, and Robert Szold, "Report of the
Reorganization Commission of the Executive of the Zionist Organization on
the Work of the Zionist Organization in Palestine," A406/4, CZA, pp. 3,
6–7, 19–20.

31 Penslar, *Zionism and Technocracy*, p. 146.

32 de Lieme, et al., "Report of the Reorganization Commission," p. 15.

33 de Lieme, et al., "Report of the Reorganization Commission," pp. 14ff.,
40ff.

34 de Lieme, et al., "Report of the Reorganization Commission," pp. 40ff., 47.

35 de Lieme, et al., "Report of the Reorganization Commission," p. 46.

36 de Lieme, et al., "Report of the Reorganization Commission," p. 45.

37 *Report of the Reorganization Commission of the Executive of the Zionist
Organization on the Work of the Zionist Organization in Palestine* (New York:
Zionist Organization of America, 1921), p. 71.

38 de Lieme, et al., "Report of the Reorganization Commission," p. ix.

39 de Lieme, et al., "Report of the Reorganization Commission," pp. 9ff.,
37ff.

40 Confidential note, attached to de Lieme, et al., "Report of the Reorganization Commission," p. 2.

41 See Lavsky, *Yesodot ha-taḳtsiv la-mif al ha-Tsiyoni*.

42 Nehemia de Lieme and Julius Simon, letter of resignation, January 20,
1921, amended to "Report of the Reorganization Commission," pp. 70–74,
A406/24, CZA.

43 Metser, *Gibush ma'arekhet ha-minum ha-tsiburi ha-Tsiyoni*, pp. 45–73.

44 Burt, *Two Jewish Justices*, p. 15.

45 Even in his published correspondence with Julius Simon, the Israeli
historian Evyatar Friesel largely avoids discussing the commission's work;
see Julius Simon, *Certain Days*; in addition to the studies of Lavsky and
Metser, one of the few other places the report is mentioned is in Shapiro's
Leadership of the American Zionist Organization, in a footnote, p. 142.

46 Louis Brandeis, letter to Julian Mack, December 23, 1921, A405/92, CZA;
undated memo from Julian Mack, probably around April 20, 1921,
A 404/231, CZA; Stephen S. Wise to Chaim Weizmann, April 24, 1921, A
404/231, CZA; Zip Szold to Louis Brandeis, August 24, 1928: "It has been

pointed out to me that if I and others likeminded with me resign, in this event we will be delivering Hadassah over to those whose sole interest will be to use it as a tool. This argument seems cogent to me, but thus far my personal reaction is that I cannot negotiate with men in whom I have no confidence, and I shall therefore be forced to withdraw" (Brandeis collection, Folder 1, Box 1, HA).

47 See Halpern, *A Clash of Heroes*, pp. 218 and 284, n. 66.
48 Stephen S. Wise to Richard Gottheil, June 7, 1921, MSS col. 49 3/5, AJA.
49 Stephen S. Wise, letter to Justine and Lee [his children], April 10, 1928, A 243/20, CZA.
50 Stephen S. Wise to Richard Gottheil, December 7, 1928, MSS col. 49 3/7, AJA.
51 Robert Szold, "Reply to Mr. Ussischkin," A406/2, CZA.
52 Louis Brandeis to Julian Mack, December 23, 1921, A405/92, CZA.
53 Samuel Rosensohn was a New York attorney and Zionist activist who was closely associated with Brandeis.
54 Samuel Rosensohn, letter to Felix Frankfurter, April 28, 1921, A 264/34, CZA; see also Louis Lipsky to J. Mack, April 19, 1921, A 405/17, CZA.
55 Nehemia de Lieme and Julius Simon, letter of resignation, January 20, 1921, amended to "Report of the Reorganization Commission," pp. 70–74, A406/24, CZA; Sol. Rosenbloom to J. Mack, May 17, 1921, A 405/17, CZA; Stephen S. Wise to Richard Gottheil, February 3, 1921, MSS col. 49 3/5, AJA.
56 "The Whispering Campaign," *New Maccabaean*, May 6, 1921, p. 2.
57 Chaim Weizmann, "Lay Down Your Arms," *New Maccabaean*, May 20, 1921, p. 23–24.
58 Weizmann, "Lay Down Your Arms," p. 24.
59 Chaim Weizmann, "The Keren Hayesod Manifesto," April 18, 1921, in *New Maccabaean*, May 6, 1921, p. 6.
60 Chaim Weizmann, address to Keren Hayesod conference, March 18, 1923, in *American Addresses of Dr. Chaim Weizmann*, preface by Samuel Untermyer (New York: Palestine Foundation Fund [Keren Hayesod], 1923), p. 14.
61 *New Palestine*, July 22, 1921, p. 1.
62 Mrs. Jacob Sobel, for the Central Committee of Hadassah, to Louis Lipsky, July 1921; Louis Lipsky to Lotta Levensohn, June 22, 1921, Record Group 4, Folder 1, Box 1, HA.
63 Louis Lipsky to Mrs. Jacob Sobel, July 15 and July 25, 1921; W. N. Seligsberg to Mrs. Jacob Sobel (a legal appraisal of Lipsky's response), August 3, 1921, all in Record Group 4, Folder 1, Box 1, HA.
64 Unsigned and unsent letter to Louis Lipsky, August 1921; Hadassah Central Committee to Officers and Members of Hadassah Chapters, September 16, 1921 (Record Group 4, Folder 1, Box 1, HA).
65 Henrietta Szold to Sophia Berger, July 23, 1923, p. 8, Record Group 7, Folder 20, Box 4, HA.
66 "Address of Justice Brandeis at Central Committee Meeting," February 22, 1922, Record Group 4, Box 2A, HA; *Palestine Progress: Monthly Bulletin of the Palestine Development Leagues*, July 1, 1923, p. 2.

67 *The Zionist Awakening: A Summary Report of the Washington Conference: Held April 29th, 1928: Issued by the Committee for ZOA Reorganization, New York*, p. 3 (A 264/68, CZA); charges are also explained in the "Report of Committee of Judges to Dr. Chaim Weizmann, President of the World Zionist Organization on the Affairs of the Zionist Organization of America," June 28, 1928, pp. 2ff., A 264/68, CZA; "Points Made by Mr. Lipsky in His Defense of Present Administration of the Zionist Organization of America at Meeting of National Executive Committee," April 15, 1928, Record Group 4, Folder 3, Box 1, HA.

68 Robert Szold, "The Need for ZOA Reorganization," *Association for the Reorganization of the ZOA, New York Conference, October 14, 1928: Report of Sessions and Program*, pp. 27–28 (A264/68, CZA); press release: "Statement by Dr. Stephen S. Wise, President of the AJC [American Jewish Congress], Rabbi of the Free Synagogue, of the Reasons for His Resignation from the Administrative and Executive Committees of the ZOA," April 2, 1928, A 243/20, CZA; press release from the Free Synagogue, New York, January 3, 1929, A 243/21, CZA.

69 Brandeis to Jacob de Haas, June 6, 1927, SC 1310, correspondence file, AJA.

70 Halperin, *Political World of American Zionism*, p. 12.

71 The preceding quotes are all from a copy of a confidential letter from Samuel Rosensohn to Louis Brandeis, October 19, 1927, Brandeis collection, Folder 1, Box 1, HA.

72 Samuel Rosensohn (to Louis Brandeis, October 19) continues: "Every program he accepted as he was ready to abandon under attack, or as a concession to those who might otherwise oppose him as president of the Organization. He yielded to Jabotinsky [leader of the right-wing Revisionists], and sacrificed the reorganization commission when Jabotinsky threatened his position. When Lipsky, [Emmanuel] Neumann, and Schmayra Levin again threatened his leadership if he did not join in an attack on the American leadership [those calling for reform, such as Stephen S. Wise], he joined that attack and destroyed the most vital force in Zionism, although he knew how necessary those men were for Zionist success in Palestine. Similarly, when he yielded to us at Basle on the question of electing a proper Executive in Palestine, he did so not because he deemed such an Executive desirable, but because he could not be elected without American support."

73 Samuel Rosensohn (to Louis Brandeis, October 19): "The general result has been to weaken, if not to destroy, the entire moral fibre of the movement. The bankruptcy of the movement must be clear and generally realized when sincere Zionists are compelled to look to [non-Zionists] Marshall and Warburg and the Jewish Agency to raise the moral tone of Zionism. Weizmann knows that he could never again be elected, and therefore is devoting all his energies to create a new Jewish Agency, for the sole purpose of securing his election as a president of the Agency. If permitted, he will sacrifice what is left of Zionism to Marshall and Warburg, if in that way he can promote his election as president of the Agency."

74 Samuel Rosensohn to Louis Brandeis, October 19, 1927; see also Henrietta

Szold to Sophia Berger, May 21, 1927, Record Group 7, Folder 20, Box 4, HA.
75 Henrietta Szold to Jessie Sampter, June 10, 1925, Record Group 7, Folder 42, Box 5, HA.
76 Quoted in Halperin, *Political World of American Zionism*, p. 13.
77 Abraham Tulin to Mitchell May, July 9, 1928, Record Group 4, Folder 2, Box 1, HA.
78 "Closing Address of Mr. Lipsky," *New Palestine*, July 13–20, 1928, p. 51.
79 "To the Delegates," *New Palestine*, June 29, 1928.
80 "L'Shalom, Dr. Weizmann," *New Palestine*, June 1, 1928, p. 563.
81 Abraham Goldberg, "Camouflage! Masquerading a Program of Destruction as Reforms," *New Palestine*, June 8, 1929, p. 599.
82 Chaim Weizmann, in *New Palestine*, June 1, 1928, p. 561.
83 Confidential memo by Jacob de Haas, January 31, 1929, A 406/2, CZA.
84 "Districts Endorse Administration: Washington Zionists Declare Local UPA Campaign Injured by Opposition Tactics," *New Palestine*, June 8, 1928, p. 605.
85 Irma Lindheim to Mrs. Pearl Franklin, April 8, 1928, p. 4, Record Group 4, Folder 7, Box 1, HA.
86 Irma Lindheim to Mrs. Pearl Franklin, April 8, 1928, p. 3, Record Group 4, Folder 7, Box 1, HA; Louis Lipsky to Nathan Sahr, March 26, 1928, Record Group 4, Folder 3, Box 1, HA; Mrs. M. Epstein, "The Political Duties of a Woman Zionist" [typescript article for *Hadassah News Letter*, May 1928]; "Clearing the Atmosphere," *Hadassah News Letter*, May 25, 1928.
87 Louis Lipsky, telegram sent by ZOA to Zionist Districts, April 1, 1928; "Letter to Chapter Presidents" from National Board of Hadassah, April 4, 1928, Record Group 4, Folder 4, Box 1, HA.
88 Louis Lipsky to Chairmen and Secretaries of Zionist Districts, June 3, 1928, containing a copy of telegram from May 31, 1928, effectively negating Hadassah as a voting bloc, Record Group 4, Folder 3, Box 1, HA; Rose L. Halprin, "The Truth in Detail," *Hadassah News Letter*, May 31, 1928, p. 2.
89 Zip Szold to the Presidents of Hadassah Chapters, May 10, 1928, Record Group 4, Folder 4, Box 1, HA.
90 Hadassah press release, May 4, 1928, Record Group 4, Folder 4, Box 1, HA.
91 "Memorandum," June 1928, Record Group 4, Folder 4, Box 1, HA.
92 Zip Szold to Presidents of Hadassah Chapters, April 13, 1928, Record Group 4, Folder 4, Box 1, HA; "Packing the Convention," *Zionist Free Press*, June 12, 1928; Zip Szold to Louis Lipsky, May 9, 1928; Meyer W. Weisgal to Zip F. Szold, May 11, 1928; Meyer W. Weisgal to Ruth Cohen, May 21, 1928, attached to Zip Szold to Meyer Weisgal, May 13, 1928; Zip Szold to Louis Lipsky, May 23, 1928; Louis Lipsky to Zip Szold, May 27, 1928; all in Record Group 4, Folder 4, Box 1, HA; see also press release for *New Palestine* (never published) "New Haven Hadassah Chapter Votes Confidence in Mrs. Lindheim: Repudiates Report It Endorsed Lipsky," Record Group 4, Folder 3, Box 1, HA.

93 Irma Lindheim, quoted in "Hadassah Convention," *New Palestine*, July 13–20, 1928, p. 52; cf. Maurice Samuel, "Women's Rights in Zionism: Equality and Special Privileges – But Not Domination," *New Palestine*, June 15, 1928, p. 627; Irma Lindheim to Pearl Franklin, April 8, 1928, Record Group 4, Folder 7, Box 1, HA; "The School of Zionism," *Hadassah Bulletin*, June 1917, pp. 11–12; *Hadassah News Letter*, May 11, 1928.

94 Abraham Goldberg, "Camouflage!," p. 599.

95 A. Coralnick, "Babbitts in Zion: A Speech that Might Have Been Delivered in Washington," *New Palestine*, May 18, 1928, p. 535.

96 Opening epigraph of Theodor Herzl's novel, *Altneuland* (Leipzig: H. Seeman Nachfolger, 1902).

97 "Editorial Comment: A Searching of Hearts on the Eve of the Days of Awe," *New Palestine*, September 7–14, 1928, p. 149.

98 Letter from Stephen S. Wise to Nahum Goldmann, July 11, 1928, A 243/20, CZA.

99 Yonathan Shapiro, *Leadership of the American Zionist Organization*, p. 106.

100 Maurice Samuel, "Men and Principles: Leaders and Part-Time Leaders," *New Palestine*, April 6, 1928, pp. 391–92.

101 A. Coralnick, "Babbitts in Zion," p. 535–36.

102 "American Zionists Welcome Dr. Weizmann: Reception in New York City Marks First Public Appearance Since Arrival Here as President of the World Zionist Organization: Louis Lipsky Scorns Zionist Detractors," *New Palestine*, April 6, 1928, p. 402.

103 Jacob de Haas, "Jewish Agency Debate Continues: Open Letter to the New Palestine: Explanations Invited of the New Formulas, Philosophy, and Objective of Zionism," January 22, 1929, in *DIGEST Number 12, Association of the Reorganization of the Zionist Organization of America*, p. 1, A 406/24, CZA.

104 Quoted in memo by Robert Szold, July 24, 1928, A 406/24, CZA.

105 "Zionist – Not Personal – Organs," *Hadassah News Letter*, June 8, 1928.

106 "Brandeis Demands Change by Zionists," *New York Times*, May 23, 1930.

107 "After the Zionist Convention," *Hadassah News Letter*, July–August 1930, p. 2.

108 *New Judaea* (July–August 1930): 206–07.

109 Chaim Weizmann to Berthold Feiwel, December 14, 1923, copy in Robert Weltsch archive, Folder 15, Box 2, AR 7185, LBI.

110 M. L. Perlzweig, "The Crisis in British Zionism: A Personal Statement," *Pioneer* (October 1932): 17.

111 Irving Howe, based on a quote from Renato Poggioli in *A Margin of Hope: An Intellectual Autobiography* (New York: Harcourt Brace Jovanovich, 1982), p. 139.

112 Perlzweig, "Crisis in British Zionism," pp. 16–17; see also "University Zionist Federation: The 'All Round Men,'" in *Pioneer* (July 1930): "we get such people as . . . the '*Keren Hayesod* Worker,' who, by their one-sidedness, actually detract from their own usefulness": p. 21.

113 Brandeis to Robert Szold, August 19, 1930, A 406/79, CZA.

114 Brandeis to E. N. Mohl, August 24, 1930, A 406/79, CZA; memo from Dr. Yassky to Mrs. Samuel Halprin, re: conversation with Justice Brandeis,

July 8, 1932, Brandeis collection, Folder 2, Box 1, HA; Brandeis to Zip Szold, August 3, 1930, Brandeis collection, Folder 1, Box 1, HA.

115 Stephen S. Wise, memo, April 25, 1928, A 243/20, CZA.

116 "Zionist Organisation and Propaganda: Programme of the Inquiry and Conference on Questions of Zionist Organisation and Propaganda," *New Judaea*, December 28, 1928, p. 58; "Fund for Political Work," *New Judaea*, November 18, 1927, p. 49; "Statement by the New Executive," *New Judaea*, October 7, 1927, pp. 1–3; "Appeal by the Zionist Executive," *New Judaea*, August 31, 1928, p. 233; Leo Lauterbach, "Organization and Propaganda: The Inquiry and Its Object," *New Judaea*, February 28, 1929, pp. 91–92.

117 Memo from Robert Szold in Stephen S. Wise file, marked "Private and Confidential," from Paris, December 17, 1920, p. 8, A 243/12, CZA.

118 Stephen S. Wise, undated memoir (1929), A 243/21, CZA.

119 The most striking documents attesting to Weizmann's boldfaced lying are the notes and letters of Julian Mack and others after the purported "deal" struck with the Brandeis faction; see Julian Mack, undated memo (probably around April 20, 1921), A 404/231, CZA; see also Louis Brandeis to [Julius] Simon, June 27, 1928, Record Group 4, Folder 2, Box 1, HA; Henrietta Szold to Alice Seligsberg, May 11, 1921, and Henrietta Szold to Alice Seligsberg, June 20, 1921, Record Group 7, Folder 47, Box 5, HA.

120 Burt, *Two Jewish Justices*, pp. 14–17.

121 "Criticisms," unsigned Hadassah memo, April 20, 1928, Record Group 4, Folder 4, Box 1, HA.

122 "Communications from Hadassah Regional Units, Chapters, Zionist Districts and Individuals on the Zionist Controversy"; Zip Szold to the Presidents of Hadassah Chapter, April 26, 1928; for an unrepresentative dissent, see (undated) copy of telegram from Mrs. Archibald Silverman (all in Record Group 4, Folder 4, Box 1, HA).

123 Rachel Natelson, "The Truth in Detail: Hadassah and the Zionist Organization," *Hadassah News Letter*, April 1928, p. 2.

124 Henrietta Szold to Jessie Sampter, January 5, 1926, Record Group 7, Folder 42, Box 5, HA; Henrietta Szold to Sophia Berger, January 3, 1927, Record Group 7, Folder 20, Box 4, HA.

125 Perlzweig, "Crisis in British Zionism," p. 17.

126 Perlzweig, "Crisis in British Zionism," all from pp. 16–17; see also "University Zionist Federation: The 'All Round Men,'" in *Pioneer* (July 1930): p. 21.

127 Hans Kohn, "Zu Frage der zionistischen Propaganda," *Der Jude* (1924): 544–48.

128 Chaim Weizmann to Robert Weltsch, February 29, 1924, p. 4; copy of letter from Weizmann to Berthold Feiwel, December 14, 1923 and January 15, 1924; Weizmann to Weltsch, January 15, 1924 (Weltsch archives, AR 7185, LBI).

129 "Zionist Students in IYAR Campaign," IYAR Campaign Press Bulletin No. 5 (1926), from Zionist Organization Central Office, London, KH 1/459/1, CZA; in general, in the wake of Germany's economic catastrophe and

resulting anti-Semitism, the fundraising appeals and announcements of Jewish donations to Zionist causes were not nearly as prominent as in America; see Robert Weltsch to Chaim Weizmann, January 28, 1924, p. 4, AR 7185, LBI; Robert Weltsch, "Zionism in Germany," *New Judaea*, January 30, 1925, p. 157.

130 Justine Wise Polier and James Waterman Wise, "A Biographical Note," in *Challenging Years: The Autobiography of Stephen Wise* (New York: G. P. Putnam's Sons, 1949), p. xi; see also Horace Kallen, "Julian Mack, 1866–1943," *American Jewish Year Book* 46 (1944), pp. 43–44; Stuart M. Geller, "Why Did Louis D. Brandeis Choose Zionism?," *American Jewish Historical Quarterly* (June 1973): 383–499, and Geller, "Louis D. Brandeis and Zionism," Rabbinic thesis (Hebrew Union College, Jewish Institute of Religion, 1970).

131 Polier and Wise, "Biographical Note," p. xvii.

132 Louis Lipsky, *Memoirs in Profile* (Philadelphia: Jewish Publication Society of America, 1975); see particularly Ben Halpern's "Foreword," pp. ix–xvii for Halpern's generous assessment of Lipsky; see also Weizmann, *Trial and Error*.

133 It should also be noted that the support of some men in the opposition was critical in the maintenance of Hadassah; through a third party, Brandeis gave $25,000 to "wipe out the Medical Unit deficit" and for "immediate Medical Unit requirements" (Dunbar, Nutter and McClennen to the ZOA, June 28, 1920; Brandeis collection, Folder 1, Box 2, HA), in addition to the $10,000 he had already given for the launch of the Malarial Unit in 1919 (Rose Jacobs, Hadassah News Letter, November–December 1931, p. 2). Despite this, Henrietta Szold was not particularly close to Brandeis personally; Henrietta Szold to Alice Seligsberg, July 9, 1930, Record Group 7, Folder 47, Box 5, HA.

4 FUNDRAISING AND CATASTROPHE

1 *Greatest Romance in History*, p. 86.

2 Adolf Boehm, *The Jewish National Fund* (The Hague: Jewish National Fund, no date), p. 70.

3 Letter from Chaim Weizmann to Robert Weltsch, February 29, 1924, pp. 4–5, in Weltsch archive, AR 7185, LBI; Weizmann to Berthold Feiwel, January 15, 1924, p. 1, AR 7185, LBI.

4 Weizmann to Berthold Feiwel, January 15, 1924, p. 2, AR 7185, LBI.

5 Boehm, *Der Palästina-Aufbaufonds* (London: Head Office of Keren Hayesod, 1923), p. 7; "Arbeit für Palästina," *JR*, September 25, 1914, p. 373; S. Bernstein, *Zionism*, pp. 48ff.

6 Opening editorial, *New Judaea*, September 26, 1924, p. 1; Nahum Goldmann, "Der dreizehnte Zionistenkongress und die Zukunft des Zionismus," *Der Jude* (1923): 56–59.

7 Louis D. Brandeis, *Jewish Rights and the Congress: Address Delivered at Carnegie Hall, New York City, January 24, 1916* (New York: Jewish Congress Organization Committee, 1916); Franz Oppenheimer, *Co-operative Colonisation in Palestine* (The Hague: Head Office of the Jewish

National Fund and the Settlement Company "Eretz Israel," no date), p. 5.

8 DD a 2/6/7/2/11, undated JNF memo [March 19, unknown year], CZA; *Erez Israel* (Vienna); S. Bernstein, *Zionism*, pp. 45–46; "Dr. Pool's Remarks," *American Hebrew*, May 25, 1917.

9 Boehm, *Jewish National Fund*, p. 16.

10 KKL 1/11, March 16, 1916, Head Office JNF to American JNF, CZA; KKL 1/12, CZA; Isidor Zar, "Constructive Relief," *American Jewish Chronicle*, November 17, 1916.

11 Goldmann, *Die drei Forderungen des jüdischen Volkes.*

12 "The Jewish People Enter," *Maccabaean* (November 1918): 313.

13 Boehm, *Der Palästina-Aufbaufonds*, p. 7; *Erez Israel* (Vienna); S. Bernstein, "Die neueste Phase der jüdischen Wanderung," *JR*, November 20, 1914, pp. 428–29.

14 S. Bernstein, *Zionism*, pp. 28ff.

15 Eli Shibi-Shai, *Ḥayim ve-ahavah be-teḳufah ha-Shabta'it ha-me'uḥeret* [Life and love in the late Sabbatean movement], M.A. thesis (Hebrew University, 1985).

16 "Resolution," *Hadassah News Letter* (November 1930): cover.

17 Chaim Weizmann, "The White Paper and the Keren Kayemeth," *Pioneer* (November 1930): 2.

18 *JR*, October 31, 1930, p. 566; Weizmann, "White Paper and the Keren Kayemeth."

19 *Der Keren Hajessod: Verfassung und Programm* (London: Head Office of the Erets Israel [Palestine] Foundation Fund, 1922), p. 6.

20 Boehm, *Jewish National Fund*, p. 70; Jessie E. Sampter, *The Key* (Jerusalem: Jewish National Fund, 1925).

21 *Maccabaean* (July 1915): 1.

22 Mendelsohn, *On Modern Jewish Politics.*

23 David Cesarani, "Zionism in England, 1917–1939," Ph.D. dissertation (Oxford University, 1986); Elias Epstein, *The Case for the Jewish National Fund: A Challenge to Zionists* (Jerusalem: Jewish National Fund, 1928), p. 3.

24 S. Landman, "Zionism in England: The Conference of the English Zionist Federation," *Monthly Pioneer* (July 1928): 26.

25 "25 Jahre Keren Kayemeth!," *JR*, August 31, 1926, p. 487; "Zehn Jahre Keren Hajessod," *JR*, November 7, 1930, p. 576; "Balfour-Feiern in der ganzen Welt," *JR*, November 8, 1927, p. 628; "Das Balfour-Dinner in London," *JR*, November 15, 1927, p. 642; "Zehn Jahre Balfour-Deklaration," *JR*, November 18, 1927, p. 648; *JR*, July 27, 1917, p. 245; "Für die Rosch Haschanah-Aktion des Keren Kayemeth Lejisrael," *JR*, September 20, 1927, p. 539; "New Propaganda Methods," *Our Fund* (Nissan 5685 [April 1925]).

26 "An die zionistische Ortsgruppen," *JR*, November 12, 1920.

27 *Report of the Emergency Fund for Palestine September 1, 1929–December 31, 1934* (Jerusalem: Jewish National Fund, 1936), p. x.

28 Stephen S. Wise, "The Tragedy of Palestine," *Pioneer* (January 1930): 13.

29 "Weizmanns Rede in New York: Das Meeting in Carnegie Hall – Felix Warburgs 50,000 Dollar-Spende," *JR*, March 6, 1925, p. 169; "Keren

Hajessod in Amerika," *JR*, January 31, 1922, p. 55; "Keren Hajessod in Amerika" and "Der Tausend-Dollar Klub," *JR*, February 21, 1922, p. 85; "Ein Rekord des Keren Hajessod in Amerika," *JR*, February 24, p. 91.

30 "Der grosse Apell," *JR*, January 20, 1922, p. 33; "Der lange Weg," *JR*, January 13, 1922, p. 19; "Stand und Weiterführung der Keren Hajessod – Arbeit in Berlin," *JR*, January 20, 1922, p. 37; "Das Echo des Keren-Hajessod-Aufrufes – Pressestimmen," *JR*, October 9, 1925, p. 667; "An die Zionisten in Deutschland!," *JR*, February 13, 1925, p. 115; "Germany's Extensive Campaign for the Jubilee Campaign: 500 Volunteers to Be Recruited," *Our Fund* (Heshvan, 5687 [October–November 1927]), p. 14.

31 "Die amerikanische Keren Hajessod-Arbeit," *JR*, May 23, 1922, p. 270.

32 Fritz Loewenstein, "Geldsammlung und Propaganda," *JR*, March 31, 1922, p. 163; "An die zionistische Ortsgruppe," *JR*, November 12, 1920; *JR*, December 29, 1920; "Neuer Kurs im amerikanischen Zionismus: Revision der Agency-Politik?," *JR*, March 2, 1926, p. 123; "Vom United Palestine Appeal," *JR*, February 15, 1927, p. 88; "Die Palästina-Kampagne," *JR*, February 24, 1928, p. 111.

33 "Die Joint-Conferenz in Chicago: Verständigung zwischen Zionisten und Nichtzionisten," *JR*, October 15, 1926, p. 573.

34 "Der amerikanische Convention," *JR*, July 21, 1922, p. 367.

35 "Der amerikanisch-jüdische Kongress," *JR*, October 23, 1923, p. 535; October 26, 1923, p. 539.

36 "Vom United Palestine Appeal," *JR*, February 15, 1927, p. 88.

37 "Die Keren Hajessodaktion in Amerika: Weizmanns Eindruck," *JR*, May 25, 1923, p. 243; "Weizmanns Amerika-Reise," *JR*, October 26, 1926, p. 597; "Für die Universität Jerusalem. Reden Warburgs und Weizmanns in New York," *JR*, January 14, 1927, p. 23.

38 "Das Recht auf Einwanderung," *JR*, June 13, 1930, p. 312.

39 "Die 6 Millionen Dollar-Kampagne," *JR*, February 14, 1930, p. 84.

40 Although it was admitted that there would be difficulties, the article contended that Americans would still be interested in the Keren Hayesod if they were convinced that it was a sound political investment: "Die Wirtschaftskrise in Amerika," *JR*, August 26, 1930, p. 440.

41 "The Carnegie Hall Demonstration," *Maccabaean* (January 1918): 1; "Three Historic Gatherings," *Maccabaean* (January 1918): 20–24.

42 "Die Jahreskonferenz der English Zionist Federation," *JR*, August 1, 1922, p. 390; "Keren Hajessod in England," *JR*, April 14, 1922, p. 172.

43 F. H. Kisch, "Activities of the Emergency Fund," *Pioneer* (October 1930): 8–9.

44 *Pioneer* (November 1930): iii.

45 "Der Keren Kayemeth in Frankreich," *JR*, February 20, 1925, p. 139; "Bulletin du Keren-Hajessod," *Menorah*, February 10, 1924, p. 46; "Das Keren Hajessod-Bankett in Paris," *JR*, February 4, 1927, p. 66; *La Nouvelle Aurore*, October 1, 1925, p. 15; "L'oeuvre du Keren Hajessod," *Menorah*, July 1, 1928, p. 201.

46 Robert Weltsch to Chaim Weizmann, January 28, 1924, p. 4, AR 7185, LBI.

47 *JR*, August 28, 1923, p. 503.
48 "Zur Krise in Deutschland," *JR*, October 24, 1924, p. 599.
49 *JR*, October 16, 1923, p. 526.
50 *Jewish Chronicle*, August 28, 1914, p. 17; September 4, 1914, pp. 5, 10; September 21, 1914, pp. 10–11.
51 M. Altschuler, "Russia and Her Jews – The Impact of the 1914 War," *Wiener Library Bulletin* (1973/74): 12–16.
52 Boehm, *Jewish National Fund*, p. 11.
53 *Jewish Chronicle*, July 31, 1914, p. 7.
54 Interview with Max Nordau, in *Celebrities of Our Time*.
55 Boehm, *Jewish National Fund*, pp. 11–12.
56 See Mordecai Eliav, ed., *Ba-matsor uva-matsok: Erets Yisra'el be-Milḥemet ha-'olam ha-rishonah* [Siege and distress: Erets Israel during the First World War] (Jerusalem: Ben Zvi Institute, 1991); Nathan Efrati, *Mi-Mashber le-tiḳvah: ha-Yishuv ha-Yehudi be-Erets Yisra'el be-Milḥemet ha-'olam ha-rishonah* [From crisis to hope: the Jewish community in Erets Israel during World War One] (Jerusalem: Yad Ben Zvi, 1991).
57 Louis Brandeis, "To the Zionists of America," *Maccabaean* (September 1914): 98–99.
58 Boehm, *Der Palästina-Aufbaufonds*, p. 7.
59 "AUFRUF!," *JR*, May 25, 1917.
60 "News from the Homeland," *Maccabaean* (May 1917): 240.
61 *Palestine During the War: Being a Record of the Preservation of the Jewish Settlement in Palestine* (London: Zionist Organisation, 1921), pp. 39–40.
62 "News from the Homeland," *Maccabaean* (May 1917): 240.
63 "Distress in Palestine," *Maccabaean* (October 1917): 376.
64 *Palestine During the War*, p. 20.
65 *Palestine During the War*, p. 32.
66 "Conditions in Palestine," *Maccabaean* (May 1915): 93.
67 Osias Thon, "Die Verwüstung und der Aufbau," *JR*, December 1, 1916, p. 395; S. Bernstein, *Zionism*, pp. 87ff.; Leo Rosenberg, "Jerusalems 'dritte Zerstörung,'" *JR*, November 20, 1914, p. 427; *Palestine During the War*, pp. 33–34.
68 *Palestine During the War*.
69 KKL 1/39, April 23, 1915, CZA.
70 KKL 1/9, "JNF of Am. to the Hague," January 28, 1915, CZA; Isaac Rubin to Head Office (JNF), October 7, 1914, KKL 1/8, CZA.
71 KKL 1/11, February 17, 1916, CZA.
72 "JNF of Am. to Hague," July 2, 1916, KKL 1/11, CZA; "The 'Forwarts' and Zionism," *Maccabaean* (January 1916): 2.
73 "JNF Bur. of Am.," December 14, 1915, KKL 1/11, CZA.
74 Letter from JNF Head Office to American JNF, December 1, 1916, KKL 1/11, CZA.
75 "An die Mitglieder des Landesvorstands! Bericht über die Keren Hajessod-Arbeit zur Sitzung des Landesvorstandes am 9. Januar 1921," AR 7185, LBI; "UNSERE HILFSAKTION," *JR*, September 11, 1914; "JNF of Am. to Hague," January 28, 1915, KKL 1/9, CZA.
76 "Nationale Hilfe," *JR*, February 23, 1917, p. 67.

77 "Die Konferenz des jüdischen 'Volkshilfkomitees' in Amerika," *JR*, January 12, 1917, pp. 16–17.

78 Herbert Parzen, "The United Palestine Appeal," *Herzl Year Book*, vol. VII (New York: Herzl Press, 1971), p. 380.

79 Boehm, *Der Palästina-Aufbaufonds*, p. 12.

80 Henrietta Szold to Alice Seligsberg, July 18, 1921, Record Group 7, Folder 47, Box 5, HA.

81 C. N. Bialik, "Zionist Propaganda: The Dangers of Exaggeration," *Pioneer* (June 1932): 6–7.

82 "Dignity of Appeal," *Our Fund* (Ab–Elul 5685 [July–August 1925]), pp. 83–84.

83 Hans Kohn, "The Technique of Collection: Olmütz Conference Favours Combination," *New Judaea*, September 26, 1924, p. 11; "Entangling Funds," *New Judaea*, September 26, 1924, pp. 2–3; DD a 2/3/4/1/4, "Second Quarterly Report of the Executive of the Zionist Organisation to the Actions-Committee for the Period 1st January–31st March 1928 with Monthly Report for April 1928," pp. 58ff., CZA.

84 "JNF Committee in England to the Hague," April 23, 1915, KKL 1/39, CZA.

85 "Dignity of Appeal."

86 "JNF of America to the Zionist Organizations," November 1914, KKL 1/9, CZA.

87 "Dignity of Appeal."

88 Isaac Rubin to JNF Head Office, October 7, 1914, KKL 1/8, CZA.

89 KKL 1/41, "Hague to the Eng. Zion. Fed.," October 13, 1917, CZA.

90 KKL 1/11, July 2, 1916, "JNF of Am. to Hague," CZA.

91 KKL 1/40, August 20, 1916, memo from JNF Comm. of Eng. to the Hague (Zionist Office), CZA; KKL 1/11, December 14, 1915; memo from JNF Bur. of America to the Hague; letter from the Hague, January 12, 1916; the Head Office suggested that the American office might wish to keep quieter about its fundraising, because not everyone wanted to "demonstrate his sympathy with the Zionist program."

92 Tschlenow, *Der Krieg, die Russische Revolution und der Zionismus*, pp. 6ff.; KKL 1/86, March 28, 1916, "Jüdische Nationalfonds, Sammelstelle für Österreich," CZA; "Die Hilfsaktion der österreichischen Zionisten für galizieschen Flüchtlinge," *JR*, December 4, 1914, p. 446; "Die Tätigkeit des Hilfskomitees der zionistischen Vereinigung für Deutschland," *JR*, December 11, 1914, p. 454.

93 Steven J. Zipperstein, "The Politics of Relief: The Transformation of Russian Jewish Communal Life During the First World War," *Studies in Contemporary Jewry*, 6 (1988), pp. 22–40; Altschuler, "Russia and Her Jews," p. 15.

94 S. Bernstein, *Zionism*, pp. 49ff., 51; J. Hodess, "Failure of Relief Conference," *New Judaea*, September 26, 1924, pp. 4–5.

95 KKL 1/40, July 27, 1916, memo from the Hague to JNF Comm. for England, CZA; KKL 1/9, circular, November 1914, CZA.

96 "Arbeit für Palästina," *JR*, September 25, 1914, p. 373.

97 *Greatest Romance in History*, pp. 86–88.

98 *Greatest Romance in History*, p. 50.
99 "Auf dem Wege zum jüdische-amerikanischen Kongress," *JR*, January 5, 1917, p. 1.
100 *Der Keren Hajessod*, pp. 5–6.
101 *New Judaea*, March 13, 1925, p. 203.
102 "From JNF Comm. of Eng. to Hague," August 20, 1916, KKL 1/40, CZA.
103 *Palestine During the War*; S. Bernstein, *Zionism*, pp. 51ff.; "Criticism of the Institute of Jewish Studies," *New Judaean*, January 30, 1925, p. 155.
104 Boehm, *Der Palästina-Aufbaufonds*, pp. 10ff.; here the "normalization" of Jewish Palestine is promised within twenty years.
105 "What to Do," *New Judaea*, October 10, 1924, p. 19; Nahum Sokolow, opening speech delivered before the Thirteenth Zionist Congress, August 6, in Carlsbad, DD a 2/1/1/13, CZA.
106 S. Bernstein, *Zionism*, pp. 77ff.
107 Epstein, *Case for the Jewish National Fund*, pp. 6ff.
108 Nahum Sokolow, opening address to the Seventeenth Zionist Congress, July 14, 1931, in DD a 2/1/1/17, CZA; Boehm, *Jewish National Fund*, pp. 45–46.
109 Kohn, "The Technique of Collection: Olmütz Conference Favours Combination," p. 11; "Entangling Funds," pp. 2–3; DD a 2/3/4/1/4, "Second Quarterly Report of the Executive of the Zionist Organisation to the Actions-Committee for the Period 1st January–31st March 1928 with Monthly Report for April 1928," pp. 58ff., CZA.
110 "A Call to Action," *Maccabaean* (November 1917): 384–85.
111 "The Jaffa Events," circular letter to the Members of the Actions Committee and Presidents of Federations, DD a 2/3/4/1/4, p. 7, CZA.
112 Henrietta Szold to Jessie Sampter, September 13, 1929, Record Group 7, Folder 44, Box 5, HA.
113 Address of Miss Henrietta Szold, Thursday, November 14 [1929], A125/10, p. 24, CZA.
114 Hugo Bergmann, *Jawne und Jerusalem* (Berlin: Jüdischer Verlag, 1919), pp. 55ff.; Maurice Samuel, "The Nature of Avukah," *Avukah Annual* (1928), p. 10; cf. S. Bernstein, *Zionism*, pp. 80ff.
115 "Neue Wege der Finanzierung," *JR*, September 19, 1930, p. 490; "Die Palästina-Campagne in Amerika," *JR*, January 30, 1931, p. 48.
116 "Die zionistische Finanzkrise," *JR*, January 9, 1931, p. 8.
117 Nahum Sokolow, Opening Speech Delivered Before the Thirteenth Zionist Congress, August 6, in Carlsbad, p. 2, DD a 2/1/1/13, CZA.

5 "FROM SWAMP TO SETTLEMENT": RURAL AND URBAN UTOPIAN VISIONS OF PALESTINE

1 Judah L. Magnes, "Note: Palestine – A Country of Extremes," Jerusalem, February 13, 1923, in *Dissenter in Zion*, edited by Arthur A. Goren (Cambridge, Mass., and London: Harvard University Press, 1988), p. 206.
2 Gertrude Van Tijn, "Oh Life of Joy and Sorrow, Laughter and Tears," p. 189.

3 This language reflects both the Basel Program, the founding document of the Zionist Organization of 1897, and the Balfour Declaration of 1917.

4 See Dan Horowitz, "Before the State: Communal Politics in Palestine Under the Mandate," in *The Israeli State and Society: Boundaries and Frontiers*, edited by Baruch Kimmerling (Albany: State University of New York Press, 1989), pp. 28–65; Baruch Kimmerling, *Zionism and Territory: The Socio-Territorial Dimensions of Zionist Politics* (Berkeley, Calif.: Institute of International Studies, 1983), pp. 1–105; Moshe Lissak, ed., *Toldot ha-Yishuv ha-Yehudi be-Erets Yisra'el me-az ha-'Aliyah ha-rishonah* [The history of the Jewish community in Erets Israel since 1882 (the period of the British mandate, part I)] (Jerusalem: Bialik Institute, 1993).

5 Lindheim, *Immortal Adventure*, pp. 60–61.

6 Carl E. Schorske, *Fin-de-Siècle Vienna: Politics and Culture* (New York: Vintage, 1980), pp. xx–xxvii; Norman L. Kleeblatt, ed., *The Dreyfus Affair, Art, Truth, and Justice* (Berkeley: University of California Press for the Jewish Museum, 1987), 1–24. In the German Zionist organs there are numerous announcements for slide shows and films, and discussions of their contents; see *JR*, April 18, 1919, p. 215; "Der Palästina-Film," *JR*, May 19, 1922, p. 266; "Das neue jüdische Palästina," *JR*, December 5, 1922, p. 633; "Ansprache von einem Palästina-Film," *JR*, December 7, 1923, p. 592; "Der Palästina-Film des Keren Hajessod," *JR*, October 31, 1924, p. 617; "Der neue Keren Hajessod-Film," *JR*, June 1, 1926, p. 308; "Ein Film von Jugenddorf," *JR*, December 13, 1927, p. 706; "Der neue Palästina-Film," *JR*, November 13, 1928, p. 632; announcement for "Ein grosser Kultur-film. Frühling in Palästina. Der Aufbau der jüdischen Heinstätte," January 27, 1929, DD a 2/6/7/2/11, CZA. The audience for the films was typically much broader than the official Zionist membership.

7 See Marsha Rozenblit, *The Jews of Vienna: Assimilation and Identity, 1867–1914* (Albany: State University of New York Press, 1983), pp. 99, 113, 4–5.

8 No author, "Das neue Gesicht Palästinas," *JR*, August 26, 1932, p. 326.

9 "New Features: The Palestine Photo Correspondence," *Our Fund* 3, pp. 56–57.

10 "A Pictorial Review of the Jewish National Fund," *Maccabaean* (December 1916): 106–08.

11 *This is the Land . . . The Spell of Palestine* (London: Jewish National Fund, no date); *Erez Israel* (London: Head Office of the Keren Hayesod, no date); *Jüdische Leistungen in Palästina. Tatsachen und Zahlen*, 3rd edn. (Berlin: Keren Hayesod Central European Division, no date); *Das Neue Palästina* (Berlin: Keren Hayesod Central European Division, 1921); *Altneuland* (Berlin: Keren Hayesod Central European Division, no date); *Jewish Progress in Palestine*; *Jewish Colonisation in Erez-Israel: After Ten Years Keren Hayesod* (Jerusalem: no publisher, 1930); *Palästina Aufbau* (Jerusalem: Keren Hayesod, 1928); *Palästina Aufbaufonds* (Berlin: Keren Hayesod, 1928); *Palästina und der Neubeginn jüdischen Lebens* (Berlin: Keren Hayesod, no date); *Aufbau: Blätter des Keren Kajemeth Lejisrael* (Berlin: Jewish National Fund, 1924); Boehm, *Der Palästina-Aufbaufonds*. Had I realized when I began this research that there would be a number of booklets with

the same, or nearly the same title and routinely missing publication information, I would have recorded the catalogue numbers from the archive, in order to make their retrieval easier. Most of them can be found in either the Central Zionist Archives or the Wiener Library at Tel Aviv University.

12 "Mengen Bilder von Otto Wallisch," *PBK* (May 1931): 5; Boehm, *Der Palästina-Aufbaufonds*, pp. 19–22, 30, 34, 37–40; "Palästina-Statistik in Bildern," *JR*, March 27, 1931, p. 152.

13 Ernst Mechner, "Das neue Gesicht Palästinas," *JR*, August 26, 1932, p. 326; Fritz Noack, "Zionistische Propaganda," *JR*, January 13, 1920, p. 18; Julius Berger, "Ist die Propaganda unserer Fonds zeitgemass?" in *JR*, January 18, 1927, p. 34, and January 27, 1927, pp. 40–41; Robert Goldstein, "Advertising the Zionist Movement," "Letters to the Editor," *Maccabaean* (January 1917): 135.

14 I have attempted to apply the model used by Kevin Starr in *Material Dreams: Southern California Through the 1920s* (New York: Oxford University Press, 1990), p. vii–viii.

15 Lindheim, *Immortal Adventure*, pp. 59–60.

16 Lindheim, *Immortal Adventure*, p. 183.

17 Lindheim, *Immortal Adventure*, p. 189.

18 In the voluminous literature on anti-Semitism, George Mosse's treatment in *The Crisis of German Ideology* (New York: Grossat and Dunlap, 1978) remains most instructive, although several important modifications have appeared; see Peter Pulzer, *The Rise of Political Anti-Semitism in Germany and Austria*, rev. edn. (Cambridge, Mass.: Harvard University Press, 1988), esp. pp. 337–50; Jacob Katz, *From Prejudice to Destruction: Anti-Semitism, 1700–1933* (Cambridge, Mass.: Harvard University Press, 1982). On the contradiction between the German embrace and rejection of modernity in institutional mythologies, to which anti-Semitism was central, see Jeffrey Herf, *Reactionary Modernism: Technology, Culture, and Politics in Weimar and the Third Reich* (Cambridge: Cambridge University Press, 1990), esp. pp. 231–44.

19 There is also little reason to believe that the reality of Jewish farmers would have done anything to alter the stereotype, as the reality of courageous German Jewish soldiers in the First World War did not prevent accusations that Jews shirked their service. On the historical bases of Jews being "assimilated" into the middle classes in Germany and the obstacles in the way of agricultural occupations, see Sorkin, *Transformation of the German Jewry*, pp. 26–27, 36–39, 86, 88, 108, 117–19, 150–54; Meyer, *Origins of the Modern Jew*; Jacob Katz, *Out of the Ghetto: The Social Background of Jewish Emancipation* (New York: Schocken, 1978). I will not deal here with anti-Semitism on the part of agrarians in general or the Bund der Landwirthe (Farmers' League); see Mosse, *Crisis of German Ideology*, pp. 28, 222; Geoff Eley, *From Unification to Nazism: Reinterpreting the German Past* (Boston: Allen and Unwin, 1986), pp. 130–40; Uriel Tal, *Christians and Jews in Germany: Religion , Politics, and Ideology in the Second Reich, 1870–1914*, translated by Noah Jonathan Jacobs (Ithaca and London: Cornell University Press, 1975), pp. 88, 129–33, 141, 233–35, 242–46.

20 *Blau-Weiss Führer: Leitfaden für die Arbeit im Jud. Wanderbund "Blau-Weiss"* (Berlin: Bundesleitung, 1917), partially quoted in "German-Speaking Jews and Zionism," *LBI News* [Winter 1987]), p. 6.

21 See Barbara Miller Lane, *Architecture and Politics in Germany, 1918–1945* (Cambridge: Harvard University Press, 1968), p. 41; Detlev Peukert, *Die Weimarer Republik: Krisenjahre der klassischen Moderne* (Frankfurt a.M.: Suhrkamp, 1987); I am indebted to Gerard Kleinfeld for this observation.

22 See Boehm, *Der Palästina-Aufbaufonds*, p. 40.

23 See, for example, the illustration in Berkowitz, *Zionist Culture*, p. 120. Heinrich York-Steiner designed the card; Carl Pollak, a university student who helped with the daily operations of the Zionist main office, drew the picture; see *Die Welt*, September 10, 1897, 16; the poor grade of the pictures, however, did not seem to diminish the delegates' enthusiasm in seeing and possessing their first Jewish national artifacts. The London *Jewish Chronicle* made special note of the appearance of the Congress post-card, and included a reproduction of it in their report. At the final session, the concluding scenes included "a brisk sale of commemorative postcards"; *Jewish Chronicle* (London), September 3, 1897, p. 10; *Die Welt*, September 10, 1897, p. 16.

24 See Theodor Herzl, "Eröffnungsrede zum ersten Kongress," in *Theodor Herzls zionistische Schriften* (Berlin-Charlottenberg: Jüdischer Verlag, 1908), p. 227; Leon Simon, *Ahad Ha-Am*, p. 105; *Mizrahi* medals collection, Box 2, CZA.

25 See the official postcards of the First through Sixth Zionist Congresses, Congress folders, Printed Material Collection, CZA.

26 Boehm, *Der Palästina-Aufbaufonds*, p. 10.

27 See the bibliography of Davis Trietsch's *Palästina Handbuch* (Berlin-Schmargendorf: Orient-Verlag, 1910), which went through several editions.

28 Cf. cover of "Spezialnummer: Keren Hajessod," *PBK* (January 1932): 23; postcard, "Die genossenschaftliche Siedlung En Charod," 'En Ḥarod file; postcards, views of 'En Ḥarod, 'En Ḥarod file, CZA; Max Heller, *My Month in Palestine: Impressions of Travel* (New York: Bloch, 1929), p. 27.

29 See *Jüdische Turnzeitung* (May 1900): 1, and (June 1908): 109; Georg Hecht, *Der Neue Jude* (Leipzig: Gustav Engel Verlag, 1911), pp. 113ff.; *Jewish Chronicle*, September 12, 1913, p. 23.

30 See also untitled photograph, *Die Welt*, November 26, 1897, p. 9; "Jüdische Feldarbeiter beim Auackern des Bodens" in Trietsch, *Bilder aus Palästina*, p. 78; "Ernte-Arbeiten auf einem der Nationalfonds-Güter in Galilaea" in *Spenden-Buch des Jüdischen Nationalfonds*, A2/6/7/1, CZA.

31 See also "Erntezeit im Emek Jesreel: Heimkehr vom Felde im Jugenddorf Kfar Jeladim," *PBK* (August 1930): 1; "Kinereth: Heueinfuhr," in Keren Hayesod pamphlet, 1927; Shapira, *Land and Power*.

32 See also "Kinereth: Unkrautvernichtung"; "Kinereth: Im Gemüsegarten," in Keren Hayesod pamphlet, 1927.

33 "Ein Traktor auf dem Feld," *Aufbau: jüdische illustrierte Zeitung* (September 1924): 7; Postcard, "615. Merchawjah," Mehaviah file, CZA; "Arbeiter-innenfarm für landwirtschaftliche Ausbildung bei Ness-Zionah (1930). Bewasserung im jungen Orangenhain," Keren Hayesod pamphlet, 1931;

"A Modern Machine in an Old Land," in Lindheim, *Immortal Adventure*, opposite p. 224.

34 "Das Gesicht des neuen Erez Israel," *PBK* (June 1932): 1; photo "Schechunath Borochov, Kindergarten," in *Erez Israel* (London); Lindheim, *Immortal Adventure*, pp. 115ff.; Ruth B. Fromenson, "The Palestine Supplies Bureau," *Hadassah News Letter* (March 1928): 11.

35 "Der Metamorphose vom Galuthjuden zum Erez-Israeljuden," *JR*, March 24, 1922, p. 152.

36 "Arbeiterinnen beim Bau der Carmelstrasse in Tel-Aviv (1928)," *Palästina Aufbau*; images from WIZO pamphlet, 1934; see, for example, *PBK* (September 1930); *Kalendar 5687 (1926–27)*, Keren Kayemeth Leisrael, cover photograph, "Landwirtschaftliche Mädchenschule in Nahalal"; cf. Deborah Bernstein, *Struggle for Equality* and *Pioneers and Homemakers*.

37 J. L. Avi-Sigla, "The Court House," *New Palestine*, May 31, 1929, p. 461; "Jüdisch–arabische Cooperation," *JR*, April 20, 1928, p. 223.

38 Heller, *My Month in Palestine*, p. 223.

39 Lindheim, *Immortal Adventure*, p. 105.

40 Lindheim, *Immortal Adventure*, pp. 57–58.

41 Heller, *My Month in Palestine*, pp. 185–90.

42 Lindheim, *Immortal Adventure*, pp. 63–64.

43 Heller, *My Month in Palestine*, pp. 25–26.

44 Oppenheimer, *Co-operative Colonisation in Palestine*, p. 7; see Penslar, *Zionism and Technocracy*.

45 Lindheim, *Immortal Adventure*, p. 69.

46 Lindheim, *Immortal Adventure*, p. 134.

47 See Adolf Friedemann and Hermann Struck, *Palästina: Reisebilder* (Berlin: Bruno Cassier, 1904), p. 31; J. Oettinger, "Zur Frage des siedlungs-genossenschaftlichen Experiments," *Neue Jüdische Monatshefte*, July 10, 1917, pp. 561–65; Franz Oppenheimer, "Soziologische Tagebuchblätter," *Neue Jüdische Monatshefte*, January 10, 1917, pp. 201–02.

48 See Boehm, *Die Zionistische Bewegung bis zum Ende des Weltkrieges I*, 2nd edn. (Berlin: Jüdischer Verlag, 1915), pp. 239–40.

49 J. B. Orr and J. A. Crichton, "The Possibilities of Developing Agriculture in Palestine," *Monthly Pioneer* (February 1929): 8–9.

50 Aaron Aaronsohn, "The Jewish Agricultural Experiment Station and its Programme" and Arthur Ruppin, "The Return of the Jews to Agriculture" in Israel Cohen, ed., *Zionist Work in Palestine* (London and Leipzig: T. Fischer Unwin, 1911; reprinted as *Zionist Work in Palestine by Various Authorities*; Westport, Conn.: Hyperion Press, 1976), pp. 114–20, 137–42; Josef Gerstman, *Kultur- und Bildungsfortschritte unter den Juden Palästinas* (Munich: Max Steinebach Buch- und Kunstverlag, 1909), p. 19.

51 J. H. Kann, *Erez Israel: Das jüdische Land* (Cologne and Leipzig: Jüdischer Verlag, 1909), p. 153.

52 "Sons of the Emek," *Jewish Colonisation in Erez Israel*; see also "Land-wirtschaftliche Kolonisation," *PBK*, 1, p. 5; "Threshing the Crops at Nuris," p. 18; "Palestine and Near East Exhibition and Fair, Tel Aviv, April 1929," *Monthly Pioneer* (April 1929): 4.

53 Laqueur, *History of Zionism*, p. 209.

54 See Rodrigue, *Images of Sephardi and Eastern Jewries*, pp. 1–4.

55 See Elias Auerbach, *Palästina als Judenland* (Berlin and Leipzig: Jüdischer Verlag, 1912); Heller, *My Month in Palestine*, pp. 31ff.; cf. Shmuel Almog, ed., *Zionism and the Arabs* (Jerusalem: Historical Society of Israel and Zalman Shazar Center, 1983), "Foreword" by Shmuel Ettinger: "All the authors refute the widespread contention according to which the Zionist movement as a whole – save for small and marginal groups within it – did not take into account the Arabs dwelling in *Eretz Israel* and ignored the Arab question altogether" (p. viii).

56 Heller, *My Month in Palestine*, p. 208; see also *Monthly Pioneer* (June 1928): 1.

57 "Araber," *PBK*, 1, pp. 19–20.

58 "Zivilisierung der Kolonisation. Eindrücke einer Reise durch den Emek," *JR*, June 17, 1930, p. 322; Hubert Auhagen, "Jüdische Kolonisation in Syrien," *Neue Jüdische Monatshefte*, February 25, 1917, pp. 269–74; S. Zemach, *Jüdische Bauern: Geschichten aus dem neuen Palästina* (Vienna and Berlin: R. Loewitt-Verlag, 1919).

59 "Anträge zur Araberfrage," 1921, Robert Weltsch collection, AR 7185, Folder 6, Box 2, LBI; "Erez Israel: Die arabische Konferenz in Haifa," *JR*, January 14, 1921, p. 20; Robert Weltsch, "Jahresrückschau 5690," in Friedrich Thieberger and Felix Weltsch, eds., *Jüdischer Almanach auf das Jahr 5691* (Prague: Keren Keremet L'Israel, 1930–1): 39–43; "Palästina und die panarabische Föderation," *JR*, May 29, 1923, p. 251; "Für eine jüdisch–arabische Entente," *JR*, June 1, 1923, p. 259.

60 Ad for "Die Islamische Welt," *JR*, December 21, 1917; the call to understand the Arabs and Islam on their own terms came up repeatedly in editorials in *Hadassah News Letter*.

61 See Hugo Bergmann, "Die arabische Frage in der Arbeiterschaft: Neue organisatorische Probleme," *JR*, February 10, 1925, p. 111; Joseph Friedfeld, "Zur Geschichte der arabische Nationalbewegungs," *JR*, April 28, 1925, p. 303, and May 22, 1925, p. 366.

62 Heller, *My Month in Palestine*, p. 25.

63 Lindheim, *Immortal Adventure*, p. 180.

64 F. H. Kisch, "Palestine Report: Presented to the General Council of the Zionist Organisation of its Meeting London on May 5, 1927," DD a 2/3/4/1/4, CZA.

65 "Erez-Israel. Die arabische Konferenz in Haifa. Antizionistische Kundgebung," *JR*, January 14, 1921, p. 20; Robert Weltsch, "Jahresrückschau 5690"; Irma Lindheim, "Messages to the Convention," *Hadassah News Letter* (December 1929): 13–14; Arthur Ruppin, "Palestine and the Jews: An Address Delivered Before the Sixteenth Zionist Congress," *New Palestine*, August 23, 1929, p. 74; J. Nefach, "Die arabischen Parteien," *JR*, December 16, 1919, p. 696.

66 "The Palestine Mandate: Arab Demand for Ratification," press release, July 17, 1922, ZO [Zionist Office], London, DD 2/3/4/1/4, CZA.

67 "Political Report of the Executive – March–May 1932," May 23, 1932, from the JA [Jewish Agency], London, DD a 2/3/4/1/4, CZA; E.M.E. [?], "The Growth of Arab Goodwill," *New Judaea*, December 19, 1924, p. 112.

68 Julian Meltzer, "Palestine Month by Month: More Outrages," *Pioneer* (April 1932): 19.

69 "Arab Delegation in Cambridge," press release, November 24, 1921, ZO (Zionist Office), London, DD a 2/3/4/1/4, CZA; "Zur Stellung der Araber" and "Gründung einer Schule für arabische Kinder," *JR*, September 16, 1919, p. 506.

70 "Arab Criticism of Arab Delegation," press release, December 8, 1921, ZO (Zionist Office), London, DD a 2/3/4/1/4, CZA.

71 Chaim Weizmann, "Civilization Versus the Desert," *Monthly Pioneer* (January 1930): 9.

72 Lindheim, *Immortal Adventure*, pp. 222–23.

73 "Spezialnummer. Wir Bauen! Neues Leben blüht auf den Ruinen," *PBK* (December 1930): 1; *PBK* (April 1931): 1.

74 Ernst Müller, review of *A. D. Gordon: Briefe aus Palästina* (Berlin: Welt-Verlag, 1919), in *Der Jüdische Wille*, pp. 216–17; Mabel Maas, "Palestine in the Shade," *New Judaea*, February 27, 1925, pp. 190–91.

75 See also "Bilder vom Leben der Araber in Palästina," *PBK* (March 1930): 4; "Junger Araber," *PBK* (December 1929): 2; see Lotta Levensohn, "Women of Palestine," *Hadassah News Letter* (May–June 1930): 3; *Hadassah News Letter* (September–October 1930): 2; Samuel Sambursky, "Der Weg der Verständigung," and A. Reitenberg, "Juden und Araber in Palästina," *Der Jüdische Student* (November 1929): 18–27.

76 J. Nefach, "Die arabischen Partien," *JR*, December 16, 1919, p. 696; "Jüdisch–arabische Cooperation," *JR*, April 20, 1928, p. 223; "Die kooperative Bewegung in Palästina. Jüdisch–arabisch Zusammenarbeit?," *JR*, August 1, 1930, p. 396; Marcel Lew, "Palästinakurse," *Der Jüdische Student* (April–May 1921): 112–15; "Jews and Arabs at Peace," press release, January 12, 1922; "Improved Relations Between Arabs and Jews," press release, January 25, 1922, ZO (Zionist Office), London, DD a 2/3/4/1/4, CZA.

77 "Der Aufmarsch der Araberfreunde: Die Arbeit der Untersuchungs-kommission," *JR*, December 3, 1929, p. 636. In Zionist media in the West, though, the British were treated quite respectfully, if not reverentially; see *PBK* (October 1928): 1.

78 "Zur Eröffnung der Nationalbibliothek," *JR*, April 25, 1930, p. 219; "Der Fortschritt der Kolonisation," *JR*, May 9, 1930, p. 246.

79 Boehm, *Der Palästina-Aufbaufonds*.

80 Cover, Keren Hayesod pamphlet, 1922; "So erobern wir Palästina," *PBK* (February 1930): 1.

81 "Veranstaltung des jüdischen Nationalfonds. Filmaufführung. Das Leben in den jüdischen Kolonien Palästinas," *JR*, March 15, 1918, p. 83; "Film Matinee des Jud. Nationalfonds," *JR*, March 2, 1922, p. 225; "Das neue jüdische Palästina," *JR*, December 5, 1922, p. 633; "Der Palästina-Film des Keren Hajessod," *JR*, October 31, 1924, p. 617; "Der neue Keren Hajessod-Film," *JR*, June 1, 1926, p. 308.

82 *JR*, April 18, 1919, p. 215; "Palästinawoche in Nürnburg," *JR*, January 9, 1920, p. 10; "Palästina-Woche," *JR*, March 8, 1921, p. 134.

83 "Die Palästina-Woche des Jüdischen Nationalfonds," *JR*, May 27, 1919, p. 299.

84 Berkowitz, *Zionist Culture*, chapter 7.

85 "Beth Sefer Reali Ibri Haifa," *Menorah* [French], October 13, 1923, p. 423.

86 Ittamar Ben-Avi, "We Young Palestinians: To the Jewish Youth of America," *Maccabaean* (June–July 1917): 261.

87 "Haifa, die Stadt der Zukunft," *PBK* (September 1931): 2.

88 Lindheim, *Immortal Adventure*, pp. 211–12.

89 Lindheim, *Immortal Adventure*, pp. 211–12.

90 Heller, *My Month in Palestine*, p. 55.

91 "Spezialnummer. Industrie in Palästina," *PBK* (March 1931); Cyril Henriques, "Industrial Development of Palestine," *Monthly Pioneer* (March 1929): 13–15; "Fourth Grand Exhibition at Tel Aviv," *Monthly Pioneer* (May 1929): 12–13; *Pioneer* (June 1931): 12–13; "Palestine and Near East Exhibition and Fair, Tel Aviv, April 1929," *Monthly Pioneer* (April 1929): 4.

92 "Jüdisch–arabische Cooperation," *JR*, April 20, 1928, p. 223.

93 "In Lager Ruthenbergs. Palästinas weisse Köhle," *JR*, January 15, 1929, p. 23; "Sondernummer: Rutenberg," *PBK* (June 1929).

94 "The Rutenberg Romance: An Account of the Victorious Struggle of the Famous Jewish Engineer to Give Electric Power and Light to Palestine," *Palestine Pictorial Service* (December 1926): 8; "The Future of Water Power in Palestine: Interview with Mr. Pinchas Rutenberg, Director of the Palestine Electric Corporation," *Monthly Pioneer* (March 1929): 12, 23.

95 Lindheim, *Immortal Adventure*, pp. 270–71.

96 Heller, *My Month in Palestine*, p. 124.

97 Heller, *My Month in Palestine*, pp. 136–37.

98 "Herzl Street in Tel-Aviv (Jaffa)," in Israel Cohen, *Zionist Work in Palestine* (1911 edn.), p. 172; see Berkowitz, *Zionist Culture*, pp. 150–51; Yosef Katz, "Ideology and Urban Development: Zionism and the Origins of Tel Aviv, 1906–1914," *Journal of Historical Geography* 12, 4 (1986): 404–24.

99 Van Tijn, "Oh Life of Joy and Sorrow, Laughter and Tears," p. 189.

100 See also "Tel-Aviv. General View," and "Tel-Aviv. Allenby Road" in *Erez Israel* (London). See Zipperstein, *Elusive Prophet*, pp. 317–18.

101 Heller, *My Month in Palestine*, p. 130.

102 Julian Mack to family, July 31, 1923, p. 3, MSS col. 262, 1/6, AJA.

103 Heller, *My Month in Palestine*, p. 126.

104 See Arthur Ruppin, "Der erste jüdische Stadt. Tel Awiw, seine Entwicklung und Zukunft," *JR*, March 3, 1925, p. 161.

105 Heller, *My Month in Palestine*, pp. 128–29.

106 Heller, *My Month in Palestine*, p. 91.

107 Ernst Simon, "Kulturproblem und religiöse Frage in Palästina," *JR*, June 27, 1930, p. 340.

108 Heller, *My Month in Palestine*, p. 192.

109 Hortense Levy, "How They Live in Palestine," *Hadassah News Letter* (November–December 1932): 11–12.

110 Lindheim, *Immortal Adventure*, pp. 84–85.

111 "Die hebräische Universität in Jerusalem," *PBK* (July 1932): 62–63; *PBK* (March 1929): 1.

112 "Zur Eröffnung der Nationalbibliothek," *JR*, April 25, 1930, p. 219; *Palästina Aufbau*; *Jüdische Leistungen in Palästina*.

113 "Repräsentative jüdische Bauten in Palästina," *PBK* (October 1928): 3; *PBK* (July 1929): 4.

114 Heller, *My Month in Palestine*, p. 126.

115 See also *PBK* (May 1930): 5, 16, 20; "Einwanderinnenheim in Tel-Aviv," *Palästina Aufbau*.

116 Heller, *My Month in Palestine*, pp. 166–70.

117 Lindheim, *Immortal Adventure*, p. 89.

118 "Zur Eröffnung der Nationalbibliothek," *JR*, April 25, 1930, p. 219; "Der Fortschritt der Kolonisation," *JR*, May 9, 1930, p. 246.

119 In the field of cultural studies (from the 1970s through the 1990s), one typically finds Zionism subsumed – if it is discussed at all – into a category of a predictably "orientalizing" discourse which simply imposed its will on Palestine and its people. But this is more misleading than informative, on several counts. Most important, the view of Zionism as similar to most "colonizing" powers usually assumes a backward glance from 1948 or later. The movement, which was more of a challenge to, rather than a part of, "hegemonic discourse," had amassed shockingly little power until its "War of Independence" in 1947–48; see Edward Said, *Orientalism* (New York: Vintage, 1976), p. 221; Thomas Richards, *The Imperial Archive: Knowledge and the Fantasy of Empire* (London and New York: Verso, 1993); cf. Efron, *Defenders of the Race*, p. 3.

120 Lindheim, *Immortal Adventure*, p. 214.

121 Chaim Weizmann, "Civilisation Versus the Desert," *Monthly Pioneer* (January 1930): 8.

122 The most thoughtful treatment of this subject is Sander Gilman, *Jewish Self-Hatred: Anti-Semitism and the Hidden Language of the Jews* (Baltimore: Johns Hopkins University Press, 1986).

123 Cover, *Der Aufbau des jüdischen Palästina*, KKL pamphlet, 1922, with etching "Aus einer jüdischen Kolonie" by Hermann Struck.

6 NATIONALIZED TOURISM IN PALESTINE

1 See chapter 7 in this volume.

2 "70613 Palästinareisende im Jahre 1924," *JR*, March 24, 1925, p. 219; "1200 Personen in einem Tage," *JR*, March 31, 1925, p. 237.

3 Typically the ships dropped anchor in Haifa and the passengers visited Jerusalem; the bulk of passengers came from the United States and Central Europe; see "Executive der Jewish Agency, Materielien, Palästina-Touristik, May 1930, 71. JA 31, DD a 2/3/4/1/4/, CZA; "Die Palästinensische Touristensaison 5688," *JR*, November 18, 1927, p. 651. On the basis of limited evidence, it seems that tourism to Palestine and Israel did not usually suffer from internal strife until the 1973 war; see Bernard Reich and Gershon Kieval, *Israel: Land of Tradition and Conflict* (Boulder: Westview, 1993), p. 531; Robert W. McIntosh, *Tourism*

Principles, Practices, and Philosophies (Columbus, Ohio: Grid, 1972), p. 41.

4 See Naomi Cohen, *The Year After the Riots*.

5 George Young, *Tourism: Blessing or Blight?* (Harmondsworth: Penguin, 1973), p. 24; see Foster Rhea Dulles, *Americans Abroad: Two Centuries of European Travel* (Ann Arbor: University of Michigan Press, 1964), pp. 153–54; F. W. Ogilvie, *The Tourist Movement: An Economic Study* (London: P. S. King and Son, 1933), p. 221.

6 Paul Bernard, *Rush to the Alps: The Evolution of Vacationing in Switzerland* (New York: Columbia University Press, 1978), p. 176.

7 The history of travel and tourism has generated a significant body of scholarship, much of it dealing with literature of the pre-modern periods; work dealing with contemporary history tends to focus on theoretical implications of tourism and the intersection with imperialism and colonialism: see Eric J. Leed, *The Mind of the Traveler: Gilgamesh to Global Tourism* (New York: Basic, 1991); Stephen Greenblatt, *Marvelous Possessions: The Wonder of the New World* (Chicago: University of Chicago Press, 1991); Mary Louise Pratt, *Imperial Eyes: Travel Writing and Transculturation* (London and New York: Routledge, 1992); Nicholas Howe, *Migration and Mythmaking in Anglo-Saxon England* (New Haven and London: Yale University Press, 1989). The best general, theoretical treatment is John Urry, *The Tourist Gaze: Leisure and Travel in Contemporary Societies* (London: Sage, 1990); Urry is particularly helpful in illuminating the relationships between the increasing attention to tourism and post-structuralist theory; see also Dean MacCannell, *Empty Meeting Grounds: The Tourist Papers* (London: Routledge, 1992); Louis Vascek and Gail Buckland, *Travelers in Ancient Lands: A Portrait of the Middle East, 1839–1919* (Boston: New York Graphic Society, 1981); James C. Simmons, *Passionate Pilgrims: English Travelers to the World of the Desert Travelers* (New York: William Morrow, 1987); Ogilvie, *Tourist Movement*; Jost Krippendorf, *The Holiday Makers: Understanding the Impact of Leisure and Travel*, translated by Verz Andrassy (London: Heinemann, 1987); Philip Pearce, *The Social Psychology of Tourist Behaviour* (Oxford: Pergamon, 1982); Peter E. Murphy, *Tourism: A Community Approach* (New York and London: Methuen, 1985); A. J. Burkart and S. Medlik, *Tourism: Past, Present, and Future* (London: Heinemann, 1974); Robert W. McIntosh, *Tourism Principles, Practices, and Philosophies*. Along with the general aversion to discussing Jews, Palestine, and Israel, there is almost total ignorance of tourism and travel among Muslims and other non-Christians by those purporting to engage in universal arguments; one of the few exceptions is Louis Turner and John Ash, *The Golden Hordes: International Tourism and the Pleasure Periphery* (London: Constable, 1975).

8 Jonathan Culler, *Framing the Sign: Criticism and Its Institutions* (Oxford: Basil Blackwell, 1988), p. 153.

9 The explicit discussions relating tourism to Zionism tend to emphasize the contemporary, phenomenological aspects of non-Jewish tourism, as opposed to historical development; see Glenn Bowman, "The Politics of Tour Guiding: Israeli and Palestinian Guides in the Occupied Territories,"

in *Tourism and the Less Developed Countries*, edited by David Harrison (London: Bellhaven, 1992), pp. 121–34; Erik Cohen, "Arab Boys and Tourist Girls in a Mixed Jewish–Arab Community," *International Journal of Comparative Sociology*, 12, 4 (1971): 217–33; Saul Katz, "The Israeli Researcher-Guide: The Emergence and Perpetuation of a Role," *Annals of Tourism Research*, 12 (1985): 49–72; Michael Wolffsohn, *Eternal Guilt? Forty Years of German–Jewish–Israeli Relations*, translated by Douglas Bokovay (New York: Columbia University Press, 1993), pp. 114–18.

10 See Thomas A. Idinopulos, *Jerusalem Blessed, Jerusalem Cursed: Jews, Christians, and Muslims in the Holy City from David's Time to Our Own* (Chicago: Ivan R. Dee, 1991); Dale Eickelman and James Piscatori, eds., *Muslim Travelers: Pilgrimage, Migration, and the Religious Imagination* (Berkeley and Los Angeles: University of California Press, 1990); Juan Campo, *The Other Sides of Paradise: Explorations into the Religious Meanings of Domestic Space in Islam* (Columbia: University of South Carolina Press, 1991), pp. 139–65; Y. Portath, *The Emergence of the Palestinian-Arab National Movement, 1918–1929* (London: Frank Cass, 1974).

11 "Palästina-Reisen," *JR*, February 12, 1924, p. 77.

12 "1200 deutsche Touristen in Palästina (Führung durch den Palestine Lloyd)," *JR*, June 8, 1928, p. 325. On the historical construction of sites of "Christian memory" in the Holy Land, see Maurice Halbwachs, "The Legendary Topography of the Gospels in the Holy Land," in *On Collective Memory*, pp. 193–235.

13 Dean MacCannell, *Empty Meeting Grounds*, p. 1.

14 Dean MacCannell remarks, without explanation, that "In 'The Holy Land,' the tour has followed in the path of the religious pilgrimage and is replacing it." As opposed to replacement, it is more accurate to see it as modified; see his *The Tourist: A New Theory of the Leisure Class* (New York: Schocken, 1976), p. 43.

15 Amos Elon, *The Israelis: Founders and Sons* (New York: Penguin, 1981), pp. 280–89; Yaacov Shavit, "Archaeology, Political Culture, and Culture in Israel," in *Archaeology in Israel*, edited by Laurence Silberstein (New York: New York University Press, forthcoming).

16 See Michel Vovelle, *Ideologies and Mentalities*, translated by Eamon O'Flaherty (Chicago: University of Chicago Press, 1990), pp. 45, 89.

17 James Heller, preface to Max Heller, *My Month in Palestine*, p. xi.

18 David Lowenthal, *The Past Is a Foreign Country* (Cambridge: Cambridge University Press, 1985), p. xvii.

19 Roy Elston, "Travel in the New Palestine," *Monthly Pioneer* (February 1929): 17.

20 *La Nouvelle Aurore*, June 20, 1924, p. 12; "1200 deutsche Touristen in Palästina."

21 *New Judaea*, September 26, 1914, p. 10; Fritz Loewenstein, "Der deutsche Zionismus und Palästina," *JR*, August 29, 1924, p. 493.

22 Egon Rosenberg, "Palästinafahrten des KJV," *Der Jüdische Student* (October 1930): 3.

23 See chapter 5 in this volume and Berkowitz, *Zionist Culture*, pp. 119–64.

24 Naomi Shepherd, *The Zealous Intruders: From Napoleon to the Dawn of*

Zionism – the Explorers, Archaeologists, Artists, Tourists, Pilgrims, and Vision-aries Who Opened Palestine to the West (San Francisco: Harper and Row, 1988).

25 Given that tourism "is a complex and highly fragmented activity," many avenues of investigation necessarily remain open; see Ray Bar-On, *Travel and Tourism Data: A Comprehensive Research Handbook on the World Travel Industry* (Phoenix and New York: Oryx Press, 1989), p. 3.

26 Harrison, *Tourism and the Less Developed Countries*; Douglas Pearce and Richard Butler, eds., *Tourism Research: Critiques and Challenges* (New York: Routledge, 1993).

27 Piers Brendon, *Thomas Cook: 150 Years of Popular Tourism* (London: Secker and Warburg, 1991), pp. 129, 138–39. See this book for the history of the name of Thomas Cook Ltd.

28 Shepherd, *Zealous Intruders*; John Pudney, *The Thomas Cook Story* (London: Michael Joseph, 1953), pp. 181–92.

29 "1200 deutsche Touristen in Palästina."

30 Roy Elston, "Travel in the New Palestine," *Monthly Pioneer* (February 1929): 17; W. Basil Worsfold, *Palestine of the Mandate* (London: T. Fisher Unwin, 1925), p. 97.

31 "Weekly Letter No. 8 – from the Jewish Agency," no date, p. 6, in Robert Weltsch archive, AR 7185, LBI; *New Judaea*, September 26, 1914, p. 10.

32 Lowenthal, *The Past is a Foreign Country*, p. xix.

33 Fritz Loewenstein, "Palästina Touristik," *JR*, January 8, 1926, p. 14.

34 "Palästina Touristen-Organisation," *JR*, November 12, 1926, p. 640.

35 On the question of the "quest for authenticity" see Philip Pearce, *The Ulysses Factor: Evaluating Visitors in Tourist Settings* (New York, Berlin, and Heidelberg: Springer-Verlag, 1988), pp. 162–93; MacCannell, *The Tourist*, p. 49, cited in Urry, *Tourist Gaze*, pp. 8–9.

36 See Lesley Hazleton, *Jerusalem, Jerusalem: A Memoir of War and Peace, Passion, and Politics* (New York: Penguin, 1987), p. 5.

37 "Die Alijah aus Deutschland," *JR*, March 23, 1923, p. 142.

38 Before Thomas Cook organized tours to Palestine, in the 1850s most of the British-based trips to Palestine were conducted by the company of Henry Gaze; in the late 1860s the Middle East was thought to be "the most lucrative travel market yet to appear; see Edmund Swinglehurst, *The Romantic Journey: The Story of Thomas Cook and Victorian Travel* (New York, Evanston, San Francisco, London: Harper and Row, 1974), p. 174; Brendon, *Thomas Cook*, pp. 120–21.

39 "Brief aus Palästina," *JR*, April 27, 1923, pp. 199–200; see Swinglehurst, *Romantic Journey*.

40 Maxine Feifer, *Tourism in History: From Imperial Rome to the Present* (New York: Stein and Day, 1985), p. 188.

41 "Brief aus Palästina."

42 Emmanuel Newman to Leo Hermann, May 9, 1924; Leo Hermann to Louis Lipsky, April 1, 1924; L. Stein to L. Hermann, March 7, 1924; KH 1/273, CZA.

43 James Buzard, *The Beaten Track: European Tourism, Literature, and the Way*

to "Culture" (Oxford: Oxford University Press, 1993); see Turner and Ash, *Golden Hordes,* pp. 51–59.

44 See Susan Sontag, *On Photography* (Harmondsworth: Penguin, 1979), p. 24, quoted in Urry, *Tourist Gaze,* pp. v, 138–41.
45 "Tourism in Palestine," *New Judaea,* November 7, 1924, p. 68.
46 "Cooks Palästinareisen," *JR,* November 7, 1924, p. 634.
47 "Neue Formen der Palästina-Touristik," *JR,* June 28, 1927, p. 367.
48 Turner and Ash, *Golden Hordes,* pp. 56–58; Brendon, *Thomas Cook,* p. 96.
49 "New Propaganda Features: Cheap Palestine Tour," *Our Fund* (Tevet 5686 [January 1926]), p. 37; "1200 deutsche Touristen in Palästina"; "Die Touristen-Saison in Palästina," *JR,* May 23, 1924, p. 300.
50 "Fabreline" advertisement, *Hadassah News Letter* (March 1927): 27.
51 Ad in *JR,* December 20, 1929, p. 683.
52 "Coronia's Winter Tour," announcement reprinted from the *New York Times* in *Hadassah News Letter* (February 1921): 1; Cunard Line advertisement, *Hadassah News Letter* (March 1928): back cover.
53 Advertisement for "The Palestine Express Company Ltd.," *JR,* September 18, 1925, p. 627.
54 "Vereinigung von Palästina Express Company und Palestine Lloyd Ltd.," *JR,* November 17, 1925, p. 759.
55 "Palästina-Amt und Palästina-Lloyd," *JR,* August 12, 1927, p. 463.
56 "New Propaganda Features: Cheap Palestine Tour."
57 Advertisements for "Mittelmeer- und Orientreise," *JR,* August 28, 1925, p. 2; *JR,* September 4, 1925, p. 603; "Orientreisen," *JR,* October 14, 1927, p. 381.
58 All in "Editorial Comments: Palestine Tours and Exhibition," *Monthly Pioneer* (February 1929): 4.
59 See chapter 3 in this volume.
60 Julius Berger, "Hin-Propaganda oder Her-Propaganda. Beitrag sum Sokolow-Monat der Zionistischen Organisation, 1931," DD 2/3/4/1/4, CZA.
61 Joseph Hirsch, "Das Hotelwesen," *JR,* December 11, 1925, p. 813.
62 "Palästina-Reisen," *JR,* February 12, 1924, p. 77; "Palästina Touristen-Organisation," *JR,* November 12, 1926, p. 640; see Paul Bernard, *Rush to the Alps.*
63 Hirsch, "Das Hotelwesen."
64 Report of address by Apfel, "Die Touristik in Palästina," pp. 681–82.
65 Apfel, "Die Touristik in Palästina," p. 682.
66 Van Tijn, "Oh Life of Joy and Sorrow, Laughter and Tears," pp. 191–92, LBI.
67 D. MacCannell, "Staged Authenticity: Arrangements of Social Space in Tourist Settings," *American Sociological Review,* 79 (1973): 589–603.
68 Van Tijn, "Oh Life of Joy and Sorrow, Laughter and Tears," p. 191.
69 "Das Hotelwesen in Tel Awiw," *JR,* July 15, 1927, p. 400.
70 "Frühlingsfahrt nach Palästina," *JR,* November 19, 1929, p. 610.
71 See chapter 7 in this volume.
72 "Hotel 'King David' in Jerusalem," *JR,* January 13, 1931, p. 16.

73 "Touristenempfang in Palästina," *JR*, April 20, 1928, p. 221; "Die Touristen-Saison," *JR*, March 12, 1926, p. 149.

74 "Palästinatouristen," *JR*, March 30, 1928, p. 188.

75 Henrietta Szold to Jessie Sampter, February 25, 1922, Record Group 7, Folder 44, Box 5, HA.

76 Letters of Julian Mack to family, July 18, August 1 and 2, 1923, MSS coll. 262, 1/6, AJA.

77 Maurice Pekarsky, "Avukah: Today and Tomorrow (Pre-Convention Thoughts)," *Avukah Bulletin* (December 1931): 3.

78 For the place of these institutions within the greater scheme of Zionist settlement, see Penslar, *Zionism and Technocracy*; Berkowitz, *Zionist Culture*, pp. 144–64.

79 Greenblatt, *Marvelous Possessions*, p. ix.

80 Herman Melville, *The Writings of Herman Melville*, vol. XV, edited by Harrison Hayford, Hershel Parker, and G. Thomas Tanselle (Evanston: Northwestern University Press and Newberry Library, 1989), journal entry for January 1857, p. 88. Elizabeth Renker traced this reference.

81 Shavit, "Archaeology, Political Culture, and Culture in Israel"; Magen Broshi, "Archaeological Museums in Israel: Reflections on Problems of National Identity," in *Museums and the Making of "Ourselves": The Role of Objects in National Identity*, edited by Flora Kaplan (Leicester: Leicester University Press, 1994), pp. 314–89; Neil Silberman, *Digging for God and Country: Exploration, Archeology, and the Secret Struggle for the Holy Land, 1799–1917* (New York: Knopf, 1982); Silberman, *Between Past and Present: Archaeology, Ideology, and Nationalism in the Modern Middle East* (New York: Henry Holt, 1989); Silberman, *A Prophet from Amongst You: The Life of Yigael Yadin: Soldier, Scholar, and Mythmaker of Modern Israel* (Reading, Mass.: Addison-Wesley, 1993).

82 In the accounts of different schools of archaeology, there is little attention to larger issues outside the framework of the discipline; see Phillip King, *American Archaeology in the Mideast: A History of the American Schools of Oriental Research* (Philadelphia: American Schools of Oriental Research, 1983), p. 101.

83 King, *American Archaeology*, pp. 15ff.

84 King, *American Archaeology*, p. 7.

85 King, *American Archaeology*, p. 55.

86 Kathleen Kenyon, *Digging up Jerusalem* (London and Tonbridge: Ernest Benn, 1974), pp. 32–34.

87 R. A. S. Macalister, *A Century of Excavation in Palestine* (New York: Arno, 1977 [reprint of 1925 edition]), p. 21.

88 Macalister, *Century of Excavation in Palestine*, p. 72; Gideon Oftrat-Friedlander, "The Bezalel Museum," in Nurit Shilo-Cohen, ed., *Bezalel, 1906–1929* (Jerusalem: Israel Museum, 1983), p. 359.

89 King, *American Archaeology*, pp. 96–108.

90 Silberman, *Between Past and Present*.

91 Lindheim, *Immortal Adventure*, p. 167.

92 "Repräsentative jüdische bauten in Palästina," *PBK* (October 1928): 3; *PBK* (July 1924): 4.

93 Berkowitz, *Zionist Culture*, pp. 167–85.
94 See Berkowitz, *Zionist Culture*, pp. 157–60.
95 Macalister, *Century of Excavation in Palestine*, pp. 66–67.
96 Campo, *Other Sides of Paradise*.
97 Heller, *My Month in Palestine*, p. 26.
98 "Die Eröffnung des Hafens in Haifa," *JR*, November 3, 1933, p. 745.
99 Joshua Neumann, "My Trip Through Palestine," *Young Judaean* (November 1914): 1–4; (December 1914): 5–9, (January 1915): 9–12.
100 Myriam Harry, *A Springtide in Palestine* (London: Ernest Benn, 1924); Lindheim, *Immortal Adventure*. Harry's book was translated (from the French) into German as *Das kleine Mädchen von Jerusalem* in 1928.
101 Advertisement enclosed in *Hadassah News Letter* (March 1928), emphasis in the original.
102 Harry, *A Springtide in Palestine*, pp. 147, 110.
103 Paul Goodman, "A Springtide in Palestine," *New Judaea*, November 7, 1924, p. 70; *Menorah* (Paris), October 15, 1922, pp. 51–53; "Les Saintes Meres," *Menorah* (Summer 1931): 83; advertisement in *JR*, April 4, 1928, p. 200.
104 Joseph Hirsch, "Das Hotelwesen," *JR*, December 11, 1925, p. 813.
105 Walter Turnowsky, "Werbung durch Reisen," *JR*, September 8, 1931, p. 428; "New Propaganda Features: Cheap Palestine Tour," *Our Fund* (Tevet 5686 [January 1926]), p. 37.
106 "American Tourists Visit Palestine," *Hadassah News Letter* (October 1927): 11.
107 "Für Palästinatouristen," *JR*, January 4, 1927, p. 12.
108 "Hin-Propaganda oder Her-Propaganda. Beitrag sum Sokolow-Monat der Zionistischen Organisation, 1931," DD 2/3/4/1/4, CZA.
109 "Touristenempfang in Palästina," *JR*, April 20, 1928, p. 221.
110 "Wer kommt mit? 25 freie Palästina Reisen für die Jugend," *JR*, February 11, 1927, p. 86; "Jugend-Preisausschreiben des Keren Kajemeth Leisrael," *JR*, February 18, 1927, p. 101.
111 "Lord Balfours Empfang in Tel Awiw," *JR*, April 4, 1925, p. 249; "Masaryk in Palästina," *JR*, April 26, 1927, p. 236.
112 "Touristen in Palästina," *JR*, May 6, 1927, p. 256; "Einstein in Palästina," *JR*, February 16, 1923, p. 75; "Touristenempfang in Palästina," *JR*, April 20, 1928, p. 221.
113 "Kein Palästina Tourist aus Polen," *JR*, February 26, 1926, p. 117.
114 "In Erwartung der Touristen-Saison," *JR*, January 5, 1926, p. 3; Fritz Loewenstein, "Palästina-Jugendfahrt," *JR*, July 20, 1928, p. 414; "Palästina-Studentreise," *JR*, November 25, 1924, p. 674; "Palästinafahrt des KJV (Früjahr 1930)," *Der Jüdische Student* (November 1929): 4.
115 "Summer Cruise," *Hadassah News Letter* (April 1927): 4.
116 "Come to Palestine," advertisement of the American Economic Committee for Palestine tour, *Hadassah News Letter* (January–February 1933): 4.
117 Nima H. Alderblum, "Palestine on Shipboard. A Unique Summer Trip to Palestine," *Hadassah News Letter* (December 1926): 10.
118 "American Tourists Visit HMO [Hadassah Medical Organization] Institutions," *Hadassah News Letter* (February 1927): 3.

119 See Billie Melman, *Women's Orients: English Women and the Middle East, 1718–1918: Sexuality, Religion, and Work* (Ann Arbor: University of Michigan Press, 1992); Pratt, *Imperial Eyes*, pp. 102–07.

120 Leed, *Mind of the Traveler*, pp. 11–129.

121 Mignon L. Rubenovitz, "Zionist Education for Hadassah," *Hadassah News Letter* (March–April 1932): 3, 15.

122 Right-wing tours did not take on a regular form until after the rise of Menahem Begin in the 1970s; see Bowman, "Politics of Tour Guiding."

123 "A Travel Seminar for Palestine," in Irma Lindheim file, Nearprint file, Biographies, AJA.

124 Advertisement for "Educational Travel Institute," *Young Judaean* (March 1924): back cover.

125 See Marion Kaplan, *The Making of the Jewish Middle Class: Women, Family, and Identity in Imperial Germany* (New York: Oxford University Press, 1992).

126 See Victor Turner, *From Ritual to Theatre: The Human Seriousness of Play* (Baltimore: Johns Hopkins University Press, 1992), p. 55.

127 Alderblum, "Palestine on Shipboard," p. 10.

128 Campo, *Other Sides of Paradise*, pp. 159–60.

129 Heller, *My Month in Palestine*, p. 29.

130 "Beginn der Touristen-Saison in Palästina," *JR*, January 14, 1927, p. 27.

131 "Neuer Touristenstrom," *JR*, October 28, 1932, p. 417.

132 Circular letter from Thomas Cook & Son, quoted in Alderblum, p. 10.

133 "Hin-Propaganda oder Her-Propaganda. Beitrag zum Sokolow-Monat der Zionistischen Organisation, 1931," DD 2/3/4/1/4, p. 4, CZA.

134 *New Judaea*, September 26, 1914, p. 10.

135 Roy Elston, "Travel in the New Palestine," *Monthly Pioneer* (February 1929): 17.

136 Advertisement for "BP Tours – British Pal. and Eastern Tours, Ltd.," *Monthly Pioneer* (October 1932): 23.

137 See Bernard, *Rush to the Alps*, p. viii.

138 "Palästina Touristen-Organisation," *JR*, November 12, 1926, p. 640.

139 "Hin-Propaganda oder Her-Propaganda," DD 2/3/4/1/4, CZA.

140 See Yerushalmi, *Zakhor*, pp. 43–44.

141 See Lowenthal, *The Past Is a Foreign Country*, p. 412.

142 Bowman, "Politics of Tour Guiding," pp. 121, 134.

143 Paul Tillich, "Mind and Migration," *Social Research* 4 (1937): 295–305, quoted in Howe, *Migration and Mythmaking*, p. 6; I have borrowed liberally from Howe's use of Tillich.

7 IDEALISM, REALISM, AND SOCIABILITY IN WESTERN ZIONIST YOUTH ORGANIZATIONS

1 Van Tijn, "Oh Life of Joy and Sorrow, Laughter and Tears," p. 30; see Ruth M. M. Hoogeswoud-Verschoor, "The First Years of the Zionist Youth Movement in the Netherlands," in *Dutch Jewish History: Proceedings of the Fifth Symposium on the History of the Jews of the Netherlands, Vol. III*, edited

by Jozeph Michman (Jerusalem and Assen/Maastricht: Hebrew University and Van Gorcum, 1993), pp. 309–20.

2 See "Zionism: The Coming Generation," *New Judaea*, December 5, 1924, p. 91; "Men and Matters: The Zionist Summer School," *Pioneer* (September 1930): 8.

3 Hubert Pollack, "Am Scheidewege," *Der Jüdische Student* (January–February, 1930): 14; Aaron Berman, *Nazism, the Jews, and American Zionism*, pp. 18–19.

4 Walter Laqueur, *Young Germany: A History of the German Youth Movement* (London: Routledge and Kegan Paul, 1962), p. xi.

5 Peter D. Stachura, *The German Youth Movement, 1900–1945* (London and Basingstoke: Macmillan, 1981), p. 1.

6 John Springhall, *Youth, Empire, and Society: British Youth Movements, 1883–1940* (London: Croom Helm, 1977); Michael Rosenthal, *The Character Factory: Baden-Powell and the Origins of the Boy Scout Movement* (New York: Pantheon, 1986).

7 David I. Macleod, *Building Character in the American Boy: The Boy Scouts, YMCA, and Their Forerunners, 1870–1920* (Madison: University of Wisconsin Press, 1983); Harold P. Levy, *Building a Popular Movement: A Case Study of the Public Relations of the Boy Scouts of America* (New York: Russell Sage Foundation, 1944).

8 Cf. Hans Kohn, "The Young Zionist Movement: A Successful Conference at Dantzic," *New Judaean*, October 10, 1924, p. 28.

9 Poppel, *Zionism in Germany*; Lavsky, *Be-țerem pur'anut*; Moshe Zimmerman, "Jewish Nationalism and Zionism in German-Jewish Students' Organisations," *Year Book XXVII of the Leo Baeck Institute* (1982): 129–53; Zimmerman's analysis ends at World War I.

10 See Glenn R. Sharfman, "Whoever Has the Youth, Has the Future: The Jewish Youth Movement in Germany, 1900–1936: A Study in Ideology and Organization," Ph.D. dissertation (University of North Carolina at Chapel Hill, 1989), for the most astute and comprehensive treatment.

11 Chanoch Rinott, "Major Trends in Jewish Youth Movements in Germany" and Werner Rosenstock, "The Jewish Youth Movement," *Year Book XIX of the Leo Baeck Institute* (1974): 77–105.

12 Zimmerman, "Jewish Nationalism and Zionism," pp. 132, 134–53; see also Marsha L. Rozenblit, "The Assertion of Identity – Jewish Student Nationalism at the University of Vienna Before the First World War," *Year Book XXVII of the Leo Baeck Institute* (1982): 171–86.

13 Rinott, "Major Trends in Jewish Youth Movements," p. 78; Julius Berger, "Gesinnung und Kenntnis: Ein Beitrag zur zionistischer Erziehungsfrage," *JR*, April 6, 1917, p. 115.

14 Stachura, *German Youth Movement*, p. 85.

15 The main non-Zionist rival of the Kameraden was the Deutsch-Jüdisch Jugend-Gemeinschaft (DJJG); see Werner Rosenstock, pp. 97–102.

16 Stachura, *German Youth Movement*, pp. 85–87; on Buber's influence, see George L. Mosse, "The Influence of the Volkish Idea on German Jewry," in Mosse, *Germans and Jews: The Right, the Left, and the Search for a "Third Force" in Pre-Nazi Germany* (Detroit: Wayne State University Press, 1987),

pp. 77–115; Maurice Friedman, *Martin Buber's Life and Work: The Early Years, 1878–1923* (New York: E. P. Dutton, 1981), pp. 228–30.

17 Herbert Nussbaum, "Weg und Schicksal eines deutschen Juden" (typescript), ME 478, LBI.

18 Stachura, *German Youth Movement*, pp. 85–87.

19 "German-Speaking Jews and Zionism," *LBI News* (Winter 1987): 6.

20 Karl Glaser, introduction to *Blau-Weiss Liederbuch* (Berlin: Jüdischer Verlag, 1914), partially quoted in "German-Speaking Jews and Zionism", p. 4.

21 See Berkowitz, *Zionist Culture*, pp. 20–23.

22 Henry Buxbaum, quoted in Monika Richarz, ed., *Jewish Life in Germany: Memoirs from Three Centuries*, translated by Stella P. Rosenfeld and Sidney Rosenfeld (Bloomington and Indianapolis: Indiana University Press, 1991), p. 304.

23 Glaser, introduction to *Blau-Weiss Liederbuch*, partially quoted in "German-Speaking Jews and Zionism", p. 4.

24 "University Zionist Federation," *Pioneer* (June 1932): 21.

25 *Blau-Weiss Führer*, partially quoted in "German-Speaking Jews and Zionism", p. 14.

26 To a certain extent, this view is consistent with Gershom Scholem's analysis of Blau-Weiss as expressed in the periodical *Blau-Weiss Brille* edited by Scholem and Erich Brauer; three issues appeared between 1915–16, and Scholem's "Jüdische Jugendbewegung" in *Der Jude* (March 1917): 822–24; see Rinott, "Major Trends in Jewish Youth Movements," p. 88; and David Biale, *Gershom Scholem: Kabbalah and Counter-History* (Cambridge: Harvard University Press, 1982). Rinott notes that Scholem "did not do justice" to the movement in claiming that it lacked commitment (p. 89); furthermore, Scholem himself did not reflect on his own immersion in the world of German culture.

27 The attitude toward Eastern Jews was highly ambivalent, to say the least; see Aschheim, *Brothers and Strangers*; Wertheimer, *Unwelcome Strangers*; Trude Maurer, *Die Entwicklung der jüdische Minderheit in Deutschland (1780–1933): neuere Forschungen und offene Fragen* (Tübingen: M. Niemeyer, 1992) and Maurer, *Ostjuden in Deutschland, 1918–1933* (Hamburg: H. Christians Verlag, 1986); S. Adler-Rudel, *Ostjuden in Deutschland, 1880–1940: zugleich eine Geschichte der Organisationen die sie betreuten* (Tübingen: Mohr, 1959).

28 *Blau-Weiss Führer*, p. 6.

29 *Blau-Weiss Führer*, p. 13.

30 *Blau-Weiss Führer*, p. 8.

31 *Blau-Weiss Führer*, p. 6.

32 *Blau-Weiss Führer*, p. 12.

33 "Kowno-Fahrt," *Der Jüdische Pfadfinder* (May 1927): 12–13.

34 Stachura, *German Youth Movement*, pp. 71–81, 85–93.

35 *Blau-Weiss Führer*, pp. 11, 8.

36 *Hamischmar. Vom Leben der Jüngeren im Blau-Weiss* (Berlin: Bundesleitung des Blau-Weiss, 1925), p. 46.

37 *Blau-Weiss Führer*, p. 26.

38 Biale, *Gershom Scholem*, p. 66–69.

39 *Blau-Weiss Führer*, p. 7; Helene Hanna Cohn, "Die Frau in der national-jüdischen Jugendbewegung," *JR*, September 27, 1918, p. 303.
40 Edith Lachmann, "Eine zionistische Mädchenbewegung," *JR*, March 15, 1927, p. 133.
41 Biale, *Gershom Scholem*, p. 68.
42 *Blau-Weiss Führer*, p. 13.
43 Levy, *Building a Popular Movement*, pp. 21, 25.
44 *Blau-Weiss Führer*, p. 8. See Chaim Schatzker, "The Jewish Youth Movement in Germany, 1900–1933," Ph.D. dissertation (Hebrew University of Jerusalem, 1969); by Schatzker's definition, an authentic "youth movement" is removed from political considerations; see Rinott, "Major Trends in Jewish Youth Movements," pp. 92ff.
45 *Blau-Weiss Führer*, p. 10.
46 "Das Bundesgesetz von Prunn," *Blau-Weiss Blätter: Führerzeitung* (December 1922): 26–30.
47 Rinott, "Major Trends in Jewish Youth Movements," pp. 85ff.
48 Stachura, *German Youth Movement*, pp. 88–89.
49 Nussbaum, "Weg und Schicksal eines deutschen Juden," pp. 8, 13–15; "Die Zusammenarbeit mit dem Blau-Weiss," *Der Jüdische Student* (November 1926): 93.
50 *New Judaea*, November 7, 1924, p. 67.
51 Nussbaum, "Weg und Schicksal eines deutschen Juden," p. 13.
52 "Hechaluz: Fortschritte in Giwath Brenner," *JR*, January 24, 1933, p. 33.
53 Heinz Boss, "Deutsche Juden in Erez Israel," *JR*, February 17, 1933, p. 66.
54 *Hamischmar*, pp. 268–70.
55 *Der Jüdische Pfadfinder* (May 1927).
56 Richard Markel, "Brith Haolim: Der Weg der Alija des jung-jüdischen Wanderbundes (JJWB)," *Bulletin des Leo Baeck Instituts* 9, 34 (1966): 119–89.
57 Stachura, *German Youth Movement*, p. 89.
58 Herbert Foerder and Siegfried Kanowitz, "Zur Kartellarbeit. Rückblick und Ausblick," *Der Jüdische Student* (February 1927): 10–13.
59 "Jugendbewegung: Aufhebung der Fusion zwischen KJV und Blau-Weiss" and Moritz Bileski, "Post Festum," *JR*, February 6, 1923, p. 60; "Die Zusammenarbeit mit dem Blau-Weiss," *Der Jüdische Student* (November 1926): 93.
60 "Jugendbewegung: Das Gesetz des Blau-Weiss," *JR*, February 16, 1923, p. 77.
61 Herbert Foerder, "Die Aufgaben des KJV," *Der Jüdische Student* (June/July 1925): 109; almost the same words were used by Richard Lichtheim in "Kurzer Rückblick," *Der Jüdische Student* (January–February 1930): 9.
62 Reinharz, *Fatherland or Promised Land*, p. 34.
63 See Konrad Jarausch, *Students, Society, and Politics in Imperial Germany: The Rise of Academic Illiberalism* (Princeton: Princeton University Press, 1982); Norbert Kampe, *Studenten und "Judenfrage" in deutschen Kaiserreich: die Entstehung einer akademischen Tragerschicht des Antisemitismus* (Göttingen: Vanderhöck and Ruprecht, 1988); Michael Kater, *Studentenschaft und Rechtsradikalismus in Deutschland, 1918–1933: Eine sozialgeschichtliche Studie*

zur Bildungskrise in der Weimarer Republik (Hamburg: Hoffmann and Campe, 1975); Geoffrey Giles, *Students and National Socialism in Germany* (Princeton: Princeton University Press, 1985).

64 Walter Gross, "The Zionist Students' Movement," *Year Book IV of the Leo Baeck Institute* (1959): 145.

65 On the cultural-historical context, see Kevin McAleer, *Dueling: The Cult of Honor in Fin-de-Siècle Germany* (Princeton: Princeton University Press, 1994) and Ute Frevert, *Ehrenmänner: Das Duell in der bürgerlichen Gesellschaft* (Munich: C. H. Beck, 1991).

66 Gross, "Zionist Students' Movement," p. 145.

67 For the Viennese background, see Rozenblit, "Assertion of Identity."

68 Reinharz, *Fatherland or Promised Land*, p. 35. The KZV was established by the group Hasmonea, which claimed to be the first "purely Zionist students' society" (founded in Berlin in 1902) and Jordania (Munich, 1905); "Kartell jüdischer Verbindungen (KJV), in *Encyclopaedia Judaica* (1971 edition), vol. X, p. 805; "Die Verschmelzung von BJC und KZV," *Der Jüdische Student* (November 1914).

69 "Kartell-Convent der Verbindungen deutscher Studenten jüdischer Glaubens (K-C)," in *Encyclopedia Judaica* (1971 edition), vol. X, p. 804.

70 Karl Glaser, "Die national-jüdische Jugendbewegung in Deutschland," *JR*, October 4, 1918, p. 309.

71 "Kartell jüdischer Verbindungen," in *Encyclopaedia Judaica*; for typical examples of extreme Palestino-centrism, see D. Nachmannsohn, "Eindrücke von der Chargiertentagung," *Der Jüdische Student* (October–November 1920): 221–22, and Julius Lewinsohn, "Das zionistische Bildungsproblem," *Der Jüdische Student* (November 1926): 96–103.

72 "Turn-und Sportfest der national-jüdischen Jugend Berlins," *JR*, June 13, 1919, p. 334; Paul Hirsch, "Turnen und Sport im KJV," *Der Jüdische Student* (March 1921): 53–55; "Der 7. Kartelltag findet am 27. und 28. Februar 1927 in Berlin[statt]" and Fritz Engel, "Bericht des Turn und Sport Ressorts," *Der Jüdische Student* (February 1927): 6, 21.

73 Quoted in Poppel, *Zionism in Germany*, pp. 132–33.

74 Gross, "Zionist Students' Movement," p. 145.

75 Gross, "Zionist Students' Movement," p. 146.

76 Franz Meyer, "Die Organisation der Erziehung," *Der Jüdische Student* (March 1921): pp. 41–45; "Führerkurs des Jung-jüdischen-Wanderbundes," *JR*, January 4, 1927, p. 12; David Nachmannsohn, "Bericht des Unterrichts-Ressorts, in *Der Jüdische Student* (February 1927): 17.

77 Siegfried Kanowitz, "Stoffe und Methode unseres Unterrichts," *Der Jüdische Student* (February 1926): 16.

78 David Nachmannshohn, "Bericht des Unterrichts-Ressorts," *Der Jüdische Student* (February 1927): 18–19.

79 Jessie Sampter, *A Course in Zionism* (New York: no publisher [Hadassah?], 1915).

80 Samuel Sambursky, "Der Stand des Hebräischen im Kartell," *Der Jüdische Student* (April–May): 106; cf. "Erziehung und Unterricht," *Der Jüdische Student* (April–May 1921): 99–103.

81 Leo Olitzki, "Referat über Erziehungsarbeit, in *Der Jüdische Student* (October–November 1920): 223–31; see Sorkin, *Transformation of the German Jewry* and George L. Mosse, *German Jews Beyond Judaism* (Bloomington: Indiana University Press, 1988).

82 Gustav Witkowsky, "Der Prophetismus als Kulturgeschichtliches Problem," *Jüdische Wille*, 1 (1918): 87–107.

83 Poppel, *Zionism in Germany*, pp. 132–35; Moshe Zimmerman refers to the *Alte Herren* as "veterans," p. 138.

84 Walter Pinner, "Organisationsfragen," *Der Jüdische Student* (March 1917).

85 The basic chronology, but not the analysis, is found in "Kartell jüdischer Verbindungen."

86 "Halbjahresbericht des Präsidums," *Der Jüdische Student* (July 1929): 7.

87 "An die Alten Herren des KJV," *Der Jüdische Student* (March 1923): 41.

88 Erich Hurwitz, "Die zukünftige Gestaltung des KJV," *Der Jüdische Student* (February 1927): 32.

89 "Auch ein Beitrag zur Altherrenfrage," *Der Jüdische Student* (June 1926): 56–58.

90 "Halbjahresbericht des Präsidums"; "Bericht über den X. Kartelltag in Dresden," *Der Jüdische Student* (January–February 1930): 23.

91 Gross, "Zionist Students' Movement," p. 146.

92 "Die Zusammenarbeit mit dem Blau-Weiss," *Der Jüdische Student* (November 1926): 92–94; Justus Schloss, "Fragen der Kartelliwirklichkeit," *Der Jüdische Student* (December 1929): 5–7.

93 Hurwitz, "Die zukünftige Gestaltung des KJV," p. 31. Keith Pickus argues that membership in various nationalist societies represented but one dimension of a complex identity for European Jewish students; see Pickus, "Jewish University Students in Germany: The Construction of a Post-Emancipation Identity," Ph.D. dissertation (University of Washington, 1993).

94 Bruno Perl, "Dritter Kartelltag des KJV in Leipzig," *JR*, January 11, 1921, pp. 16–17; Moritz Bileski, "KT [Kartell Tage] Referat über Dienstpflicht und Keren Hajessod," *Der Jüdische Student* (March 1921): 51; "IYAR Campaign Press Bulletin No. 5," from Zionist Organization Central Office London, KH 1/459/1, CZA; "An die zionistische Jugend in Deutschland!," *JR*, February 24, 1925, p. 145.

95 Fritz Sternberg, "Wissenschaftliche Arbeit für den Zionismus," *Der Jüdische Wille* (1918): 84–87.

96 M. Y. Gavrieel, "Judarabisch Konfederation," *Der Jüdische Student* (August–September 1930): 6; "Die arabischen Partien in Palästina" and "Die arabische Press," *Der Jüdische Student* (May–June 1930): 9–12; Samuel Sambursky, "Der Weg der Verständigung" and A. Reitenberg, "Juden und Araber in Palästina," *Der Jüdische Student* (November 1929): 18–22; Justus Schloss, "Palästina und die arabische Welt" and "Der arabische Aufstand in Palästina und seine Konsequenzen für Erez-Israel," *Der Jüdische Student* (October 1929): 9–20.

97 Richard Lichtheim, "Was ist zionistische Politik?," *Der Jüdische Student* (February 1931): 31; Hans Capell, "Betrachtungen nach dem Camp," *Der Jüdische Student* (November 1926): 104–05.

98 *Jewish Academy* [publication of the Inter-University Jewish Federation of Great Britain and Ireland (IUJFGBI)] (November 1927): 7–9; M. Solomon, "The Present Position of the UZF," *Pioneer* (August–September 1931); in 1932, the British university students' "academic program" was very simple and undeveloped, consisting of "1. Main waves of Jewish migration; 2. Messianic ideas and movements in Israel; 3. The XIX Century and Jewish Nationalism; 4. Objections to Zionism and how to answer them; 5. The Palestine Mandate" (p. 2).

99 "University Zionist Federation: Half-Yearly Bulletin," *Pioneer* (August 1930): 22–24.

100 "University Zionist Federation," *Pioneer* (October 1931): 17–18.

101 "University Zionist Federation," *Pioneer* (July 1930): 21; "University Zionist Federation," *Pioneer* (May 1932): 20.

102 "University Zionist Federation," *Pioneer* (December 1931): 24; "University Zionist Federation," *Pioneer* (October 1932): 24; "University Zionist Federation," *Pioneer* (September 1930): 21; "University Zionist Federation," *Pioneer* (March 1930): 20; "University Zionist Federation," *Pioneer* (April 1930): 20; "University Zionist Federation," *Pioneer* (September 1929): 21; "University Zionist Federation," *Pioneer* (November 1931): 24.

103 "University Zionist Federation," *Pioneer* (June 1932): 21; *Jewish Academy*, p. 9; "University Zionist Federation," *Pioneer* (March 1932): 21.

104 "University Zionist Federation," *Pioneer* (April 1932): 15.

105 Program: Second Annual Zionist Summer Course Under the Auspices of the Intercollegiate Zionist Association of America, July 15–19, 1918, Box 2, Nearprint file, special topics, Zionism, AJA.

106 "University Zionist Federation," *Pioneer* (January 1932): 18. In February 1933 it was reported that a "Hebrew session" had become a "regular feature of the UZF annual conference"; it seems, however, to have been a single lecture: "University Zionist Federation," *Pioneer* (February 1933): 24.

107 "University Zionist Federation, in *Pioneer* (March 1932): 21.

108 Stuart Cohen, *English Zionists and British Jews*, pp. 129–30; see also Joseph Brainin, "English and Zionist Tradition: Leon Simon, the Introducer of Zionism into England's University Life," *Monthly Pioneer* (December 1928): 20.

109 Stuart Cohen, *English Zionists and British Jews*, p. 130.

110 See chapters 5 and 6 in this volume.

111 *Magazine* (of the IUJFGBI) (December 1925): 9.

112 Rudi R. Hecht, "Zur Frage der Hebräischen Universität," *Der Jüdische Student* (May 1931): 5; Egon Rosenberg, "Palästinafahrten des KJV," *Der Jüdische Student* (October 1930): 3; "Palästinafahrt des KJV (Frũjahr 1930)," *Der Jüdische Student* (November 1929): 4.

113 There were at least three different Zionist groups named "Habonim"; in Montreal, the "Zionist Order Habonim," apparently intended for university students, was founded in 1923 as a vehicle of fundraising for the Keren Hayesod: Bernard Figler, *From Mandate to State, 1923–1948: The Story of the Zionist Order Habonim* (Montreal: no publisher, 1951), pp. 11–13, 16. The best known is the youth wing of Ha-Po'el ha-tsa'ir in North America:

see J. J. Goldberg and Elliot Kings, eds., *Builders and Dreamers: Habonim Labor Zionist Youth in North America* (New York: Herzl Press, 1993).

114 "University Zionist Federation," *Pioneer* (January 1930): 23.
115 "University Zionist Federation," *Pioneer* (April 1932): 15.
116 Wesley Aron, "Habonim," *Pioneer* (November 1930): 20.
117 Rebecca Sieff, "The Youth Movement in England," *New Judaea*, December 5, 1924, pp. 100–01.
118 All from Sieff, "Youth Movement in England," pp. 100–01.
119 Julian Mack to family, July 31, 1923, MSS col. 262 1/6, AJA.
120 Cecil I. Dorrian, "Palestine as Seen by an American Writer," *American Hebrew*, October 22, 1920, pp. 678–79.
121 "University Zionist Federation," *Pioneer* (February 1932): 23.
122 *Magazine* (of the Inter-University Jewish Federation of Great Britain and Ireland) (December 1925): 7.
123 "University Zionist Federation," *Pioneer* (February 1932): 23.
124 "Zionist – Not Personal – Organs," *Hadassah News Letter*, June 8, 1928; see chapter 8 in this volume.
125 *Palestine During the War*, p. 6.
126 "Sub-Convention of the Intercollegiate Zionist Association," *Maccabaean* (August 1917): 334.
127 Harshav, *Language in Time of Revolution*, p. 110.
128 E. Hinden and E. P. Bradlow, "University Zionist Federation," *Pioneer* (March 1930): 20.
129 "University Zionist Federation," *Pioneer* (January 1932): 18.
130 "University Zionist Federation," *Pioneer* (October 1932): 24.
131 "University Zionist Federation," *Pioneer* (March 1931): 24; "University Zionist Federation," *Pioneer* (November 1932): 2.
132 *Jerubbaal: Eine Zeitschrift der jüdischen Jugend* (1918–19): 461. John Hoberman thoughtfully sent me this item.
133 Van Tijn, "Oh Life of Joy and Sorrow, Laughter and Tears," p. 30. Van Tijn worked as a translator in the Jewish National Fund Head Office at the Hague.
134 Richard Hofstadter argues that one of the reasons why anti-intellectualism is so prominent in American thought is because of incessant self-criticism; see Hofstadter, *Anti-Intellectualism in American Life* (New York: Vintage, 1963).
135 The Avukah Summer School (Second Annual Session), Camp Scopus, Lake George, New York, June 19 to July 3, 1931, American Student Zionist Federation, Box 5, Nearprint file, special topics, Zionism, AJA.
136 "Summer School Offers Attractive Prospectus," *Avukah Bulletin* (March 1931): 1.
137 "A Call to Service" (leaflet), the Intercollegiate Zionist Association, Box 2, Nearprint file, special topics, Zionism, AJA; *Kadimah* (New York: Federation of American Zionists, 1918).
138 Marie Syrkin, "The New Youth Movement," *New Palestine*, August 14, 1925, p. 140.
139 Syrkin, "New Youth Movement," p. 140.
140 Prospectus of the Summer Agricultural Course Under the Auspices of the

Intercollegiate Zionist Organization and the National Farm School (Bucks County, PA), July 11–August 20, 1920, Box 2, Nearprint file, special topics, Zionism, AJA.

141 Syrkin, "New Youth Movement," p. 140.
142 Morris Rivlin, "Avukah," *New Palestine*, August 14, 1925, p. 139.
143 Rivlin, "Avukah," p. 139.
144 Samuel Blumenfeld, "Whither Avukah?" in *Avukah Bulletin* (December 1931): 3.
145 See John Higham, *Send These to Me: Immigrants in Urban America*, rev. edn. (Baltimore: Johns Hopkins University Press, 1984), pp. 205–08.
146 Mitchell Salem Fisher, "Zionism and the Religion of Youth," *Avukah Annual* (1928): 14.
147 Syrkin, "New Youth Movement," p. 140.
148 Blumenfeld, "Whither Avukah?," p. 3; see also Sidney Jacobi, "The Four Million," *Avukah Bulletin* (December 1931): 3.
149 Emmanuel Neumann, "The Policies of Young Judaea," *Young Judaean* (July 1916): 322.
150 Samuel Blumenfeld, "A Resolution That Failed," *Avukah Annual* (1929): 36.
151 Blumenfeld, "Whither Avukah?" p. 3.
152 Maurice Samuel, "The Nature of Avukah," *Avukah Annual* (1928): 9–10.
153 S. L. Halkin, "What Ails Our Jewish American Youth?" *Avukah Annual* (1928): 24–25.
154 "Chapter Activities," *Avukah Bulletin* (March 1931): 3.
155 Blumenfeld, "Whither Avukah?" p. 3.
156 The United Palestine Appeal was the name given to the American branch of the Keren Hayesod, in conjunction with the Jewish National Fund, in 1925.
157 Maurice Pekarsky, "Avukah: Today and Tomorrow (Pre-Convention Thoughts)," *Avukah Bulletin* (December 1931): 3.
158 Maurice Pekarsky, "A Message from the President," *Avukah Bulletin* (February 1932): 4.
159 *Avukah Bulletin* (February 1932): 1.
160 Solomon Abramov, "Problems of Avukah Cultural Work," *Avukah Bulletin* (February 1932): 2–4.
161 Leo W. Schwartz and James Waterman Wise, "Zionism and the Jewish National Home: A Syllabus," Box 3, Nearprint file, special topics, Zionism, AJA.
162 "Talkies of Palestine and of Professor Einstein at National Office," *Avukah Bulletin* (March 1931): 4.
163 *The Challenge of Avukah* [pamphlet], Box 3, Nearprint file, special topics, Zionism, AJA; Samuel Blumenfeld, "Hebrew in the High School and College Curriculum," *Avukah Annual* (1928): 12.
164 "A University Women's Group in Hadassah," *Hadassah News Letter* (November [?] 1923), no pagination.
165 *Hadassah News Letter* (December 1925): 14.
166 Lillian Weiss, "Cultural Fellowship of the Junior Hadassah," *Hadassah News Letter* (March–April 1930): 10.

167 Henrietta Szold to Jessie Sampter, September 4, 1930, Record group 7, Folder 44, Box 5, HA; Henrietta Szold to Jessie Sampter, June 10, 1925, Record Group 7, Folder 42, Box 5, HA.

168 Henrietta Szold to Rose Jacobs, [fragment of letter, probably around 1934], Record Group 7, Box 5, HA.

169 Blumenfeld, "Whither Avukah?" p. 3.

170 Benjamin Itkowitz, "Avukah, American Student Labor-Zionist Federation," *Avukah Bulletin* (April 1932): 2; "Chapter Activities," *Avukah Bulletin* (May 1931): "A debate on the subject 'Revisionism is Beneficial to Zionism' was held in the ENY chapter," p. 7.

171 "Avukah Luncheon, July 2nd: Convention of American Student Zionist Federation Will be Followed by Important Luncheon Conference," *New Palestine*, June 29, 1928, p. 698.

172 "Chapter Activities," *Avukah Bulletin* (May 1931): 7; "Sixth Annual Convention Gives New Impetus to Zionist Activity in Indianapolis," *Avukah Bulletin* (February 1932): 2.

173 Judith Klein, *Der deutsche Zionismus und die Araber Palästinas: Eine Untersuchung der deutsch-zionistischen Publikationen, 1917–1938* (Frankfurt: Campus Verlag, 1982).

174 "Professor Albert Einstein Gives Avukah Students Views on Palestine in International Broadcast: Organization Selected for Exclusive Radio Address," *Avukah Bulletin* (December 1930): 1. Einstein was a member of B'rith Shalom.

175 "Sixth Annual Convention Gives New Impetus to Zionist Activity in Indianapolis," *Avukah Bulletin* (February 1932): 2.

176 Schwartz and Wise, "Zionism and the Jewish National Home," p. 21.

177 Benjamin Itkowitz, "Avukah, American Student Labor-Zionist Federation," *Avukah Bulletin* (April 1932): 2.

178 *Hadassah Bulletin*, November 23, 1914, p. 1.

179 David Schneeberg, "Five Years of Young Judaea," *Young Judaean* (May–June 1913): 24; "Federation and Hadassah," *Young Judaean* (December 1916): 115–16.

180 "Young Judaea," in *Encyclopedia of Zionism and Israel*, vol. II, edited by Raphael Patai (New York: Herzl Press/McGraw-Hill, 1971), p. 1250.

181 *Young Judaean* (January 1918): 1; "The Story of the Keren Ha-Yesod," *Young Judaean* (April 1921): 193, 209.

182 "Young Judaea Must Go On!," *Young Judaean* (January 1921): 121; "YJ Convention," *Young Judaean* (August 1923): 256; Schneeberg, "Five Years of Young Judaea," p. 24.

183 "Young Judaea," in *Encyclopedia of Zionism and Israel*, vol. II, p. 1250.

184 "The Young Judaea Banquet," *New Palestine*, November 7, 1924, p. 291.

185 *Young Judaean* (March–April 1915): 1.

186 *Young Judaean* (November 1915): back cover.

187 See Roger A. Fischer, *Tippecanoe and Trinkets Too: The Material Culture of American Presidential Campaigns, 1828–1924* (Urbana and Chicago: University of Illinois Press, 1988), pp. viii–ix; Biale, *Gershom Scholem*, p. 53.

188 "Avukah Convention: Summary Report of Proceedings of Third Annual Convention of Avukah, American Student Zionist Organization at

Pittsburgh, June 28, 29, 30, 1928, as Submitted by the Avukah National Office," *New Palestine*, July 13–20, 1928, p. 55; "Avukah's Anniversary," *New Palestine*, June 6, 1930, pp. 347–48.

189 *Avukah Annual* (1928): 1.

190 *Program for American Jews* (New York: Avukah, 1938); Shoshana Harris Sankowsky, *Short History of Zionism* (No. 3. Avukah Program) (No place: American Student Zionist Federation, 1936), pp. 50–51, Box 5, Nearprint file, special topics, Zionism, AJA; Solomon Abramov, "Problems of Avukah Cultural Work," in *Brandeis Avukah Annual of 1932: A Collection of Essays on Contemporary Zionist Thought* (Boston: Stratford, 1932), pp. 627–41.

191 "Sixth Annual Convention Gives New Impetus to Zionist Activity in Indianapolis," *Avukah Bulletin* (February 1932): 2.

192 "Chapter Activities," *Avukah Bulletin* (December 1931): 7.

8 COLD EMBRACE: THE RECEPTION OF HADASSAH AND ORGANIZED EUROPEAN WOMEN ZIONISTS

1 See, e.g., Ellen M. Umansky, "Spiritual Expressions: Jewish Women's Religious Lives in the Twentieth-Century United States," in Baskin, *Jewish Women*, p. 273.

2 Aaron Berman, *Nazism, the Jews and American Zionism*, p. 18; Davidman and Tenenbaum, *Feminist Perspectives on Jewish Studies*.

3 Prestel, "Frauen und die zionistische Bewegung."

4 See chapter 3 in this volume.

5 See Yonathan Shapiro, *Leadership of the American Zionist Organization*, pp. 204–06; Urofsky, *American Zionism from Herzl to the Holocaust*, pp. 342–44; the papers of Hadassah have rarely been consulted. There is now an exemplary guide for future research, L. D. Geller, *The Henrietta Szold Papers in the Hadassah Archives, 1875–1975* (New York: Hadassah, 1982).

6 "Kinder in neuer Heimat. Vor 50 Jahren und heute" (accompanied by a picture of Henrietta Szold on the cover), *JR*, April 2, 1935, p. 1.

7 Although the full implications will not be discussed in this chapter, the theoretical model from which I draw is from Joan Wallach Scott, *Gender and the Politics of History* (New York: Columbia University Press, 1988), p. 10, and Scott, "Women's History," in *New Perspectives on Historical Writing*, edited by Peter Burke (State College, Penn.: Penn State University Press, 1991), pp. 42–66.

8 See Marion Kaplan, *Jewish Feminist Movement in Germany*; and Kaplan, *Making of the Jewish Middle Class*, pp. 208–27; Berkowitz, "Transcending 'Tsimmes and Sweetness.'"

9 The problem is alluded to in Mosse, *Nationalism and Sexuality*, p. 42, Lesley Hazleton, *Israeli Women: The Reality Behind the Myths* (New York: Simon and Schuster, 1977), p. 95, and Jay Y. Gonen, *A Psychohistory of Zionism* (New York: Meridian, 1976), p. 141; David Biale, *Eros and the Jews: From Biblical Israel to Contemporary America* (New York: Basic, 1992).

10 See "General Report," *Women's International Zionist Organization: Report for the Period 1923–1925 for the Third International Zionist Conference*, p. 3; Helena Weissberg to [?] Cohen, July 15, 1912, Z3/983, CZA; Edith Lachmann to ZZ [Zionistische-Zentralkomitee], November 23, 1913, Z3/983, CZA; Otto Warburg to Arthur Ruppin, April 22, 1914, L1/20, CZA; Hazleton, *Israeli Women*, pp. 15–37; cf. Rachel Katznelson-Rubashow, ed. *The Plough Woman: Records of the Pioneer Women of Israel*, translated by Maurice Samuel (New York: Nicholas L. Brown, 1932); *Pioniere und Helfer* 2 (November 1928): 10; Lina Wagner Tauber, August 14, 1912, Z3/983, CZA.

11 Paula Hyman, "The History of European Jewry: Recent Trends in the Literature," *Journal of Modern History* 54, 2 (June 1982): 303–19; Rozenblit, *Jews of Vienna*, p. 163; and Harriet P. Freidenreich, *Jewish Politics in Vienna* (Bloomington: Indiana University Press, 1991), p. 59, 236. Margalit Shilo provides the most comprehensive treatment of early Zionist women in "The Women's Farm at Kinneret, 1911–1917: A Solution to the Problem of the Working Woman in the Second Aliya," *Jerusalem Cathedre* (1981): 246–83. Yehuda Eloni, in *Zionismus in Deutschland: von den Anfängen bis 1914* (Gerlingen: Bleicher, 1987), briefly traces only one of three organizations, the Jüdisch-Nationale Frauen-vereinigung, pp. 144–48. Women Zionists are mentioned in passing in the leading work on German-Jewish women, Marion Kaplan's *Jewish Feminist Movement in Germany*; see also Bristow, *Prostitution and Prejudice*; and Linda Gordon Kuzmack, *Women's Cause: The Jewish Women's Movement in England and the United States, 1881–1933* (Columbus: Ohio State University Press, 1990), pp. 5–6.

12 See Rosalie Gassman-Sherr, *The Story of the Federation of Women Zionists of Great Britain and Ireland* (London: Federation of Women Zionists, 1968); Fay Grove-Pollak, ed. *The Saga of a Movement: WIZO, 1920–1970* (No place: Department of Organization and Education of WIZO, no date).

13 *Die Welt*, November 18, 1898, p. 12; emphasis in the original.

14 Miriam Scheuer and Wera Levin, eds., *Women in the Zionist World* (No place: Women's International Zionist Organization Instruction and Information Center, no date), p. 3; Rozenblit, *Jews of Vienna*, p. 163; *Statuten der Jüdisch-nationalen Frauenvereinigung zu Berlin*, no date, CZA.

15 See Susan Tananbaum, "Generations of Change: The Anglicization of Russian-Jewish Immigrant Women in London, 1880–1939," Ph.D. dissertation (Brandeis University, 1991); Black, *Social Politics of Anglo-Jewry*.

16 Tananbaum, "Generations of Change," pp. 251–66.

17 Else Rabin, "The Jewish Woman in Social Service in Germany," in *The Jewish Library*, vol. III, edited by Leo Jung (New York: The Jewish Library, 1934), pp. 271–72.

18 Rabin, "Jewish Woman in Social Service," p. 276; *Protokoll der gemeinsamen Vertreter-Versammlung des Verbandes jüdischer Frauen und des Verbandes jüdischer Frauen für Kulturarbeit in Palästina vom 12. November 1929*, p. 12; Rabin, p. 272; "Notiz," Organisation der zionistische Arbeit unter den Frauen 1911–1917, Z3/983, CZA.

19 Rabin, "Jewish Woman in Social Service," pp. 296–98; Bonnie S. Anderson and Judith P. Zinsser, *A History of Their Own: Women in Europe from Prehistory to the Present, Volume II* (New York: Harper and Row, 1988), p. 176; see Dennis B. Klein, *Jewish Origins of the Psychoanalytic Movement* (Chicago and London: University of Chicago Press, 1985), pp. 72–84; announcements, Jüdisch-nationale Frauenvereinigung, May 1914, February 21, 1911, 3/1/2/5, CZA.

20 Betti Leszczynsky to Sarah Thon, May 16, 1911, L2/257II, CZA; Rabin, "Jewish Woman in Social Service," p. 303.

21 Van Tijn, "Oh Life of Joy and Sorrow, Laughter and Tears," p. 7.

22 Announcement, "Bund zionistisches Frauen," September 16, 1925, 3/1/2/5, CZA; Rabin, "Jewish Woman in Social Service," p. 306–07; Rahel Straus, "The Importance of Our Work for the Promotion of Health in Palestine," *Report of the Jewish Women's League for Cultural Work in Palestine for 1913*, CZA; Rahel Straus, *Wir lebten in Deutschland: Erinnerungen einer deutschen Jüdin, 1880–1933* (Stuttgart: Deutsche Verlags-Anstalt, 1962).

23 Announcement, Jüdisch-nationale Frauenvereinigung, June 1915; announcement, Bund zionistischer Frauen in Deutschland Ortsgruppe Berlin: Jüdisch-nationale Frauenvereinigung, January 12, 1926; Grove-Pollak, *Saga of a Movement*, p. 67; Nanny Margulies-Auerbach, *Frauenarbeit und Volksbewegung* (Vienna: Keren Keyemet L'Israel, 1920), pp. 29–32; Betti Leszczynsky to Otto Warburg, July 14, 1911, L1/20, CZA; Gassman-Sherr, *Story of the Federation of Women Zionists*, p. 18.

24 One of the few studies that includes women in the more general discussion is Penslar, *Zionism and Technocracy*.

25 Thon's husband, Jacob, was the assistant director of the Palestine Office of the Zionist Organization, under Arthur Ruppin; Shilo, "Women's Farm at Kinneret," p. 256; Scheuer and Levin, *Women in the Zionist World*, p. 17; "Übersicht über die Institutionen der Weltorganisation zionistischer Frauen (WIZO) in Palästina," in *Palästina-Fragen*, pp. 66–68; Grove-Pollak, *Saga of a Movement*, 66; Rose G. Jacobs, "Beginnings of Hadassah," in *Early History of Zionism in America*, edited by Isidor S. Meyer (New York: Arno, 1977), p. 233.

26 Shilo, "Women's Farm at Kinneret"; Penslar, *Zionism and Technocracy*, pp. 126–27.

27 Nadia Stein, *Women in Eretz Israel*, translated by D. C. Adler Hobman (London: Women's International Zionist Organization, 1927), p. 5; *Pioneers and Helpers*, 3 (May 1928): 6; Gerda Arlosoroff-Goldberg, ed., *Palästina-Fragen* (Zurich: Women's International Zionist Organization, 1929), pp. 5ff.; Marie Syrkin, preface to Ada Maimon, *Women Build a Land*, translated by Shulamith Schwarz-Nardi (New York: Herzl Press, 1962), pp. 13–14; Shilo, "Women's Farm at Kinneret," p. 272; Mrs. Otto Warburg to Arthur Ruppin, April 15, 1914, L2/77I, CZA; Betti Leszczynsky to Sara Thon, January 2, 1914, A 148/37, CZA; Gordon Craig, *The Germans* (New York: G. P. Putnam's Sons, 1982), p. 147, in reference to the general history of women in Germany; Miriam Schach, *Asher itam hithalakhti* [Those with whom I walked], (Tel-Aviv: Dvir, 1951).

28 "Bericht VJFKP," no date, 3/1/2/5, CZA; "Programm für zionistische Frauenvereine," no date [probably around 1911], Z3/983, CZA; announcement of "Jüdisch-nationale Frauenvereinigung," May 1914, 3/1/2/5, CZA; undated letter from Edith Lachmann to Heinrich Margulies, A 392/2, CZA; Arthur Handtke to Edith Lachmann, December 4, 1913, Z3/983, CZA; Jenny Blumenfeld, "Referat," November 12, 1929, Berlin, 3/1/2/5, CZA; *Korrespondenzblatt des Verbandes jüdischer Frauen für Palästina Arbeit*, no date, pp. 3ff.; 3/1/2/5, CZA; *Palästina-Aufbau und Frauenarbeit* (London: World Organization of Zionist Women, no date), p. 19; Edith Lachmann to Margulies, March 14, 1914, A 392/2, CZA.

29 Jenny Blumenfeld, "Referat."

30 *JR*, May 4, 1920, p. 219; Anitta Müller-Cohen, "Das System der jüdischen Frauenräte," *JR*, February 22, 1924, p. 100; Anitta Müller-Cohen, "Frauenfrage in Palästina," *JR*, July 24, 1925, p. 502; Rebekah Kohut, *My Portion (An Autobiography)* (New York: Thomas Seltzer, 1925), pp. 271–72.

31 "Ruppin-Persitz-Abend der Frauen," *JR*, September 2, 1930, p. 458.

32 It was not unusual for Helena Hanna Thon's articles to appear as front-page news in the Zionist press: "Frauenarbeit in Palästina," *JR*, October 17, 1924, p. 591.

33 Jacobs, "Beginnings of Hadassah," p. 233.

34 On the British Zionist background, see Stuart Cohen, *English Zionists and British Jews*; David Cesarani, ed., *The Making of Modern Anglo-Jewry* (Oxford: Basil Blackwell, 1990).

35 See chapter 2.

36 "Das jüdische Leben in Palästina: der Kampf gegen der Frauenwahlrecht," *JR*, July 15, 1919, p. 386.

37 Gassman-Sherr, *Story of the Federation of Women Zionists*, p. 5.

38 Rachel Gruenspan to Sara Thon, July 23, 1913, L2/258/I, CZA.

39 Gassman-Sherr, *Story of the Federation of Women Zionists*, p. 7.

40 Henrietta Szold to Sophia Berger, July 23, 1923, p. 8, Record Group 7, Folder 20, Box 4, HA.

41 Gassman-Sherr, *Story of the Federation of Women Zionists*, pp. 9–10.

42 *In Memorium: Henrietta Irwell* (published privately, no date); Gassman-Sherr, *Story of the Federation of Women Zionists*, pp. 7, 16.

43 Gassman-Sherr, *Story of the Federation of Women Zionists*, pp. 9–10.

44 Gassman-Sherr, *Story of the Federation of Women Zionists*, p. 17.

45 Gassman-Sherr, *Story of the Federation of Women Zionists*, p. 21.

46 Frau Dr. Maisel Schochat, "Frauenarbeit in Palästina," *Volk und Land* (February 6, 1919): 162–70, and "Eine Rede an junge Zionistinnen," *Volk und Land* (May 3, 1919): 562–66; *Women's International Zionist Organisation, Report for the Period 1923–1925 for the Women's International Zionist Conference*, pp. 4–5; *Pioniere und Helfer*, 2 (November 1928): 10; *Tätigkeitsbericht 1929–1931 an die VI. Konferenz in Basel, 22.–28. Juni 1931*, WIZO, p. 14; promotional booklets, Verband jüdischer Frauen für Kulturarbeit in Palästina, 3/1/2/5, CZA; announcement, "Was will der Verband jüdischer Frauen für Kulturarbeit in Palästina?," January 1922; Scheuer and Levin, *Women in the Zionist World*, p. 17; *Protokoll der gemeinsamen*

Vertreter-Versammlung, p. 12; "Woman Marches On," *Pioneer and Helpers*, 1 (January 1931): 15; "Welfare Work for Women and Children in Palestine," WIZO, no date.

47 *Arbeiterinnen Erzählen: Kampf und Leben in Erez Israel*, edited by Hechaluz (Berlin: Deutscher Landesverband, 1935); "Literarisch Sondernummer," *Pioniere und Helfer*, 1 (January 1929); *Pioneers and Helpers*, 3 (February 1932): 13; *Protokoll der gemeinsamen Vertreter-Versammlung*, p. 7; Martha Hofmann, "Culture and Propaganda," *WIZO: REPORT of the 5th Biennial Conference in Zurich, July 1929*, p. 33.

48 Ada Fishman, "Earth – Mother of All Living," *Pioneer and Helpers*, 4 (May 1932): 14; Bogen, in *Plough Woman*, p. 219.

49 "Jüdische Frauenkundgebung Programm," postcard announcement of Bund zionistischer Frauen in Deutschland, May 15, 1926, CZA.

50 See, e.g., Jeffrey Fleck, *Character and Context: Studies in the Fiction of Abramovitsh, Brenner, and Agnon* (Chico, Calif.: Scholars Press, 1984), pp. 60–85; "Woman Marches On," *Pioneer and Helpers*, 1 (January 1931): 15; Katznelson-Rubashow, *Plough Woman*, pp. 141–45, 150–51, 180, 189, 193, 212; Mrs. I. M. Sieff, in *WIZO: REPORT of the 5th Biennial Conference in Zurich, July 1929*, p. 37.

51 Scheuer and Levin, *Women in the Zionist World*, p. 11.

52 Naomi Ben-Asher, *Great Jewish Women Throughout History: A Course of Study in Seven Outlines* (New York: Education Department, Hadassah, 1954), p. 40; Scheuer and Levin, *Women in the Zionist World*, p. 7.

53 See chapter 7 in this volume; "Jüdische frauen!," announcement, Verband jüdischer Frauen für Kulturarbeit in Palästina, May 1924, 3/1/2/5, CZA; "Kennen Sie das Programm unseres Verbandes?," Verband jüdischer Frauen für Kulturarbeit in Palästina, 3/1/2/5, CZA; "Bericht VJFKP," no date, 3/1/2/5, CZA; *Pioneers and Helpers*, 4 (October 1928): 19; David Vital, *The Future of the Jews*, p. vii; "Ein Brief zum Geleit," *Pioniere und Helfer*, 1 (January 1927): 1; on the contemporary ramifications, see Eliezer D. Jaffe, *Givers and Spenders*.

54 *15. Bericht des Verbandes jüdischer Frauen für Kulturarbeit in Palästina*, 3/1/2/5, CZA; Bath-Shewa Saslawsky, "Aufgaben der Wanderlehrerin," in *Palästina-Fragen*, pp. 53ff.; "Das jüdische Leben in Palästina: Die hebräischen Kindergärten in Jerusalem," pp. 468–69; founding announcement of the Verband jüdischer Frauen für Kulturarbeit in Palästina, "VJFKP – Aufruf!," 3/1/2/5, CZA; Betti Leszczynsky, "Abschrift eines Briefes an die Vertauens und Vorstandesbande," April 2, 1911, L2/257 II, CZA; announcement, Jüdische-nationale Frauen Vereinigung, 3/1/2/5, CZA; "Fragments – from the letters and notebooks of Shoshanah Bogen," in *Plough Woman*, pp. 216–17; *Der Neue Weg: Monatsschrift der jüdischen sozialdemokratischen Arbeiter-Organisation Poale Zion in Deutschland* (December 1924–August 1925); "25 Years – Dedicated to Building Israel in the Spirit of the Torah," Mizrachi Women's Organization, 1950, DD 3/1/2/8, CZA.

55 Minutes: Board of Directors of the JNF Bureau for America, December 17, 1914, KKL1/9, CZA.

56 *Keren Hayesod (Palestine Foundation Fund): What It Has Done, What It Has to Do and What You Should Do*, issued by the Keren Hayesod Committee of the English Zionist Federation, no date [around 1922].
57 See chapter 7 in this volume; "Medizinische Hilfe für Palästina," *JR*, September 8, 1916, p. 300; *JR*, October 18, 1916, p. 343; "Aus Palästina," *JR*, January 19, 1917, p. 28.
58 "Palästina: Ein Konflikt zwischen Ussischkin und der 'Hadassah'," *JR*, December 9, 1919, p. 681; "Der Disziplinbruch der 'Hadassah,'" *JR*, January 6, 1920, p. 4; "Brief aus Palästina," *JR*, May 4, 1923, p. 209.
59 Henrietta Szold to Alice Seligsberg, May 11, 1921, Record Group 7, Folder 47, Box 5, HA.
60 Henrietta Szold to Alice Seligsberg, June 20, 1921, Record Group 7, Folder 47, Box 5, HA.
61 "Dr. Weizmann über die 'Hadassah,'" in *JR*, January 15, 1924, p. 24.
62 "'Hadassah' und die syrischen Flüchtling," *JR*, December 11, 1925.
63 Werner Senator, "Observations and Proposals regarding the Activities and Methods of Administration and Organization of the Jewish Agency for Palestine," no date [around 1923], DD 2/3/4/1/4, CZA.
64 Felix Danziger, "Die separatorische Tendenz der Hadassah," *JR*, May 25, 1927, p. 296, and Danziger, "Noch einmal: Die Hadassah gegen die Zionistische Organisation," *JR*, June 21, 1927, p. 350; "Ein Konflikt mit der Hadassah," *JR*, February 11, 1927, p. 85.
65 "Der Konflikt innerhalb Hadassah," *JR*, September 2, 1927, p. 499.
66 Nadja Stein, "Hadassah News Letter," *JR*, August 3, 1927, pp. 446–47, and M. Turnowsky, "Frauenarbeit," p. 447.
67 Nadja Stein, "Lernt von der Hadassah," *JR*, April 4, 1928, pp. 203–04.
68 "The Hadassah Issue," *Pioneer Woman*, September 1930, pp. 2–3.
69 Sophie Udin, "Henrietta Szold," *Pioneer Woman*, November 1930, pp. 4–5.
70 "Eine neue Palästina-Exekutive," *JR*, September 13, 1927, p. 522; "Der Schluss des Kongresses," *JR*, September 16, 1927, p. 529.
71 "Demand Removal of Zionist Heads: Speakers at Washington Meeting Accuse Am. Leaders of Mismanagement: Reorganization is Sought: Resolution Offered by Felix Frankfurter is Adopted by Representatives of 45 Cities," *New York Times*, April 30, 1928, p. 7.
72 Felix Danziger, "Gegen die Hadassah," *JR*, July 13, 1928, p. 399.
73 Maurice Samuel, "Women's Rights in Zionism: Equality and Special Privileges – But Not Domination," *New Palestine*, June 15, 1928, p. 627; "Miss Szold über Konsolidierung," *JR*, May 8, 1928, p. 252.
74 "Miss Szold über Konsolidierung," p. 252.
75 "Districts Endorse Administration: Washington Zionists Declare Local UPA Campaign Injured by Opposition Tactics," *New Palestine*, June 8, 1928, p. 605; Irma Lindheim to Mrs. Pearl Franklin, April 8, 1928, p. 3, Record Group 4, Folder 7, Box 1, HA; Louis Lipsky to Nathan Sahr, March 26, 1928, Record Group 4, Folder 3, Box 1, HA; Mrs. M. Epstein, "The Political Duties of a Woman Zionist" [typescript article for *Hadassah News Letter*, May 1928]; "Clearing the Atmosphere," *Hadassah News Letter*, May 25, 1928.

76 Louis Lipsky, telegram sent by ZOA to Zionist Districts, April 1, 1928; "Letter to Chapter Presidents" from National Board of Hadassah, April 4, 1928, Record Group 4, Folder 4, Box 1, HA. See chapter 3 in this volume for a detailed discussion of this conflict.

77 Louis Lipsky to Chairmen and Secretaries of Zionist Districts, June 3, 1928, containing a copy of telegram from May 31, 1928, effectively negating Hadassah as a voting bloc, Record Group 4, Folder 3, Box 1, HA; Rose L. Halprin, "The Truth in Detail," *Hadassah News Letter*, May 31, 1928, p. 2; Zip Szold to the Presidents of Hadassah Chapters, May 10, 1928, Record Group 4, Folder 4, Box 1, HA.

78 Hadassah press release, May 4, 1928, Record Group 4, Folder 4, Box 1, HA. An internal memo succinctly stated the failings of the ZOA: "1. It has not increased the membership in the Zionist Organization. 2. It is not able to draw to itself sufficient forces to work for Palestine. 3. It is not representative of all classes of American Jewry. 4. It has lowered the tone of Zionism in America": "Memorandum," June 1928, Record Group 4, Folder 4, Box 1, HA.

79 Irma Lindheim, quoted in "Hadassah Convention," *New Palestine*, July 13–20, 1928, p. 52, emphasis in the original; cf. Maurice Samuel, "Women's Rights in Zionism: Equality and Special Privileges – But Not Domination," *New Palestine*, June 15, 1928, p. 627.

80 Irma Lindheim to Pearl Franklin, April 8, 1928, Record Group 4, Folder 7, Box 1, HA.

81 "The School of Zionism," *Hadassah Bulletin*, June 1917, pp. 11–12.

82 *Hadassah News Letter*, May 11, 1928.

83 For the larger American context, see Bremner, *American Philanthropy*, pp. 116–35; see also Odendahl, *Charity Begins at Home*, pp. 138–60.

84 Berkowitz, *Zionist Culture*, pp. 165–87.

85 Manja Ostrowski, "Sozial Arbeit oder Philanthropie? Frauenarbeit in Palästina," *JR*, August 23, 1927, p. 480.

86 Anitta Müller-Cohen, "Menschenschutz und Menschenökonomie in Palästina," *JR*, 1927, p. 739.

87 Dash, *Summoned to Jerusalem*, p. 159.

88 See chapter 1 in this volume.

89 Henrietta Szold to the National Board of Hadassah, March 23, 1929, A125/383, CZA.

90 Henrietta Szold to Mrs. Robert Szold, January 16, 1929, A125/383, pp. 2–3, CZA.

91 Cf. Israel Sieff, *Memoirs* (London: Weidenfeld and Nicolson, 1970), p. 123.

92 "Sokolow Month" speeches: Romanna Goodman, "Women in the Zionist Organization," 1931, DD a 2/3/4/1/4, CZA; *Korrespondenzblatt des Verbandes jüdischer Frauen für Palästina Arbeit*, no date, pp. 3ff.; Hedwig Gellner, "Programm," in *Palästina-Fragen*, pp. 7ff.; Lina Wagner Tauber, August 14, 1912, Z3/983, CZA; *4. Bericht des Verbandes jüdischer Frauen für Kulturarbeit in Palästina, Berlin, January 1912*, pp. 7, 10.

93 Betti Leszczynsky to Arthur Ruppin, December 15, 1911, L1/20, CZA; Katznelson-Rubashow, *Plough Woman*, pp. 141–43, 156; Gellner, "Programm," p. 8; Ada Fischman, *Die Arbeitende Frau in Erez-Israel:*

Geschichte der Arbeiterinnenbewegung in Palästina, 1904–1930 (Tel Aviv: Women's International Zionist Organization, 1930), pp. vi, 129, 164; S. Bernstein, *Zionism*, p. 50.
94 See Scott, "Women's History," p. 50.

CONCLUSION

1 Robert Weltsch, "Zum Aufbau des Volkes: Wir und die Idee," *JR*, December 15, 1922, p. 647.
2 Boehm, *Jewish National Fund*, p. 68.
3 Laurence Silberstein, "Cultural Criticism, Ideology, and the Interpretation of Zionism: Toward a Post-Zionist Discourse," working draft, p. 2.
4 Silberstein, "Cultural Criticism, Ideology, and the Interpretation of Zionism," p. 1.
5 Yosef Gorny, "'Aḥdut ha-'avodah, 1919–1930. Ideology and Practice," Ph.D. dissertation (Tel Aviv University, 1970), p. ix. See Martin Buber, "Epilogue: An Experiment that Did Not Fail," in *Paths in Utopia*, translated by R. F. C. Hall (Boston: Beacon, 1958), in which he speaks of the cooperative movement in Palestine, exemplified by the *Kibuts* and the *Kevutsa*, as "a signal non-failure" (p. 142): "I cannot say: a signal success. To become that, much has still to be done. Yet in this way, in this kind of tempo, with such setbacks, disappointments, and new ventures, the real changes are accomplished in this our mortal world" (p. 148). Cf. Gerson Shafir, *Land, Labor, and the Origins of the Israeli–Palestinian Conflict, 1882–1914* (Cambridge: Cambridge University Press, 1989). I wish to thank Laurence Silberstein for these references.
6 Henrietta Szold to the National Board of Hadassah, March 23, 1929, A125/383, CZA.
7 Chaim Weizmann to Robert Weltsch, February 29, 1924, AR 7185, LBI; "Amerikanisch-zionistische Diskussion," in *JR*, February 10, 1931, p. 71.
8 Lindheim, *Immortal Adventure*.
9 Penslar, *Zionism and Technocracy*.
10 Finkielkraut, *Imaginary Jew*.
11 Sigmund Freud to Theodor Herzl, September 28, 1902, HVIII/247, CZA.
12 "Die Schicksalstunde des deutschen Judentums," *JR*, November 9, 1923, p. 557.
13 Boehm, *Jewish National Fund*, p. 18.
14 Boehm, *Jewish National Fund*, p. 70.
15 Helena Hanna Thon, "Eine Enzyklopädie der Schnorrerei," *JR*, November 23, 1928, p. 651.
16 Mendelsohn, *On Modern Jewish Politics*, p. 109.
17 L. Jaffe, *Activities and Aims of the KH* (Jerusalem: Keren Hayesod, 1932), p. 3.
18 Jaffe, *Activities and Aims of the KH*, pp. 14–15.
19 Boehm, *Der Palästina-Aufbaufonds*, p. 12.
20 This was evident before the outbreak of the First World War; see Marjorie Lamberti, "From Coexistence to Conflict: Zionism and the Jewish

Community in Germany, 1897–1914," *Year Book XXVII of the Leo Baeck Institute* (1982): 53–86.

21 Chaim Weizmann to Robert Weltsch, February 29, 1924, AR 7185, LBI.
22 Boehm, *Jewish National Fund*, p. 54.
23 Chaim Weizmann to Robert Weltsch, January 15, 1924, p. 4, AR 7185, LBI.
24 Chaim Weizmann to Robert Weltsch, January 15, 1924, pp. 4–5, AR 7185, LBI.
25 Boehm, *Jewish National Fund*, p. 70.
26 Louis Brandeis to Robert Szold, August 19, 1930, A406/79, CZA.
27 Frankel, "Modern Jewish Politics East and West (1840–1939): Utopia, Myth, Reality," in Gitelman, *Quest for Utopia*, p. 95.

Bibliography

ARCHIVES AND LIBRARIES

American Jewish Archives, Cincinnati, Ohio [AJA]
American Jewish Historical Society, Waltham, Massachusetts
Central Zionist Archives, Jerusalem [CZA]
Hadassah Archives, New York [HA]
Jewish National Library, Jerusalem
Klau Library, Hebrew Union College – Jewish Institute of Religion, Cincinnati
Leo Baeck Institute, New York [LBI]
New York Public Library
The Ohio State University Libraries, Columbus, Ohio
Tel Aviv University Library
Wiener Library, Tel Aviv

PRIMARY SOURCES

PERIODICALS

American Hebrew
American Jewish Historical Quarterly
Aufbau: jüdische illustrierte Zeitung
Avukah Annual
Avukah Bulletin
Blau-Weiss Blätter
Blau-Weiss Brille
Boston Hebrew
Hadassah Bulletin
Hadassah News Letter
Jerubbaal: Eine Zeitschrift der jüdische Jugend
Jewish Academy
Jewish Chronicle
Jewish Criterion
Jewish Tribune
Der Jude
Der Jüdische Pfadfinder
Jüdische Rundschau [JR]

Der Jüdische Student
Jüdische Turnzeitung
Der Jüdische Wille
Jüdischer Nationalkalendar
Karnanu
Korrespondenzblatt des Verbandes jüdischer Frauen für Palästina Arbeit
Maccabaean
Magazine of the Inter-University Jewish Federation of Great Britain and Ireland
Manchester Guardian
Menorah
Monthly Pioneer
Neue Jüdische Monatshefte
Der Neue Weg: Monatsschrift der jüdischen sozialdemokratischen Arbeiter-Organisation
    Poale Zion in Deutschland
New Judaea
New Maccabaean
New Palestine
New York Times
La Nouvelle Aurore
Our Fund
Palästina Aufbau
Palästina-Bilder-Korrespondenz [PBK]
Palästina Fragen
Palestine Pictorial Service
Palestine Progress: Monthly Bulletin of the Palestine Development Leagues
Pioneer
Pioneers and Helpers
Pioniere und Helfer
Social Research
Der Tag
Die Tat
Volk und Land
Die Welt
Yedioth Hadassah
Young Judaean
Young Zionist
Zionist Free Press

BOOKS, PAMPHLETS, ARTICLES

Abramov, Solomon. "Problems of Avukah Cultural Work," in *Brandeis Avukah Annual of 1932: A Collection of Essays on Contemporary Zionist Thought.* Boston: Stratford, 1932 (pp. 627–41).

Altneuland. Berlin: Keren Hayesod Central European Division, no date.

Arbeiterinnen Erzählen: Kampf und Leben in Erez Israel, edited by Hechaluz. Berlin: no publisher, 1935.

Arlosoroff-Goldberg, Gerda. *Palästina Fragen.* Zurich: Women's International Zionist Organization, 1929.

Auerbach, Elias. *Palästina als Judenland*. Berlin and Leipzig: Jüdischer Verlag, 1912.

Aufbau: Blätter des Keren Kajemeth Lejisrael. Berlin: Jewish National Fund, 1924.

Der Aufbau des jüdischen Palästina. No place: Keren Keremet L'Israel, 1922.

Der Aufbau Palästinas und das deutsche Judentum: Reden-Aufsaetze-Dokumente. Berlin: Keren Hayesod, 1922.

Balfour, Arthur James. *Opinions and Arguments from Speeches and Addresses of the Earl of Balfour, 1910–1927*. Garden City, N. Y.: Doubleday, Doran, and Co., 1928.

Speeches on Zionism by Balfour, edited by Israel Cohen. London: Arrowsmith, 1928.

Berger, Julius. *Ostjüdische Arbeiter im Kriege. Sonderabdruck aus Volk und Land*. Berlin: no publisher, 1919.

Bergmann, Hugo. *Jawne und Jerusalem*. Berlin: Jüdischer Verlag, 1919.

Bernstein, S. *Zionism, Its Essential Aspects, and Its Organisation*. Copenhagen: Copenhagen Office of the Zionist Organisation, 1919.

Blau-Weiss Führer: Leitfaden für die Arbeit im Jud. Wanderbund "Blau-Weiss." Berlin: Bundesleitung, 1917.

Blau-Weiss Liederbuch. Berlin: Jüdischer Verlag, 1914.

Blumenfeld, Kurt. *Erlebte Judenfrage: Ein Vierteljahrhundert deutscher Zionismus*. Stuttgart: Deutsche Verlags-Anstalt, 1962.

Im Kampf um den Zionismus: Briefe aus fünf Jahrzehnten. Edited by Miriam Sambursky and Jochanan Ginat. Stuttgart: Deutsche Verlags-Anstalt, 1976.

Boehm, Adolf. *The Jewish National Fund*. The Hague: Jewish National Fund, no date.

Der Palästina-Aufbaufonds (Keren Hajessod). London: Head Office of Keren Hayesod, 1923.

"Zionistische Arbeit in Palästina," in *Erez Israel. Sondernummer: Die Kriegslandspende* (Vienna).

Die zionistische Bewegung. Tel Aviv: Hozaah Ivrith, 1935–37.

Die Zionistische Bewegung bis zum Ende des Weltkrieges I. 2nd edn. Berlin: Jüdischer Verlag, 1915.

Brandeis, Louis D. *Half Brother, Half Son: The Letters of Louis D. Brandeis to Felix Frankfurter*. Edited by Melvin Urofsky and David Levy. Norman: University of Oklahoma Press, 1991.

Jewish Rights and the Congress: Address Delivered at Carnegie Hall, New York City, January 24, 1916. New York: Jewish Congress Organization Committee, 1916.

Letters of Louis D. Brandeis, vols. I–V. Edited by Melvin Urofsky and David Levy. Albany: State University of New York Press, 1971–78.

Zionism and Patriotism. New York: Federation of American Zionists, 1915.

Buber, Martin. *A Land of Two Peoples: Martin Buber on Jews and Arabs*. Edited by Paul Mendes-Flohr. New York: Oxford University Press, 1983.

Paths in Utopia, translated by R. F. C. Hall. Boston: Beacon, 1958.

Cohen, Israel, ed. *Zionist Work in Palestine*, edited by Israel Cohen. London and Leipzig: T. Fischer Unwin, 1911. Reprinted as *Zionist Work in Palestine by Various Authorities*, edited by Israel Cohen. Westport, Conn.: Hyperion Press, 1976.

Cohen, Reuss. *Die politische Bedeutung des Zionism*, in *Pro Palästina: Schriften des Deutschen Komitees zur Förderung der jüdischen Palästinasiedlung*. Berlin: Reimar Hobbing, 1918.

de Lieme, Nehemia, Julius Simon, and Robert Szold. "Report of the Reorganization Commission of the Executive of the Zionist Organization on the Work of the Zionist Organization in Palestine." A406/4, CZA.

Das deutsche Judentum. Seine Partien und Organisationen: eine Sammelschrift. Berlin and Munich: Neue Jüdische Monatshefte, 1919.

Einstein, Albert. *About Zionism*. Edited and translated by Leon Simon. London: Soncino, 1930.

The World As I See It (originally published as *Mein Weltbild*), translated by Alan Harris. New York: Covici Friede, 1934.

Epstein, Elias M. *The Case for the Jewish National Fund: A Challenge to Zionists*. Jerusalem: Jewish National Fund,1928.

Erez Israel. London: Head Office of Keren Hayesod, no date.

Erez Israel: Sondernummer: Die Kriegslandspende. Vienna: Jewish National Fund, 1916.

Fingerman, Jakob. *Die Flucht aus Jerusalem*. Berlin and Vienna: R. Loewitt Verlag, 1919.

Fischman, Ada. *Die Arbeitende Frau in Erez-Israel: Geschichte der Arbeiterinnenbewegung in Palästina, 1904–1930*. Tel Aviv: Women's International Zionist Organization, 1930.

Friedemann, Adolf, and Hermann Struck. *Palästina: Reisebilder*. Berlin: Bruno-Cassier, 1904.

Fuchs, Eugen. *Um Deutschtum und Judentum*. Frankfurt a.M.: Verlag Kaufmann, 1919.

"General Report," *Women's International Zionist Organization: Report for the Period 1923–1925 for the Third International Zionist Conference*.

Gerstman, Josef. *Kultur- und Bildungsfortschritte unter den Juden Palästinas*. Munich: Max Steinebach Buch- und Kunstverlag, 1909.

Goldmann, Nahum. *The Autobiography of Nahum Goldman: Sixty Years of Jewish Life*. Translated by Helen Serba. New York: Holt, Rinehart, and Winston, 1969.

Die drei Forderungen des jüdischen Volkes. Berlin: Jüdischer Verlag, 1919.

Mein Leben als deutscher Jude. Munich: Langen Müller, 1980.

Gordon, A. *Briefe aus Palästina*. Berlin: Welt-Verlag, 1919.

The Greatest Romance in History. New York: Keren Hayesod, 1922.

Gronemann, Sammy. "Erinnerungen." Manuscript in Leo Baeck Institute, New York.

Grove-Pollak, Fay, ed. *The Saga of a Movement: WIZO, 1920–1970*. No place: Department of Organization and Education of Women's International Zionist Organization, no date.

Hamischmar. Vom Leben der Jüngeren im Blau-Weiss. Berlin: Bundesleitung des Blau-Weiss, 1925.

Harry, Myriam. *A Springtide in Palestine*. London: Ernest Benn, 1924.

Hecht, Georg. *Der Neue Jude*. Leipzig: Gustav Engel Verlag, 1911.

Heller, Max. *My Month in Palestine: Impressions of Travel*. New York: Bloch, 1929.

Herzl, Theodor. *Altneuland*. Leipzig: H. Seeman Nachfolger, 1902.

The Complete Diaries of Theodor Herzl. 5 vols. Edited by Raphael Patai and translated by Harry Zohn. New York: Herzl Press and Thomas Yoseloff, 1960.

Der Judenstaat: Versuch einer modernen Lösung der Judenfrage. Leipzig and Vienna: M. Breitenstein's Verlag-Buchhandlung, 1896.

Theodor Herzl's Zionist Writings. 2 vols. Translated by Harry Zohn. New York: Herzl Press, 1973–75.

Theodor Herzl's zionistische Schriften. Berlin-Charlottenberg: Jüdischer Verlag, 1908.

Howe, Irving. *A Margin of Hope: An Intellectual Autobiography*. New York: Harcourt Brace Jovanovich, 1982.

In Memorium: Henrietta Irwell. Published privately, no date.

Jabotinsky, Vladimir. *Die jüdischer Legion im Weltkrieg*. Berlin: Jüdischer Verlag, 1930.

The Story of the Jewish Legion. Translated by Samuel Katz. New York: Bernard Ackerman, 1945.

Turkey and the War. London: T. Fischer Unwin, 1917.

Jaffe, L. *Activities and Aims of the KH*. Jerusalem: Keren Hayesod, 1932.

Jewish Colonisation: Erez Israel 30 Years Keren Kayemet. No place: Jewish National Fund, 1931.

Jewish Colonisation in Erez Israel: After Ten Years Keren Hayesod. Jerusalem: no publisher [Keren Hayesod?], 1930.

Jewish Pioneering in Palestine (What Our Haluzim are Doing). No place: Palestine Foundation Fund Keren Hayesod, 1922.

Jewish Progress in Palestine: Four Years' Work of Keren Hayesod. London: Palestine Foundation Fund, Keren Hayesod, 1925.

Die Juden im Krieg: Denkschrift des jüdischen sozialistischen Arbeiterverbandes Poale-Zion an das Internationale Sozialistische Bureau. The Hague: no publisher, 1917.

Jüdische Leistungen in Palästina: Tatsachen und Zahlen. 3rd edn. Berlin: Keren Hayesod Central European Division, no date.

Jüdisches Archiv. Vienna: R. Loewitt, 1915.

Kadimah. New York: Federation of American Zionists, 1918.

Kallen, Horace. "Julian Mack, 1866–1943," *American Jewish Year Book* 46 (1944): 35–46.

Kann, J. H. *Erez Israel: Das jüdische Land*. Cologne and Leipzig: Jüdischer Verlag, 1909.

Kanowitz, Siegfried. "Zionistische Jugendbewegung," Sonderdruck aus *Die neue Jugend*. Berlin: Zionistische Vereinigung für Deutschland, 1928.

Katznelson-Rubashow, Rachel, ed. *The Plough Woman: Records of the Pioneer Women of Israel*, translated by Maurice Samuel. New York: Nicholas L. Brown, 1932.

Der Keren Hajessod: Verfassung und Programm. London: Head Office of the Erets Israel (Palestine) Foundation Fund, 1922.

Keren Hayesod (Palestine Foundation Fund): What It Has Done, What It Has to Do, and What You Should Do. Keren Hayesod Committee of the English Zionist Federation, no date [around 1922].

Keren Hayesod: Tatsachen und Bilder aus dem neuen jüdischen Leben in Palästina. Jerusalem: no publisher [Keren Hayesod?], 1927.

Klatzkin, Jakob. *Probleme des modernen Judentums.* Jüdischer Verlag, Berlin 1918.

Kohut, Rebekah. *My Portion (An Autobiography).* New York: Thomas Seltzer, 1925.

Krewer, M. *Die Zukunft Palästinas.* Kovno: 1928.

Krimsky, Joseph. *Pilgrimage and Service, 1918–1919.* Published privately, no date.

Land und Arbeit: Zum 10-jährigen Jubilaeum der zionistischen Arbeiter-organisation Hapoeel Hazaier. Berlin: Verlag Hapoeel Hazaier, 1918.

Landauer, Karl, and Herbert Weil. *Die zionistische Utopie.* Munich: Hugo Schmidt, 1914.

Levinger, Elma. *Fighting Angel.* New York: Behrman, 1946.

Lichtheim, Richard. *Die Geschichte des deutschen Zionismus.* Jerusalem: Rubin Mass, 1954.

Lindheim, Irma. *The Immortal Adventure.* New York: Macaulay, 1928.

Parallel Quest: A Search of a Person and a People. New York: Thomas Yoseloff, 1962.

Lipsky, Louis. *Memoirs in Profile.* Philadelphia: Jewish Publication Society of America, 1975.

Lowenthal, Marvin, ed. *Henrietta Szold: Life and Letters.* New York: Viking, 1942.

Magnes, Judah L. *Dissenter in Zion.* Edited by Arthur A. Goren. Cambridge, Mass., and London: Harvard University Press, 1988.

Margulies-Auerbach, Nanny. *Frauenarbeit und Volksbewegung.* Vienna: Keren Keremet L'Israel, 1920.

Markel, Richard. "Brith Haolim: Der Weg der Alija des jung jüdischen Wanderbundes (JJWB)," *Bulletin des Leo Baeck Instituts* 9, 34 (1966): 119–89.

Das Neue Palästina. Berlin: Keren Hayesod Central European Division, 1921.

Nussbaum, Herbert. "Weg und Schicksal eines deutschen Juden." Manuscript in Leo Baeck Institute, New York.

Oppenheimer, Franz. *Co-operative Colonisation in Palestine.* The Hague: Jewish National Fund and the Settlement Company "Eretz Israel," no date.

Merchavia: A Jewish Cooperative Settlement in Palestine. New York: Jewish National Fund, 1914.

Palästina Aufbau und Frauenarbeit. London: World Organization of Zionist Women, no date.

Palästina Aufbaufonds. Berlin: Keren Hayesod, 1928.

Palästina und der Neubeginn jüdischen Lebens. Berlin: Keren Hayesod, no date.

Palestine During the War: Being a Record of the Preservation of the Jewish Settlement in Palestine. London: Zionist Organisation, 1921.

Patterson, J. H. *With the Judaeans in the Palestine Campaign.* London: Hutchinson, 1922.

With the Zionists in Gallipoli. New York: George Doran and Co., 1916.

Program for American Jews. New York: Avukah, 1938.

Protokoll der gemeinsamen Vertreter-Versammlung des Bundes zionistischer Frauen und des Verbandes jüdischer Frauen für Kulturarbeit in Palästina vom 12. November 1929.

Protokoll des XV. Delegiertentages des zionistischen Vereinigung für Deutschland. Berlin: Jüdischer Verlag, 1919.

Report of the Emergency Fund for Palestine Sept. 1, 1929–December 31, 1934. Jerusalem: Jewish National Fund, 1936.

Report of the Reorganization Commission of the Executive of the Zionist Organization on the Work of the Zionist Organization in Palestine. New York: Zionist Organization of America, 1921.

Rosenfeld, Max. *Die Zukunft Palästinas.* Vienna and Berlin: R. Loewitt Verlag, 1919.

Roth, Paul. *Die politische Entwicklung in Kongresspolen während der deutschen Okkupation.* Leipzig: K. F. Köhler Verlag, 1919.

Rothschild, Eli, ed. *Meilensteine: Vom Wege des Kartells jüdischer Verbindungen (KJV) in der Zionistischen Bewegung.* Tel Aviv: Presidium of the KJV, 1972.

Ruppin, Arthur. *Der Aufbau des Landes Israel.* Berlin: Jüdischer Verlag, 1919.

The Jews in the Modern World. London: Macmillan, 1934.

Salaman, Redcliffe N. *Palestine Reclaimed: Letters from a Jewish Officer in Palestine.* London: George Routledge and Sons, and New York: E. P. Dutton, 1920.

Sampter, Jessie. *A Course in Zionism.* New York: no publisher [Hadassah?], 1915.

The Key. Jerusalem: Jewish National Fund, 1925.

Samuel, Maurice. *What Happened in Palestine: The Events of August, 1929, Their Background and Their Significance.* Boston: Stratford, 1929.

Sankowsky, Shoshana Harris. *Short History of Zionism.* (No. 3 Avukah Program]). American Student Zionist Federation, 1936.

Schach, Miriam. *Asher itam hithalakhti* [Those with whom I walked]. Tel-Aviv: Dvir, 1951.

Scheuer, Miriam, and Wera Levin, eds. *Women in the Zionist World.* No place: Women's International Zionist Organization Instruction and Information Center, no date.

Scholem, Gershom. "Jüdische Jugendbewegung," *Der Jude* (March 1917): 822–24.

Segall, Jacob. *Die deutschen Juden als Soldaten im Kriege, 1914–1918: Eine statistische Studie.* Berlin: Philo-Verlag, 1922.

Sieff, Israel. *Memoirs.* London: Weidenfeld and Nicolson, 1970.

Simon, Julius. *Certain Days.* Edited by Evyatar Friesel. Jerusalem: Israel Universities Press, 1971.

Soskin, S. E. *Kleinsiedlung und Bewasserung: die neue Siedlungsform für Palästina.* No. 4, Nationalfonds-Bibliothek. Berlin: Jüdischer Verlag, 1920.

Stein, Nadia. *Women in Eretz Israel,* translated by D. C. Adler Hobman. London: Women's International Zionist Organization, 1927.

Straus, Eduard. *Judentum und Zionismus.* Frankfurt a.M.: J. Kaufmann Verlag, 1919.

Straus, Rahel. "The Importance of Our Work for the Promotion of Health in Palestine," *Report of the Jewish Women's League for Cultural Work in Palestine for 1913.*

Wir lebten in Deutschland: Erinnerungen einer deutschen Jüdin, 1880–1933. Stuttgart: Deutsche Verlags-Anstalt, 1962.

Die Tätigkeit des Wiener Palästina. Amtes. 1922.

Tätigkeitsbericht 1929–1931 an die VI. Konferenz in Basel. 22.–28. Juni 1931. Women's International Zionist Organization.

Tannenbaum, Eugen, ed., *Kriegsbriefe deutscher und österreichischer Juden.* Berlin: Neuer Verlag, 1915.

Thieberger, Friedrich, and Felix Weltsch, eds. *Jüdischer Almanach auf das Jahr 5691.* Prague: Keren Keyemet L'Israel, 1930.

This is the Land . . . The Spell of Palestine. London: Jewish National Fund, no date.

Trietsch, Davis. *Bilder aus Palästina.* Berlin: Orient-Verlag, no date.

Jüdische Frauenarbeit und Frauenberufe für Palästina. Mährisch-Ostrau: Zionistischen Distriktskomitee für Mähren und Schlesien, 1919.

Palästina Handbuch. Berlin-Schmargendorf: Orient-Verlag, 1910.

Tschlenow, E. W. *Der Krieg, die Russische Revolution und der Zionismus.* Copenhagen: Copenhagen Bureau of the Zionist Organization, 1917.

Ulitzur, A. *Two Decades of Keren Hayesod: A Survey in Facts and Figures 1921–1940.* Jerusalem: Erets Israel (Palestine) Foundation Fund Keren Hayesod, 1940.

V[an] Tijn, Gertrude. "Oh Life of Joy and Sorrow, Laughter and Tears." Manuscript in Leo Baeck Institute, New York.

Weizmann, Chaim. *American Addresses of Dr. Chaim Weizmann.* Preface by Samuel Untermyer. New York: Palestine Foundation Fund (Keren Hayesod), 1923.

The Letters and Papers of Chaim Weizmann, II, edited by Meyer Weisgal (general ed.). London: Oxford University Press, 1971.

Trial and Error: The Autobiography of Chaim Weizmann, 2nd edn. New York: Schocken, 1966 (originally published in 1949).

Weizmann der Führer: Anlässlich seines Besuches in Brünn im Januar 1925. Prague [?]: Keren Hayesod in Czechoslovakia, 1925.

Wise, Stephen. *Challenging Years: The Autobiography of Steven Wise.* New York: G. P. Putnam's Sons, 1949.

[Stephen S.] Wise: Servant of the People: Selected Letters. Edited by Carl Voss. Philadelphia: Jewish Publication Society of America, 1969.

Women's International Zionist Organization: Report for the Period 1923–1925 for the Women's International Zionist Conference.

Worsfold, W. Basil. *Palestine of the Mandate.* London: T. Fisher Unwin, 1925.

Zemach, S. *Jüdische Bauern: Geschichte aus dem neuen Palästina.* Vienna and Berlin: R. Loewitt-Verlag, 1919.

Zionistisches Handbuch, edited by Gerhard Holdheim. Berlin: Bureau of the Zionist Organization, 1923.

SECONDARY SOURCES

PERIODICALS

AJS Review
American Historical Review
American Jewish Historical Quarterly
American Jewish Year Book
American Sociological Review

Bulletin des Leo Baeck Institute
English Historical Review
German Quarterly
German Studies Review
Historische Zeitschrift
Jerusalem Cathedre
Jerusalem Quarterly
Jewish Social Studies
Journal of Contemporary History
Journal of Israel History
Journal of Jewish Sociology
Journal of Modern History
Journal of the American Academy of Religion
Journal of Women's History
Judaism
LBI News
Modern Judaism
Representations
Shofar
Signs
Studies in Contemporary Jewry
Studies in Zionism
Ha-Tsiyonut
Wiener Library Bulletin
Yearbook of the Leo Baeck Institute
Zion
Z'manim

BOOKS, CHAPTERS, ARTICLES

Adams, Michael C. C. *The Great Adventure: Male Desire and the Coming of World War I.* Bloomington: Indiana University Press, 1990.

Adler-Rudel, S. *Ostjuden in Deutschland, 1880–1940: zugleich eine Geschichte der Organisationen die sie betreuten.* Tübingen: Mohr, 1959.

Alderman, Geoffrey. *Modern British Jewry.* Oxford: Oxford University Press, 1992.

Almog, Shmuel, ed. *Zionism and History: The Rise of a New Jewish Consciousness.* New York: St. Martin's Press, 1987.

   Zionism and the Arabs. Jerusalem: Historical Society of Israel and Zalman Shazar Center, 1983.

Altschuler, M. "Russia and Her Jews – The Impact of the 1914 War," *Wiener Library Bulletin,* 27 (1973/74): 12–16.

Anderson, Bonnie S., and Judith P. Zinsser. *A History of Their Own: Women in Europe From Prehistory to the Present, Volume II.* New York: Harper and Row, 1988.

Aschheim, Steven. *Brothers and Strangers: The East European Jew in German and German-Jewish Consciousness.* Madison: University of Wisconsin Press, 1982.

Avineri, Shlomo. *The Making of Modern Zionism: The Intellectual Origins of the Jewish State.* New York: Basic, 1981.

Avni, Haim. *Argentina and the Jews: A History of Jewish Immigration.* Translated by Gila Brand. Tuscaloosa: University of Alabama Press, 1991.

Baker, Adrienne. *The Jewish Woman in Contemporary Society: Transitions and Traditions.* New York: New York University Press, 1993.

Barnard, Harry. *The Forging of an American Jew: The Life and Times of Judge Julian W. Mack.* New York: Herzl Press, 1974.

Bar-On, Ray. *Travel and Tourism Data: A Comprehensive Research Handbook on the World Travel Industry.* Phoenix and New York: Oryx Press, 1989.

Baskin, Judith R., ed. *Jewish Women in Historical Perspective.* Detroit: Wayne State University Press, 1991.

Ben-Asher, Naomi. *Great Jewish Women Throughout History: A Course of Study in Seven Outlines.* New York: Education Department, Hadassah, 1954.

Berkowitz, Michael. "The Invention of a Secular Ritual: Western Jewry and Nationalized Tourism in Palestine, 1922–1933," in *The Seductiveness of Jewish Myth: Challenge or Response,* edited by Daniel Breslauer. Albany: State University of New York Press, 1997 (pp. 69–91).

"Transcending 'Tsimmes and Sweetness': Recovering the History of Zionist Women in Central and Western Europe," in Sacks, *Active Voices* (pp. 41–62).

Zionist Culture and West European Jewry Before the First World War. Cambridge: Cambridge University Press, 1993.

Berman, Aaron. *Nazism, the Jews, and American Zionism, 1933–1948.* Detroit: Wayne State University Press, 1990.

Berman, Russell. *Cultural Studies of Modern Germany: History, Representation, and Nationhood.* Madison: University of Wisconsin Press, 1993.

Modern Culture and Critical Theory: Art, Politics, and the Legacy of the Frankfurt School. Madison: University of Wisconsin Press, 1990.

Bernard, Paul. *Rush to the Alps: The Evolution of Vacationing in Switzerland.* New York: Columbia University Press, 1978.

Bernstein, Deborah. *The Struggle for Equality: Urban Women Workers in Prestate Israeli Society.* New York: Praeger, 1987.

Bernstein, Deborah, ed. *Pioneers and Homemakers: Jewish Women in Pre-State Israel.* Albany: State University of New York Press, 1992.

Bernstein, Herman. *Celebrities of Our Time.* London: Hutchinson, 1924.

Biale, David. *Eros and the Jews: From Biblical Israel to Contemporary America.* New York: Basic, 1992.

Gershom Scholem: Kabbalah and Counter-History. Cambridge: Harvard University Press, 1982.

Black, Eugene C. *The Social Politics of Anglo-Jewry, 1880–1920.* Oxford: Basil Blackwell, 1989.

Bowman, Glenn. "The Politics of Tour Guiding: Israeli and Palestinian Guides in the Occupied Territories." In *Tourism in the Less Developed Countries,* edited by David Harrison. London: Bellhaven, 1992 (pp. 121–34).

Breines, Paul. *Tough Jews: Political Fantasies and the Moral Dilemma of American Jewry.* New York: Basic, 1990.

Bremner, Robert H. *American Philanthropy*, 2nd edn. Chicago: University of Chicago Press, 1988.

Brendon, Piers. *Thomas Cook: 150 Years of Popular Tourism*. London: Secker and Warburg, 1991.

Brenner, Michael. *The Renaissance of Jewish Culture in Weimar Germany*. New Haven: Yale University Press, 1995.

Breuer, Mordechai. *Modernity Within Tradition: The Social History of Orthodox Jewry in Imperial Germany*, translated by Elizabeth Petuchowski. New York: Columbia University Press, 1992.

Bristow, Edward J. *Prostitution and Prejudice: The Jewish Fight Against White Slavery, 1880–1939*. New York: Schocken, 1983.

Broshi, Magen. "Archaeological Museums in Israel: Reflections on Problems of National Identity." In *Museums and the Making of "Ourselves": The Role of Objects in National Identity*, edited by Flora Kaplan. Leicester: Leicester University Press, 1994 (pp. 314–89).

Burkart, A. J., and S. Medlik. *Tourism: Past, Present, and Future*. London: Heinemann, 1974.

Burt, Robert A. *Two Jewish Justices: Outcasts in the Promised Land*. Berkeley and Los Angeles: University of California Press, 1988.

Buzard, James. *The Beaten Track: European Tourism, Literature, and the Way to "Culture"*. Oxford: Oxford University Press, 1993.

Campo, Juan. *The Other Sides of Paradise: Exploration into the Religious Meanings of Domestic Space in Islam*. Columbia: University of South Carolina Press, 1991.

Caplan, Neil. "Zionist Visions in the Early 1930s," *Studies in Contemporary Jewry*, vol. 4 (1988): 232–49.

Cesarani, David. *The Jewish Chronicle and Anglo-Jewry, 1841–1991*. Cambridge: Cambridge University Press, 1994.
    "Zionism in England, 1917–1939." Ph.D. dissertation. Oxford University, 1986.

Cesarani, David, ed. *The Making of Modern Anglo-Jewry*. Oxford: Basil Blackwell, 1990.

Cheyette, Bryan. *Constructions of "The Jew" in English Literature and Society: Racial Representations, 1875–1945*. Cambridge: Cambridge University Press, 1993.

Clark, Ronald W. *Einstein: The Life and Times*. New York: World, 1965.

Clifford, James. *The Predicament of Culture: Twentieth-Century Ethnography, Literature, and Art*. London and Cambridge, Mass.: Harvard University Press, 1988.

Cohen, Erik. "Arab Boys and Tourist Girls in a Mixed Jewish–Arab Community," *International Journal of Comparative Sociology*, 12, 4 (1971): 217–33.

Cohen, Mitchell. *Zion and State: Nation, Class, and the Shaping of Modern Israel*. Oxford: Basil Blackwell, 1987.

Cohen, Naomi W. *American Jews and the Zionist Idea*. New York: KTAV, 1975.
    The Year After the Riots: American Responses to the Palestine Crisis of 1929–1930. Detroit: Wayne State University Press, 1988.

Cohen, Stuart A. *English Zionists and British Jews: The Communal Politics of Anglo-Jewry, 1895–1920*. Princeton: Princeton University Press, 1982.

Craig, Gordon. *The Germans*. New York: G. P. Putnam's Sons, 1982.

Culler, Jonathan. *Framing the Sign: Criticism and Its Institutions*. Oxford: Basil Blackwell, 1988.

Dash, Joan. *Summoned to Jerusalem: The Life of Henrietta Szold*. New York: Harper and Row, 1979.

Dawson, Nelson L., ed. *Brandeis and America*. Lexington: University of Kentucky Press, 1989.

Davidman, Lynn, and Shelly Tenenbaum, eds. *Feminist Perspectives on Jewish Studies*. New Haven and London: Yale University Press, 1994.

de Haas, Jacob. *Theodor Herzl: A Biographical Study*, 2 vols. Chicago and New York: Leonard, 1927.

Dothan, Shmuel. *A Land in the Balance: The Struggle for Palestine, 1918–1948*. Translated by Jeffrey Green. Tel Aviv: MOD, 1993.

Dugdale, Blanche. *Arthur James Balfour*. New York: G. P. Putnam's Sons, 1937.

Dulles, Foster Rhea. *Americans Abroad: Two Centuries of European Travel*. Ann Arbor: University of Michigan Press, 1964.

Dunker, Ulrich. *Der Reichsbund jüdischer Frontsoldaten, 1919–1938: Geschichte eines jüdischen Abwehrvereins*. Dusseldorf: Droste Verlag, 1977.

Efrati, Nathan. *Mi-Mashber le-tikvah: ha-Yishuv ha-Yehudi be-Erets Yisra'el be-Milḥemet ha-'olam ha-rishonah* [From crisis to hope: the Jewish community in Erets Israel during World War I]. Jerusalem: Ben Zvi Institute, 1991.

Efron, John. *Defenders of the Race: Jewish Doctors and Race Science in Fin-de-Siècle Europe*. London and New Haven: Yale University Press, 1994.

Egremont, Max. *Balfour: A Life of Arthur James Balfour*. London: Collins, 1980.

Eickelman, Dale, and James Piscatori, eds. *Muslim Travelers: Pilgrimage, Migration, and the Religious Imagination*. Berkeley and Los Angeles: University of California Press, 1990.

Eksteins, Modris. *Rites of Spring: The Great War and the Birth of the Modern Age*. London: Black Swan, 1990.

Elam, Yigal. *Ha-Sokhnut ha-Yehudit: Shanim rishonot* [The Jewish Agency: the formative years]. Jerusalem: Ha-Sifriyah ha-Tsiyonit, 1990.

Eley, Geoff. *From Unification to Nazism: Reinterpreting the German Past*. Boston: Allen and Unwin, 1986.

Eliav, Mordecai, ed. *Ba-matsor uva-matsok: Erets Yisra'el be-Milḥemet ha-'olam ha-rishonah* [Siege and distress: Erets Israel during the First World War]. Jerusalem: Ben Zvi Institute, 1991.

Elon, Amos. *The Israelis: Founders and Sons*. New York: Penguin, 1981.

Eloni, Yehuda. *Zionismus in Deutschland: von der Anfängen bis 1914*. Gerlingen: Bleicher, 1987.

Encyclopaedia Judaica. Jerusalem: Encyclopedia Judaica, Keter, 1971. 16 vols.

Encyclopedia of Zionism and Israel, edited by Raphael Patai. New York: Herzl Press/McGraw-Hill, 1971. 2 vols.

Feifer, Maxine. *Tourism in History: From Imperial Rome to the Present*. New York: Stein and Day, 1985.

Feingold, Henry L. *The Jewish People in America, Volume V. A Time for Searching: Entering the Mainstream, 1920–1945*. Baltimore: Johns Hopkins University Press, 1992.

Figler, Bernard. *From Mandate to State, 1923–1948: The Story of Zionist Order Habonim*. Montreal: no publisher, 1951.

Fineman, Irving. *Woman of Valor*. New York: Simon and Schuster, 1961.

Finkielkraut, Alain. *The Imaginary Jew*, translated by Kevin O'Neil and David Suchoff. Lincoln: University of Nebraska Press, 1994.

Fischer, Roger. *Tippecanoe and Trinkets Too: The Material Culture of American Presidential Campaigns, 1828–1924*. Urbana and Chicago: University of Illinois Press, 1988.

Fleck, Jeffrey. *Character and Context: Studies in the Fiction of Abramovitsh, Brenner, and Agnon*, Chico, Calif.: Scholars Press, 1984.

Frankel, Jonathan. "Modern Jewish Politics East and West (1840–1939): Utopia, Myth, Reality." In Gitelman, *Quest for Utopia* (pp. 81–103).

"The Paradoxical Politics of Marginality: Thoughts on the Jewish Situation During the Years 1914–1921," *Studies in Contemporary Jewry*, 4 (1988): 3–21.

Frankel, Jonathan, and Steven Zipperstein, eds. *Assimilation and Community: The Jews in Nineteenth-Century Europe*. Cambridge: Cambridge University Press, 1992.

Freidenreich, Harriet P. *Jewish Politics in Vienna*. Bloomington: Indiana University Press, 1991.

Frevert, Ute. *Ehrenmänner: Das Duell in der bürgerlichen Gesellschaft*. Munich: C. H. Beck, 1991.

Friedman, Alan J., and Carol C. Donley. *Einstein as Myth and Muse*. Cambridge: Cambridge University Press, 1989.

Friedman, Maurice. *Encounter on a Narrow Ridge: A Life of Martin Buber*. New York: Paragon, 1991.

Martin Buber's Life and Work: The Early Years, 1878–1923. New York: E. P. Dutton, 1981.

Martin Buber's Life and Work: The Middle Years, 1923–1945. New York: E. P. Dutton, 1983.

Friesel, Evyatar. "Brandeis' Role in American Zionism Historically Reconsidered," *American Jewish History* 69, 1 (1979): 34–59.

"Lel ha-mashber ben Weizmann le-ven Brandeis" [The crisis in leadership between Weizmann and Brandeis]. *Ha-Tsiyonut* 4 (1975): 146–64.

Ha-Mediniyut ha-Tsiyonit le-aḥar hats'harat Balfour, 1917–1922 [Zionist policy after the Balfour Declaration, 1917–1922]. Tel Aviv: Tel Aviv University Press, 1977.

"Pinsk and Washington," *Studies in Contemporary Jewry*, 6 (1990): 326–30.

Fussell, Paul. *The Great War and Modern Memory*. New York and London: Oxford University Press, 1975.

Gaisbauer, Adolf. *Zionismus und jüdischer Nationalismus in Österreich, 1882–1918*. Vienna–Cologne–Gratz: Böhlau Verlag, 1988.

Gal, Allon. "Brandeis, Judaism, and Zionism," in *Brandeis and America*, edited by Nelson L. Dawson. Lexington: University Press of Kentucky, 1989.

Brandeis of Boston. Cambridge: Harvard University Press, 1980.

"Brandeis's View on the Upbuilding of Palestine, 1914–1923," *Studies in Zionism* 6 (Autumn 1982): 216–38.

"In Search of a New Zion: A New Light on Brandeis's Road to Zionism," *American Jewish History* 68, 1 (1978): 19–31.

"Independence and Universal Mission in Modern Jewish Nationalism: Comparative Analysis of European and American Zionism (1897–1948)," *Studies in Contemporary Jewry*, vol. 5 (1989): 242–74.

"Medinat Yisra'el ha-ide'alit be-ene Hadasah, 1945–1955" [The ideal State of Israel in the eyes of Hadassah, 1945–1955], *Yahadut Zémanenu* 4 (1987): 157–70.

"The Mission Motif in American Zionism (1898–1948)," *American Jewish History* 75 (June 1986): 363–85.

Gartner, Lloyd. "Anglo-Jewry and the Jewish International Traffic in Prostitution, 1885–1914," *AJS Review* 78 (1982–83): 129–78.

Gaskell, Ivan, "History of Images." In *New Perspectives on Historical Writing*. Edited by Peter Burke. University Park, Pennsylvania: Pennsylvania State University Press, 1991 (pp. 168–92).

Gassman-Sherr, Rosalie. *The Story of the Federation of Women Zionists of Great Britain and Ireland*. London: Federation of Women Zionists, 1968.

Geller, L. D. *The Henrietta Szold Papers in the Hadassah Archives, 1875–1975*. New York: Hadassah, 1982.

Geller, Stuart M. "Louis D. Brandeis and Zionism." Rabbinic thesis. Hebrew Union College – Jewish Institute of Religion, 1970.

"Why Did Louis D. Brandeis Choose Zionism?," *American Jewish Historical Quarterly* (June 1973): 383–499.

Gellner, Ernest. *Nations and Nationalism*. Ithaca: Cornell University Press, 1992.

Gidal, Nahum. "Jews in Photography," *Leo Baeck Institute Year Book XXXII* (1987): 437–53.

Giles, Geoffrey. *Students and National Socialism in Germany*. Princeton: Princeton University Press, 1985.

Gilman, Sander. *Jewish Self-Hatred: Anti-Semitism and the Hidden Language of the Jews*. Baltimore: Johns Hopkins University Press, 1986.

The Jew's Body. New York and London: Routledge, 1991.

Gilner, Elias. *War and Hope: A History of the Jewish Legion*. New York: Herzl Press, 1969.

Gitelman, Zvi, ed. *The Quest for Utopia: Jewish Political Ideas and Institutions Through the Ages*. Armonk, N. Y.: M. E. Sharpe, 1992.

Goldberg, J. J., and Elliot Kings, eds. *Builders and Dreamers: Habonim Labor Zionist Youth in North America*. New York: Herzl Press, 1993.

Gonen, Jay Y. *A Psychohistory of Zionism*. New York: Meridian, 1976.

Goode, William J. *The Celebration of Heroes: Prestige as a Social Control System*. Berkeley and Los Angeles: University of California Press, 1978.

Gorny, Yosef. "Aḥdut ha-'avodah, 1919–1930. Ideology and Practice." Ph.D. dissertation. Tel Aviv University, 1970.

Aḥdut ha-'avodah, 1919–1930: ha-yesodot ha-ra'yoniyim veha-shiṭah ha-medinit [Aḥdut ha-'avodah, 1919–1930: its intellectual bases and its political system]. Tel Aviv: Tel Aviv University Press, 1973.

From Rosh Pina and Degania to Demona: A History of Constructive Zionism, translated by John Glucker. Tel Aviv: MOD, 1989.

Zionism and the Arabs 1882–1948: A Study of Ideology. Oxford: Clarendon Press, 1987.

Shutafut u-ma'avaḳ: Chaim Weizmann u-tenu'at ha-'avodah ha-Yehudit be-Erets Yisra'el [Partnership and conflict: Chaim Weizmann and the Jewish labor movement in Palestine]. Tel Aviv: Tel Aviv University Press, 1976.

Greenblatt, Stephen. *Marvelous Possessions: The Wonder of the New World.* Chicago: University of Chicago Press, 1991.

Greenfeld, Liah. *Nationalism: Five Roads to Modernity.* Cambridge: Harvard University Press, 1992.

Gross, Walter. "The Zionist Students' Movement," *Year Book IV of the Leo Baeck Institute.* (1959): 143–64.

Halbwachs, Maurice. *On Collective Memory*, edited and translated by Lewis Coser. Chicago: University of Chicago Press, 1992.

Hall, Peter Dobkin. *Inventing the Nonprofit Sector and Other Essays on Philanthropy, Voluntarism, and Nonprofit Organizations.* Baltimore: Johns Hopkins University Press, 1992.

Halperin, Samuel. *The Political World of American Zionism.* Detroit: Wayne State University Press, 1961.

Halpern, Ben. *A Clash of Heroes: Brandeis, Weizmann, and American Zionism.* New York: Oxford University Press, 1987.

The Idea of the Jewish State, 2nd revised edn. Cambridge: Harvard University Press, 1969.

Hammer, Gottlieb. *Good Faith and Credit.* New York, London, and Toronto: Cornwall, 1985.

Harrison, David, ed. *Tourism and the Less Developed Countries.* London: Bellhaven, 1992.

Harshav, Benjamin. *Language in Time of Revolution.* Berkeley and Los Angeles: University of California Press, 1993.

Hazleton, Lesley. *Israeli Women: The Reality Behind the Myths.* New York: Simon and Schuster, 1977.

Jerusalem, Jerusalem: A Memoir of War and Peace, Passion, and Politics. New York: Penguin, 1987.

Herf, Jeffrey. *Reactionary Modernism: Technology, Culture, and Politics in Weimar and the Third Reich.* Cambridge: Cambridge University Press, 1990.

Hertzberg, Arthur, ed. *The Zionist Idea: A Historical Analysis and Reader.* New York: Athenaeum, 1977.

Higonnet, Margaret, Jane Jenson, Sonya Michel, and Margaret Collins Weitz, eds. *Behind the Lines: Gender and the Two World Wars.* New Haven: Yale University Press, 1987.

Higham, John, ed. *Ethnic Leadership in America.* Baltimore: Johns Hopkins University Press, 1978.

Send These to Me: Immigrants in Urban America. rev. edn. Baltimore: Johns Hopkins University Press, 1984.

Hobsbawm, E. J. *Nations and Nationalism Since 1780: Programme, Myth, Reality.* New York and Cambridge: Cambridge University Press, 1992.

Hobsbawm, E. J., and Terence Ranger, eds. *The Invention of Tradition*. New York: Cambridge: Cambridge University Press, 1983.

Hoff, Mascha. *Johann Kremenezky und die Gründig des KKLs*. Frankfurt a.M.: Peter Lang, 1986.

Hoffman, Charles. *The Smoke Screen: Israel, Philanthropy, and American Jews*. Silver Spring, Md.: Eschel, 1989.

Hofstadter, Richard. *The American Political Tradition and the Men Who Made It*. New York: Vintage, 1960.

Anti-Intellectualism in American Life. New York: Vintage, 1963.

Holton, Gerald, and Yehuda Elkana, eds. *Albert Einstein: Historical and Cultural Perspectives*. Princeton: Princeton University Press, 1982.

Holub, Robert. *Reception Theory: A Critical Introduction*. London and New York: Methuen, 1984.

Hoogeswoud-Verschoor, Ruth M. M. "The First Years of the Zionist Youth Movement in the Netherlands." In *Dutch Jewish History: Proceedings of the Fifth Symposium on the History of the Jews of the Netherlands, Vol. III*, edited by Jozeph Michman. Jerusalem and Assen/Maastricht: Hebrew University and Van Gorcum, 1993 (pp. 309–20).

Horowitz, Dan. "Before the State: Communal Politics in Palestine Under the Mandate." In *The Israeli State and Society: Boundaries and Frontiers*, edited by Baruch Kimmerling. Albany: State University of New York Press, 1989 (pp. 28–65).

Howe, Nicholas. *Migration and Mythmaking in Anglo-Saxon England*. New Haven and London: Yale University Press, 1989.

Howes, Justin, and Pauline Paucker. "German Jews and the Graphic Arts," *Leo Baeck Institute Year Book XXXIV* (1989): 443–74.

Hyman, Paula. "The History of European Jewry: Recent Trends in the Literature," *Journal of Modern History* 54, 2 (June 1982): 303–19.

"Was There a 'Jewish Politics' in Western and Central Europe?" In Gitelman, *Quest for Utopia* (pp. 105–17).

Idinopolis, Thomas A. *Jerusalem Blessed, Jerusalem Cursed: Jews, Christians, and Muslims in the Holy City from David's Time to Our Own*. Chicago: Ivan R. Dee, 1991.

Iser, Wolfgang. "The Reading Process: A Phenomenological Approach." In *Critical Theory Since 1965*, edited by Hazard Adams and Leroy Searle. Tallahassee: University Presses of Florida, 1980.

Jacobs, Rose. "Beginnings of Hadassah," in *Early History of Zionism in America*, edited by Isidor S. Meyer. New York: Arno, 1977 (pp. 228–44).

Jaffe, Eliezer D. *Givers and Spenders: The Politics of Charity in Israel*. Jerusalem: Ariel, 1985.

Jaher, Fredric Cople, ed. *The Rich, the Well Born, and the Powerful: Elites and Upper Classes in History*. Urbana: University of Illinois Press, 1973.

Jarausch, Konrad. *Students, Society, and Politics in Imperial Germany: The Rise of Academic Illiberalism*. Princeton: Princeton University Press, 1982.

Jauss, Hans Robert. *Literatur als Provokation*. Frankfurt a.M.: Suhrkamp, 1970.

Kadish, Sharman. *Bolsheviks and British Jews: The Anglo-Jewish Community, Britain, and the Russian Revolution*. London: Frank Cass, 1992.

Kampe, Norbert. *Studenten und "Judenfrage" in deutschen Kaiserreich: die Entstehung einer akademischen Tragerschicht des Antisemitismus.* Göttingen: Vandenhöck and Ruprecht, 1988.

Kaplan, Marion. *The Jewish Feminist Movement in Germany: The Campaigns of the Jüdischer Frauenbund, 1904–1938.* Westport, Conn.: Greenwood, 1979.

    The Making of the Jewish Middle Class: Women, Family, and Identity in Imperial Germany. New York: Oxford University Press, 1992.

Karp, Abraham, J. *To Give Life: The UJA in the Shaping of the American Jewish Community.* New York: Schocken, 1981.

Kater, Michael. *Studentenschaft und Rechtsradikalismus in Deutschland, 1918–1933: Eine sozialgeschichtliche Studie zur Bildungskrise in der Weimarer Republik.* Hamburg: Hoffmann and Campe, 1975.

Katz, Jacob. *From Prejudice to Destruction: Anti-Semitism, 1700–1933.* Cambridge: Harvard University Press, 1982.

    Out of the Ghetto: The Social Background of Jewish Emancipation. New York: Schocken, 1978.

Katz, Saul. "The Israeli Researcher-Guide: The Emergence and Perpetuation of a Role," *Annals of Tourism Research,* 12 (1985): 49–72.

Katz, Yosef. "Ideology and Urban Development: Zionism and the Origins of Tel Aviv, 1906–1914," *Journal of Historical Geography* 12, 4 (1986): 404–24.

Kenyon, Kathleen. *Digging up Jerusalem.* London and Tonbridge: Ernest Benn, 1974.

Kepnes, Steven. *The Text as Thou: Martin Buber's Dialogical Hermeneutics and Narrative Theology.* Bloomington: Indiana University Press, 1992.

Kepnes, Steven, ed. *Postmodern Interpretations of Judaism: Deconstructive and Constructive Approaches.* New York: New York University Press, forthcoming.

Kimmerling, Baruch. *Zionism and Territory: The Socio-Territorial Dimensions of Zionist Politics.* Berkeley, Calif.: Institute of International Studies, 1983.

King, Phillip. *American Archaeology in the Mideast: A History of the American Schools of Oriental Research.* Philadelphia: American Schools of Oriental Research, 1983.

Kleeblatt, Norman L., ed. *The Dreyfus Affair, Art, Truth, and Justice.* Berkeley: University of California Press for the Jewish Museum, 1987.

Klein, Dennis B. *Jewish Origins of the Psychoanalytic Movement.* Chicago and London: University of Chicago Press, 1985.

Klein, Judith. *Der deutsche Zionismus und die Araber Palästinas: Eine Untersuchung der deutsch-zionistischen Publikationen, 1917–1938.* Frankfurt: Campus Verlag, 1982.

Knee, Stuart. *The Concept of Zionist Dissent in the American Mind, 1917–1941.* New York: Robert Speller and Sons, 1979.

Kohn, Hans. *Living in a World Revolution.* New York: Trident, 1964.

Kolatt, Israel. *Ide'ologyah u-metsi'ut bi-tenuat ha-'avodah be-Erets Yisra'el, 1905–1919* [Ideology and reality in the labor movement in the land of Israel, 1905–1919]. Ph.D. dissertation. Hebrew University, 1964.

Kornberg, Jacques. *At the Crossroads: Essays on Ahad Ha-Am.* Albany: State University of New York Press, 1983.

Kozodoy, Ruth, David Sidorsky, and Kalman Sultanik, eds. *Vision Confronts Reality: Historical Perspectives on the Contemporary Jewish Agenda.* New York: Herzl Press, 1989.

Krippendorf, Jost. *The Holiday Makers: Understanding The Impact of Leisure and Travel.* Translated by Verz Andrassy. London: Heinemann, 1987.

Kutscher, Carol Bosworth. "The Early Years of Hadassah, 1912–1921." Ph.D. dissertation. Brandeis University, 1976.

Kuzmack, Linda Gordon. *Women's Cause: The Jewish Women's Movement in England and the United States, 1881–1933.* Columbus: Ohio State University Press, 1990.

Lamberti, Marjorie. "From Coexistence to Conflict: Zionism and the Jewish Community in Germany, 1897–1914," *Year Book XXVII of the Leo Baeck Institute* (1982): 53–86.

Lane, Barbara Miller. *Architecture and Politics in Germany, 1918–1945.* Cambridge: Harvard University Press, 1968.

Laqueur, Walter. *A History of Zionism.* New York: Holt, Rinehart, and Winston, 1972.

  Young Germany: A History of the German Youth Movement. London: Routledge and Kegan Paul, 1962.

Lavsky, Hagit. *Be-ṭerem pur'anut: darkam ve-yiḥudam shel Tsiyone Germanyah, 1918–1932* [Before catastrophe: the unique path of Zionism in Germany, 1918–1932]. Jerusalem: Magnes Press, Hebrew University, Ha-Sifriyah ha-Tsiyonit, 1990.

  "The Distinctive Path of German Zionism," *Studies in Contemporary Jewry,* vol. 6 (1990): 254–71.

  Yesodot ha-taḳtsiv la-mif'al ha-Tsiyoni: Va'ad ha-tsirim, 1918–1921 [The budgetary bases of the Zionist enterprise, 1918–1921]. Jerusalem: Ben Zvi Institute, 1980.

Leed, Eric J. *The Mind of the Traveler: Gilgamesh to Global Tourism.* New York: Basic, 1991.

Lehn, Walter and Uri Davis. *The Jewish National Fund.* London: Kegan Paul International, 1988.

Levene, Mark. *War, Jews, and the New Europe: The Diplomacy of Lucien Wolf, 1914–1919.* Oxford: Littman, 1992.

Levine, Etan, ed. *Diaspora: Exile and the Jewish Condition.* New York: Scribner, 1983.

Levy, Harold P. *Building a Popular Movement: A Case Study of the Public Relations of the Boy Scouts of America.* New York: Russell Sage Foundation, 1944.

Lipstadt, Deborah E. "The Zionist Career of Louis Lipsky, 1900–1921." Ph.D. dissertation. Brandeis University, 1976.

Lissak, Moshe, ed. *Toldot ha-Yishuv ha-Yehudi be-Erets Yisra'el me-az ha-'Aliyah ha-rishonah* [The history of the Jewish community in Erets Israel since 1882 (the period of the British mandate, part I)]. Jerusalem: Bialik Institute, 1993.

Lowenthal, David. *The Past Is a Foreign Country.* Cambridge: Cambridge University Press, 1985.

Lucas, Noah. *The Modern History of Israel.* London: Weidenfeld and Nicolson, 1974.

Luz, Ehud. *Parallels Meet: Religion and Zionism in the Early Zionist Movement, 1882–1904*. Philadelphia: Jewish Publication Society of America, 1988.

McAleer, Kevin. *Dueling: The Cult of Honor in Fin-de-Siècle Germany*. Princeton: Princeton University Press, 1994.

Macalister, R. A. S. *A Century of Excavation in Palestine*. New York: Arno, 1977 (reprint of a 1925 edn.).

MacCannell, Dean. *Empty Meeting Grounds: The Tourist Papers*. London: Routledge, 1992.

"Staged Authenticity: Arrangements of Social Space in Tourist Settings," *American Sociological Review*, 79 (1973): 589–603.

The Tourist: A New Theory of the Leisure Class. New York: Schocken, 1976.

McIntosh, Robert W. *Tourism Principles, Practices, and Philosophies*. Columbus, Ohio: Grid, 1972.

Mackay, Ruddock. *Balfour: Intellectual Statesman*. Oxford: Oxford University Press, 1985.

Macleod, David I. *Building Character in the American Boy: The Boy Scouts, YMCA, and Their Forerunners, 1870–1920*. Madison: University of Wisconsin Press, 1983.

Mattenklott, Gert. *Bilderdienst*. Munich: Rogner and Bernhard, 1976.

Maurer, Trude. *Die Entwicklung der jüdische Minderheit in Deutschland (1780–1933): neuere Forschungen und offene Fragen*. Tübingen: M. Niemeyer, 1992.

Ostjuden in Deutschland, 1918–1933. Hamburg: H. Christians Verlag, 1986.

Medding, Peter Y. "The 'New Jewish Politics' in the United States: Historical Perspectives," in Gitelman, *Quest for Utopia* (pp. 119–53).

"The Politics of Jewry as a Mobilized Diaspora," in *Culture, Ethnicity, and Identity: Current Issues in Research*, edited by William C. Mcready. New York: Academic Press, 1983 (pp. 195–207).

Melman, Billie. *Women's Orients: English Women and the Middle East, 1718–1918: Sexuality, Religion, and Work*. Ann Arbor: University of Michigan Press, 1992.

Mendelsohn, Ezra. *The Jews of East Central Europe Between the World Wars*. Bloomington: Indiana University Press, 1987.

On Modern Jewish Politics. New York: Oxford University Press, 1993.

Zionism in Poland: The Formative Years, 1915–1926. New Haven: Yale University Press, 1981.

Metser, Jacob. *Gibush ma'arekhet ha-minum ha-tsiburi ha-Tsiyoni: 1919–1921* [Crystallization of the Zionist public finance plan: 1919–1921]. Jerusalem: Hebrew University Press, 1976.

Hon le'umi le-vayit le'eumi, 1919–1921 [National capital for a national home, 1919–1921]. Jerusalem: Hebrew University Press, 1979.

Metser, Jacob, and Nahum Gross. "Public Finance in the Jewish Economy in Interwar Palestine," *Research in Economic History* 3 (1978): 87–159.

Meyer, Michael. *The Origins of the Modern Jew: Jewish Identity and European Culture in Germany, 1749–1824*. Detroit: Wayne State University Press, 1984.

Miller, Donald H. "A History of Hadassah, 1912–1935." Ph.D. dissertation. New York University, 1968.

Mitchell, W. J. T. *Iconology: Image, Text, Ideology*. Chicago and London: University of Chicago Press, 1987.

Morris, Benny. *1948 and After: Israel and the Palestinians*. Oxford: Clarendon Press, 1990.

Mosse, George. *The Crisis of German Ideology*. New York: Grosset and Dunlap, 1978.

—— *German Jews Beyond Judaism*. Bloomington: Indiana University Press, 1988.

—— "The Influence of the Volkish Idea on German Jewry," in Mosse, *Germans and Jews: The Right, the Left, and the Search for a "Third Force" in Pre-Nazi Germany*. Detroit: Wayne State University Press, 1987 (pp. 77–115).

—— *The Jews and the German War Experience, 1914–1918*. New York: Leo Baeck Institute, 1977.

—— *Nationalism and Sexuality: Respectability and Abnormal Sexuality in Modern Europe*. New York: Howard Fertig, 1985.

Murphy, Peter E. *Tourism: A Community Approach*. New York and London: Methuen, 1985.

Myers, David. *Re-inventing the Jewish Past: European Jewish Intellectuals and the Zionist Return to History*. New York: Oxford University Press, 1995.

Navon, Yitzhak. "On Einstein and the Presidency of Israel," in *Albert Einstein, Historical and Cultural Perspectives: The Centennial Symposium in Jerusalem*. Princeton, N. J.: Princeton University Press, 1982.

Nicosia, Francis. "Revisionist Zionism in Germany (I) – Richard Lichtheim and the Landesverband der Zionisten-Revisionisten in Deutschland, 1926–1933," *Leo Baeck Institute Year Book XXXI* (1986): 209–40.

—— *The Third Reich and the Palestine Question*. Austin: University of Texas Press, 1985.

Odendahl, Teresa. *Charity Begins at Home: Generosity and Self Interest Among the Philanthropic Elite*. New York: Basic, 1990.

Ogilvie, F. W. *The Tourist Movement: An Economic Study*. London: P. S. King and Son, 1933.

Owen, Roger. *State, Power, and Politics in the Making of the Modern Middle East*. 1992.

Pais, Abraham. *Subtle is the Lord: The Science and Life of Albert Einstein*. New York: Oxford University Press, 1982.

Parzen, Herbert. "The United Palestine Appeal," *Herzl Year Book*, vol. 7 (1971): 355–93.

Pearce, Douglas, and Richard Butler, eds. *Tourism Research: Critiques and Challenges*. New York: Routledge, 1993.

Pearce, Philip. *The Social Psychology of Tourist Behaviour*. Oxford: Pergamon, 1982.

—— *The Ulysses Factor: Evaluating Visitors in Tourist Settings*. New York, Berlin, and Heidelberg: Springer-Verlag, 1988.

Penslar, Derek. *Zionism and Technocracy: The Engineering of Jewish Settlement in Palestine, 1870–1918*. Bloomington and Indianapolis: Indiana University Press, 1991.

Peukert, Detlev. *Die Weimarer Republik: Krisenjahre der klassichen Moderne*. Frankfurt a.M.: Suhrkamp, 1987.

Pickus, Keith. "Jewish University Students in Germany: The Construction of a Post-Emancipation Identity." Ph.D. dissertation. University of Washington, 1993.

Poppel, Stephen M. *Zionism in Germany, 1897–1933: The Shaping of a Jewish Identity*. Philadelphia: Jewish Publication Society of America, 1977.

Portath, Y. *The Emergence of the Palestinian-Arab National Movement, 1918–1929*. London: Frank Cass, 1974.

Pratt, Mary Louise. *Imperial Eyes: Travel Writing and Transculturation*. London and New York: Routledge, 1992.

Prestel, Claudia. "Frauen und die Zionistische Bewegung (1897–1933): Tradition oder Revolution?" in *Historische Zeitschrift* 258 (1994): 29–71.

Pudney, John. *The Thomas Cook Story*. London: Michael Joseph, 1953.

Pulzer, Peter. *The Rise of Political Anti-Semitism in Germany and Austria*. rev. edn. Cambridge, Mass.: Harvard University Press, 1988.

Rabin, Else. "The Jewish Woman in Social Service in Germany," in *The Jewish Library*, vol. III, edited by Leo Jung. New York: The Jewish Library, 1934 (pp. 268–310).

Rabinowicz, Oscar K. *Fifty Years of Zionism: A Historical Analysis of Dr. Weizmann's "Trial and Error"*. London: Robert Anscombe, 1950.

Raphael, Marc Lee. *A History of the United Jewish Appeal, 1939–1982*. Providence: Brown University Press, 1982.

Rapoport-Albert, Ada and Steven Zipperstein, eds. *Jewish History: Essays in Honour of Chimen Abramsky*. London: Peter Halban, 1988.

Reich, Bernard, and Gershon Kieval. *Israel: Land of Tradition and Conflict*. Boulder: Westview, 1993.

Reinharz, Jehuda. *Chaim Weizmann: The Making of a Statesman*. New York: Oxford University Press, 1993.

Chaim Weizmann: The Making of a Zionist Leader. New York: Oxford University Press, 1985.

Fatherland or Promised Land: The Dilemma of the German Jew, 1893–1914. Ann Arbor: University of Michigan Press, 1975.

"Science in the Service of Politics: The Case of Chaim Weizmann During the First World War," *English Historical Review* (July 1985): 572–603.

Reinharz, Jehuda, ed. *Dokumente zur Geschichte des deutschen Zionismus, 1882–1933*. Tübingen: J. C. B. Mohr, 1981.

Richards, Thomas. *The Imperial Archive: Knowledge and the Fantasy of Empire*. London and New York: Verso, 1993.

Richarz, Monika, ed. *Bürger auf Widerruf: Lebenszeugnisse deutscher Juden, 1780–1945*. Munich: C. H. Beck, 1989.

Jewish Life in Germany: Memoirs from Three Centuries. Translated by Stella P. Rosenfeld and Sidney Rosenfeld. Bloomington and Indianapolis: Indiana University Press, 1991.

Rinott, Chanoch. "Major Trends in Jewish Youth Movements in Germany," *Year Book XIX of the Leo Baeck Institute*. (1974): 77–105.

Rodrigue, Aron. *Images of Sephardi and Eastern Jewries in Transition: The Teachers of the Alliance Israélite Universelle*. London and Seattle: University of Washington Press, 1993.

Rose, Norman. *Chaim Weizmann: A Biography.* New York: Viking-Penguin, 1986.

Rosen, Ruth. *The Lost Sisterhood: Prostitution in America.* Baltimore: Johns Hopkins University Press, 1982.

Rosenkranz, Zev. "Albert Einstein be-'ene Tsiyone Germanyah, 1919–1921" [Albert Einstein in the eyes of the German Zionists, 1919–1921], in *Yehude Weimar: hevrah be-mashber ha-moderniyut, 1918–1933* [Weimar Jewry and the crisis of modernization, 1918–1933]. Edited by Oded Heilbronner. Jerusalem: Magnes Press, 1994.

Rosenstock, Werner. "The Jewish Youth Movement," *Year Book XIX of the Leo Baeck Institute.* (1974): 77–105.

Rosenthal, Michael. *The Character Factory: Baden-Powell and the Origins of the Boy Scout Movement.* New York: Pantheon, 1986.

Rothschild, Eli, ed. *Meilensteine: vom Wege des Kartells jüdischer Verbindungen in der Zionistischen Bewegung.* Tel Aviv: Presidium of the KJV, 1972.

Rozenblit, Marsha L. "The Assertion of Identity – Jewish Student Nationalism at the University of Vienna Before the First World War," *Year Book XXVII of the Leo Baeck Institute* (1982): 171–86.

The Jews of Vienna: Assimilation and Identity, 1867–1914. Albany: State University of New York Press, 1983.

Sachar, Howard M. *A History of the Jews in America.* New York: Knopf, 1992.

Sacks, Maurie, ed. *Active Voices: Women in Jewish Culture.* Urbana: University of Illinois Press, 1995.

Said, Edward. *Culture and Imperialism.* New York: Knopf, 1993.

Orientalism. New York: Vintage, 1976.

The Question of Palestine. Vintage, 1980.

Salmon, Yosef, ed. *Dat ve-Tsiyonut: 'imutim rishonim: kovets ma'amarim* [Religion and Zionism: first encounters.] Jerusalem: ha-Sifriyah ha-Tsiyonit al yad ha-Histradrut ha-Tsiyonit ha-'olamit, 1990.

Sarna, Jonathan. *JPS: The Americanization of Jewish Culture, 1888–1988.* Philadelphia: Jewish Publication Society of America, 1989.

Schatzker, Chaim. "The Jewish Youth Movement in Germany, 1900–1933." Ph.D. dissertation. Hebrew University, 1969.

Schorske, Carl E. *Fin-de-Siècle Vienna: Politics and Culture.* New York: Vintage, 1980.

Scott, Joan Wallach. *Gender and the Politics of History.* New York: Columbia University Press, 1988.

"Women's History," in *New Perspectives on Historical Writing*, edited by Peter Burke. State College, Penn.: Penn State Press, 1991 (pp. 42–66).

Segev, Tom. *The Seventh Million: The Israelis and the Holocaust*, translated by Haim Watzman. New York: Hill and Wang, 1992.

Serle, Geoffrey. *John Monash: A Biography.* Melbourne: Melbourne University Press, 1985.

Shafir, Gerson. *Land, Labor, and the Origins of the Israeli–Palestinian Conflict, 1882–1914.* Cambridge: Cambridge University Press, 1989.

Shaltier, Eli. *Pinchas Rutenberg: Hayim u-zemanim, 1879–1942, vol. I.* Tel Aviv: Am Oved, 1990.

Shapira, Anita. *Berl: The Biography of a Socialist Zionist.* Translated by Haya Galai. New York: Cambridge University Press, 1984.

Land and Power: The Zionist Resort to Force, 1881–1948, translated by William Templer. New York: Oxford University Press, 1992.

Ha-ma'avak ha-nikhzav: 'avodah 'Ivrit, 1929–1939 [The futile struggle: Hebrew labor, 1929–1939]. Tel Aviv: Tel Aviv University Press, 1977.

Shapiro, Robert D. *A Reform Rabbi in the Progressive Era: The Early Career of Stephen S. Wise.* New York and London: Garland, 1988.

Shapiro, Yonathan. *Leadership of the American Zionist Organization, 1897–1930.* Urbana: University of Illinois Press, 1971.

Sharfman, Glenn R. "Whoever Has the Youth, Has the Future: The Jewish Youth Movement in Germany, 1900–1936: A Study in Ideology and Organization." Ph.D. dissertation. University of North Carolina at Chapel Hill, 1989.

Shavit, Yaacov. "Archaeology, Political Culture, and Culture in Israel." In *Archaeology in Israel,* edited by Laurence Silberstein. New York: New York University Press, forthcoming.

Jabotinsky and the Revisionist Movement, 1925–1948. London: Frank Cass, 1988.

The New Hebrew Nation: A Study in Israeli Heresy and Fantasy. London: Frank Cass, 1987.

Shepherd, Naomi. *The Zealous Intruders: From Napoleon to the Dawn of Zionism – the Explorers, Archaeologists, Artists, Tourists, Pilgrims, and Visionaries Who Opened Palestine to the West.* San Francisco: Harper and Row, 1988.

Shibi-Shai, Eli. *Ḥayim ve-ahavah be-tekufah ha-Shabta'it ha-me'uḥeret* [Life and love in the late Sabbatean movement]. M.A. thesis. Hebrew University, 1985.

Shilo, Margalit. "The Women's Farm at Kinneret, 1911–1917: A Solution to the Problem of the Working Woman in the Second Aliya," *Jerusalem Cathedre* (1981): 246–83; also published in Deborah Bernstein, *Pioneers and Home-makers* (pp. 119–43).

Shilo-Cohen, Nurit, ed. *Bezalel, 1906–1929.* Jerusalem: Israel Museum, 1983.

Shimoni, Gideon. *Jews and Zionism: The South African Experience, 1910–1967.* New York: Oxford University Press, 1980.

"Poale Zion: A Zionist Transplant in Britain (1905–1945)," *Studies in Contemporary Jewry,* vol. 2 (1986): 227–69.

The Zionist Ideology. Hanover, N. H.: Brandeis University Press of the University Press of New England, 1995.

Shimoni, Gideon, and Hayim Avni, eds. *Ha-Tsiyonut u-mitnagdeha ba-'am ha-Yehudi: kovets ma'amarim* [Zionism and its Jewish opponents.] Jerusalem: ha-Sifriyah ha-Tsiyonit, 1990.

Shlaim, Avi. *Collusion Across the Jordan.* Oxford: Oxford University Press, 1988.

Silberman, Neil. *Between Past and Present: Archaeology, Ideology, and Nationalism in the Modern Middle East.* New York: Henry Holt, 1989.

Digging for God and Country: Exploration, Archeology, and the Secret Struggle for the Holy Land, 1799–1917. New York: Knopf, 1982.

A Prophet from Amongst You: The Life of Yigael Yadin: Soldier, Scholar, Myth-maker of Modern Israel. Reading, Mass.: Addison-Wesley, 1993.

Silberstein, Laurence. "Cultural Criticism, Ideology, and the Interpretation of Zionism: Toward a Post-Zionist Discourse," in Kepnes, *Postmodern Interpretations of Judaism.*

Martin Buber's Social and Religious Thought: Alienation and the Quest for Meaning. New York: New York University Press, 1989.

Silver, Daniel Jeremy. *Images of Moses.* New York: Basic, 1982.

Simmons, James C. *Passionate Pilgrims: English Travelers to the World of the Desert Travelers.* New York: William Morrow, 1987.

Simon, Leon. *Ahad Ha-Am: Asher Ginzberg, A Biography.* Philadelphia: Jewish Publication Society of America, 1960.

Smith, Anthony. *The Ethnic Origins of Nations.* Oxford and Cambridge, Mass.: Basil Blackwell, 1993.

Sokolow, Florian. *Nahum Sokolow: Life and Legend.* London: Jewish Chronicle Publications, 1975.

Sokolow, Nahum. *History of Zionism, 1600–1918.* New York: KTAV, 1969.

Sontag, Susan. *On Photography.* Harmondsworth: Penguin, 1979.

Sorin, Gerald. *The Jewish People in America. A Time For Building: The Third Migration, 1880–1920.* Baltimore and London: Johns Hopkins University Press, 1992.

Sorkin, David. *The Transformation of the German Jewry, 1780–1840.* New York: Oxford University Press, 1987.

Springhall, John. *Youth, Empire, and Society: British Youth Movements, 1883–1940.* London: Croom Helm, 1977.

Stachura, Peter D. *The German Youth Movement, 1900–1945.* London and Basingstoke: Macmillan, 1981.

Starr, Kevin. *Material Dreams: Southern California Through the 1920s.* New York: Oxford University Press, 1990.

Stein, Kenneth. *The Land Question in Palestine, 1917–1939.* Chapel Hill: University of North Carolina Press, 1984.

Stock, Ernest. *Partners and Pursestrings: A History of the United Israel Appeal.* Lanham, Md.: University Press of America, 1987.

Strum, Philippa. *Brandeis: Beyond Progressivism.* Lawrence: University of Kansas Press, 1993.

Louis D. Brandeis: Justice of the People. Cambridge: Harvard University Press, 1984.

Swinglehurst, Edmund. *The Romantic Journey: The Story of Thomas Cook and Victorian Travel.* New York, Evanston, San Francisco, London: Harper and Row, 1974.

Syrkin, Marie. Preface to Ada Maimon, *Women Built a Land,* translated by Shulamith Schwarz-Nardi. New York: Herzl Press, 1962.

Tagg, John. *The Burden of Representation: Essays on Photographies and Histories.* Amherst: University of Massachusetts Press, 1988.

Tal, Uriel. *Christians and Jews in Germany: Religion, Politics, and Ideology in the Second Reich, 1870–1914,* translated by Noah Jonathan Jacobs. Ithaca and London: Cornell University Press, 1975.

Tananbaum, Susan. "Generations of Change: The Anglicization of Russian-Jewish Immigrant Women in London, 1880–1939." Ph.D. dissertation. Brandeis University, 1991.

Tartakover, David, ed. *Herzl in Profile: Herzl's Image in the Applied Arts*. Tel Aviv: Tel Aviv Museum, 1979.

Teitelbaum, Gene. *Justice Louis D. Brandeis: A Bibliography of Writings and Other Materials on the Justice*. Littleton, Colo.: Fred B. Rothman and Co., 1988.

Turner, Louis, and John Ash. *The Golden Hordes: International Tourism and the Pleasure Periphery*. London: Constable, 1975.

Turner, Victor. *From Ritual to Theatre: The Human Seriousness of Play*. Baltimore: Johns Hopkins University Press, 1992.

Urofsky, Melvin. *American Zionism from Herzl to the Holocaust*. Garden City, N. Y.: Anchor/Doubleday, 1975.

A Voice that Spoke for Justice: The Life and Times of Stephen S. Wise. Albany: State University of New York Press, 1982.

We Are One! American Jewry and Israel. Garden City, N. Y.: Anchor/Doubleday, 1978.

Urofsky, Melvin, ed. *Essays in American Zionism, 1917–1948*. New York: Herzl Press, 1978.

Urry, John. *The Tourist Gaze: Leisure and Travel in Contemporary Societies*. London: Sage, 1990.

Vascek, Louis and Gail Buckland. *Travelers in Ancient Lands: A Portrait of the Middle East, 1839–1919*. Boston: New York Graphic Society, 1981.

Vereté, Mayir. *From Palmerston to Balfour: Collected Essays of Mayir Vereté*. Edited by Norman Rose. London and Portland: Frank Cass, 1992.

Vital, David. *The Future of the Jews*. Gambridge, Mass.: Harvard University Press, 1990.

The Origins of Zionism. Oxford: Clarendon Press, 1975.

Zionism: The Crucial Phase. Oxford: Clarendon Press, 1987.

Zionism: The Formative Years. Oxford: Clarendon Press, 1982.

Vovelle, Michel. *Ideologies and Mentalities*, translated by Eamon O'Flaherty. Chicago: University of Chicago Press, 1990.

Wertheimer, Jack. *Unwelcome Strangers: East European Jews in Imperial Germany*. New York and Oxford: Oxford University Press, 1987.

White, Hayden. *The Content of the Form: Narrative Discourse and Historical Representation*. London and Baltimore: Johns Hopkins University Press, 1992.

Metahistory: The Historical Imagination in Nineteenth-Century Europe. Baltimore: Johns Hopkins University Press, 1993.

Wolffsohn, Michael. *Eternal Guilt? Forty Years of German–Jewish–Israeli Relations*, translated by Douglas Bokovay. New York: Columbia University Press, 1993.

Woocher, Jonathan. *Sacred Survival: The Civil Religion of American Jews*. Bloomington: Indiana University Press, 1986.

Yerushalmi, Yosef. *Zakhor: Jewish History and Jewish Memory*. New York: Schocken, 1989.

Yisraeli, David. "The Struggle for Zionist Military Involvement in the First World War, 1914–1917," in *Bar Ilan Studies in History*, edited by Pinhas Artzi. Ramet-Gan: Bar Ilan University Press, 1978.

Young, George. *Tourism: Blessing or Blight?* Harmondsworth: Penguin, 1973.

Zebel, Sydney. *Balfour: A Political Biography*. Cambridge: Cambridge University Press, 1973.

Zechlin, Egmont. *Die deutsche Politik und die Juden im Ersten Weltkrieg*. Göttingen: Vandenhöck and Ruprecht, 1969.

Zeitlin, Rose. *Henrietta Szold*. New York: Dial, 1952.

Zerubavel, Yael. "The Politics of Interpretation: Tel Hai in Israeli Collective Memory," *AJS Review* 16 (Spring–Fall 1991): 133–59.

Recovered Roots: Collective Memory and the Making of Israeli National Tradition. Chicago: University of Chicago Press, 1995.

Zerubavel, Yael, Barry Schwartz, and Bernice Barnett. "The Recovery of Masada: A Study in Collective Memory." In *Sociological Quarterly* 27, 2 (1986): 147–64.

Zimmerman, Moshe. "Jewish Nationalism and Zionism in German-Jewish Students' Organisations," *Year Book XXVII of the Leo Baeck Institute*. (1982): 129–53.

Zipperstein, Steven. *Elusive Prophet: Ahad Ha-Am and the Origins of Zionism*. Berkeley and Los Angeles: University of California Press, 1993.

"The Politics of Relief: The Transformation of Russian Jewish Communal Life During the First World War," *Studies in Contemporary Jewry*, vol. 6 (1988): 22–40.

Index

agriculture, 93–99, 102–09, 121, 122–23
  aforestation, 62, 137
  funding for, 106–07
  German-sponsored projects, 166
  and land reclamation, 105, 106–07
  limited value of, 62
  photographic portrayal of, 97–99
  and "plague of locusts" (1917), 84
  Zionist emphasis on, 95, 111, 135, 145
Ahad Ha-Am (Asher Ginsburg), 26
Alderblum, Nima, 141
Allenby, Field Marshal Edmund, 9–10
Allied powers, 7, 8, 18
  see also World War I; World War II
Altneuland (Theodor Herzl), 109
American Hebrew (non-Zionist journal),
    163
American Jewish Joint Distribution
    Committee (JDC, "the Joint"), 17,
    19, 57
American Jewish Relief Committee, 19, 20
American Red Cross, 17, 45
American Schools of Oriental Research, 136
American Zionist Federation, 45
American Zionist Medical Unit, see
    Hadassah
American Zionist Organization, see Zionist
    Organization of America (ZOA)
anti-defamation, 196
anti-Semitism
  in Austria and Germany, 18, 24, 52,
    53–54, 76, 151
  and Balfour Declaration, 34
  and credit to Jewish troops, 9–10
  Einstein on, 52–53
  in France, 18
  and fundraising, 78–79
  and Jews in cities, 94
  organizations defending against, 154,
    155, 174
  in Poland, 21, 82
  and prostitution, 15

  in Russian Empire, 7, 18, 82, 89
  travel bureaus and, 129, 130, 131
  Turkish, 83–84
  in United States, 82
  US accusations of, 18
  Zionist experience in Palestine (1920s),
    84
  see also pogroms; stereotypes
ANZAC (Australian and New Zealand)
    forces, 9
Arab riots (1929–30), 55, 72, 78, 121, 172
  Brandeis speech on, 42
  and fundraising, 57, 80, 89
  ostensible cause of, 136
  and tourism, 125
  Zionist perception of, 104, 159
  see also Arab–Zionist relations
Arab–Zionist relations, 27, 103–05, 111
  "Arab problem," 104–05
  conflict, 110, 112, 118, 121, 128, 171
    (see also Arab riots, 1929–30)
  conflict minimized, 89, 105
  Jewish sympathy for/understanding of
    Arabs, 55, 89–90, 139, 159, 172,
    187
Arabs, Palestinian
  British bias toward, 138
  culture recognized, 104
  nationalism of, 104, 105, 171–72
  and tourist trade, 128
  see also Arab riots (1929–30); Arab–
    Zionist relations
archaeology, 136–37, 138, 142
Aronson family, 83
Artamanen (German youth group), 149
Australia, Zionism in, 9
Austria, 8, 18, 149, 180
  Jewish troops from 13, 14, 16, 20
  Zionism in, 7, 11, 178
Avineri, Shlomo, 40, 48
Avukah, 166–72, 173–74
Avukah Bulletin, 170

Great Depression, 50, 81, 90, 125
individualism, Jewish propensity for,
    89
stock market crash, 72, 81
education, *see* intellectual life
Egremont, Max, 29
Egypt, tours/pilgrimages to, 127, 128, 129
Einstein, Albert, 140, 172
as hero of Zionist movement, 26, 27,
    48–55, 197
Einstein Forest (Palestine), 50
Eksteins, Modris, 16
Elam, Yigal, 3, 61
Elon, Amos, 136
England, *see* Britain
English Zionist Federation, 75, 88, 160
"Ladies' Committee," 183
Erets Israel, 126, 129, 154, 161, 164,
    233n4
emigration from, 163
Zionist pride in, 194
see also Yishuv, the
Europe, Zionist movement in, 91, 177, 195
center of, under Weizmann, 182
dormancy of (in France and
    Switzerland), 2, 81, 126
women in, 178–86, 188, 193
World War I and, 24
see also Austria; Britain; Eastern
    European Jewry; France; Germany

Fabreline cruise company, 131
farming, *see* agriculture
Fascism, 171, 174
Federation of Women Zionists (FWZ,
    Britain), 182, 183, 184
Feingold, Henry, 57
feminism, *see* women
films, *see* visual images of Palestine
Finkielkraut, Alain, 6, 196
Fishman, Ada, 184
forests
aforestation practices, 62, 137
Memorial (Palestine), 32, 50, 52
Forverts! (periodical), 84
France, Anatole, 17
France, 8, 18, 154
Jewish troops in, 16, 19
Zionism in, 2, 81, 126
Franco-Prussian War (1870–71), 16
Frank, Leo, 82
Frankel, Jonathan, 7, 200
Frankfurter, Felix, 36
Freidenreich, Harriet, 178
Friesel, Evyatar, 221n45

fundraising
Arab riots and, 57, 80, 89
British, 75, 80, 88
catastrophe and, 57, 77–90
charity/relief versus nation-building, 6,
    58, 75, 77, 78, 84–87, 121, 175,
    190–91
consolidation of, 57
criticism of efforts, 58–59, 61–69,
    74–76, 85–86, 90
seen as treason, 69–70, 189
diaspora Jews and, 4, 77, 80–81, 89, 90,
    105, 185, 190, 198, 220n28
economic conditions and, 50, 72, 81, 90
Einstein and, 50
"Emergency Funds," 80, 86
and false expectations, 89–90
"Flag-Day," 84
German, 80, 88
Hadassah and, 58, 65–66, 74–75,
    78–79, 90, 186, 187–88
for land purchase, 106–07
need for emphasized, 194
pessimism about expressed, 198
phonograph records used in, 181
priorities of, 84, 86–87
and propaganda, 83, 87–88, 106, 138,
    140, 170
resistance to change and, 73–74
sick-care fund (Kupat Holim), 73, 187,
    193
tourism and, 127, 135, 139–40, 144–45
US, *see* Zionism, American
Weizmann and, 59–60, 77, 79, 81, 85,
    199
women and, 90 (*see also* Hadassah)
World War I, 84–85, 86, 87
for Yishuv, 61–63, 83, 87, 89, 184
visual portrayal of needs, 105–06
by youth groups, 159, 165, 173, 174

Gal, Allon, 48
Gandhi, Mahatma, 157
Gaze, Henry (British travel company),
    243n38
gender as issue, 15, 48, 74, 176, 180, 197
see also women
German Jews
versus Eastern European Jews, 53,
    59–60, 71, 74, 151
Einstein on, 52–54
in German army (World War I), 12,
    13–14, 15–16, 18, 243n19
national consciousness of, 15–16, 93
in the Yishuv, 154

Printed in the United States
57997LVS00003B/192

9 780521 894203